In the Ring
With
Tommy Burns

Adam J. Pollack

WIN BY KO

Win By KO Publications

Iowa City

In the Ring With Tommy Burns

Adam J. Pollack

(ISBN-13): 978-0-9799822-3-1

(hardcover: 55# acid-free alkaline paper)

Library of Congress Control Number: 2011933044

Includes footnotes, appendix, and index.

Cover design by Gwyn Snider ©

Manufactured in the United States of America.

Win By KO Publications

Iowa City, Iowa

winbykopublications.com

Contents

Preface:
The Chameleon

This is book six in my *Reigns of Fame and Shame* heavyweight championship series. For those of you have read *John L. Sullivan: The Career of the First Gloved Heavyweight Champion*, *In the Ring With James J. Corbett*, *In the Ring With Bob Fitzsimmons*, *In the Ring With James J. Jeffries*, and *In the Ring With Marvin Hart*, you know my style. This is an attempt to clear up misconceptions and misinformation about this champion's boxing career by using mostly local next-day primary sources written by those who actually saw Tommy Burns box live. I hope this book paints a better, more complete and accurate portrait of this underrated fighter based on what was said at the time of his career. You are about to experience Tommy Burns' career journey as a boxer, his trials and tribulations, blow by blow and fight by fight.

Like Bob Fitzsimmons, Tommy Burns was a man who defied convention and categorization. He was a boxer who grew, adapted and changed with time. At times he was listed as being from Canada, Detroit, Chicago, and various places on the west coast like Seattle, Portland, and Los Angeles. He was of French Canadian, German, and Italian heritage. He was Canadian, but learned to box in the United States. He was born Noah Brusso, but during his boxing career changed his name to Tommy Burns.

For most of his early career, also like Bob Fitzsimmons, Brusso was a 158-pound middleweight. But then he became a heavyweight. He had lost a middleweight fight, but then won the heavyweight championship in his next fight.

Even as a full-blown heavyweight, Burns usually only weighed between 170 and 180 pounds. He was history's shortest heavyweight champion, standing only 5'7" tall. Because of his small size, most experts, writers, and even opponents tended to underestimate him.

Despite these seeming handicaps, Burns had long arms, solid punching power, a particularly strong right hand, a good chin, sturdy balance, good conditioning, and an unusual amount of strength for a man of his size. He was well-schooled both offensively and defensively. He was a fairly aggressive puncher who liked working in close on the inside, but he could also be a slick boxer, moving around on the outside, demonstrating his good sense of range and timing, knowing how to position himself and when to fire his punches. His versatility enabled him to defeat a myriad of styles and opponents.

Tommy Burns would become known as a fighting champion who defended the title quite often. Over time, he earned respect. However, like

Marvin Hart, because he followed in the wake of an undefeated all-time great legend in James Jeffries, it took quite some time for Burns to gain full acceptance as a champion and admiration as a fighter. James Jeffries was a hard act to follow. In fact, non-Americans may have admired Burns the most. Regardless of perspective, Tommy Burns was determined to make as much money from the boxing game as possible, and he was quite successful from this point of view.

The Brusso/Burns career is also significant from a sociological perspective. He fought black fighters at a time when many drew the color line. When the money was right, he was willing to break this social rule in order to fight the era's top contender. He was the first heavyweight champion of the gloved era to break the color line in a heavyweight championship fight, and the only white heavyweight champion to do so in a title defense until the late 1930s, nearly 30 years after Burns.

CHAPTER 1

Noah Brusso –
The Canadian
Michigan Middleweight

Tommy Burns was born Noah Brusso on June 17, 1881 in Hanover, Ontario, Canada. He was the 12th of 13 children, born to a Canadian cabinet-maker named Fredrick Brusso, and his wife, Sofa Dankert.[1] Burns said his father was French and his mother German. Some reports said Noah was a French Canadian, while others said he was actually of Italian descent.[2] The family was poor, and they moved around Ontario a great deal. Burns said that while he was still very young, the family moved to Chesley, Ontario.

In school, Brusso often liked to fight with his fellow students, and he found that he was good at it. His fighting, and perhaps the need for money, caused his mother to pull him out of school at age 10, when Noah began working as a finisher in a furniture factory. He also washed freight wagons at the train station. Brusso continued having a few street fights on occasion.

As he grew up, even from a young age, the athletic Brusso enjoyed participating in sports, and usually excelled. His eventual great physical endurance and strength came from years of lacrosse, tennis, soccer, hockey, and speed skating, those sports having been Brusso's lifelong pastimes in Canada. Brusso was known as a very good skater, and enjoyed participating in races. His other favorite activity was lacrosse, which was Canada's national sport since the 1860s. Such sports helped him develop powerful legs and also toughened him up. Brusso claimed that by the time he was 12 years old, he was good enough to play for the town lacrosse team, even though the next youngest player was 19 years old.[3]

After Brusso's father died in 1896, 15-year-old Noah took a job in a molding foundry. During that time, his mother remarried. Brusso's stepfather was verbally and physically abusive, not hesitant to use violence for discipline. He eventually kicked Noah out of the home at age 17. Brusso

---

1 Burns, Tommy, *Scientific Boxing and Self Defence*, Health & Strength (London, 1908), 163; McCaffery, Dan, *Tommy Burns: Canada's Unknown World Heavyweight Champion*, James Lorimer & Co. Ltd. (Toronto, 2000), 11.
2 *San Francisco Chronicle*, August 31, 1905; *National Police Gazette*, March 24, 1906.
3 *National Police Gazette*, March 24, 1906. McCaffery at 15-19. Burns at 163.

moved to Hespeler, and worked in a wool mill, spinning yarn and weaving cloth. He continued participating in sporting events.

The athletic Brusso claimed to have won third place in the Ontario Skating Championship tournament. It requires only one glance at his powerful-looking legs to realize that he was likely a very strong skater.

However, during this time, Brusso's true passion was lacrosse, a game at which he excelled. Noah played goalie for the local lacrosse team. Lacrosse was a particularly violent sport, and Brusso got into his fair share of fights during games. Noah was well-known for his violent propensities, although he eventually learned to hold them in check to a certain degree so that he would not be ejected from so many games. He claimed to have played for the Galt team which won the 1898 Western Ontario lacrosse championship.

TOMMY BURNS,
with lacrosse racket, as he played on the team at Galt, Ontario, in the years before he became a prize fighter.

In 1899, at age 18, Noah moved up to the semi-professional lacrosse ranks. He began playing as a forward, and continued his on-field fistfights. His fistic talent and ability to defeat much larger men gained him notoriety.

A story often told was that Brusso's parents lived in Preston, a few miles from Galt. An 18-year-old Brusso went to school, but showed little inclination for books. He often went down to Galt to play lacrosse, and was a first-class goalkeeper, particularly with his broad shoulders and long arms. In one exhibition game against the Bright team, when a 30-year-old 200-pound Bright player who was a blacksmith by trade tried to set himself up to score, Brusso threw him over his hip into the nets. The angered big fellow was prevented from fighting Noah, but told him that he would pulverize him after the game. Later that evening, the two fought it out with their fists, and Brusso knocked him out.[4]

Another version of this story said the fight happened after a soccer game, and that Brusso was living in Hespeler at the time. News of this deed caused the Hespeler boxing club's teacher C.M. Schultz to invite Brusso to join their club, which he did. Brusso may have had some sort of amateur career, because it was years later said that "he couldn't find enough amateurs to stand up before him, so he had to turn professional." However, in the late 1890s, Brusso mostly just boxed and fought for fun in impromptu scraps.[5]

When Burns was a boxing champion, it was said that he was one of the best men in the country at lacrosse, the biggest sport in Canada. He had formerly played with the champion Galt team of Ontario at age 16, and was the youngest player in the Canadian League. Even during his professional boxing career, when he lived in the United States, Burns would play lacrosse with teams in Michigan, Washington, and Oregon.[6]

In around 1900, Brusso moved to Mount Forest, Ontario, where he painted houses to earn a living, and played lacrosse for that town's team. He continued his on-field fights. In fact, the local coach, George Allen, supplied the team with boxing gloves during their training so they would be prepared for the fights that seemed integral to the sport.

When the season ended, Brusso worked as a bouncer in a tavern in Sarnia, Ontario. He next worked on a Great Lakes steamer, where he defeated the ship's steward, a bully, in a fistfight. However, that got him fired.

Brusso left the steamer at Detroit, Michigan, in the United States, and began working there as a dockhand, and then as a painter. Painting made him relatively good money, so he decided to remain in Detroit.

To obtain some exercise, Noah became a member of the Detroit Athletic Club. Before long, he joined the local lacrosse team, and quickly gained a reputation for having no fear about mixing it up with the toughest players. An impressed sports writer eventually told Brusso that he should

---

4 *Los Angeles Herald*, February 13, 1907.
5 McCaffery at 19-20; *National Police Gazette*, March 24, 1906.
6 *Los Angeles Times,* November 4, 1906.

consider fighting for a living. He told Noah that he was mean enough for it, and had the killer instinct.

Brusso was introduced to Sam Biddle, a fight promoter and former boxer. Noah began training under his tutelage, at Biddle's gymnasium.[7]

Although Brusso and several semi-primary sources (likely based upon Brusso's assertions) consistently claim that he began his professional boxing career in 1900, the known primary source evidence supports that that Brusso began his professional boxing career in 1902, when he was 20 years old. It is possible that he had additional fights before then, but the dates have not been found. Interestingly, the bouts he claimed to have had in 1900 turned out to be rematches in 1902, according to Brusso. It is quite possible that Brusso first fought these men in 1902, and that the rematches, if any, took place later.

Although he was born a Canadian, Noah Brusso began his professional boxing career in America, in the Detroit, Michigan area. At the time, James J. Jeffries was the world heavyweight champion. Noah Brusso was just a middleweight. Like Marvin Hart, he first developed local notoriety by fighting and winning quite often, usually by knockout. At the start of his pro career, he used his given name of Brusso.

Brusso's first known professional fight was against a black fighter, perhaps befitting because Burns would become the first gloved era heavyweight champion to break the color line in a formal title defense once he was champion. Other champions during their ascendancy to the throne were willing to fight blacks, but once they became champion, none defended against blacks.[8]

Speaking several years later about the start of his career, Brusso said, "I went to a fight in Detroit one night and liked it. A few days later I joined the Detroit Athletic Club and boxed as an amateur. About three months after that I went to a fight as a spectator. Instead of occupying a seat near the ringside I became one of the principals." Apparently, someone didn't show up, so Brusso was convinced to step in as a substitute.[9]

The black fighter against whom Noah Brusso made his pro debut was named Fred Thornton, who was also a Canadian, from Windsor. A secondary source indicates that in 1900, fellow black fighter Young Peter Jackson had knocked out Thornton in the 6th round. Another secondary source claims that "Thunderbolt" Thornton had two dozen victories to his credit.[10]

---

7 McCaffery at 22-32; *New York Herald*, December 21, 1908.
8 Jeffries did as champion box Hank Griffin in a 4-round exhibition bout, so technically, if Griffin had knocked him out, Hank would have been champion. However, the limited duration gave the bout less of a championship quality than Jeff's more typical scheduled 20 or 25-round fights.
9 *San Francisco Evening Post*, August 14, 1905.
10 Boxrec.com; McCaffery at 33.

The local press described Brusso as a likable chap from Delray, which was a Detroit area neighborhood. Early in his career, Brusso was generally listed as fighting out of Delray or Detroit. He was a Detroit Canadian.

The Noah Brusso-Fred Thornton bout took place on January 16, 1902 before a crowd of 250 at Delray, Michigan's Handloser's Hall.

The local press reported that early in the bout, "Brosso" or "Kid Brossou" got to colored boxer Fed Thornton's nerve and hit him at will, although Brusso was cautious. During the 5th round, Brusso dropped Thornton with a right (or right and left) on the chin. After the "colored lad" rose at the count of nine, all but out, a sheriff's deputy entered the ring and stopped fight. The authorities did not want to allow a true knockout. The bout was awarded to Brusso.

> [Brosso] had done most of the leading throughout and had his man practically at the end of his rope. Brosso gave a good exhibition, but showed his lack of experience in leaving openings that a more aggressive man than Thornton could have used to advantage. The bout was a fast and interesting one throughout. They met at catchweights, the white lad having quite a bit the better of it on this point.[11]

A semi-local report out of Jackson, Michigan said that Larry Coleman promoted the show. Before the bouts started, the 14 deputy sheriffs on hand announced that knockouts were barred. "Brousso" and Thornton worked their arms like pistons as they whirled about the ring. It was nip and tuck during the first 4 rounds, with Thornton having perhaps just a shade the better of matters. Between rounds, Kid Kennedy advised Brousso.

In the 5th round, like a flash, Brousso landed a hard left to the neck that sent Fred's head back. A follow-up punch to the stomach doubled him up, and then a right to the jaw dropped him. Thornton just beat Referee Wellman's 10-count, but was sent down again by stiff jab to the face. At that point, Deputy Sheriff L.P. Muffat jumped through the ropes to stop it and prevent a true ten-count knockout. "Thornton was knocked down and out as far as anybody could tell."[12]

Pugilism was flourishing in the Delray/Detroit area. Less than a month after the Thornton fight, on February 5, 1902, the Detroit Athletic Club hosted its first winter smoker, for members only at its gymnasium. 500 club members were in attendance. The scheduled 8-round wind-up featured Delray's whirlwind Noah Brusso versus Detroit's Billy Walsh. Jack Collins

---

11 *Detroit Free Press, Detroit Times,* January 17, 1902. It is possible that Brusso began his career earlier and that he fought Thornton twice. A source reporting in 1904 indicated that Thornton and Brusso fought twice in Delray, Brusso the first time winning in 6 rounds, the second time stopping him in the 5th round. It is unknown when the previous bout took place, if it did, or whether it was just the product of Brusso's faulty memory. *Milwaukee Daily News,* October 6, 1904.
12 *Jackson Daily Citizen,* January 18, 1902.

officiated as the announcer. William Considine and James McCafferty acted as timekeepers.

According to the local *Detroit Free Press*, up to and including the 3rd round, they fought a hurricane battle, although Walsh appeared timid, and Brusso was easily the better man. At one point during the 3rd round, both men simultaneously went through the ropes, putting the ring out of business and necessitating a five-minute delay while the platform was strengthened.

In the 4th round, Brusso attempted to end matters, and knocked Walsh down twice. He was landing at will. Just as the bell sounded, the men clinched and broke away. Brusso later claimed that he did not hear the gong, so he struck Walsh just as Billy started to go to his corner. Referee Coffin did not allow the foul.

In the 5th round, Brusso had him all but out, and in his eagerness to land a finishing blow, he struck Walsh while he was on his knees, committing another foul that was overlooked. Walsh refused to continue, and so the referee gave Brusso the decision.[13]

The *Detroit Evening News* said the bout drew both hisses and laughter. The "suburbanite" "Brusso seemed to prefer to use foul tactics rather than fair, but his ways were overlooked by the referee."[14]

According to semi-local papers, the two men knocked each other through the ropes and fiercely pounded on one another in a very exciting bout. Brusso fouled twice; hitting Walsh once after the gong had rung, and once while Walsh was on his knees. The referee allowed neither of the foul claims, and so when Walsh refused to continue, Brusso was awarded the victory.[15]

In early March, Brusso was scheduled to box a 10-round rematch against Fred Thornton at Weiler's Hall, 1171 Russell Street. It was said that Brusso and Thornton had met some time ago in a fast fight and that Brusso had won. However, on this occasion, for whatever reason, on very short notice, Brusso's opponent changed. Hence, Brusso's belief that he fought Thornton twice might have been in error, when in fact he fought another black fighter who subbed in for Thornton.[16]

One month after the Walsh bout, on March 3, 1902 in Detroit, Delray's Noah Brusso took on Harry Peppers, another black fighter, in a scheduled 8-round bout. According to secondary sources, Peppers had been fighting since at least 1892. Amongst his bouts with recognizable opponents, Peppers' results included: 1894 KO4 Dan Hickey; 1896 D10 Jack Stelzner; 1897 L10 Australian Billy Smith, ND6 Jack Bonner, and LKOby19 George Byers; 1898 LKOby2 Ed Dunkhorst, LKOby1 Joe Butler, and D6 Jimmy

---

13 *Detroit Free Press*, February 5, 6, 1902.
14 *Detroit Evening News*, February 6, 1902.
15 *Grand Rapids Evening Press, Saginaw Evening News*, February 6, 1902.
16 *Detroit Today* (a.k.a. *Detroit Times*), March 3, 1902.

Watts; 1899 L6 Jack Root, D6 George Grant, KO6 Frank "Dutch" Neal (who died four days later as a result of injuries suffered in this bout), and LKOby2 Jack Bonner; 1901 LKOby3 Young Peter Jackson, and 1902 W6 Jim Driscoll and D6 Jack Beauscholte. Ironically, in early 1898, Peppers drew the color line against a boxer of his own race. "Peppers is the first colored boxer who ever drew the color line with a boxer his own color, and he is being laughed at by everybody connected with the sport." However, he had fought black fighters before and after that. Brusso was taking on a fighter with far more experience than he, and one who had experience against quality fighters.[17]

Harry Peppers

Against Brusso, Peppers went to the mat eight times in the 1st round, although Brusso only truly sent him there once. It appeared that Peppers was intentionally dropping to save himself from punishment. In the 2nd round, Peppers continued to fall until he finally "bumped into a stiff jolt which toppled him over and this time he quit for keeps."

Harry had tasted Noah's power and thought that discretion was the better part of valor. It was opined that it would be in the sport's best interests if in the future the local promoters tabooed the less than courageous Peppers. Still, the victory was significant, given Peppers' experience, having gone 19 rounds with Byers and the full 6 with Root. The fact that subsequently that year Peppers would fight Billy Stift to a 10-round draw and lose a 6-round decision to Mike Schreck was further evidence that Noah Brusso's punch had some pop in order to make Harry Peppers quit in 2 rounds.[18]

A mere two days after the Peppers bout, on March 5, 1902, before a crowded gymnasium at the Detroit Athletic Club, in a scheduled 6-round bout, Delray's Noah Brusso met Detroit's Archie Steele. They were said to be nearly the same weight. Owing to the demand of outsiders/non-

17 *Louisville Evening Post*, March 16, 1898; Cyberboxingzone.com; Boxrec.com.
18 *Detroit Evening News*, *Detroit Free Press*, March 4, 1902. Boxrec.com.

members for admission, the club sold a limited number of tickets at a half dollar each. Members were admitted for free.

From the start, Brusso attacked furiously and had the best of matters. Steele quickly realized that he had little chance to win. Therefore, Archie repeatedly clinched to save himself from punishment, and deliberately hit low every time they clinched.

In the 2nd round, Steele absorbed some punishment, but continued hitting below the belt. Steele had fouled at least a dozen times. Finally, Referee Eddie Ryan disqualified him, no one being more pleased than Steele, who was happy to be out of the bout. "It is evident that Noah Brusso, of Delray, has every local boxer of his weight frightened." Two fighters in a row had looked for early exits from their bouts with Brusso, one simply by quitting, Peppers, and another, Steele, by de facto quitting by intentionally fouling in order to get himself disqualified.[19]

During the early part of his boxing career, Brusso fell in love with Nellie Sweitzer. The two saw each other for some time, but Brusso eventually drifted apart from her, feeling that potential marriage with her might hinder his career as a professional boxer. He was determined to climb to the profession's top ranks. At that time, most believed that women weakened fighters. Brusso also felt that the responsibilities of marriage might force him to choose another less speculative profession. So, according to Brusso, he eventually gave up the love of his life.[20]

In the meantime, one month after his victory over Steele, on Friday April 4, 1902 at Handloser's Hall in Delray, under the auspices of the River Rouge Athletic Club, in the wind-up, Brusso fought a rematch with Billy Walsh. 500 people witnessed the bouts. Five deputy sheriffs were on hand, but they did not interfere. Billy Considine refereed.

Brusso and Walsh hammered each other for 6 rounds, "the former earning the decision by a good margin." Another paper said, "Brusso beat Walsh in six rounds of fierce fighting." It is unclear whether Brusso knocked him out or won a points decision.[21]

Just two weeks later, on April 18, 1902 before a crowd that filled the Detroit Athletic Club's gymnasium, in the main event, Brusso took on Bay City's Ed Sholtrau (also spelled Sheltrau or Sholtreau) in a fight advertised as being for the Michigan State Middleweight Championship. The bout was "one of much local interest." Sholtrau was touted as a very promising middleweight. "Sholtreau had beaten a lot of men and weighed 10 pounds more than the Delray boy, who is practically a novice."[22]

---

19 *Detroit Free Press, Detroit Times* (a.k.a. *Detroit Today*), *Detroit Evening News,* March 4 - 6, 1902. The local papers said his name was Archie Steele. Some later called him George Steele.
20 McCaffery at 43-44.
21 *Detroit Free Press, Detroit Evening News,* April 5, 1902.
22 *West Bay City Times-Press,* April 17, 1902; *Detroit Free Press,* April 18, 1902; *Detroit Evening News,* April 19, 1902.

The fight lasted just 1 minute and 35 seconds. When the gong rang, the men sparred and did some footwork, feeling each other out for about a minute. They danced away and came together again. Just as Sholtrau stepped in, Brusso came to him and landed a right hook that caught him on the point of the chin. It did not look to be a hard blow, but it was well placed and Sholtrau dropped "like a dog playing dead." It was the first real blow of the contest, and it functionally ended the bout.

Sholtrau came up wobbly at eight. He rushed into another jaw punch that dropped him again. Brusso decked him again and again. Ed would either land on his face or the back of his head, but he was game, and kept rising. Upon the fourth or fifth knockdown, Referee Eddie Ryan stopped the bout "and cheated the ambulance," although Sholtrau might have continued for 20-30 more seconds had he been allowed to do so. When Sholtrau rose to walk to his corner, he traveled in a circle, his legs being all but gone. Nothing could have prevented a knockout. It took some time for him to get his bearings again.

Once again, Noah Brusso had demonstrated his punching power. "Brusso has been learning a lot of late and he now looks to be the best of any of the middleweights around here."[23]

One month later, Brusso fought a rematch with Sholtrau, who was also known as "The Bay City Brawler." Sholtrau claimed that his 1st round knockout loss to Brusso was a fluke. He wanted the rematch.[24]

This was the final card of the boxing season at the Detroit Athletic Club's gymnasium. Eddie Ryan would manage the show as usual. Members would be admitted for free, but outsiders would be charged an admission fee.[25]

Brusso and Sholtrau fought again at the packed Detroit Athletic Club on May 16, 1902, in a scheduled 10-round bout. It was the card's main event and final fight.[26]

This time, it was a very good fight. In the 1st round, it looked like the bout would be a repeat of their first match. Brusso landed a right that made Sholtrau dizzy. However, Ed hung on and survived the round.

Thereafter, Brusso led and was the aggressor. In the 3rd round, Sholtrau began improving and hit Brusso's body, distressing him. Still, Brusso had won the first few rounds.

However, in the 4th round, Sholtrau knocked Brusso down with a body blow. Sholtrau's body shots hurt Brusso, and he chased Noah around the ring. He continued doing so through the 6th round. A body punch in the 6th almost knocked Brusso through the ropes. Ed landed more body punches

23 *Detroit Free Press, Detroit Evening News,* April 19, 1902.

24 *Detroit Free Press,* May 15, 16, 1902; *Detroit News,* May 16, 1902. *The Detroit News* said that the last time Brusso and Sholtreau fought the bout was settled before the timer's watch got fairly started. Sholtreau was apparently an experienced fighter with 20 victories under his belt. McCaffery at 44.

25 *Jackson Citizen Patriot,* May 10, 1902.

26 *Detroit News,* May 16, 1902.

in the 7th round as well. Noah was doing less leading and landing during these rounds.

However, although Brusso was not as good as Sholtrau from the 4th to the 7th rounds, it was also said that Noah's punches hurt more, and he frequently landed. Brusso's "work was truer." Hence, these rounds were not one-sided.

Brusso had lost the middle rounds, but from the 8th round on, he came out fresher and started forcing matters. In the 9th round, Brusso rushed and did well. The 10th round was fierce, and, like the 9th, very much in Brusso's favor. At the end of the bout, Brusso had Sholtrau in a bad way. Noah Brusso showed that he could finish well.

Referee Ed Ryan awarded Brusso the close decision. "There was very little criticism of the award, though Sholtrau might have been given a draw without any injustice being worked." Noah had found it to be a much tougher task than he probably anticipated coming into the fight. Overall, Sholtrau lacked Brusso's speed and ability to land cleanly. Otherwise, he might have won. During the middle of the bout, Sholtrau was the aggressor and took the lead, but his slowness cost him chances. The "nonpareil" Brusso had narrowly earned the victory with his good start and strong finish, and harder and cleaner punches.[27]

During this time, Brusso began seeing a lady named Irene Peppers. She allegedly attended Noah's fights dressed as a man. They eventually got married the following year, on November 2, 1903, but divorced six months later.[28]

Following the tough Sholtrau rematch, continuing his monthly fighting clip, next up for the now 21-year-old Brusso was Dick Smith, another local fighter. They fought in Mount Clemens, Michigan on June 27, 1902, in a scheduled 10-round bout advertised as being for the Michigan State Welterweight Championship. Welterweight? Although the weights were not reported, it is possible that Brusso made 147 pounds.

One month earlier, on the undercard of Brusso-Sholtrau II, Dick Smith had scored a KO3 over Big Earl Thompson. In April, on the undercard of Brusso-Walsh II, Smith had defeated Fred Wellman in 6 rounds. The well-respected Smith was actually the betting favorite over Brusso.[29]

According to the *Detroit Free Press*, the 1st round was entertaining. When the 2nd round was halfway complete, "Brusso got to Smith when he was a trifle off his guard, and sent over what appeared to be a not very stiff blow. It reached Smith's jaw and sent him over backwards. His head hit the boards and the count was almost superfluous, Smith being unable to rise for

27 *Detroit Free Press, Detroit News,* May 17, 1902. The *Detroit Free Press* spelled it Sholtrau, while the *Detroit News* spelled it Sholtreau.

28 One secondary source believes that Irene Peppers might have been Harry Peppers' sister. If so, Noah Brusso was not afraid of having an interracial relationship. However, she may have just had the same last name. This is unclear. McCaffery at 50-52.

29 *Detroit Free Press,* May 17, 1902, June 27, 1902.

some time after its completion." Once again, Noah Brusso had shown that his punches had pop.

Smith claimed that it was the unpadded ring that really caused his defeat. He wanted a rematch. His friends called the 2nd round knockout blow a fluke. Certainly though, Brusso had been demonstrating effective punching power on a consistent basis.[30]

The semi-local *Jackson Citizen Patriot* reported that it was anybody's fight up to the point in the 2nd round that Brusso landed a left swing which sent Smith into dreamland for five minutes.[31]

Dick Smith got his wish, and they fought a rematch a mere twelve days later, on July 9, 1902, again in Mt. Clemens. Tom McCune was originally supposed to fight Brusso, but he pulled out, claiming that he had insufficient time to get into shape. Therefore, the recently defeated Smith filled in. Back then, there were no suspensions after being knocked out.[32]

Brusso started off the bout trying to repeat his previous knockout success against his foe, but Smith hung tough and took a pounding in the 1st round. After that round, Smith managed to come back, fight hard, and make it an exciting fight. However, Brusso had the better of it all the way. Brusso dropped Smith twice in the 9th round, only the bell saving him. Smith was again game in the 10th round, but Brusso dropped him three more times in that round. Smith managed to survive and Brusso was awarded the clear 10-round decision.[33]

Regarding the heavyweight fight scene, in late July 1902, in their rematch held in San Francisco, heavyweight champion James J. Jeffries scored a KO8 over former champion Bob Fitzsimmons.

For the first time, Noah Brusso ventured outside of Michigan to fight, taking on Jack O'Donnell on September 19, 1902 in Butler, Indiana. The *National Police Gazette* and the *Jackson Citizen Patriot* reported that one of the most scientific prize fights ever held in Northern Indiana occurred at Butler on Friday, September 19 at midnight, in which Noah Brusso, of Detroit, welterweight champion of Michigan, knocked out Jack O'Donnell, of Cleveland, Ohio, in the 11th round. James Foley acted as referee.[34]

On October 21, Brusso and Reddy Phillips agreed to fight in Lansing, Michigan in two weeks. Phillips wanted the bout to be held at 154 pounds, but Brusso thought that was too low, given their limited training time. They agreed to weigh in no more than 158 pounds at ringside, right before the fight. There would be a $100 side bet in addition to a purse.[35]

30 *Detroit Free Press,* June 28, 1902.
31 *Jackson Citizen Patriot,* June 28, 1902.
32 *Detroit Free Press,* July 8, 1902.
33 *Detroit Free Press, Detroit News,* July 10, 1902.
34 *National Police Gazette,* October 11, 1902; *Jackson Citizen Patriot,* September 22, 1902. The November 1, 1902 edition of the *National Police Gazette* had a photo of Brusso with a caption that read, "Says he's the welterweight champion of Michigan."
35 *Jackson Citizen Patriot,* October 22, 1902.

On Friday, October 24, 1902, Brusso announced that a carnival of boxing would take place that evening at his gymnasium on Michigan Avenue. He was set to spar 5 rounds each with Earl Thompson and a fighter named Moore (likely Billy Moore). Brusso's main sparring partner, Jimmy Duggan, would also spar with two others. Brusso was preparing for the Phillips bout.[36]

On November 6, 1902 at the Lansing Athletic Club in Lansing, Michigan, Brusso took on "Reddy" Phillips in a scheduled 10-round bout. According to the local *Lansing Daily Journal*, a crowd of 500 was on hand, with folks coming from all over Michigan, including Detroit, Jackson, Ionia and Mason. Before the fight, odds of $100 to $50 were offered on Brusso, the favorite, with no takers.

NOAH BRUSSO

The main event was late to start, owing to the fact that when the gloves were handed to the fighters, the box contained three right-handed mitts and only one left. It took a messenger nearly half an hour to return with another left-handed glove.

The fight was mostly tame. In the 1st round, they showed respect for one another, primarily using cautious taps. By the 2nd round, it was obvious that Brusso was the cleverer of the two. He was quick in eluding Phillips' dangerous swings, which only landed once or twice. Both were careful though, and neither wanted to mix it up. This continued in the 3rd round.

The 4th round opened with Phillips leaping from his corner and rushing at Brusso, but Noah sidestepped the attack. They clinched, and Phillips flagrantly hit Brusso in the back. The crowd howled "foul," and did not stop their complaints until the referee halted matters for a moment to inform the house, "If I was to give the decision on every break of a technical rule, there would be no fight."

In the 5th round, Phillips landed a left uppercut to the jaw that sent the Canadian back. However, not much else of note took place. The 5th through 7th rounds were hotter than the first four, but neither man received any punishment, and the mixes were infrequent and tame. The 8th round was again cautious, so the referee informed the boxers that unless they woke up, there would be no decision.

---

36 *Detroit Tribune*, October 24, 1902.

As a result of the referee's ultimatum to liven up matters, the 9th round was the hottest of the fight, and the first with real fighting. Three quarters of the fighting that was done in the bout was done in the 9th round. Brusso attacked and forced Phillips into a corner until Reddy clinched. After breaking, Phillips' lead was blocked and Brusso landed on the chest. They clinched again and Phillips went to the ropes. Brusso then landed several hard punches to the body and head that functionally put Phillips out of the contest. Noah rained additional forceful blows on his face and side. They clinched, broke clean, and again Brusso broke down Phillips' guard, landing his right to the chin and then left to the neck. The round closed with the two sparring, but Phillips was plainly "all in." At the bell, Reddy dropped into his corner. Fatigued, outclassed, and too exhausted to continue, Phillips retired, and his corner threw up the sponge. Referee Quealey awarded Brusso the bout.

The local *Lansing Daily Journal* opined, "Had Phillips gone in for the tenth round, he undoubtedly would have been knocked out. A blow on the kidney had taken the strength out of him and he was in no condition for another round." Brusso had been cautious, pecking away for 8 rounds, and then essentially pummeled Phillips into submission with one round of hard fighting.[37]

The semi-local Detroit newspapers reported that Reddy Phillips fought gamely and gave Brusso a hard contest, but that Noah was the more skillful and better conditioned. Phillips became very tired in the 7th round and was quite groggy at the end of the round. He managed to hang on until the 9th round, when he "threw up the sponge" and retired.

Despite the reports that Phillips had quit after the 9th round, the following morning Phillips called the *Detroit Evening News* office and said the reason he could not continue was that he fell off the stage in the 9th round and had injured himself. However, the local account did not back his claim.[38]

The *National Police Gazette* reported that Detroit clubs were offering purses for a bout between Brusso and Al Weinig. However, one promoter asked, "Who is Brusso? How much would he draw in Fort Erie? ... How much? Not enough to pay me for putting out the bills." He questioned Brusso's drawing powers. Still, Brusso was on the rise, having won at least eleven fights in a row in less than a year. Local promoters were using him as the main event about every month or so. There was also some local discussion of a possible bout with Billy Moore, but the fight did not materialize until late the following year.[39]

---

37 *Lansing Daily Journal*, November 7, 1902.
38 *Detroit Today* (a.k.a. *Detroit Times*), October 25, November 7, 1902; *Detroit Free Press, Detroit Evening News*, November 7, 1902.
39 *National Police Gazette*, December 13, 1902.

Former heavyweight champion James J. Corbett was in Detroit, sparring and working out there for one week in early December 1902. He was anticipating a rematch with champion James Jeffries. On December 9, 1902, Corbett sparred for a short time with Harry Nederlander and also mixed it up for 10 minutes with middleweight Noah Brusso.

Afterwards, Corbett had "considerable praise" for the Detroit boys, as well as advice. Of his sparring with Brusso, "The bout was very fast, and after it was over the ex-champion had some good words for the local boy. 'He settles his muscles too much,' said Corbett. 'Let him overcome that and he will be heard from. He can certainly hit some.'"[40]

Corbett had sparred Jeffries on Jeff's way up the ladder, and now Noah Brusso had the honor of having been in the ring with the former champ. His showing and Corbett's compliments gave Brusso confidence. He took Corbett's advice and worked on relaxing his muscles more. Years later, Brusso said he sparred with Corbett several times that week and learned something new each time.[41]

On Friday, December 26, 1902 at Detroit's Light Guard Armory, on a card sponsored by the Metropolitan Athletic Club, Brusso fought Tom McCune for the Michigan State Middleweight Championship. Amongst his bouts, McCune had an 1897 D4 Dave Sullivan; 1899 LKOby12 Philadelphia Jack O'Brien; and 1900 W6 Young Peter Jackson. He was coming off a late 1902 KO2 Bobby Thompson and L10 Jimmy Duggan. He had at least 19 pro bouts of experience.[42]

Although Brusso was heavier, stronger, and younger, McCune had the superior experience, height, and reach, and therefore was the favorite going into the bout.

It was a fast and clean middleweight fight, with both men surprisingly speedy. McCune kept away from Brusso's powerful right hand and contented himself with lefts to the body. There was not much hard work until the 3rd round.

In the 4th round, Brusso dropped McCune.

In the 5th round, both went down. Brusso had scored another knockdown, but perhaps in trying too eagerly to follow up, Noah ran into a right swing and "almost went through the floor." When he rose, Noah was more wobbly than McCune, who tried but could not land the finishing blow.

The 6th round was a breathing spell for both men.

To that point, it was an even fight. McCune was a clever boxer, both offensively and defensively. "Brusso used more caution than in most of his

---

40 *Detroit Free Press,* December 8 - 10, 1902; *Detroit Times,* December 9, 10, 1902. Corbett did not appear at the DAC gym on the 8th, disappointing fans. He first put on gloves with club members on the 9th.
41 *Los Angeles Herald,* November 23, 1906.
42 Boxrec.com.

earlier contests. He had the punch, however, and every clean blow that he landed counted in speeding the close of the encounter."

Brusso cut loose again in the 7th round, rushing after McCune, working his left for the jaw. Noah was superior inside, and was landing, mostly using his left. When McCune was near the ropes, Brusso landed a hard left hook to the jaw, hurting Tom. Noah then landed a lighter blow of the same punch. McCune circled back to ring center, but Brusso feinted a left and then landed a straight right to the jaw that dropped McCune "as though he had come through the roof."

McCune rose, but was nearly out, and Brusso easily decked him again with another right. McCune gamely got up again, but it was obvious that he was in no state to continue, so Referee Terry McGovern stopped it with 20 seconds left in the 7th round.

Tom McCune was a very clever boxer, but was outmatched whenever they had mixed it up, because Brusso was the superior puncher. One reporter said Brusso had improved immensely, particularly in his defensive work, which formerly was his weak point. Noah was able to evade and cover-up very cleverly, avoiding McCune's long left. He had also demonstrated improved offensive speed and the power that counts, having hurt McCune with a left hook and finishing him with a straight right.[43]

One semi-local source said the club had instructed Referee McGovern to stop the bouts when one contestant was clearly beaten. This robbed the show of any brutality and gave the spectators great satisfaction. Some referees would not terminate a bout until a fighter was down for the full ten seconds. Although no decisions were necessary that evening, the club had appointed two judges to act along with the referee to award any potential decisions.[44]

At the end of his first year of professional boxing, Noah Brusso had a record of 12-0 with at least 8 knockouts. Clearly, Brusso had skill and power.

During his free time, Brusso liked to ice skate, and it was said that he was one of the fastest skaters in the city to patronize the rinks.

Noah Brusso's first bout of 1903 was considered a very big step up in class, when he took on Cincinnati southpaw Mike Schreck. According to a secondary source, Schreck was undefeated. He was vastly more experienced than Brusso, with fifty pro bouts of experience compared to Brusso's twelve, and he had fought a high level of opposition. His recent career included 1902 D6 Jack "Twin" Sullivan, D6 and W6 Hugo Kelly, W6 Harry Peppers (over whom Burns scored a KO2), and a January 12, 1903 W6 Jack Beauscholte (who in 1901 Marvin Hart had stopped in the 10th round), just four days prior to the Brusso fight.[45] Schreck would be a prominent fighter

43 *Detroit Free Press, Detroit News,* December 27, 1902.
44 *Jackson Citizen Patriot,* December 27, 1902.
45 Boxrec.com.

on the boxing scene in the years to come. Brusso regarded the bout to be the most important of his career up to that point.

The local newspaper said,

> [Schreck is] one of the most successful boxers of the present season. Schreck has been beating all of the Chicago men, his list of victims including Jim Driscoll, Jack Beauscholte, Gloomy Spencer and Harry Peppers. He is matched to box Hugo Kelly next week. Schreck and Kelly have met twice, once for a draw and once for a decision to Schreck.[46]

The Brusso-Schreck bout took place at Detroit's Light Guard Armory on January 16, 1903. Terry McGovern refereed. It was a scheduled 10-round bout at 156 pounds. The local paper said Brusso would be lighter than he had been for any previous battle. Schreck was reported to weigh 156 pounds, and Brusso was likely about the same. They fought in a 24-foot-ring. 3,000 spectators witnessed the fight, which was the main event and final bout of the card.[47]

Schreck's southpaw style was unique from what Brusso was accustomed to fighting. From the beginning, Schreck rushed matters and chased after Brusso, who moved about the ring. It

Mike Schreck

seemed as if they were playing a game of tag. Schreck went after him like a tiger, with his head down and bent nearly double, playing for the ribs with a wide left swing that missed. Brusso landed several light punches on the jaw. Noah kept up his stiff-arm right leads for the face, mostly missing. He failed to use his left, despite the fact that there were openings for its use.

Beginning in the 2nd round, after they clinched, Schreck would side-step or spin over to the side and then shoot a left, although Brusso was usually able to evade the blow.

---

46 *Detroit Free Press*, January 16, 1903.
47 *Detroit Today*, January 15, 16, 1903.

Halfway through the fight, Schreck began attacking the body with more success. By the 7th round, Brusso looked tired as a result of the continual stiff lefts that Schreck had landed on his body. However, one paper said that honors were even for 7 rounds.

Through the first 8 rounds, Schreck did the forcing, with Brusso blocking and unsuccessfully trying to land his right. Brusso tried hard and often to land his right, but Schreck avoided it every time, primarily by ducking. Brusso either missed when Mike ducked, or he was short, or he only landed a glancing blow. Brusso used his left very little, although Schreck appeared to be open for jabs.

In the 8th round, Schreck's body punches had Brusso in distress. Just before the bell, Schreck finally raised his left from the body up to the jaw and knocked Brusso down for a nine-count. Just as he rose, the bell came to his rescue.

In the 9th round, showing his recuperative powers, Brusso came up fresh and rushed in like a whirlwind, which is what one paper opined he should have done earlier. Brusso twice landed his hard right to the jaw, which staggered and shook up Schreck, causing him to hang on. Schreck stalled just enough to get out of danger. Weakened by the early continuous body attack, Brusso slowed up, allowing Mike to take up the pursuit again.

In the 10th round, Brusso again hurt Schreck, but once again was unable to follow up and finish him. For most of the round, Schreck did the leading.

One local paper said the judges gave the 10-round decision to Schreck, "who fairly earned it." Another said that on "general results, leads and lands, it was Schreck's bout." Still a third newspaper said Brusso only lost the bout "by a slight margin." Noah had suffered his first defeat, albeit by a close decision to a far more experienced fighter.

It was said that Brusso had failed to gain the decision over Schreck as a result of his failure to follow up at critical moments. Still, the "west sider" was willing and displayed more than a little science and very fast footwork, doing much of the leading as well. Brusso's winning right hand punch started a hundred times for the Ohioan's jaw with sufficient force to put him to sleep, but Schreck's crouching attitude and low duck found Noah's glove pointing at the stars.

One local writer called it a "slashing bout." Another said the fight was interesting, but "at times slow, owing to the inability of either man to land effectively, and to holding, Brusso being the one most at fault in the latter respect." He seemed a bit nervous and not as strong in his first battle with a man of reputation. However, the defeat was not considered a discredit to Brusso, given that he had fought relatively well against a left-handed fighter with far more experience.

Schreck was described as "awkwardly clever; he is very resourceful and game to the last. He can cut loose about 40 different ways." Another writer felt that despite his billing, Schreck was not so much clever but "so awkward that he puts a clever man at sea. He is left-handed, and he comes in side-on, so to speak, making it hard for a boxer who sees him in action for the first time to get to him. Such cleverness as Schreck did show was in ducking." Brusso "found it difficult to map out a plan of campaign against Schreck, who is one of the most awkward boxers in the ring."[48]

The local press was still quite high on Brusso. A couple days after the bout, the *Detroit Free Press* said that despite his first loss, Brusso's reputation had actually been enhanced rather than damaged. He made a good showing and stood up through 10 hard rounds against a good man. "He could have made more by forcing the fight in its early stages, and he might have reached Schreck had he been coached on the use of his left hand. In a second meeting there is no doubt that he would make a better showing." Noah Brusso showed promise.[49]

Back in the ring again in his typical once-a-month fighting pace, on February 13, 1903 at the Delray Athletic Club, Brusso took on Boston's Jim O'Brien, who claimed to be the brother of either Dick O'Brien or Jack O'Brien, depending on the source. They agreed to box at 160 pounds.[50]

O'Brien lasted the full 10 rounds, but was given a "sound trouncing" by Brusso, who was the easy decision winner of the fierce bout. Jim O'Brien was not clever, but game. He rarely used his right hand. Brusso battered him at will and landed his heavy right to the jaw, but could not put him out. "Nothing short of an ax would have knocked out Jim O'Brien." Noah kept up a steady hail of blows and had him at his mercy all the way. O'Brien scattered his gore all over the ring, the spectators, and his opponent.

Brusso did finally drop O'Brien in the 10th round, but Jim managed to get up at eight and finished the round as gamely as he had fought all along. Referee Lavigne awarded Brusso the 10-round decision.[51]

The following month, on March 25, 1903 at Handloser's Hall in Delray, Michigan, Brusso took on two men in rematches on the same day. Brusso contracted to stop both Dick Smith and Reddy Phillips one after the other, each within 6 rounds. This was the type of feat that if successfully achieved, would bring him big publicity. Brusso had previously fought both: 1902 KO2 and W10 Smith, and 1902 KO9 Phillips. The self-imposed task was risky, given that both opponents had lasted more than 6 rounds in Brusso's most recent meetings with them, and Brusso would have to deal with the fatigue of having fought one before meeting the other fresh man, which could also affect his pacing in the first bout. Clearly, Brusso had courage and confidence. One woman was in attendance.[52]

---

48 *Detroit Free Press, Detroit News, Detroit Times,* January 17, 1903.
49 *Detroit Free Press,* January 18, 1903.
50 *Detroit Free Press, Detroit Today,* February 13, 1903.
51 *Detroit Free Press, Detroit Times,* February 14, 1903. Brusso and Jim O'Brien would fight again a few years later, in 1906, when Brusso was heavyweight champion.
52 *Detroit Free Press,* March 25, 1903.

This time, Dick Smith held his own in the 1st round, though Brusso had the better of it. Smith led in the 2nd round, but Brusso willingly mixed it. After Smith landed a heavy body shot, Brusso retaliated with a right to the nose that dropped Smith. The gong saved him. In the 3rd round, Brusso attacked and scored two knockdowns in quick succession, using his right. He finished matters with a right to the jaw that put Smith down and out.

After Smith left the ring, Reddy Phillips was up. From the start of their bout, Phillips was a dirty fighter, fouling in every way imaginable, especially by consistently hitting on the break, despite the referee's cautions. He made no effort to fight fairly.

Brusso had the better of the 1st round, though Phillips landed some hard blows. The fouls continued in the 2nd, and when Brusso went in to finish him, Phillips deliberately kicked Noah in the groin. The whole crowd saw it and hissed. Referee Considine immediately disqualified Phillips and chased him from the ring. One writer said Phillips fought more like a dog than a human.[53]

Another local newspaper's version said there was obviously something personal between Brusso and Phillips, and they were out to settle their differences. Brusso grabbed Phillips by the throat, landing a battering ram right while holding. Phillips responded by kicking and appeared anxious to bite as well. The referee quickly disqualified Phillips.[54]

Brusso had achieved his self-imposed task of defeating two men within 6 rounds each, one right after another, via KO3 and DQ2.

On April 18, 1903 in Detroit, Brusso was scheduled to box Horace Thompson in an exhibition bout.[55]

Just for some contextual flavor, the following day's newspaper said the telephone had been growing astronomically. In 1892, there were 552,720 Bell instruments in use. By the conclusion of 1902, the number had increased to 3,150,320.[56]

After defeating two solid fighters on the same night, for the first time in his career, Brusso was inactive for several months. In the spring of 1903, Noah moved and began living in Houghton, Michigan. He joined the Portage Lake lacrosse club.

There was some discussion of a potential Brusso-Jack Beauscholte bout to be held at Windsor, Ontario (just over the border from Detroit) on July 3, but for some reason, it did not take place.[57]

53 *Detroit Free Press*, *Detroit News*, March 26, 1903.
54 *Detroit Times*, March 26, 1903.
55 *Detroit Free Press*, April 18, 1903. Secondary sources report that on April 18, 1903 in Detroit, Brusso stopped Earl Thompson in the 3rd round. However, a local source merely said that Brusso was scheduled to box an exhibition with Horace Thompson. Black heavyweight Big Earl Thompson had fought on the Brusso–Sholtrau II undercard, when Dick Smith stopped him in the 3rd round. Whether Brusso fought Earl or Horace Thompson and whether it was just an exhibition is unclear. Semi-primary-source reports of Brusso's record do not list this bout. *Detroit Free Press*, May 17, 1902; McCaffery at 70.
56 *Detroit Free Press*, April 19, 1903.
57 *Rockford Daily Register-Gazette*, June 30, 1903.

Brusso scheduled an August 25 bout at 158 pounds against Chicago's Jerry Driscoll, to be held at the Port Huron Club (northeast of Detroit). However, for whatever reason, this bout did not take place either.[58]

In August 1903 in San Francisco, heavyweight champion James Jeffries knocked out Jim Corbett in the 10th round of their rematch. About that time, a black fighter named Jack Johnson, who was the colored heavyweight champion, was being noticed as a possible contender to the crown. However, Jeff said that he would not defend the title against a black fighter.[59] At that time, Jeffries did not draw a great deal of criticism from the press. Although Johnson was a good, skillful boxer, his style was less than entertaining, and he was not seen as a very big threat. It was years later said, "As most of Johnson's important battles were merely won on points, Jeffries has not been very much criticized for passing the negro up." Still, Johnson would remain prominent on the heavyweight fight scene for years to come.[60]

On September 25, 1903 before a good-sized crowd at the Amphidrome in Houghton, Michigan, Noah Brusso took on Jimmy Duggan, who held a 1902 W10 over Tom McCune. Duggan had fought on the undercard of Brusso-Schreck, having looked good in defeating Brooklyn's Eddie Cain in a 10-round decision, utilizing his aggressive style. It was said that Duggan could both hit and withstand punishment, and was a very promising fighter. Duggan had once been a Brusso sparring partner.[61]

The local *Houghton Daily Mining Gazette* said that Jimmy Duggan of Detroit would defend his title of middleweight champion of Michigan against Noah Brusso of Houghton. Of course, Brusso had already won that title, not Duggan, but even back then, anyone could simply claim they were a champion of some sort. For marketing purposes, promoters often liked to claim that a type of championship was involved, as they still do.

The local paper said Brusso was a former Detroiter, but had resided in Houghton since last spring, coming there to play lacrosse with the Portage Lakes. It said that Brusso's record was 16-1.[62] Noah was described as young, strong, and fast.

> Duggan is still young, but he has been at the fighting game since he was a boy and has figured in 30 battles. He has beaten Harry Fails, who fought Johnny Thompson during the Hancock tournament, in three rounds. Harry Lemmons, the colored fighter who was brought up at that time to beat up Bud Higgins, went down before Jimmy in

58 *Bay City Evening Times, Jackson Citizen Patriot*, August 17, 1903, *Flint Daily Journal*, August 18, 1903.
59 *Police Gazette*, September 5, 1903.
60 *Police Gazette*, October 13, 1906.
61 *Detroit Free Press*, January 17, 1903, January 18, 1903; *Milwaukee Daily News*, October 6, 1904.
62 Of course, if this paper is correct, then several of the bouts that Brusso/Burns later claimed took place from 1900-1901 actually happened in 1902, because this record matches the known bouts that took place since 1902.

three rounds and Jim Popp lasted the same length of time. Duggan fought a draw with Mike Ward and has gained decisions over Tom McCune and Eddie Cain.[63]

Billy Moore of Syracuse seconded Duggan, and he challenged the winner. Frank Ellingwood was in Brusso's corner.

Brusso entered the ring early, while Duggan did not appear for some time. Brusso's physical form appeared magnificent. Duggan had the physique as well, but proved to be clumsier in his actions.

The fight was Brusso's from the start. The 1st round was fast. In the 2nd round, Brusso twice dropped Duggan for nine seconds. In the 3rd round, it was plain that Brusso would eventually win. Duggan showed up better in the 4th round, "which provided a give and take mill of the slashing variety and it was anybody's round." They fought fiercely. However, it was all Brusso after this round.

By the 6th round, Duggan was bloody, and before the fight was over, Brusso had him looking like a chopping block. At the close of the 8th round, Brusso looked fresh as a daisy, while Duggan was bleeding from the mouth and nose. He displayed gameness, however, which made the crowd pull for him.

Early in the 9th round, Brusso forced matters. He sparred for an opening, and after a minute or so, Noah landed a right and left to the jaw and Duggan went to the canvas in a heap. Referee Gessler counted him out, and Billy Moore carried Jimmy to his corner.

It had been 9 rounds of fierce fighting. The large crowd considered it one of the best bouts they had ever seen. Brusso's showing marked him as a comer in the fighting game. It was also said that if Noah accepted Billy Moore's challenge that the Amphidrome would not hold the crowd that would want to see the fight.[64]

As hoped for, soon thereafter, Brusso arranged a 10-round catchweight match with Billy Moore, to be held in Houghton one month after the Duggan fight. Moore and Brusso had once given a sparring exhibition together. After the Brusso-Duggan bout, Moore, who had worked Duggan's corner, said that he would make Brusso "look like thirty cents." Noah made no boasts. Brusso was much larger, but size was not the only consideration.

> Moore is a fighter, a clever boxer and has had years of ring experience where Brusso is still comparatively a novice. Brusso will have to fight harder than he did Friday night to whip the little man from Syracuse. There are a few people in Houghton who have seen Moore go and they are unanimous in the opinion that Brusso has his work cut out for him to beat the smaller man.

---

63 *Houghton Daily Mining Gazette*, September 25, 1903. The paper was also known as the *Portage Lake Mining Gazette*. It catered to Houghton and Calumet, MI.
64 *Houghton Daily Mining Gazette*, September 26, 1903.

Brusso would be trained by Frank Ellingwood, "who has conditioned him for most of his fights." Jimmy Duggan would train Moore. Duggan argued that he did not lose the Michigan State Middleweight Championship to Brusso, owing to the fact that Noah had fought above the middleweight limit.[65]

Those who saw Moore sparring with Duggan noted Moore's clear superiority over Jimmy. Moore was training hard and promised to be in the very best condition for the Brusso bout. His showing gained Moore many backers. However, Brusso's friends were still confident that Noah was a wonder.[66]

In the meantime, just over two weeks after the Duggan fight, Brusso took an interim tune-up bout. On October 12, 1903 in Sault Sainte Marie, Michigan, Brusso fought Jack Hammond in a scheduled 10-round bout at the Soo opera house. Hammond's career included: 1898 LKOby2 Jack Root; 1899 KO5 Reddy Phillips and D10 Jim Watts; 1900 LKOby2 Root; and 1903 LKOby2 Jack Beauscholte.[67]

The local *Sault Sainte Marie Evening News* noted that both men had defeated Tom McCune: Brusso in 7 rounds and Hammond in 4 fierce rounds. Since then, Brusso had improved wonderfully. "He is a strong, well built man, quick with his hands

Jack Hammond

and shifty on his feet. He is game to the core." It should also be noted that Hammond stopped Reddy Phillips in 5 rounds, whereas Brusso did so in 9 rounds, and then in 2 rounds via disqualification.

Jack Hammond was described as willing and fast, and had been working hard during the last few weeks preparing for the bout. His flesh was solid as a rock, and his frequent wrestling, boxing, and bag punching had increased his speed of hand and foot. Hammond was sure that he would emerge victorious.[68]

---

65 *Houghton Daily Mining Gazette*, September 29, 1903.
66 *Houghton Daily Mining Gazette*, September 30, 1903.
67 Boxrec.com; *Detroit Today*, October 13, 1903.
68 *Sault Sainte Marie Evening News*, October 10, 1903.

The afternoon of the fight, Brusso claimed to be weighing 151 pounds and said that he never felt better. Hammond said that he too never felt better in his life, and was down nearly to Brusso's weight. He expected to win.[69]

That evening, before the fight, when Brusso threw off his sweater and overcoat, everyone admired his clean-cut and muscular figure. Still, Hammond was bigger and had a considerable height and reach advantage. He looked quite big as he stood next to Brusso.

In the 1st round, Hammond took the fight to the crouching Brusso, launching hard blows. Hammond landed a hard left, but Brusso smiled and sparred. Noah did not work as hard, content to throw light left jabs and the occasional right to the body, boxing smartly and holding himself in reserve. Jack worked hard and was too eager. He fired hard jabs, some of which landed, while others were partially blocked and didn't bother Brusso at all. Hammond remained the aggressor, but was met with stinging jabs in the face and hard rights on the body, with the occasional right cross to the jaw, Brusso's favorite blow. Near the end of the round, Noah sent in a left jab and crossed over the right like a streak of lightning, catching Jack on the mouth, causing his lip to puff up.

When the 2nd round began, Hammond was puffing from his own exertions. Brusso was cool and gliding around on his feet, working both hands with wonderful speed. Hammond jabbed and ripped up a right to the body, but the blows had no effect. A hard left from Brusso sent Jack's head back. Hammond seemed strong, however, and came in fiercely again, only to catch a right on the neck that sent him down for a nine-count. As he watched the referee count, Brusso stood back with his hands behind his back.

When Hammond rose, he landed a hard left which sent Brusso's head back. He was still game. About a minute later, Brusso again sent over his right and Hammond went down for the second time. Again Jack came back strong, and at the close of the round, both were fighting hard. Hammond rushed and Brusso side-stepped. There was considerable clinching, as neither was inclined to give much ground.

Hammond began the 3rd round with a rush, going after his man with both hands. However, Brusso was too quick with his feet and hands. Suddenly Brusso sent a right to the neck and Jack staggered. Another right sent him down. Confident that the fight was over, Brusso went to his corner and began putting on his coat before the count was concluded. Hammond was all out and indeed the fight was at an end.

The local paper called it the fastest fight ever seen in Sault Sainte Marie. While it lasted, the men went at it strongly, but Brusso was too quick and Hammond failed to elude Noah's powerful right.

---

69 *Sault Sainte Marie Evening News,* October 12, 1903.

Brusso, who is a wonderfully quick man both with hands and feet was in and out and around, ducking, dodging and hitting with both right and left so fast it was impossible to follow his blows. Hammond stood up gamely and with his advantage in height and reach landed some hard blows on Brusso but they didn't seem to bother his opponent any.[70]

Brusso had speed, power, footwork, defense, and a chin.

Next up for Brusso was the Billy Moore fight, scheduled to be held just twelve days later, back in Houghton. Both men were training hard. "Brusso will make about 156 pounds and Moore will enter the ring several pounds lighter." Jimmy Duggan continued training Moore, the Syracuse fighter, while Frank Ellingwood continued working with Brusso. Both fighters were confident of victory.[71]

Brusso had the advantages in height, reach, and weight. However, Moore was a very clever boxer, with much more experience than Brusso, having been boxing since about 1896. The lightweight Moore's record included notable fights such as 1898 D12 George McFadden, KO7 Tommy Cleary, and L20 Tommy White; 1899 LKOby5 McFadden; 1900 KO4 Jack Downey; and 1903 LKOby1 McFadden. The reporters expected a fast fight.[72]

On Saturday October 24, 1903 at Houghton, Michigan's Amphidrome, Noah Brusso fought Billy Moore. The combatants entered the ring at 10:30 p.m.

The local *Houghton Daily Mining Gazette* gave its report. The fight was fast and furious from the opening bell. Up to the 7th round, it was a give and take matter, each man boring in and keeping a rapid pace. "Brusso's well known assortment of left jabs was repeatedly used without any appreciable effect on Billy's countenance." While Noah did most of the rushing, he found Moore waiting for him every time.

During the 7th round, it looked bad for Billy. Brusso hit him with several hard left jabs, but Moore brightened up in the last few seconds and at the bell was fresh and fast again.

They rushed together in the 8th round and stayed at it. The round closed with honors even, with both showing some fatigue as a result of their fast work.

---

70 *Sault Sainte Marie Evening News*, October 13, 1903. *Detroit News, Detroit Today, Detroit Free Press*, October 13, 1903.

71 *Houghton Daily Mining Gazette*, October 22, 1903.

72 *Houghton Daily Mining Gazette*, October 24, 1903. Some have incorrectly claimed that Billy Moore was a black southpaw, but in fact this was the white right-handed Billy Moore from Syracuse. There was a black lightweight named Billy Moore from St. Louis. Some have confused the two. The local report did not mention his race or style, which they typically did for mixed race fights, and also if something was unusual about their style.

Early in the 9th round, Moore crossed his right to Brusso's mouth and drew the first blood of the fight. This stirred up Noah and he went at Billy like a demon, but they were still on even terms at the end of the round.

The 10th and final round was fought at a fast clip, but both were still fresh when the bell rang.

Referee George Getchell's draw decision was generally popular with the big crowd, although both boxers and their adherents claimed victory. Neither of the men showed any effects from their hard work. They had put up a fight worthy of the money the crowd spent, and the patrons left satisfied. Brusso claimed victory on points, but the crowd on the whole agreed with the draw decision. "Moore exhibited science all the way through the bout, saving himself repeatedly from Noah's nasty left jabs. Brusso retains all the prestige he gained by defeating Duggan."[73]

The semi-local *Sault Sainte Marie Evening News* reported that "Billy" Moore of Syracuse, New York had put up a surprisingly good fight against Brusso of Houghton. From the 1st round, Moore was "there with the goods." Both men claimed victory, but the referee's draw decision was generally satisfactory.

> The honors were so even throughout the match that the referee could not conscientiously give any other decision. Both men fought cleverly and hard and all through there was a continual and lively exchange of blows. Both were aggressive at the beginning, but in the latter rounds Moore played a waiting game and let Brusso do most of the leading. Moore proved himself a clever dodger and his foot and head work saved him from many vicious swings.[74]

There were discussions for a rematch. Neither was satisfied by the result, and their clever bout had been sufficiently entertaining that fans would attend a rematch. However, Moore insisted that Brusso make 150 pounds, which Noah felt was too low. "Brusso weighed in at about 156 pounds last Saturday night, while Moore only tipped the scales at 138 ½. Moore wants Brusso to come down to 150 before they meet again, but the Houghton man has not yet agreed to do so." Hence the rematch did not take place.[75]

According to secondary sources, on November 8, 1903 in Sault Sainte Marie, Brusso took on Jack Butler. Butler had results such as: 1899 LKOby7 George Gardner; 1900 L20 Kid Carter and LKOby1 Jack Bonner; 1902 LDQ9 Young Peter Jackson and L15 George Cole; and 1903 LND6 Philadelphia Jack O'Brien and ND6 Joe Butler.

---

73 *Houghton Daily Mining Gazette*, October 25, 1903.
74 *Sault Sainte Marie Evening News*, October 26, 1903.
75 *Sault Sainte Marie Evening News*, October 28, 1903.

Brusso allegedly knocked out Butler in the 2nd round, significant because Butler had lasted longer with men like Gardner, Carter, and O'Brien, all very good fighters.[76]

Secondary and semi-primary sources also claim that Brusso next fought a rematch with Jack O'Donnell in Evanston, Illinois on November 25, 1903. O'Donnell had been stopped by Brusso in 1902 in the 11th round. This time, Brusso allegedly scored another KO11 over O'Donnell.

That same day, in San Francisco, 40-year-old Bob Fitzsimmons won the world light-heavyweight championship with a W20 over George Gardner.

A couple days later, Michigan middleweight champion Brusso was in Grand Rapids, Michigan, along with his manager, R.C. Smith of New York, who was trying to arrange matches for Brusso with either Billy Campbell or Mike Schreck. "Smith says he thinks he has a comer in Brusso. The latter, although only 21, has whipped everybody he has met, thus far." Of course, Brusso had lost to Schreck, but managers, fighters, and newsmen often took liberties with the facts, even as they do today.[77]

While in Grand Rapids, as Brusso was walking on a trail with his trainer/sparring partner Frank Ellingwood of Houghton, a bullet passed through Ellingwood's hat and Frank immediately dropped to the ground. A hunter approached. He had mistaken Ellingwood for a deer.

> Brusso proceeded to teach him a severe lesson by giving a number of his famous right hand swings and uppercuts. The same lesson was [given] out to the fellow's partner only a few minutes later. Both were at first inclined to be sarcastic, but they acted differently after the pugilist got through with them.[78]

On December 31, 1903 in the main event at the Detroit Athletic Club, Noah Brusso fought a rematch with Tom McCune. In 1902, Burns had stopped McCune in the 7th round. The scheduled weight for this 10-round bout was 152 pounds, "the lightest Brusso has ever done, and a very good figure for McCune," who was naturally smaller than Brusso. Hence, Noah Brusso was actually a junior middleweight.[79]

The first 2 rounds were uneventful, although one local paper said McCune had the better of matters.

In the 3rd round, McCune dropped Brusso with a right to the jaw, and Brusso took a six-count. McCune also landed a good right to the body during that round.

---

76 This fight has not been confirmed by a primary source, although semi-primary sources list the bout on his record. This author was not able to find a report on the bout in the *Sault Sainte Marie Evening News*. Some have claimed that Butler was a black fighter, but they may have confused him with another Jack Butler, who was white.

77 *Grand Rapids Evening Press*, November 27, 1903.

78 *Sault Sainte Marie Evening News*, December 1, 1903.

79 *Detroit Free Press*, December 31, 1903.

However, the 4th round was all Brusso's. He came back strong and started jabbing well, soon having McCune's face covered with blood. Brusso landed five hard blows to the head and body and once allegedly threw McCune to the floor, although some said Brusso had decked him. McCune took a nine-count, perhaps indicating that he had been dropped.

The 5th and 6th rounds were tame. Brusso tried to land his right, but McCune was able to elude it.

In the 7th round, McCune landed a hard right that dazed Brusso. However, Brusso slowed McCune with a stiff stomach punch.

The 8th round featured the best give-and-take slugging of the bout. Brusso landed his hard, damaging right, and the bell helped McCune a lot.

McCune was fatigued in the 9th round. He stalled a lot to kill time, but whenever he was in distress, he would lash out with a swing or stiff jab that kept Noah respectful. Still, Brusso won the round.

Early in the 10th round, McCune landed three strong rights to the head, but Brusso came back and won the remainder of the round. Neither was hurt at the end.

Referee Ed Ryan awarded Brusso the 10-round decision. One writer said Brusso was stronger for most of the fight, but did not show marked superiority. Another observer said Brusso's victory was "hair-line." Some questioned the decision, feeling that it was so close that it should have been a draw. Overall, it was a somewhat even bout that was rather tame, with perhaps a slight edge for Brusso. Both showed respect for each other's right, which made it more of a jabbing contest. It was fast and had plenty of action, but it was not of the fierce-slugging hard-punching order. Neither man fought impressively. Perhaps the low weight had told on Brusso, who previously had been reluctant to agree to fight so low. After all, he had knocked out McCune the first time they had met, at a higher weight.[80]

The semi-local *Grand Rapids Evening Press* reported that the bout was rather tame in view of Brusso's reputation as a slugger, but that Brusso had won the decision.

> McCune scored a knockdown in the third, and Brusso sent McCune to the mat in the next round. In the ninth and tenth Brusso had the advantage. Outside of these rounds it was a very even contest. McCune was wary and Brusso kept away from the other man's right as much as possible.[81]

It had been a fairly good 1903 for Noah Brusso. That year, he had won at least seven fights, lost only one decision, and had drawn in another bout. Not bad for a very busy fighter who took on some tough customers. To that point in his two-year professional career, the 22-year-old Brusso was at least 18-1-1, although he may have had three or four more victories.

---

80 *Detroit Free Press, Detroit News,* January 1, 1904.
81 *Grand Rapids Evening Press,* January 1, 1904.

CHAPTER 2

A Name-Changing Near-Death Experience

Noah Brusso's first 1904 bout was held on January 28 at the Detroit Athletic Club, against Buffalo's Ben O'Grady. The night before, O'Grady gave a private exhibition with Harry Nicholson. He was big, strong, and willing to mix it, and had a good punch, but lacked speed. "One thing that O'Grady showed is that he will rough it and make the milling fast." It was a scheduled 10-round bout at 158 pounds.[82]

Before the fight started, the supremely confident O'Grady, looking fat and beefy, loudly asked his seconds if he ought to hit Brusso as hard as he could. He asked, "Shall I kill him?" His intimidation tactics proved to be ironic. They shook hands at 9:49 p.m.

1 – O'Grady was not trained for a hard battle, and his poor condition was apparent from the start. However, he was strong enough to make it interesting. Noah focused on trying to avoid Ben's wild left. Brusso dropped O'Grady once in the round, and was in control all the way. Still, O'Grady punched and fought hard enough to make Brusso cautious at all times. Ben's left was dangerous.

2 – Brusso crossed his right to the jaw and O'Grady went down for the second time in the bout. He lay prone while Referee Ed Ryan counted to eight. When Ben rose, Noah tried to finish him, but in doing so, amidst their slugging, Brusso became careless and ran into an O'Grady haymaker that put him down for part of the count.

Another local source said of the round that Brusso had the better of the slugging, flooring O'Grady three times. However, O'Grady then made a desperate rush and caught Brusso off balance, dropping Noah with a left to the head.

Both local sources agreed that after Brusso rose, they mixed it up and Brusso decked O'Grady yet again. Ben was very tired and groggy at the bell.

3 - O'Grady was weak, but aggressive. In the middle of the round, Brusso went after him, and, working O'Grady into a corner, ducked Ben's left, straightened up and landed a left, and then drove his right straight to the jaw, knocking O'Grady down. O'Grady's head hit the floor-mat hard

enough that the dull thud could be heard outside on Woodward Avenue. He was out cold.

Despite his gameness and strength, O'Grady was not a very good boxer. He left openings and was a poor judge of distance. Brusso had been in control all the way, despite being decked once.

Unfortunately, O'Grady remained unconscious for more than half an hour. He lay prostrate on the ring floor, his seconds "prying under his finger nails with knife blades to restore him, while Dr. Gurney squirted nitroglycerin into his arm, but without results for some time." The smoke-laden air of the gymnasium was not helpful either. Eventually, Ben was carried into the trophy room. Finally, he was taken to the hospital. It was believed that the bumping of his head on the mat had caused a serious concussion.

All of this "resulted in more police activity than any boxing bout hereabouts since the game was temporarily closed by a well remembered mill...over three years ago." The police arrested Brusso and his two seconds, Kennedy and Commodore, and took them to the police station, pending the results of O'Grady's injuries. At that time, a boxer could be imprisoned for killing an opponent. Assumption of the risk was no defense. O'Grady did not wake up until an hour later, while at Harper Hospital.

Brusso and his seconds spent the night in a jail cell at the Canfield Avenue police station. Brusso did not sleep, pacing the narrow cell, appearing indignant at his seconds, who snored like sailors, despite Brusso's mental anguish.

The following morning, Brusso's seconds were released when it was reported that O'Grady was out of danger, but Brusso was still being held pending O'Grady's discharge from the hospital.

In his hospital room, a reporter asked O'Grady questions, but he merely groaned and turned in his cot without opening his eyes. When asked how his head felt, Ben just moaned. The reporter asked, "Were you much hurt? Don't you know where you are? Do you remember the fight?" O'Grady responded, "Go away, you blockhead. What kind of stuff are you talking about? I never felt better in my life. Go chase yourself." He groaned again. The reporter asked, "Are you going back to Buffalo? You were beaten, you know?" O'Grady responded, "What foolishness are you giving me? You're crazy. I want to sleep." Ben refused to believe that he had been in a fight, rambling incoherently about his home and his mother. His face was scratched, torn and red. The nurses said it would be a couple days before he could leave the hospital.[83]

---

83 *Detroit Free Press, Detroit Evening News,* January 29, 1904.

Brusso's manager said that he would match his man with any 158-pound boxer in the country. "The Detroiter is more speedy now than at any time in his career."[84]

Brusso was allowed to leave the police station on January 30, having been forced to spend two nights there. O'Grady had slightly improved, but remained hospitalized.[85]

O'Grady was still at the hospital on January 31, but had not improved very much. He was ready to be discharged on February 1. Yet, he was still in the hospital as of February 2, waiting for his family to make arrangements for his return to Buffalo.[86]

Unfortunately, there had been a consistent stream of publicity about O'Grady over the course of several days, which wasn't good for boxing. It was said that the revival of the pugilistic art in Detroit during the present winter season had also brought with it a revival of the general indignation regarding the sport.

Initially, Mayor William Maybury stoutly defended boxing.

> I think it is a very small matter for people to raise any very great objection to these friendly contests, when they will flock by the thousands to the football field, where surgeons and ambulances are in attendance, and where the players are dragged from the field with broken limbs and oftentimes injuries which prove fatal.[87]

Exacerbating the current of anti-boxing sentiment, on February 2 in Detroit, black world lightweight champion Joe Gans stopped Mike Ward in the 10th round. Apparently the police had told referee Tim Hurst to stop the bout, but he waited another ten to fifteen seconds before doing so.

The next day, on February 3, 1904, Detroit Mayor Maybury did a total about-face and put a temporary halt to all boxing in the city.

> The number of boxing shows given in saloons has been steadily increasing, and, because of the youth of many contestants, has been regarded as a source of danger. This, with the O'Grady affair, Tim Hurst's work in the tenth round on Tuesday night, and one or two other circumstances, caused the mayor to call a halt for the present.

The police commissioner was ordered to suspend all boxing permits. The mayor said, "When the police say 'Stop' the referee should do it like that... I realize that it is a very popular sport, and that many of our best people enjoy it. But these affairs must be conducted right." It was believed to be a temporary ban, and that boxing would be allowed to resume under proper restrictions.[88]

---

84 *Detroit Free Press,* January 30, 1904.
85 *Detroit Free Press, Detroit News Tribune,* January 31, 1904.
86 *Detroit Free Press,* February 1, 2, 1904.
87 *Detroit News-Tribune,* January 31, 1904.
88 *Detroit Free Press,* February 4, 1904.

The following day, on February 4, Michigan State Governor Aaron Bliss got in on the act and announced that knock-out bouts were barred. Boxing could only be fought for points.[89] On the 5th, a boxing show in Ypsilanti, Michigan was not allowed to proceed. The police commissioner said that "the pressure was so great that he must order the bouts stopped." 600 fans had to leave. "This kills boxing here."[90]

The press noted, "The boxing structure…seemingly secure, came down with a crash this week." The impression was that the mayor wanted some changes made to the game. The O'Grady affair was referenced. Some opined that it was not improper equipment that caused his injuries, but the fact that he was "a man who was not fitted for a severe strain." Still, others said that even if he was in the best shape, Brusso hit so hard that he could have been hurt anyhow. "From the length of time that O'Grady is taking to recover, it would seem probable that, if perfectly trained, he could not get into shape for battle with a man who hits as Brusso does."[91]

Perhaps not entirely coincidentally, the next day, it was announced that eighteen clubs from around the country had met in Detroit and formed the National Boxing Association. Its object was stated to be the regulation of the boxing game, control of the boxers, and adjustment of the scale of weights. All boxers would have to pay registration fees and honor their contracts or be suspended by the organization, with clubs subject to similar discipline. Weigh-ins were to be held at 3 p.m. on the day of the fight. Middleweight remained at 158 pounds, light heavy 175, and heavyweight everything above 175 pounds.[92]

As a result of all the controversy, bad publicity, anti-boxing politics, legal impediments to the sport, and possibly fear of criminal prosecution, Noah Brusso left Michigan and went to Chicago, Illinois. He also changed his name to Tommy Burns, which likely was motivated by both legal concerns and marketing considerations. Some have suggested that he did not want his upset and embarrassed mother to know that he was continuing in the boxing profession. He would not return to box in the Detroit area for well over a year.

Obviously, the timing of his decision to change his name after the O'Grady bout was not coincidental, but what he changed it to was the result of marketing considerations. At that time, fighters often changed their names for business reasons. Some changed their names to give them a more, or less, or even different ethnic sound, depending on what they thought would make them more popular with the crowds. Since Irish fighters were considered to be good, and the crowds often supported them, a lot of boxers gave themselves Irish names. For example, Tommy Ryan

89 *Detroit Free Press*, February 5, 1904.
90 *Detroit Free Press*, February 6, 1904.
91 *Detroit Free Press*, February 7, 1904.
92 *Detroit Free Press*, February 8, 1904.

was actually a Jewish fighter named Joseph Youngs. Noah Brusso had an Italian sounding origin, and at that time, prejudice towards Italians was high. In fact, one 1903 edition of the *Police Gazette* said,

> It is amusing to note the way in which the crowd at a ringside receives the different nationalities of fighter. There is always a hearty cheer and earnest backing for the Irishman; grins and good-humored tolerance for the German, and virulent hostility to the Italian and the negro. Put a boy of any other race in with an Italian, and everybody in the house who is not himself of Italian origin at once begins to root frantically against the son of ancient Rome. It is to the credit of the Italians that they have pushed so far forward against such adverse influences.[93]

"Burns" was a name whose origins came from the British Isles, and was not likely to elicit any prejudice.

In late February, in Chicago it was reported,

> 'Tommy Burns,' the assumed name under which a well-known eastern middleweight is traveling, will box George Shrosbree. It is safe to say that half the gathering will recognize 'Burns' when he steps into the ring and that his incognito, assumed for business reasons, will be quickly dissipated.[94]

Another local Chicago paper, when stating his name, unlike other names on the card, put quotes around the name of "Tommy Burns," signifying that it knew that it was not his real name.[95]

On February 26, 1904 at Chicago's Battery D, Brusso, now called Burns, knocked out George Shrosbree in the 5th round of their 158-pound bout. One local paper said that it was "Ed Burns, fighting under an assumed name." Apparently, Brusso was using the name of Tommy Burns, but telling them that he really was Ed Burns. However, the *Chicago Record-Herald* specifically reported that Noah Brusso was going under the name of Tom Burns. It also referenced the fact that he had knocked out O'Grady with almost fatal results.[96]

How did Brusso come up with those names? There was a Detroit lightweight named Ed Burns who had been fighting at that time.[97] Who was Tommy Burns? He was a popular jockey. His victories had often been published in the *Detroit Free Press*.[98] Admittedly, this is just guess-work as to

---

93 *Police Gazette*, August 22, 1903.
94 *Chicago Chronicle*, February 26, 1904.
95 *Chicago Daily Tribune*, February 26, 1904.
96 *Chicago Daily Tribune, Chicago Record-Herald*, February 27, 1904.
97 Ed Burns had fought Mike Schreck to a 1901 10-round draw in Cincinnati, and, in March 1902, in Detroit, he fought William McPartland to a 10-round draw. His name was referenced the same day as the report of Brusso's disqualification victory over Archie Steele, and he fought McPartland shortly thereafter. *Detroit Free Press*, March 6, 1902; Boxrec.com.
98 *Detroit Free Press*, July 9, 1902.

how Brusso came up with the names. One thing that is clear is that Noah Brusso would thereafter primarily be known as Tommy Burns; despite the fact that most knew it was not his given name, and some occasionally referenced his real name.

Burns had boxed Shrosbree on the undercard of the 6-round-draw main event between Jack Root and George Gardner, two top 170-pound fighters. Also present at the fights were contenders Philadelphia Jack O'Brien and Jack Johnson. Bob Fitzsimmons was scheduled to box an exhibition there the following evening. That's some serious talent in one town.[99]

Mike Schreck

99 *Chicago Daily News*, February 27, 1904.

The very next day after stopping Shrosbree, on February 27, 1904 in Milwaukee, Wisconsin, at the Milwaukee Athletic Club, Tommy Burns fought a rematch against the only man to have defeated him to that point: Mike Schreck of Cincinnati. Since his 1903 W10 over Brusso, Schreck's results included: 1903 L15 and D20 Hugo Kelly, KO4 Cyclone Kelly, W15 Andy Walsh, L6 Billy Stift, L6 Jack O'Brien, W6 Jack Beauscholte; and 1904 LND6 Jack "Twin" Sullivan, WND6 Jim Jeffords, and D6 George Cole, amongst others.

A couple Milwaukee papers reported that Tommy Burns was formerly known as Noah Brusso, his right name, and that he had a good local Detroit reputation as a fighter; for those who had seen him fight in Detroit had recommended him. One noted that Burns was masquerading as a Philadelphia fighter.

The M.A.C. athletic committee said it had selected Burns to fight Schreck because of Tommy's known ability to give and take punishment, and because of his fondness for hard fighting. "Brusso has made a name for himself as a man with a punch."

One local paper said, "Schreck belongs to the class of sluggers that always puts up a whirlwind fight." Another said, "Schreck is one of the hardest men in his class to beat, as was shown by his hard fight with Jack O'Brien at the C.A.A." They were scheduled to fight 6 rounds at catchweights.[100]

Schreck was a 1 to 3 favorite when he entered the ring, but those odds shifted soon after the fight began. "Burns started off like a house afire, and before one minute of the first round had ended, he had Schreck all but out. Burns rained blow after blow upon the Cincinnatian and he had him completely at his mercy."

Burns held his advantage in the 2nd through 4th rounds, once even dropping Schreck for a count. "For four rounds Brusso made the man that held Jack O'Brien even look like a novice handicapped with a combination of tied hands and stage fright." Throughout those 4 rounds, Burns jabbed with his left and crossed with his right with such telling effect that Schreck was on the defensive all the time, staggering repeatedly. He was given no opportunity to set himself.

However, Burns slowed his terrific pace, which gave Schreck an opportunity to show his usual form and give Tommy a very hard fight in the final two rounds. A series of wild swings to the body took away a great deal of Tommy's steam.

According to the local *Milwaukee Sentinel*, in the 6th round, Burns was twice sent to the canvas. Although he was tired, each time Burns rose as quickly as he could. Both men were quite fatigued at the end, staggering and

---

100 *Milwaukee Daily News, Milwaukee Free Press, Milwaukee Sentinel,* February 27, 1904.

reeling about, locked in each other's arms. Neither one appeared to have a knockout blow in the last minute.

The *Milwaukee Free Press* saw the final frames a bit differently. It said that although Schreck did well in the 5th and 6th rounds, Burns held his own and fought back desperately. It noted only one knockdown of Burns. In the last half of the 6th round, Schreck landed a lucky wallop on the point of the chin and Burns went down. He was right up again and fought back harder than ever and evened up matters by putting Schreck to the mat. It called the bout the hardest and fastest between two big men ever witnessed in Milwaukee.

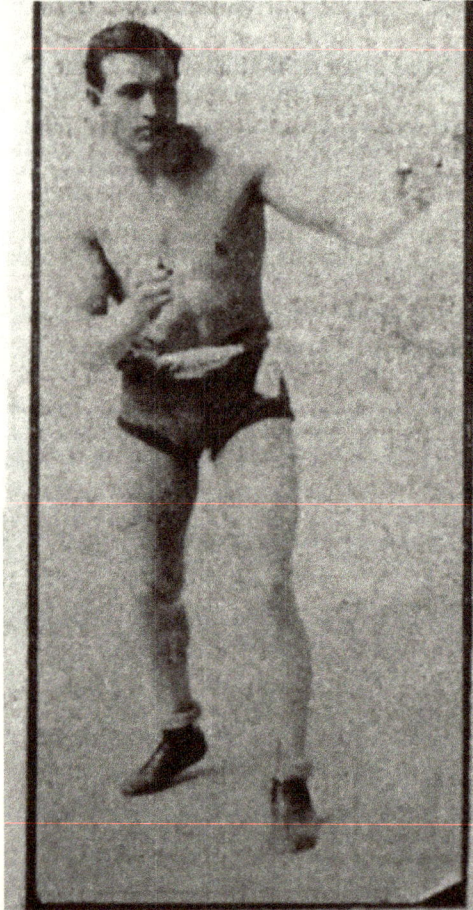

Noah Brusso.
Detroit fighter who got a draw with Mike Schreck before the M. A. C. last night.

Referee Pollack called the fight a draw, but the local press strongly disagreed, feeling that Burns had won. The *Sentinel* said Brusso had put up a great battle. He gave Schreck a beating in the first 4 rounds, which was a surprise. The "draw decision does not tell what a thorough drubbing Schreck was given." Although some spectators supported the decision, most thought that Brusso was entitled to the winner's end of the purse. "He certainly had a big lead up to the fifth round, and in the remainder of the affair stubbornly contested every point."

After the fight, when Schreck staggered down the aisle, "he looked as though he had been fighting a half dozen fighters rather than one. His face was badly marked, and one of his eyes was nearly closed. Brusso had a cut lip and his nose bled slightly. He carried no other signs of injury."

The *Milwaukee Free Press* said that but for the unfortunate knockdown in the concluding round, Burns would have received the decision. "As it was Burns was easily entitled to the long end of the purse, as he had the advantage for five out of the six rounds." It still thought that Burns had won.[101]

The *Milwaukee Daily News* said that although Burns and Schreck fought to a 6-round draw, Burns had exacted a measure of revenge, because he was the better man and had deserved the victory. Burns was called a comer.

> With the exception of one round, the Detroit lad, who travels under an assumed name, had the better of the milling. He had a left jab that Schreck could not avoid and in addition managed to land vicious swings. Schreck did not put up his usual good fight and is more than lucky for getting a draw. It looked like Burns' fight and the decision of Referee Pollack was a surprise.[102]

Hence, despite the official draw decision, subsequently the press unanimously treated the bout as a victory for Burns over Schreck.

The following month, Philadelphia Jack O'Brien won a 15-round decision over Schreck.[103] Schreck would remain a prominent contender for several years.

Less than a month after Burns-Schreck II, on March 18, 1904, back at Chicago's Battery D, Tommy Burns met the allegedly undefeated local Italian, Tony Caponi or Camponi (each paper used a different spelling); although a secondary source says that Tony had a decision loss. Caponi had a penchant for keeping matters close, for already he had four draws on his record after only two years of boxing.

The name "Tom Burns" had printed next to it "(Noah Brusso)," confirming that they knew who he really was. Burns was said to have shown "uncommon ability and endurance" in his recent bouts with Shrosbree and Schreck. One local paper claimed that the bout was scheduled at 150 pounds.[104]

That evening, Burns fought Camponi to a 6-round draw. One local paper called the Burns-Camponi middleweight bout a "rough, tough battle" that "was a case of slugging all the way.... Burns did a lot of

Tony Caponi

101 *Milwaukee Sentinel, Milwaukee Free Press,* February 28, 1904.
102 *Milwaukee Daily News,* February 29, 1904. Referee Pollack is of no relation to the author of this book.
103 *Chicago Daily Tribune,* March 11, 1904.
104 *Chicago Chronicle, Chicago Record-Herald,* March 18, 1904.

rough work and at the end was thoroughly disgusted with the decision." Noah thought that he had won but was robbed against the local fighter.

The *Chicago Record-Herald* said Brusso was a far cleverer boxer than Caponi. He used his left to draw out Caponi so as to get a chance to cross with his right. Caponi managed to duck most of the rights, but he had several narrow escapes from this combination. From the start, they fought at a whirlwind pace all over the ring. Both were a little wild, so their blows did not do much damage, and they missed most punches. The 2nd round featured considerable clinching of the hard and fast order. Caponi did most of the holding. By the 6th round, Brusso had a good shade on points, but lost it in the final round, when Caponi rushed vigorously and landed some hard wallops to the head and body. It was a hard-fought draw.

In the main event, shifty Philadelphia Jack O'Brien won a slow 6-round decision over Hugo Kelly. Some felt that a draw would have been the proper decision, while others felt that Jack had a clear margin.[105]

Having felt that he was robbed of victory with the draw decision, Burns wanted a rematch with Caponi. He got his wish when they again fought in Chicago less than one month later, on April 9, 1904. They were listed as fighting at 152 pounds.[106] One local paper said the decision in the tame 6-round bout was given to Burns, "who tapped his man to a finish." Another said it was a slow affair, but "Burns was the more scientific, and won with lots to spare." A non-local dispatch said, "Caponi was slow as an ox and Brusso showed more dancing than fighting ability." This time, the decision went to the right man.[107]

105 *Chicago Chronicle, Chicago Daily News, Chicago Daily Tribune, Chicago Record-Herald, Daily Inter Ocean,* March 19, 1904. Boxrec.com.
106 *Chicago Tribune,* April 9, 1904.
107 *Chicago Chronicle, Chicago Tribune, Boston Globe,* April 10, 1904.

CHAPTER 3

The Western Warrior

Hoping to make a name for himself out West, where boxing was thriving and did not endure quite as many legal restrictions and regulations, in April 1904, Tommy Burns traveled to Tacoma, Washington.

On April 26, 1904, Tommy was at Tacoma's Germania Hall, training for a potential fight with Dave Barry. Spectators watched Burns play a game of handball and engage in two fast 4-round sparring bouts. Larry McKenna, who was Burns' manager, and had a valid claim to the title of Pacific Coast handball champion, lost the game to Tommy. The 100 or so spectators declared it the fastest game they had ever seen.

Immediately following the handball, Burns sparred 4 rounds with Indian Joe Schildt. Tommy felt frisky, for he really went after Schildt. "The blows landed so fast and hard, that at the end of the fourth round the big Siwash was completely bewildered." Burns next sparred 4 more rounds with Bobby Johnson. At the conclusion, the impressed crowd gave Burns an ovation.[108]

TOMMY BURNS,
Who is Here Looking for Big Game.

When the Barry fight did not materialize, Burns temporarily returned to Chicago. Tommy became the manager, trainer, and sparring partner for welterweight Otto Sieloff, "the Fighting Dutchman," who was preparing for a rematch with Jerry McCarthy to be held May 24 in Utah.[109]

---

108 *Tacoma Daily News*, April 27, 1904.
109 Otto Sieloff's record included: 1898 WDQ15 Kid Carter and W6 Tom McCune; 1899 LKOby13 Spike Sullivan and L25 Kid McPartland; 1900 W10 Young Peter Jackson and LKOby9 Joe Gans; 1902

Coming from Chicago, Sieloff and Burns arrived in Salt Lake City, Utah on May 17, one week before the fight. Sieloff trained and sparred with Burns in Ogden, Utah, also known as the Junction City. Tommy was said to be a comer in the middleweight division.

While Burns was in Utah, he made several challenges, trying to obtain a fight with just about anyone, but found it difficult to make a match. Burns was willing to fight any of the locals, such as Tommy Reilly, or even Tommy Ryan or Hugo Kelly (also spelled Kelley) for the world middleweight championship. Shamrock Athletic Club manager S.J. Kelly offered Ryan and Kelly a $1,000 purse to meet Burns.[110]

On May 24, 1904 at the Salt Palace in Salt Lake City, Utah, Jerry McCarthy scored a KO10 over Otto Sieloff, avenging his 20-round decision loss to Sieloff earlier that year.

Burns continued trying to make a match in Salt Lake, but ultimately found no success. He was said to be a clever and experienced fighter who would give the fans their money's worth.[111]

In the meantime, in order to make some money, at the end of May and for the first week of June at Salt Lake's Bon Ton Vaudeville Theater, Burns gave clever sparring exhibitions with Jerry McCarthy, who had just defeated Sieloff. "They are giving boxing exhibitions at the little show house, and judging from their reception last night, the exhibitions will become popular."[112]

They next took their exhibitions to Ogden's Lyceum Theater for a week.[113]

Throughout June, potential matches were arranged for Burns, but they all fell through. On June 9 in Salt Lake, Tommy Reilly fought "Fireman" Jim Flynn to a 20-round draw. Burns was willing to fight either one of them. He was in Ogden, and said that he would remain in the Salt Lake area until July 1 unless someone accepted his challenge. Otherwise, he planned to return to Chicago. Burns was so anxious for a match that he even offered to fight Eugene Thompson at 170 pounds. Tommy was frustrated by his inability to successfully make a match.[114]

On June 24, 1904, the *Salt Lake Herald* published a letter from Burns to the sporting editor.

> I stopped over in Ogden for three weeks to get the winner of the Reilly-Flynn fight, but so far have been unable to get a match with

W6 Dave Barry and LKOby1 Kid McPartland; and 1904 W20 Jerry McCarthy, LKOby4 Honey Mellody, and D10 George Memsic. Boxrec.com.

110 *Deseret Evening News*, May 17, 21, 1904; *Salt Lake Herald*, May 18, 1904. *Salt Lake Telegram*, May 18, 19, 1904.

111 *Salt Lake Telegram*, May 26, 1904.

112 *Deseret Evening News*, May 31, 1904; *Salt Lake Telegram*, June 1, 2, 1904.

113 *Salt Lake Telegram*, June 11, 1904. In December 1905, Stanley Ketchel would score a KO12 and KO11 over McCarthy.

114 *Salt Lake Telegram*, June 18, 1904; *Salt Lake Herald*, June 22, 1904.

either one of them. Willard Bean tried to match me with Eugene Thompson, but he says I am too small for him. I will agree to stop Thompson in twenty rounds or he can take all the money. To show all the sports that my heart is in the right place, I will take on Thompson and Jack Levell on the same night, each for ten rounds, and if either one beats me they can take all the money. As for Tommy Reilly, I will fight him winner take all the money. Reilly said that if he fought anyone here it would be me, but I see that he is trying to make a match with Levell. I guess he does not want any of my game or he would meet me. Everybody is looking for easy money, but I will take on anyone in the country.

If I don't get a match here by the Fourth of July I will return to Chicago and get Jack "Twin" Sullivan or Hugo Kelley. Yours truly, TOMMY BURNS.[115]

Although no one has found a confirming primary source report, secondary sources indicate that sometime, possibly during July 1904 in Salt Lake City, Burns scored a KO1 over Joe Wardinski.[116] Semi-primary sources reporting Burns' record as of late 1904 listed the KO1 win over Wardinski, though no date was provided.[117] Most of the local press reports focused on Burns' lack of success in finding anyone willing to face him.

Apparently, a Burns fight took place on July 8, 1904 in Kemmerer, Wyoming (northeast of Salt Lake City), which previously has not been listed in his record. The *National Police Gazette* reported that Tommy Burns knocked out Hans Erickson in the 3rd round. Erickson swapped blows for the first 2 rounds, but in the 3rd, Burns "caught the Dane on the point of the jaw with a terrific left swing. That was all."[118]

By mid-July, in Utah it was said that the *San Francisco Chronicle* had reported that the Salt Lake area had one good fighter in Tommy Burns, who wanted a match with either Billy Woods or Dave Barry.[119]

Burns did not leave the Salt Lake area. Instead, he took up a position as a sparring partner for William "Cyclone" Kelly, who arrived in Salt Lake on July 18 to train for his scheduled August 1 match there with Tommy Reilly, who was coming off his 20-round draw with Jim Flynn.

Burns was sparring 4 hard rounds every afternoon with Cyclone Kelly at Willard Bean's gymnasium. Kelly was not exceptionally clever, but he had a

---

115 *Salt Lake Herald*, June 24, 1904.

116 Boxrec.com; Cyberboxingzone.com.

117 The Wardinski win was listed before Burns' bout with Cyclone Kelly, which took place on August 19, 1904, but this record has inaccuracies and lists other bouts out of order. No date is provided for the Wardinski bout. *Tacoma Daily News*, August 16, 1904; *Milwaukee Daily News*, October 6, 1904.

118 *National Police Gazette*, July 30, 1904.

119 *Deseret Evening News*, July 16, 1904, quoting the *San Francisco Chronicle*.

dangerous punch and could take punishment. Kelly liked to rush and utilize power-punching from the inside.[120]

On July 20, 1904 at Salt Lake's Utahna Park, 3,000 people attended a benefit hosted by the Local No. 99 of Theatrical Stage Employees. During the variety of entertainments given at the benefit, Tommy Burns sparred 2 rounds with Willard Bean.[121]

When the Kelly-Reilly fight did not happen, Tommy Burns soon shifted from the role of sparring partner to the role of opponent for Cyclone Kelly. However, the fight was set to be held in Tacoma, Washington, where they had been trying to make a fight for both Kelly and Burns. Having them fight each other was the solution. Folks there had seen Burns spar and train back in April, and owing to the good impression that he had made, they wanted to see him in action.

The Cyclone Kelly–Tommy Burns bout was scheduled for 20 rounds, to be held on August 19 in Tacoma, sponsored by the Tacoma Athletic Club.

The San Francisco middleweight Kelly was well known in the area as a slugger. Burns was an unknown quantity in the West, but had brought over the reputation for being a good fighter. At that point, veteran fighter Billy Lavigne was managing Burns.[122]

In early August 1904, Burns was training in Seattle, Washington, just north of Tacoma. Tommy trained and sparred with Jean Wilson and Tommy Kane on a daily basis at hose house No. 2, and their workouts usually attracted a large crowd. Tommy was heralded as a comer, with an alleged 26-1 record, the lone loss to Schreck functionally having been avenged.[123]

Benny Miles, Kelly's trainer at Seattle's Turn Verein gym, said that he would bet up to $1,000 on Kelly against Burns, the "Chicago fighter."

Initially, the boxers had agreed to weigh no more than 156 pounds at 3 p.m. on the day of the fight or forfeit a share of the receipts. However, this was eventually changed to 158 pounds at the Cyclone's insistence. The winner would be matched with Billy Woods.[124]

On August 15, Burns arrived in Tacoma from Seattle. He would finish up his training at the Spanaway Park roadhouse. The fight was scheduled to be held at Germania Hall the following Friday.[125]

It was said that Burns was a man who made friends easily and would have plenty of backing when he entered the ring to meet "one of the toughest propositions on the Pacific coast, for there is no doubt Kelly is

120 *Salt Lake Telegram, Salt Lake Herald,* July 21, 1904.
121 *Salt Lake Telegram,* July 21, 1904. Willard Bean's record included 1899 ND10 Joe Choynski and 1902 L20 Fireman Jim Flynn. Boxrec.com.
122 *Seattle Daily Times,* August 5, 11, 1904. *Tacoma Times,* August 9, 1904.
123 *Tacoma Times,* August 11, 1904.
124 *Seattle Daily Times,* August 11, 1904.
125 *Tacoma Times,* August 15, 1904.

that and then some." The attendance was expected to be big, judging by the opening sale of seats.

Tommy expressed confidence. He was doing a fair amount of road work each day. He continued training at Spanaway Lake with Jean Wilson and Tommy Kane. It was noted that Burns came from Detroit, but was born in Hanover, Ontario on June 17, 1881, and was therefore 23 years old. He stood 5'7" tall.

Kelly was said to be weighing about 160 pounds, although as with most things in boxing, without confirmation. At that point, the Cyclone was training at Germania Hall, and had a big circle of admirers, "for Kelly is undeniably fast." He sparred Professor Reed and Chris Mussen. Chris broke his hand landing a blow on Kelly's face that did not jar the Cyclone in the slightest.[126]

It was said that in San Francisco's Cyclone Kelly, the Canadian was going to encounter the scrappiest fighter he had ever met. Kelly was the same age as Burns. He stood 5'9" tall. He had been San Francisco's welterweight amateur champion from 1900 to 1902. "He turned professional in 1902, and since that time has fought over 100 battles." Some of the Kelly fights the local paper mentioned included: 1902 L10 Billy Woods; 1903 LDQ7 Tommy Ryan, D20 Jim Flynn, KO3 Jimmy Handler, D6 Jack O'Brien, D6 Larry Temple, and W6 Young Peter Jackson.[127] Secondary sources also include bouts such as: 1902 LKOby1 Dave Barry; 1903 LKOby4 Mike Schreck; and 1904 LKOby5 Billy Woods, amongst others.[128]

TOMMY BURNS, MIDDLEWEIGHT

Who will meet "Cyclone" Kelly in a twenty-round match at Germania hall Friday evening.

---

126 *Tacoma Daily News*, August 16, 1904. Newspapers often alternately spelled his name "Kelly" or "Kelley." This book will typically use "Kelly" for consistency.
127 *Tacoma Daily News*, August 17, 1904.
128 Boxrec.com.

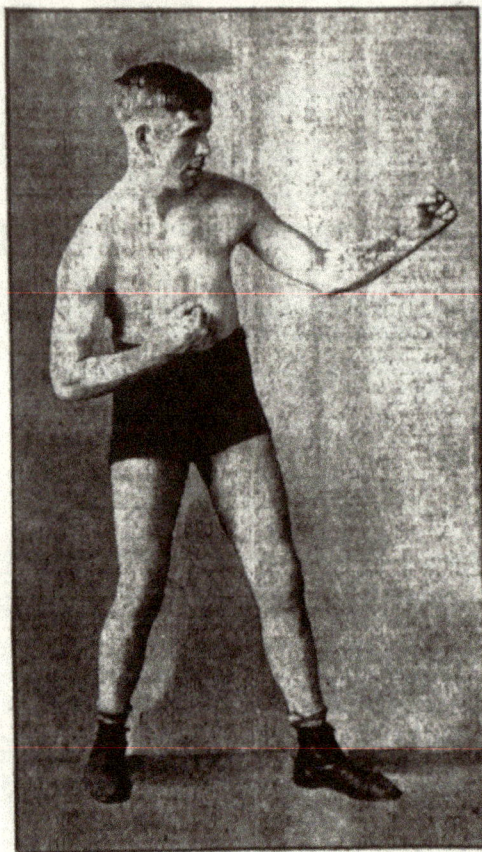

"CYCLONE" KELLY, OF SAN FRANCISCO

To meet Tommy Burns in twenty-round contest in Tacoma Friday night.

Kelly was the odds favorite at 10 to 8, owing to his much longer record and fact that folks on the West Coast were more familiar with him. Burns still had a strong following which seemed anxious to cover all the money in sight at those odds. Although Kelly was taller and heavier, Burns had the longer reach. However, Kelly's backers counted on his aggressiveness to overcome that.[129]

The *Seattle Daily Times* said the local sports were looking forward to a treat. Both fighters had been training hard and earnestly for the battle. "Burns will be slightly handicapped in weight in the coming mill but this fact does not seem to bother him in the least and some of his friends pick him to win inside of ten rounds."

Every afternoon at Kelly's training quarters, standing room was at a premium. Folks enjoyed watching him train.

> The crowd of amateurs the Cyclone takes on every day in the boxing bouts furnish knockdowns galore. So far the betting seems to favor Kelly at odds of 10 to 8, which is no doubt due to the 'Frisco fighter's record being better known here. Jimmy Carroll, the well-known athletic instructor has been selected as referee.[130]

The fight was attracting widespread attention. A special inter-urban train would take a large delegation of fight followers from Seattle over to Tacoma to witness the fight. The preliminaries would begin at 9:30 p.m.

The day of the fight, it was said,

129 *Tacoma Daily News*, August 18, 1904.
130 *Seattle Daily Times*, August 17, 1904.

Both fighters are trained to the finest point and are ready for a hard contest. Burns will enter the ring a few pounds below the weight limit of 158 pounds, but he will more than make up for the weight deficit by increased speed. The "Cyclone," on the other hand, will take advantage of the limit.[131]

Kelly remained the betting favorite. It was anticipated that the winner would meet colored middleweight Billy Woods.[132]

On August 19, 1904, Tommy Burns fought Cyclone Kelly at Germania Hall in Tacoma, Washington, in a scheduled 20-round bout sponsored by the Tacoma Athletic Club. According to the local *Tacoma Daily News*, the house was large, and the fighters were to receive 60% of the gate receipts, with 65% of that amount going to the winner and 35% to the loser.

The *Seattle Post-Intelligencer* said Burns weighed 154 pounds to Kelly's 163 pounds. *The Seattle Star* said Burns weighed 157 ¾ pounds, while Kelly weighed only a trifle under 166 pounds. Apparently, Kelly had not really attempted to make the agreed-upon weight, and was willing to pay the monetary forfeit so that he could have the weight advantage against a man with a clever reputation.

Black middleweight Billy Woods challenged the winner. One lone woman occupied a front seat, and before the fight, she sent up a big bouquet of roses to Burns.

Jimmy Carroll refereed the match, which was fought according to straight Marquis of Queensberry rules, meaning that the fighters could hit with one hand free in the clinches and on the breakaways. Hence the Queensberry rules saying: "Protect yourself at all times."

The following is an amalgamation of the round-by-round reports offered by the *Tacoma Daily News, Seattle Post-Intelligencer*, and *Seattle Star*.

Throughout the 1st round, the aggressive Burns waded in and slugged Kelly with both hands. Kelly stuck out his tongue at Burns and remarked, "I suppose you think you did something." Burns landed a terrific left under the chin and followed it with several fast rights. Kelly answered with swings that failed to land. Kelly kept covering his head with his hands. When he threw, he was wild, and Burns punished his face. Tommy's rights made the Cyclone appear sick as he waddled to his corner with blood running from his nose.

Early in the 2nd round, Referee Jimmy Carroll began breaking the men often, as Kelly did nothing but clinch. Burns frequently jabbed him. One of Burns' vicious jabs cut open Kelly's left eyebrow. However, Kelly woke up for a minute and did better. He landed one right swing on the cheek that momentarily dazed Burns, causing him to cover and spar. The Cyclone made Burns move around the ring a number of times to avoid his terrific

131 *Tacoma Times*, August 19, 1904.
132 *Seattle Star*, August 19, 1904.

lunges and swings. Burns quickly recovered though, and after he landed a vicious left uppercut, he became the aggressor again. The round closed with Burns landing jabs and rights, while Kelly appeared badly winded.

In the 3ʳᵈ round, Kelly repeatedly clinched in order to survive. Burns landed many furious jabs to the face and head. Tom cut both of Kelly's eyes. The Cyclone could not land his wild punches, but showed his ability to stand severe punishment and come back for more. He even taunted Tommy, saying things like, "You can't hit, Burns... You can't knock me out. ... I thought you were a fighter." Just before the gong rang, Burns landed a left swing to the solar plexus that badly hurt Kelly, who seemed groggy as he returned to his corner. Tom winked his eye at Kelly and said, "I see your finish now."

In the 4ᵗʰ round, after some sparring and clinching, Burns kept up his jabbing and began following Kelly, though keeping out of reach of the Cyclone's wild swings, and also avoiding clinches. Kelly left himself unprotected and vulnerable to several punishing blows that Burns landed. During this round, some thought that the fight should be stopped, for Kelly was at times staggering and reeling about. Tom was alert, watching for the opportunity to land a knockout blow.

The knockout came while Kelly was covering to protect his head from left swings, leaving his breast unprotected. Tom feinted a left at the head and then like lightning landed a terrific stiff right just under the heart, "sending his man to the dust." Kelly was counted out.

The local *Tacoma Daily News* said Burns was the crowd favorite from the start. He was obviously a clever boxer and was confident of winning. Kelly only had a hard right swing. It had knockout power, but he was not able to land it. His own guard was always open, and he was badly punished as a result. Burns outclassed him in every round, treating him as a punching bag. The fight was short and one-sided.[133]

The semi-local *Seattle Daily Times* said,

> Kelly had to be assisted to his dressing-room, while Burns was unscratched. Kelly was entirely outclassed and was knocked down and badly punished in the first round. He received a right on the jaw in the second that started him going. He rallied in the third, but was unable to land effectively on the Chicago man. In trying to keep away from another on the jaw in the fourth, he raised his guard and Burns landed a hard punch under the heart that ended the fight.[134]

The *Seattle Post-Intelligencer* said that overall, it was a one-sided fight in Burns' favor. Burns exhibited "magnificent footwork" and worked his

133 *Tacoma Daily News*, August 20, 1904.
134 *Seattle Daily Times*, August 20, 1904.

body, arms, and head "with a coolness and precision acquired through long training." Kelly only demonstrated an ability to absorb punishment.[135]

The *Seattle Star* agreed that Burns clearly outclassed Kelly from the start. Afterwards, Kelly said that Burns was the best and fastest man he had ever encountered, including Tommy Ryan. "Burns is a faster man than Ryan ever was. If Ryan ever meets Burns, Ryan will be licked." That was a high compliment indeed, for Ryan was considered to be an all-time great.[136]

The local *Tacoma Times* said Kelly was a back number, for Burns handled him with ease.

> "Cyclone" Kelly has lost his famous cyclone attachment. If he hasn't lost it entirely, he surely forgot it at his training quarters when he entered the ring with young Mr. Burns of Chicago last night. Lavigne's fighter had the Irishman's face chopped to pieces within two rounds, and was landing at will on the latter's battered nose and eyes when, in the opening of the fourth installment, he sent a right punch to the solar plexus that laid the old "war hoss" down and out.
>
> Tommy Burns made a good impression with the crowd, but Kelly was a sad disappointment to his supporters. Not once did the 'Frisco boxer land a telling blow on his adversary, the latter ducking from the Irish man's wild swings with ease. ...
>
> Billy Woods announced that he would meet the winner of the last night's go.[137]

Once again, Burns had exhibited his vaunted punishing power and defensive skills. The locals now realized that his reputation was legitimate.

In late August 1904 in San Francisco, James J. Jeffries scored a KO2 over Jack Munroe. It was Jeffries' final heavyweight championship defense.

The Washington State crowd wanted to see more of Tommy Burns. A match was arranged with the well-respected "crack Los Angeles middleweight" Billy Woods, a black fighter, to be held in mid-September, one month after the Kelly bout, at the Seattle Theatre. According to a secondary source, Woods' record included: 1902 LDQ3 Dave Barry; 1903 D20 Al Neil and D20 Joe Walcott (world welter title);[138] and 1904 KO5 Cyclone Kelly, D25 Mike Schreck,[139] and KO18 Nick Burley.[140] In 1902, Woods had been a sparring partner for heavyweight Jack Johnson before Johnson's fight with Jack Jeffries. The *Police Gazette* described Woods as an

---

135 *Seattle Post-Intelligencer*, August 20, 1904.
136 *Seattle Star*, August 20, 1904.
137 *Tacoma Times*, August 20, 1904.
138 The Woods-Walcott fight was of the hurricane kind and both inflicted severe punishment. Woods gave as well as he received in the 20-round draw. *Police Gazette*, April 25, 1903.
139 Woods-Schreck was a great fight. They mixed it up well and it was a wonder that neither was stopped. The crowd approved of the 25-round draw decision. "Woods has been winning so many fights of late that he is considered invincible." *Police Gazette*, April 23, 1904.
140 Boxrec.com.

aggressive fighter with brute strength.[141] The local press and experts certainly gave Woods a great deal of respect, and the fight was viewed as quite competitive in its inception.

BILLY WOODS

Burns' manager Billy Lavigne and Woods' manager Biddy Bishop, both of whom were famous, had engaged in a great deal of wrangling in their negotiations for the match, but had finally come to an agreement. The fighters would compete at the Seattle Theatre in a 15-round contest. They chose Charley Reno, who trained Jimmy Britt for numerous bouts, to referee. Straight Queensberry rules would govern the contest. "The men, according to their agreement, will be permitted to hit at all times until ordered to break and, when breaking, they will be allowed to hit in the breakaway." The articles called for the men to weigh in at 158 pounds at 3 p.m. on the day of the fight, and if either was overweight, he would forfeit one-half of his share of the purse. The winner was to take 65 per cent of the purse and the loser 35 per cent.

Burns trained at a Seattle fire engine house with Louie Long and Warren Zurbrick (also often spelled Zubrick). "Burns is one of the most confident young fellows in the world. He hasn't a doubt but that he can best Woods, and has it all figured out how he will turn the trick."[142]

Burns had been playing lacrosse in Seattle. He was well known in Seattle "through his good work with the lacrosse team, and his friends will give him a noisy greeting when he is introduced. Burns is said to be the best lacrosse player on the Pacific Coast, and the wielders of the stick say if the Detroit boy can fight as well as he can play lacrosse Woods will be bested." Tom's fellow lacrosse players visited his training quarters daily. Playing lacrosse had helped Burns obtain a fan following.[143]

141 *Police Gazette*, February 21, 1903.
142 *Seattle Daily Times, Tacoma Times*, September 7, 1904.
143 *Seattle Daily Times*, September 8, 1904.

Over at Pleasant Beach, where he was training, the "Black Cyclone" Woods created a good impression with visitors. He worked with dumbbells, shadow boxed and practiced footwork and defense, punched the bag, wrestled with trainer George Paris, sparred with Paris and Johnny Garrison, demonstrating his speed, punching power, and cleverness throughout, and then he jumped rope. "Woods is as light and fast as a bantam weight on his feet."

Eight days before the fight, on the morning of September 8, Woods allegedly weighed 157 pounds, one pound under the contract weight. However, in subsequent days, there were rumors that the claim was false, that he was even bigger and was struggling to make weight.[144]

Burns was demonstrating wonderful speed in his training at the engine house. Each day, he sparred with Warren Zurbrick and Louie Long. Those who observed his workouts pronounced him "a marvel of strength and cleverness, and his hard punches never fail to bring his sparring mates down when they land. Burns is a fast clean hitter and his record shows him to be a boxer who wins his decisions more decisively than merely on points." The crowds that watched his training showed their appreciation with generous applause.

The contest was generating a great deal of attention and excitement all along the Coast. It was anticipated that the theatre's seating would be taxed to its utmost capacity, judging from the great interest shown in the contest. The club management had even received orders for seats from Victoria and Vancouver. There was a large amount of wagering on the contest.

There was some talk of the winner potentially meeting Kid McCoy. However, it was said that McCoy had previously refused to meet Woods a few weeks ago, when Woods' manager offered to make a $1,000 side bet.[145]

The *Seattle Times* said Woods and Burns were both fast and aggressive, and evenly matched. Tommy Burns was "looked upon by expert ring critics to be a wonder." However, Californians thought the black fighter had the edge, for he was "rated one of the best men in the business" and called the "undisputed king of his class" in the West. Woods' work and wallop were well known on the Coast. Billy had been unable to find anyone who could give him any kind of a contest until he went against Mike Schreck, who "stood him off" for 25 rounds to a draw at Colma a short time ago. Schreck and Woods had put up a "corking good contest," the fight of Woods' life.

This reporter noted that it was known that Burns had beaten Schreck (unofficially), and therefore Burns had to be good. Burns had also easily defeated Cyclone Kelly in 4 rounds, after the Cyclone had "defeated such good men as George Cole and Hugo Kelly," fought to a draw with Philadelphia Jack O'Brien, and had given "Tommy Ryan a hard tussle for eleven grueling rounds." However, Woods had also defeated Cyclone Kelly,

144 *Seattle Daily Times*, September 9, 1904.
145 *Seattle Daily Times*, September 10, 1904.

in 8 rounds and again in 5 rounds. "To Californians who are familiar with Woods' ring record, he is figured to win, but still they believe he will have to box in his best form all the way in order to do so." Woods was the betting favorite at 10 to 9 odds.

> There are many who think Bishop's protégé [Woods] is the strongest man in the ring and the heaviest hitter of his time, barring, of course, Jim Jeffries. He is very aggressive and has wonderful speed for a boxer of his weight and strength. His vitality and endurance, which make it possible for him to stand almost any amount of punishment are scarcely less important factors. He is undoubtedly clever, and his knack of covering up effectively makes him hard to land on. These qualities have made the colored man well liked by the followers of the boxing game, and the number that predict great things for him is large.

However, it was also said,

> The Chicago lad is just the kind of a man that will give Billy a hard contest. He is an aggressive chap, stepping in all the time, with no let up. Burns has a left jab for the face that Woods will find hard to avoid and he has a wicked right cross that will get the money with anyone if it lands in the right place. Burns kept up a continual fire at Cyclone Kelly and the sports who saw the bout marveled at the speed he displayed. Eastern ring critics say that Burns would make short work of such a clever fellow as Philadelphia Jack O'Brien and, if this be true, then Woods will certainly have his hands full.

The *Seattle Times'* reporter felt that Burns' performances with their common opponents, Mike Schreck and Cyclone Kelly, stamped him the slightly better man. However, "Figuring the men from all sides, it looks to be a fairly even contest all the way and one that will surely please the audience, as both men are decidedly aggressive and seldom keep an audience waiting for an exciting round." Both of the fighters had impressed spectators with their training and excellent shape.[146]

Large crowds came to see both Burns and Woods train. On September 11, even ladies, who were usually barred from boxing exhibitions and matches, visited Tommy's training quarters at the No. 4 engine house. Tom did not want the room to be too crowded, so he was only admitting about a dozen or so spectators each day.

> Once Burns starts to work he goes at it systematically and without a let up. Yesterday he played hand ball, punched the bag, skipped the rope and boxed with his trainers [Louie Long and Warren Zurbrick] with not more than a half minute rest between times. Those who saw

---

146 *Seattle Times*, September 11, 1904.

Burns at work yesterday were surprised at the speed he showed, and it is a foregone conclusion with the visitors that he will keep Woods busy when they meet Friday night at the Seattle Theatre.

Burns was full of confidence. He said, "I am sure I will win, and I will do it as quickly as possible."

Woods was also confident, but did not do much talking. He said that he would do his best to win. "While Woods is dangerous, cool headed and quick as a cat in the ring, out of it he is pleasant and quiet. The severe course of training he has undergone has not rendered him irritable, as it does most fighters, and he is as fresh as a daisy, a sure sign that he is not overtrained." At that point, the betting was even.[147]

Many wagers were being placed. Although both men had plenty of backers, the general feeling around town was that Woods would win the contest. The question was not so much whether Billy would win, but whether or not he would stop Burns.

> Some argue that Burns, by reason of his extreme cleverness and the speed he is known to possess, will go the fifteen rounds with the crack Californian, while others are of the opinion that Woods will turn the trick inside of ten rounds. The greatest number of bets made, however, are on whether or not Woods wins inside the limit, which is fifteen rounds.

Biddy Bishop said he would bet $100 against $200 that his man Woods would win inside 15 rounds. Although he was asking for 2 to 1 odds, he would lose his money if Woods did not win by knockout, even if Billy won. Billy Lavigne said he would bet $250 at even money that Burns would win the decision.[148]

A couple days before the fight, it was said that Burns would make weight without problem and therefore would take it easy, tapering his training. Tom said, "I have studied this thing out to a nicety, and I find that Woods is a fellow that will require a good deal of work. I must keep at him all the time and never give him a chance to come to me. In other words, I must carry the contest right up to him."

Unlike Burns, Woods was still overweight and was keeping up his daily 10-mile runs. Three days before the fight, on the 13th, Woods not only ran and boxed 4 rounds with Charlie Neary, but he remained under blankets for more than 30 minutes to sweat. Afterwards, he was 2.5 pounds over the weight limit. "Whether or not such strenuous labors will impair his chances remains to be seen."

---

147 *Seattle Daily Times*, September 12, 1904.
148 *Seattle Daily Times*, September 13, 1904.

An unusually large crowd was expected to come from Portland, Oregon. Also, "It is expected that fully 500 will be over from Tacoma. Up to the present time the advance sale amounts to more than $1,200."[149]

They would be fighting for the Pacific Coast Middleweight Championship. Burns was called the best 158-pounder that had ever been developed in Chicago, "not even excepting Jack Root," which was a big compliment indeed. Both contestants were in excellent condition, and since they were evenly matched in every particular, a fine contest was expected. The fight was being called one of the most attractive bouts ever offered to a local audience. "Opinions differ as to who will win, and it appears that each has an equal number of admirers who are ready and willing to stake their good, hard dollars on their choice."[150]

The *Seattle Daily Times* said Burns might whip Woods. Many local sports thought his chances were more than good. It said that he would have as many, if not more backers, than the formidable Woods.

> At first glance the match appeared to be slightly in Woods' favor among those who make a practice of betting on such affairs, but since the ring records of the men have been inquired into more thoroughly, and since both have been watched and compared at their respective training quarters, the people have come to the conclusion that Burns has equally as good a chance of winning as has Woods, and they intend to back him with good hard dollars of the realm.

> Californians are confident their representative will win, and Woods will get much support from this contingent, but the short-enders have won so many great battles of late it makes one a bit timid in stringing a bet on the colored wonder.

Some bettors feared that the lesser-known Burns might spring a surprise on them.

> Burns is a youngster with considerable experience, he has had as many contests as Woods, and he is always in the pink of condition. He takes excellent care of himself and has a punch that will bring anyone down if it is landed in the right place. In addition to this Burns is fast and clever, and is a good ring general.

Even the referee, Charley Reno, was said to be in good shape, having been doing considerable road work to prepare himself for the contest.[151]

Although Woods had a tough time making 158 pounds, he was on weight shortly after noon on the day of the fight. Therefore, he would make weight at 3 p.m. Everyone acknowledged that Billy was in excellent condition. Still, his struggle to make weight was seen by some bettors as

149 *Seattle Daily Times*, September 14, 1904.
150 *Tacoma Times*, September 14, 1904.
151 *Seattle Daily Times*, September 15, 1904.

increasing Tommy's chances of victory. Woods said he knew that Burns was a fast and clever man with a good punch.

Tommy was so confident that he instructed his manger to bet half of his end of the purse on himself. "Burns looks the picture of good health and he says he never felt better in his life." It was expected that fully 100 members of the Seattle lacrosse team would be on hand to applaud Tommy's every punch.

Charley Neary said, "I saw Burns in the contest with Mike Schreck, and he's a great fighter. Woods is one of the best men I have ever boxed with, and it should be a fine contest." Someone who saw Burns defeat Cyclone Kelly said he thought that Burns was a great man.

Both fighters were listed as being 23 years of age, and within 1-2 inches of each other in height. It was estimated that Woods would be about 158 pounds to Burns' 156 pounds. The bouts were set to start between 8:30 p.m. and 8:45 p.m.[152]

TOMMY BURNS,
The man who will meet Billy Woods at the Seattle theatre tonight.

On Friday September 16, 1904 at the Seattle Theatre before a house of 1,500 people, Tommy Burns and Billy Woods fought 15 rounds to a draw decision. The local *Seattle Daily Times* said that "more than half the house vociferously objected to the decision" issued by Charley Reno, feeling that Burns had won. Its reporter also thought that Tommy had earned the decision.

> While Burns' blows lacked steam, and while he failed to hurt his dusky opponent, nevertheless he displayed the most cleverness, landed the most blows, put up an exhibition of footwork such as has never been seen in a Seattle ring before, and on points, deserved the decision.

---

152 *Seattle Daily Times, Seattle Post-Intelligencer*, September 16, 1904.

Of course, the above is merely the opinion of one lone man, but that same man bet his money on Woods, so there is certainly nothing prejudiced about it whatsoever.

Both men were in good condition, and it was a fast and satisfying contest. Woods assumed a very low crouching position, and Burns had difficulties getting through his guard. Woods mostly attacked the body. Burns was hurt by some body shots in the 1st round and was butted in the eye in the 2nd, which raised a welt. Tommy also hurt his right hand on the top of Woods' head, owing to the fact that he went after the head when Woods was crouching down. Other than that, Woods did no damage.

Overall, "Burns demonstrated his ability as a boxer." Quite often Woods would attempt his left to the body, but each time Burns would step in and the left arm would whip harmlessly around his body. Billy looked slow compared to the "shifty quickness of the Chicago boy." Woods was a good man, but his showing was a "disappointment," for despite being highly touted, he "couldn't catch his opponent last night any more than a fly could catch a flea."

Burns felt that he had earned the decision. "I had him a mile. I ought to spank that little referee." Tom was scheduled to catch a midnight boat for Victoria, where he had promised to play in a lacrosse game the following afternoon.

Typical in the event of a draw, the combatants split the fighters' share of the receipts, with each receiving about $700. Burns added $240 to that sum as a result of his winning wager that Woods would not stop him.[153]

The *Seattle Post-Intelligencer* said Burns had shown wonderful cleverness in blocking and in footwork, making Woods narrowly miss his punches. A large number in attendance disagreed with the draw decision. "Burns did the greater part of the leading and landed more blows." However, the other side of the house felt that "while Burns may have had the lead early in the game, Woods did the forcing in the last seven rounds, and landed more telling blows." Both came out of the fight fresh and unharmed and could have kept going, which often justified a draw. The referee said, "I gave it as I saw it, and that ends the matter. It was a very close contest, and I could not do otherwise than call it a draw." A man (unnamed) who was considered one of the best boxing critics on the coast agreed that the decision was just.

Overall, Burns lacked force in his blows and had trouble landing effectively because of Woods' peculiar crouch, but still he put up a great exhibition. "Comparing the two men as to science, the palm must go to Burns. His blocking of Woods' fierce rushes was little less than phenomenal." Woods' vicious leads did no damage, while Tom was there with both arms firing away. Billy persistently tried to land his left to the

---

153 *Seattle Daily Times*, September 17, 1904.

body, but could not land with full force. Burns was complimented on his magnificent judgment of distance, cleverly moving in and making Billy's body punches slide around his own body. Ring followers said Burns reminded them of Tommy Ryan.

> Seattle has not seen such a clever exhibition of side-stepping and avoiding blows by a hair's breadth in her history of ring contests. For fifteen rounds without a let up Burns was on the go all the time. He led and was away; he blocked and came back with a short-arm jab; he let right and left swings come with the full strength of the powerful arms of his opponent, but his body and his jaw were always just out of reach.

Burns was also said to have an accurate eye, moving about the ring like a flash, landing with precision and meeting and answering rushes with well-timed blocks and steps that placed him out of harm's way. He had an attractive, eye-pleasing style. The crowd's sympathy was with him. "In truth his foot-work and blocking were enough to inspire admiration."

Woods carried the knockout punch in either hand, but was neutralized most of the time by Burns' quickness and good judgment. He occasionally landed a hard blow, but Burns either took it well or quickly recovered. Woods' defense was good too, for he covered up nicely with his crouching style.

Some claimed that Burns broke his right hand in the 8th round, while others said it was not until the 15th round that it was hurt. In the last round, he did not use his right, and he did a lot of dancing to keep away from the determined Woods.[154]

Unlike the other two local papers, the *Seattle Star* was not impressed by the bout, and provided its own unique perspective of matters. It said the fight was dull and that the two boxers stalled through thirteen rounds until they fought with more ginger in the last two. The bout resembled a tame exhibition more than a fight. Both men were clever and defensive, so as to offset the other.

Pandemonium broke loose when the draw decision was announced. "Rotten! Rotten!" "Give us our money back!" "Oh, you thieves!" While the other papers saw this as the crowd feeling that Burns was robbed of the decision, the *Star* opined that the fans felt that they had been robbed of a good and legitimate fight. It believed that the fight had been fixed, owing to the fact that the men "dilly-dallied and danced around." The fighters continually clinched and hung on.

> When they were not doing this, Woods was giving an exhibition of a pet dog saying his prayers. With his hand over his head and doubled up like a man afflicted with chronic dyspepsia, he jumped around the

---

154 *Seattle Post-Intelligencer*, September 17, 1904.

ring and, not until the fight was nearly over, did he show any desire to force the fighting. Whenever Woods did make a pass at Burns, the latter showed his ability to take ample care of himself, for not once did the colored fighter land a telling blow. In fact neither of them got in a good, square swat. ...

The sports claim that Burns, had the decision been given according to the merits of the affair, should have been declared the winner. He forced all the fighting and showed his ability on every occasion to keep clear of the rushes of his opponent.[155]

The semi-local *Tacoma Times* reported that Burns outpointed Woods, but only got a draw. Its report echoed the *Post-Intelligencer*.[156]

Once again, Tommy Burns' stock went up, even with a draw decision. The majority felt that he had won the fight. The *San Francisco Call* reported that the there was "considerable dissatisfaction" with Referee Reno's draw decision. "Burns was much the cleverer and showed wonderful skill in blocking Woods' rushes." However, neither man was hurt in the bout.[157]

The day after the fight, Woods' manager Biddy Bishop said that both Burns and Woods were great fighters and two of the best middleweights in the world.

You should give Burns credit for being a coming champion, and at the same time credit Woods with being a past master, too, for if Burns is so good, then Woods, too, must be equally as good for going the distance with him.... Burns is deserving of great credit to last through fifteen rounds with my boy. Take a fellow that will stand up to his work and wallop and take punch for punch with Woods and he won't last through four rounds with Billy, but these clever fellows that can smother and stall and step in close and clinch, as Burns did, will always give any man a hard job to knock them out.[158]

Bishop, who managed both Woods and Young Peter Jackson, who held a knockout victory over Jack O'Brien, said that if his fighters were matched, he would pick Woods to defeat Jackson. "Billy is faster and is much harder to hit and has equally as good a punch."

Bishop gave Burns all the credit due him for his great battle against Woods. He offered no excuses, but said that he wanted a rematch. Still, Bishop felt that the decision was justified. He opined that the expectation to see Woods tear off Burns' head and his failure to do so had caused Billy to be unmercifully roasted. He said,

---

155 *Seattle Star*, September 17, 1904.
156 *Tacoma Times*, September 17, 1904.
157 *San Francisco Call*, September 17, 1904.
158 *Seattle Post-Intelligencer*, September 18, 1904.

They forget that the man in the ring with him may be equally as good a fighter, although he hasn't as good a reputation. ... My boy came heralded as the great and only Billy Woods; the fellow who had made the mighty Joe Walcott look like a deuce; the only fellow who could lick the remarkably clever "Philadelphia" Jack O'Brien, and the chap whom all the middleweights were dodging right and left. ... Almost every one of them thought Woods would wade through Burns ... These fellows didn't give Tommy credit for knowing anything about the game, and what was the result? Woods fell in for his share of roasting because he didn't dispose of Tommy in a few short rounds, when, as a matter of fact, Burns is capable of withstanding any of our best middleweights. ... Burns is a good boy, and a clever fellow. He must be a good man to stay fifteen rounds with Woods. He's entitled to much credit for his showing, but on the other hand, if Burns is such a decidedly good man as he is, then Woods should not be discredited for not knocking him out. Let me tell you and in after years you will remember what I have told you is right, both Tommy Burns and Billy Woods are two of the greatest middle weights in the world. Now wait and see if I ain't right.

I still think that Woods can beat Burns, and I stand ready at any time to arrange another match with him on the same terms as the one Friday night, and to show you that I mean business, I'll wager $1,000 that Woods beats him.

As to the decision, I will say that I think it was perfectly just. ... Ask anyone that understands the game and they will tell you whether or not it was a good decision. Immediately after the contest Jim Morrison, Tom Considine, Billy Belond, Frank Clancy, Frank Purcell, Ty Kreling and Joe Corbett, and you must admit that these men are all authorities on boxing matters, offered their opinions that the decision was a good one.[159]

However, upon reading the newspaper, Billy Belond wrote the *Times* that Biddy Bishop's statement claiming that Belond was satisfied with the Woods-Burns decision was wrong. "He says he thought Burns should have had the decision as he had all the best of the go."[160]

Burns' manager Billy Lavigne said Tommy deserved to win the fight. He said,

The bout Friday night was one of the best and most stubbornly fought contests I ever saw between two high class middleweights, and while Woods made a gallant stand all through the route of fifteen rounds, I figure that Burns had him safely in hand all the way. At no

159 *Seattle Sunday Times*, September 18, 1904.
160 *Seattle Daily Times*, September 20, 1904.

time was I apprehensive of Burns' chances of winning. There were quite a number of times during the mill when it was necessary for the referee to call Woods' attention to foul work, and the only mark Burns received during the bout was the one he received from the colored man's head in one of the mixups.

Woods was also called on several times to quit his defensive tactics and fight. Several times Burns placed himself in jeopardy trying to coax Woods out of that turtle shell style and mix matters up. My opinion is that when a boxer refuses to take any chances whatsoever and tries merely to protect himself he does so for the reason that he is up against a faster man than himself, and must take that method of defending himself.

As for the decision, I will leave it for those who were there to witness the bout to decide. Mr. Reno, who acted as referee, I know to be honest and upright in every way. He rendered his version of the bout in his own honest way, and before the bout informed both sides that he wouldn't render any hair-line decision either way. I figure the margin was far from a hair-line one and therefore claim we should have had the verdict of winner.

Burns' work against Woods pleased me greatly, and I feel safe in predicting a great future for him in the ring. He has every quality necessary to make him a leader in his class; his speed is wonderful, and it showed to splendid advantage in this battle against such a burly strong fellow as Woods is. Some were of the opinion his blows lacked force, but they must take in consideration the fact that his opponent the other night is a fighter of the hard shell order and keeps the most vital portion of himself hidden all the time, with his body drawn in and jaw covered with elbows and arms. There was little left for Burns to peck at but the top of that tough cocoanut of a head, which the colored man kept well in Burns' face all the time.

Several years ago boxers were more in the habit of side-stepping and dodging in order to avoid punishment than they are today. Nowadays a fighter thinks as much of trying to avoid a blow by stepping inside as he does of slipping away, and possibly more so. Burns is a past master at the new art of boxing: he is cool and collected all the time and has all manner of confidence in his ability, which in my opinion has all to do with a man's success in the ring.

Burns had never seen Woods in action in the ring. Lengthy stories of Woods' great prowess had little effect on the Chicago boy's confidence in his ability to win. Burns entered the ring as cool and as confident as if he were about to play a game of billiards. In meeting Woods, Burns was certainly taking on no easy proposition; besides conceding quite a number of pounds in weight and his action previous to the bout, as well as in the ring, convinces me that he is fit to cope with any man in his class--and win.[161]

A week after the fight, discussion of the Woods decision continued, which was favorable towards Burns. "Although Referee Reno declared the Burns-Woods fight a draw the other night, Seattle papers claim that Tommy should have had the long end of the purse. It is said that he did most of the leading and showed himself to be the cleverer of the two."[162]

There was some talk of Burns being matched to fight Joe Walcott in October. Tommy was anxious to meet him, although he had to await the result of Walcott's already scheduled match with Joe Gans. "Burns has long wanted to get a crack at Joseph and anyone who saw Friday night's contest will certainly admit that a go between Burns and Walcott would prove a great drawing card." On September 30, 1904, Joe Walcott fought Joe Gans to a 20-round draw. A Walcott-Burns fight was in the works. Unfortunately, shortly thereafter, Walcott accidentally shot himself in the hand and did not fight again for over a year, until 1906. What is clear, though, is that Tommy Burns was not afraid to mix it up with top black fighters or quality fighters in general.

161 *Seattle Sunday Times*, September 18, 1904.
162 *Seattle Sunday Times*, September 25, 1904.

CHAPTER 4

Taking on the Top Tier Middleweights

Just before the Burns-Woods bout, in Wisconsin, where Tommy Burns had impressed the locals with his early 1904 performance against Mike Schreck, it was said,

> One of the most promising middleweights in the country today, barring such men as Tommy Ryan, Jack O'Brien and Bob Fitzsimmons, is Tommy Burns of Detroit, Mich., formerly known to the boxing world as "Noah Brusso." ... He made such a favorable impression to the people of the Pacific coast that they are now anxious to match him against Tommy Ryan or any man in the country at his weight. There is no doubt that this same Burns will make a mark for himself, if he is properly handled and takes good care of himself. He is lightning fast on his feet and hits almost as hard as any heavyweight.[163]

Clearly, the folks in Wisconsin wanted to see more of Burns. Just three weeks after going 15 rounds with Billy Woods, in early October 1904 in Milwaukee, Wisconsin, Tommy Burns took another very big step up in opponent quality when he took on "Philadelphia" Jack O'Brien (whose original name was Joseph Hagan).

At that time, Jack O'Brien was one of the best boxers in the world. He was vastly experienced, having fought over 90 bouts. O'Brien's best weight was middleweight, but he occasionally fought light heavyweights and heavyweights. O'Brien had been boxing since at least late 1896, giving him five years more experience than Burns, but at age 26 he was only three years older than Tommy. He had fought the far superior quality of opponents, and had fought quite often. In contrast, Burns was just completing his third year as a professional. Saying there was a vast difference in experience is a huge understatement. It was said that Tom had a 28-1 record, but had avenged his one loss to Schreck (even though it was called a draw).

O'Brien's record included the who's who of boxing and is too vast to reproduce here, but a sampling of significant bouts includes: 1898 W10 Kid Carter; 1899 W20 George Cole and KO12 Tom McCune; 1900 LKOby13 Young Peter Jackson, WND6 Tommy West, and KO6 Jimmy Handler;

1901 KO11 George Chrisp, KO6 and KO1 Jack Scales, KO6 Dido Plumb, and WDQ7 Frank Craig; 1902 KO3 Andy Walsh, ND6 Joe Walcott,[164] WND6 Young Peter Jackson, KO4 George Cole, WND6 Jack Bonner, KO3 Al Neil, KO3 Yank Kenny, W6 Jack Beauscholte, W6 Billy Stift, W6 Joe Choynski,[165] WND6 and DND6 Peter Maher, DND6 Marvin Hart,[166] and KO4 Jimmy Watts; 1903 KO12 and KO4 Al Weinig, WND6 Choynski, D10 Joe Walcott, ND6 Marvin Hart,[167] ND6 George Byers, LKOby3 Al Limerick, WND6 Kid Carter, WND6 Jack "Twin" Sullivan, W6 Mike Schreck, W15 Jack "Twin" Sullivan (world middleweight title claim), WND6 Jim Jeffords, and D10 Hugo Kelly; 1904 WND6 Tommy Ryan,[168] W15 Mike Schreck, L6 Hugo Kelly, KO3 Jack "Twin" Sullivan, KO3 Kid Carter, DND6 Kid McCoy, DND6 Bob Fitzsimmons,[169] WND6 Hugo Kelly, KO2 Billy Stift,[170] and KO1 Joe Butler.[171]

Burns/Brusso (newspapers often used both names) arrived in Milwaukee on October 5, two days before the fight, with sparring partner Warren Zurbrick of Buffalo, who was said to be a first class fighter.[172]

On the 5th, Noah took a 5-mile run and boxed at Barnickle's. After his work, he tipped the beam at 154 pounds, four pounds below the 158-pound weight limit. Burns realized that O'Brien was faster than he was, but Tom figured that he had a much harder punch than O'Brien did.

Tom's manager, Billy Gee, was expected to come up from Chicago to assist him. Malachy Hogan of Chicago was selected to referee the fight.[173]

All of the local newspapers scouted the bout. The local press called O'Brien "undoubtedly the best middleweight in the business," "probably the greatest 158-pound fighter in the world today," the best man at his

---

164 There were conflicting views of O'Brien's performance against Walcott. One said it was O'Brien's fight from start to finish. O'Brien's footwork was marvelous and had Walcott bewildered and unable to land. Another account said O'Brien's performance was disgraceful as he seemed more interested in sprinting around and keeping away out of fear. *National Police Gazette*, May 3, 1902.

165 O'Brien-Choynski was a clever battle and both proved themselves masters in the art of hitting and getting away. O'Brien though had the advantage of youth, and his speed, shiftiness, and better pace, darting in and out with punches, gained him the clear decision over Choynski. *National Police Gazette*, October 25, 1902.

166 Against Hart, O'Brien won the first 4 rounds, but in the 5th he was dazed, and in the 6th he was dropped and nearly knocked out by Hart. The local newspapers agreed that it was a draw. *Philadelphia Inquirer, Philadelphia Public Ledger*, November 20, 1902.

167 Accounts vary, but the general gist is that O'Brien again won the first 4 rounds against Hart, but was dropped in the 5th and 6th rounds by body shots (possibly more than once) and had to do all that he could to survive. O'Brien "won" because Hart had contracted to knock him out. *Police Gazette*, May 23, 1903; *Louisville Times, Louisville Courier-Journal, Philadelphia Inquirer, Philadelphia Public Ledger*, May 6, 1903.

168 O'Brien had only a slight advantage over Ryan. In the 5th round, first Ryan, then O'Brien was dropped. *Detroit Free Press*, January 28, 1904.

169 In this bloody battle, O'Brien scored his jab often, but Fitz decked him in the 5th and 6th rounds. The police stopped the bout early because the fighting had grown so ferocious. *Police Gazette*, August 6, 1904.

170 An O'Brien right swing knocked Stift out. *Police Gazette*, October 8, 1904.

171 An O'Brien right to the jaw knocked out the black heavyweight Butler. *Police Gazette*, October 15, 1904. Boxrec.com. *Milwaukee Daily News*, October 6, 1904, also gave O'Brien's record.

172 *Milwaukee Sentinel*, October 4 - 6, 1904.

173 *Milwaukee Free Press*, October 6, 1904.

weight in the country, one of the cleverest, if not the cleverest, fighters in the business, the middleweight champion of England, one of the fastest men in the country, and the most active boxer in the profession, fighting more often than any other member of the boxing fraternity. Jack was without doubt as "well known throughout the fighting world as any boxer living."

Because O'Brien was so well known and had fought so often, he was said to be probably the richest boxer in the world. Just the other day, he had purchased a $20,000 home on "millionaire's row." Jack did not look the part of the boxer, especially when he went about with his high silk hat and flashy suit. Regardless of looks, he could fight.

Tommy Burns came with the reputation for being one of the most determined fighters ever. While the tough little fellow with two names (Burns/Brusso) did not have O'Brien's reputation, nevertheless he was a likely man, having proven so in his victory over Schreck. The local papers treated his draw with Schreck as a virtual victory. One paper noted that Burns gave Schreck a "whipping" last winter. The *Milwaukee Daily News* said,

> Burns...is not a top notcher, but he is good enough to give the easterner a hard game.... Burns' capacity for punishment is unlimited and he can hit as hard as the rest of them. His fight with 'Cyclone' Kelley showed that he was of the fighting stuff. Burns fought Mike Schreck here a year ago and gave the Cincinnati boy a beating.

O'Brien was a 10 to 7 favorite. Most thought he should win easily. His cleverness was likely to overcome Burns' rushes, while at the same time Jack would land his quick lefts. However, many did not expect a walkover. The *Milwaukee Free Press* said, "O'Brien has been meeting anybody and everybody in the country for two years and has always managed to gain an easy victory, but in Burns he may strike a tartar." The local *Evening Wisconsin* said it was a battle between a master of the science game and a sturdy, bull-necked youngster. O'Brien had advantages in height, reach, science, and experience. Burns had advantages in strength, hitting power, and "the knowledge that a defeat by O'Brien will not hurt him any," while a victory would project him into the limelight. Burns was listed as standing 5'7" tall and weighing 154 pounds to O'Brien's 5'10" and 158 pounds. The *Milwaukee Journal* said, "The styles of the two men differ widely. O'Brien is one of the most shifty men in the business, while Burns is just a hard-hitting willing boy, who depends more upon his punch than upon any finer points of the game to bring home the money."

The stocky Burns had a hard wallop in either hand, and was figuring that a stiff punch would slow up O'Brien, and that he would be able to hold his own after that. Burns told another reporter, "I think I have a chance with O'Brien, and I am not underestimating his ability either. I don't think that O'Brien can put me away and I know that if I can hit him he'll go to sleep.

If I land it will be all off with Jack and if I don't, he will probably outpoint me."[174]

On October 6, the day before the fight, Burns took a long run in the morning, and in the afternoon, sparred at Barnickle's with Chicago heavyweight John Willie, who had fought 6-round draws with Marvin Hart, Jack Root, and George Gardner.[175]

The scheduled 6-round Burns-O'Brien bout took place on October 7, 1904 in Milwaukee, Wisconsin, before the Badger Athletic Club at the Panorama building. O'Brien weighed in at 157 ½ pounds, while Burns tipped the beam at 154 pounds.

During the first few rounds, O'Brien was either cautious or took it easy on Burns, causing the spectators to cry, "Fake." O'Brien was too clever with his ducking and excellent footwork, utilizing his height and reach to outbox Burns. "O'Brien contented himself with bumping Burns' face into his left glove at very frequent

"Philadelphia" Jack O'Brien

intervals. He would vary it with a few straight rights either to the face or wind." Jack spoke to Tommy in the 3rd round, asking him how he liked the blows. "Towards the end of the battle he changed his tactics somewhat and hammered a number of heavy rights over Burns' heart."

The only good work Burns did was in the 6th round, when Tommy's manager, Billy Gee, sent him on the attack and told him to exchange wallops. Burns landed two unexpected hard left hooks to the jaw. The fight became lively and fast. O'Brien retaliated by attacking and punishing Burns, making a grandstand finish. O'Brien was always in the lead, as he had been

174 *Milwaukee Journal, Milwaukee Daily News, Milwaukee Sentinel, Evening Wisconsin, Milwaukee Free Press,* October 7, 1904.
175 *Milwaukee Free Press,* October 7, 1904.

throughout the bout. Another writer echoed, "During the entire distance Burns probably landed three blows which could be called clean, and two of these came in the last round, when he managed to get up spunk enough to let go a few."

The *Milwaukee Daily News* reported that it was an easy 6-round decision victory for O'Brien, for Burns could not land effectively, while Jack landed where and when he pleased.

The *Milwaukee Free Press* said Burns was no match for the clever Philadelphian, who won the decision by a large margin. O'Brien feinted Burns into many hard wallops, but Burns was game and took the punishment without flinching and always came back for more. Owing to its one-sidedness, the spectators took little interest in the bout.

The *Evening Wisconsin* said the locals got a chance to see a world champion in O'Brien demonstrate his extreme cleverness. He gave a splendid scientific exhibition. "His feinting was superb and his footwork perfection." Burns could not get inside Jack's long tantalizing left. When Burns would swing, Jack would close in, out of danger. Burns was fast on his feet, but not fast enough. O'Brien was so far ahead of Burns in the fine points of the game that he made Tommy look worse than he really was.

Two other papers were even harsher in their assessments. The *Milwaukee Sentinel* said O'Brien won a tame and disappointing bout. Referee Malachy Hogan awarded him the decision because O'Brien "completely outclassed his opponent and was entitled to the verdict." However, O'Brien never extended himself. Although he had far greater knowledge of the game, he did not attempt to show how good he was, but was content to stall along and win the verdict with as little effort as possible.

The *Milwaukee Journal* agreed that O'Brien put up a languid fight, meaning lackadaisical, listless, or spiritless. He was content to win on points, and "gave an exhibition of what a champion might do. What he might have done and what he did do, however, are two different things." Jack made a monkey of Tommy with his cleverness, without taking any chances of injuring his hands. The bout resembled an exhibition more than a fight. Nevertheless, O'Brien won easily in a one-sided walkover. Jack was never forced to do anything more than fiddle along. "At the end of the six rounds neither man was much the worse to wear, O'Brien's hair not being mussed, while Burns' eyes showed the effect of their frequent contact with O'Brien's mitts."[176]

However, the *Evening Wisconsin* disagreed with the *Journal*, saying, "Burns took a much worse beating than appeared to the crowd, for Jack's blows were sharp and cutting." At the end, Noah's eyes were decorated and his cheek was damaged, besides having sprained his left shoulder.

---

176 *Milwaukee Daily News, Milwaukee Sentinel, Milwaukee Journal, Milwaukee Free Press, Evening Wisconsin,* October 7-9, 1904.

After the fight, the gracious O'Brien said that Burns was a good man who would whip nearly all of the fighters around 160 pounds. Burns would head back to Chicago.

The *National Police Gazette* reported that the "fighting was somewhat tame, O'Brien having the better of his man in every round with the exception of the fourth, in which honors were about even."[177]

A few days after the bout, the local press reported that many spectators were disappointed that O'Brien did not put Burns away. However, the fact was that O'Brien had hit him hard, but Burns proved that he could take it. Also, O'Brien respected Burns' punching power and did not want to leave himself vulnerable to a knockout blow. Hence, he fought cautiously.

> The bout, however, was not so tame as many believe. O'Brien was easy with his man the first three rounds but some of the wallops he landed in the fourth, fifth and sixth rounds would be money getters had an ordinary man received them. Burns is a tough proposition and a hard man to put away.

> Had O'Brien been careless he might have been given a chance to regret it. Burns has a knockout in each hand…. O'Brien did just what any other wise fighter would do – give his man a whipping without taking any chances.[178]

Burns and O'Brien would meet again a couple years later, in a championship fight.

Despite continual attacks on the popular sport, former heavyweight champion John L. Sullivan said, "Boxing ain't one half as bad nor as brutal as football. … There are a lot of milk and water guys who don't know a thing about boxing, but who are knocking the game all the time."[179]

Returning to the West Coast, where he had become popular, Tommy Burns' first 1905 bout was on January 31 in Ballard, Washington, a Seattle area neighborhood, against heavyweight "Indian" Joe Schildt. Burns had sparred Schildt back in April 1904. Clearly, Tommy was not afraid of taking on bigger foes, a harbinger of things to come.

Burns was listed as 5'7" and 156 pounds to Schildt's 6'1 ½" and 210 pounds. However, Joe was said to be carrying at least 20 pounds of unnecessary fat which slowed him down and affected his condition. Regardless, Tommy was confident enough to be willing to take on a heavyweight, spotting him at least 50 pounds.

In the 1st round, Burns mostly ducked Schildt's vicious swings. By the end of the round, Joe's mouth was slightly bleeding. In the 2nd round, Burns landed several times. Schildt began covering and clinching frequently. Burns

---

177 *National Police Gazette*, October 22, 1904.
178 *Milwaukee Daily News*, October 10, 1904.
179 *Seattle Post-Intelligencer*, January 29, 1905.

would work quickly until he was given the bear hug. Tommy kept Joe going at a good enough pace such that it wore down the larger man.

In the 3rd round, Schildt alternated between swinging wildly and clinching. Tommy ducked every time. The 4th round was similar, and Joe was very tired at the end of the round, with his mouth bleeding.

Schildt was so tired in the 5th and 6th rounds that all he could do was cover and clinch; only occasionally rushing and swinging. "Near the end of the sixth Joe landed a fair blow on Burns and Tommy pretended to be groggy. Schildt went after him and Burns wobbled around for a minute, then suddenly jumped at the big fellow like a catamount, staggering him with right and left on the jaw." Tommy had used an old Fitzsimmons trick, feigning being hurt in order to draw his opponent into opening up so that he could explode with his own offense. The hurt Schildt clinched until the bell. The deputy sheriff then stepped into the ring and stopped the one-sided bout. Burns was awarded the victory.[180]

Two other local papers said the contest was a farce. The clever Burns was so superior from the start that there was nothing to the bout. Tommy was a good boxer, jabbing Schildt at will. The Indian was carrying too much weight, was too slow, and Tommy easily dodged his blows. Schildt mostly hugged until the deputy stopped it in disgust after 6 rounds.[181]

JACK "TWIN" SULLIVAN

Just over a month later, in early March in Tacoma, Washington, Burns again took on a well-respected and very experienced opponent in top middleweight Jack "Twin" Sullivan. Sullivan's over 50 bouts of experience included fights against the division's elite, including: 1902 D6 Mike Schreck, W10 George Cole, KO9 Jimmy Handler, D10 Dick O'Brien, and D6 George Byers; 1903 D15 Jack Palmer, D6 Steve O'Donnell, LND6 and L15 Jack O'Brien (world middleweight title claim); and 1904 WND6 Schreck, L6 and W20 Hugo Kelly, LKOby3 Jack O'Brien, D10 Kelly, W10 Mike Schreck, W20 Dave Barry, L20 Kid McCoy, and KO2 Nick Burley. In 1903 and 1904, Sullivan had been a sparring partner for heavyweight Jack Munroe.[182]

---

180 *Seattle Post-Intelligencer,* January 29, February 1, 1905.
181 *Seattle Daily Times, Seattle Star,* February 1, 1905.
182 Boxrec.com.

He has a style of shadow fighting all his own,

He is not much on fancy stunts, but he's there with the wallop,

He skips rope like a girl of sixteen,

He is clever at the dance

His fighting smile,

He hastens to the shower and a rub down,

He toys with his 225 lb. Indian training partner,

In his swell rags he's a handsome chap

SOME IMPRESSIONS OF TWIN SULLIVAN

Sullivan generally weighed around 154 pounds. He was in excellent shape for the Burns fight, as always. Jack said, "I am never caught napping, and it seems now as if I improved with age." Sullivan was 26 years old. His brother Dave Sullivan would spar with Jack, as well as heavyweight Indian Joe Schildt, who said that he weighed a little over 220 pounds.

Burns had been living in Portland, Oregon, even playing with a lacrosse team there. It was in Portland that he met his future wife, Julia Keating. However, he transferred to Seattle to train. He was then being handled by manager Larry McKenna.

Each day, Burns ran 8 miles and worked for an hour in the gym. He boxed with McKenna and others. Burns was confident, as always. "Sullivan is hard game, but I'll get him before it's over." McKenna did not expect it to be easy, but felt that Tommy would win. "When this fight is over, both of the men will know they have been in a fight."[183]

The two fighters met for the first time on the evening of March 5, two days before the fight. Sullivan asked Tommy, "Where did you spring from? I never heard of you as a fighter until I reached the coast." The remark seemed to anger Burns, who declared, "I may be a green one in your estimation, but I'll make you travel in record-breaking time. It'll have been a long trip from Southern California to come here to take a beating." Sullivan replied, "You back to where the green grass grows when we meet. I guess you'll be a pretty hard nut to crack, all right, all right, but when I crack it, you can gamble, it'll be good." Jimmy Carroll, manager of the hosting Tacoma Amateur Athletic Club, who introduced the men, changed the subject, and asked them who they wanted to referee, and both agreed upon Carroll.

The two boxers engaged in debate regarding whether hitting in the clinches would be allowed. Burns wanted clean breaks, while Sullivan wanted straight Queensberry rules. After agreeing to clean breaks, Sullivan remarked, "That's the way wit' t'ings. The real fighter has to come along and give the kid all the best of it. I lose a lot on that because I ain't as shifty as the boy here, but when I land him, watch out for the funeral march with the Creatore stunts."

Burns wanted to win in order to earn a rematch with Jack O'Brien. "If I should lose, I – well, I really can't say, as I have not given that side of the question any thought." Tom said it would break his heart if he lost.[184]

Burns was said to have generally weighed around 154 pounds and would not have any trouble making weight. Sullivan would have the advantage in height and weight, and was said to know every trick of the trade.[185]

The day of the fight, Sullivan said, "I will have no excuses to offer if I don't come out of the mix-up with the long end of the purse. I feel good

183 *Tacoma Daily News*, March 4, 1905.
184 *Tacoma Daily News*, March 6, 1905.
185 *Seattle Daily Times*, March 7, 1905.

and confident of winning." Burns said, "I realize that a lot of money has been wagered on me, and while I might fail to land a knockout, will win by the decision without doubt."

The local *Tacoma Daily News* said they were fighting for the middleweight championship of the world. Everyone expected a rip-roaring fight. It was anticipated that the big hall, which could seat 1,700, would be packed to the doors, owing to the fact that the bout was attracting an unusual amount of interest.[186]

Tommy Burns and Jack "Twin" Sullivan fought on March 7, 1905 at Tacoma's Germania Hall. It was a scheduled 20-round bout at 158 pounds.

Jack "Twin" Sullivan and Tommy Burns Shake Hands Before Referee Carroll.

---

186 *Tacoma Daily News*, March 7, 1905.

The *Tacoma Daily News* said a big crowd of 1,280 people (five of which were women) witnessed the fight, the biggest crowd in Germania Hall's history. On the main floor, patrons were wedged together from the sides of the ring all the way to the walls. The gallery was also thickly packed.

At ringside, the betting odds were 10 to 8 with Sullivan the favorite. Sullivan was looked after by his brother Dave Sullivan, as well as Harry Monahan, Chris Person, and Jack Lynch. Burns had Tommy Tracy, Jack Hill, and "Kirby Kid" Lampman. The main event started at 10:27 p.m.

The local *Tacoma Daily News* said the fight was hard from the first bell. Burns primarily used left jabs to the jaw and body, while Sullivan punched with both hands, showing his extremely long reach. For the first five rounds, Tommy looked awkward compared to Sullivan, who kept up a continual volley of blows to the body and head. Sullivan clinched and hooked on the breakaways, which could have caused him to be disqualified, because they had agreed to clean breaks. As the fight progressed, Burns improved.

Although Sullivan had been the betting odds favorite, Burns did well enough such that the odds shifted to even after the 10th round. Up to the 11th round, the milling was about even, with Sullivan perhaps having a shade the best of it, but after that, Tommy did most of the punishing.

The principals battered each other in vicious style throughout, particularly in the last 5 rounds, which were the most grueling of the fight. A Burns wild right cut Sullivan's eye fearfully. It immediately filled with blood and completely blinded the Twin, who was already enraged by Tommy's left jabs. What followed were "some of the most vicious exchanges of punishment imaginable."

Burns seemed to have Sullivan in distress after the 15th round, but Sullivan's generalship stood him in good stead. Jack finished the battle strong, although badly battered. Both men were tired at the final gong.

When the contest was over, Referee Jimmy Carroll announced, "Burns told me that he did not want to win this fight on a foul. I call this a draw." Carroll made the statement regarding the fouling owing to the fact that many in the crowd thought Sullivan should have been disqualified. On numerous occasions, the crowd hissed and called 'foul' because of Sullivan's tactics of hitting in the clinches after they had been ordered to break.

Afterwards, Sullivan said, "I am satisfied with the decision. I will never fight Burns or any other man with that break clean proposition, as it really is not fighting. I was in good shape and well handled, or I could never have stood the awful punches. Burns is a good man and he gave me the hardest fight I have ever had."

Burns said,

> I think I can beat him if we ever fight again. I was at a disadvantage all the time as he smashed me in the clinches and I broke clean as we had agreed to do. Those elbow and clinch upper-cuts were not love

taps by any means, and had he fought as per agreement, I would surely have won, as I would have been stronger at the finish, and could have turned the trick. I owe a lot to Tommy Tracy, who looked after me in fine style from the corner.

The next day, Referee Carroll said that although his draw decision may not meet the approval of many, he rendered it to the best of his judgment. "Burns had told me he did not want the fight on a foul, and all I could then do was to keep warning Sullivan. Both are tough fighters, and last night's go was a toss-up."

The crowd had seen 20 rounds of furious fighting. Both men took a beating, but showed their gameness. Sullivan and Burns each received $438.25, and the Tacoma Athletic Club earned $876.50.[187]

Another writer for the *Tacoma Daily News*, Willie Green, presented his observations of the bout. He said the rules, as well as Burns' youth, stamina, and physique built to resist the onslaughts of a more experienced ring general had saved Tommy from defeat. He felt that Sullivan would have done much better and defeated Burns had the rules allowed hitting in clinches. He opined that Sullivan was Burns' master in ring generalship. "Sullivan is a veteran in the art. He is slow but tricky." The Twin had short, powerful, jolting blows like Fitzsimmons, but Tommy either saw them coming and eluded them, or withstood them.

> Burns is a large-sized miniature edition of Champion Jim Jeffries – he possesses a physique that enables him to withstand punishment that would discourage any ordinary boxer. He is not a modern Jem Mace, nor a Corbett, nor a Fitzsimmons – just a big, strong, willing, brave young fellow, with a good idea of the game and a strong arm and heart.

The crowd was with Burns. When Tommy opened up a gash over the Bostonian's eye, the Burns fans went wild. However, Sullivan made many friends by his clever work. Green opined that a draw was the correct decision. "Anything but a draw would have forever killed boxing in Tacoma. Referee Carroll was wise in his decision." Burns had visibly punished Sullivan the most, but Sullivan had done most of the leading.

> Even after having seen Burns in action it is difficult to class him. Just what he would do with a man like Bob Fitzsimmons, or Tommy Ryan, or any one of the very top-notchers is a guess. He is a most willing lad. In his makeup the 'yellow' was left out. And he has a dangerous punch in either hand. His underpinning is marvelous, and his torso reminds one of the ancient gladiators pictured in their battles with the cestus, before petty kings, to the death. Built like Jeffries, he is capable of receiving as well as giving. His fighting

attitudes make almost impossible efforts to lift him from his feet. No blow save one of the knockout species would send him to the grass. He is not a tricky boxer. At in-fighting Sullivan is his master.[188]

Writers for the semi-local Seattle papers provided their own perspectives, which differed from the Tacoma paper in some respects. The Seattle newspapers confirmed that Referee Carroll claimed afterwards that Burns allegedly told him that he did not want to win on a foul, which is why he did not disqualify Sullivan for his foul tactics.

The *Seattle Daily Times* said that Sullivan fouled repeatedly by hitting in the clinches and on the breaks at least twenty times (which had been barred in the agreement). The referee simply warned and scolded Sullivan throughout.

This reporter felt that Sullivan looked slow and awkward compared with Burns, who was too clever for Sullivan. However, Tommy was also too careful, and although he made Sullivan look slow, he did not damage him very much with his punches. Tommy's jab made the crowd cheer, but it was not powerful.

During the fight, Sullivan occasionally threw a haymaker left, but generally Tommy was able to step inside or under it.

> At that Sullivan is so awkward he is clever, for his bald head slipped by a dozen right-hand smashes that would have stretched him cold on the padded ring, and he never for a moment lost his head, even when he was dripping blood and half-blinded from a cut over his left eye.

> Burns nearly copped the coin in the fifth round when he landed his right on Sullivan's chin. 'Twin' sagged at the knees and had the gong not rung the close of the round, he would have been in serious trouble… [I]n every clinch up to the ninth round Sullivan either sent a short jolt to the chin or used his elbows in cuffing Tommy about the head. The crowd was simply frantic, and howled and hissed and cursed the referee and Sullivan.

Burns opened a big cut over Jack's left eye in the 15th round, which nearly closed the eye. However, Sullivan showed cleverness in covering up and stalling, and Burns did not sufficiently follow-up. When Tommy did land his right occasionally, Sullivan would grunt or the blood would flow from the cut over his left eye.

Although Sullivan's left eye was dripping with blood, he came on strong during the last two to three rounds, which perhaps earned him the 20-round draw.

---

188 *Tacoma Daily News*, March 8, 1905.

However, the pro-Burns crowd hooted and hollered when the decision was announced. Sullivan was so overjoyed that he bounced across the ring and kissed Tommy's cheek. Burns was unmarked and fresh at the end.

Most at ringside felt that Burns deserved the decision, but this reporter opined that a draw was all right because Sullivan was still fresh at the end and was looking better during the closing rounds than at any other time. If Burns had "gone in and made a slam-bang fight of it he would have won, for he was the stronger man of the two, and by far the faster."[189]

The *Seattle Post-Intelligencer* said the "fight was a series of clinches from start to finish. Sullivan repeatedly fouled Burns." Sullivan was an in-fighter, and either could not or would not comport himself within the rules. The crowd hissed him. "Few persons in the big crowd were well satisfied with the decision of the referee. Burns was the favorite with the house and had done the leading all through the go." However, Burns only really opened up and went after him twice in the bout. "He tried his much-talked of double shift but once and landed it. He was cautious and took no chances with Sullivan." Still, few expected Sullivan to last after the first three rounds, for he was groggy several times. Sullivan's left eye was cut and closed by one of Tommy's rights. Burns was shorter, but seemed to have the reach advantage. However, Sullivan showed great ring generalship.[190]

The *Seattle Star* said the fight was a good one from start to finish, but Sullivan was inclined to fight dirty. A large crowd from all over the Northwest was in attendance, including 500 from Seattle. Before the fight, odds of 10 to 7 were offered on Sullivan, the favorite. After the 5th round, a lot of Burns money came in sight, but found no takers willing to bet on Sullivan.

From the start, Sullivan used his elbows on Tommy's chin and stomach. The referee warned him no less than nine times during the first 4 rounds. The referee's warnings had no effect on Sullivan, who roughed it whenever he found an opportunity. Burns complained to the referee time after time. The crowd hurled all sorts of epithets towards Sullivan, and called for Carroll to separate the men, which he finally did.

Burns appeared weary in the 14th through 16th rounds, but rallied after that, and with repeated left jabs tore open a gash in the eye and brought blood from the nose. Tom had Sullivan groggy in at least two of the final rounds, although Jack finished appearing fresher. By the bout's conclusion, Carroll was smeared with blood.

Burns said this was the second time that he had been robbed on the West Coast (the Woods fight being the other one). "I had him out twice and should have won on points." Sullivan said that he was used to infighting more, and admitted that Tommy had a "strong lightning left."

189 *Seattle Daily Times*, March 8, 1905.
190 *Seattle Post-Intelligencer*, March 8, 1905.

Despite Referee Carroll's claim that he would have awarded the fight to Burns had Tommy not told him that he did not want to win on a foul, the next-day *Seattle Star* published a letter from Burns wherein he disputed Carroll's claim. He said,

> Mr. Carroll stated that I told him that I did not wish to win the bout through a foul. This is absolutely wrong. I would be very foolish to make such a statement. When I enter the ring to box a man I do so to win that boxing match, whether by a knockout, on points, or if the other man is rough enough to foul me and box in a mean and dirty manner [via disqualification]. In other words, I want all that is coming to me. I cannot understand why Mr. Carroll made such a statement. The people in attendance at the bout know who should have been given the decision. Mr. Carroll can never referee another match in which I am one of the principals. I won the fight last night through fouls alone. I am willing to meet Sullivan again, winner to take all, Jack Grant to referee. TOMMY BURNS.[191]

Clearly, the Burns-Sullivan bout had been a competitive fight between two really good fighters. The patrons felt that Burns deserved victory. Once again, Tommy Burns' stock did not drop as a result of a draw. Quite the contrary, the West Coast press and fans wanted to see more of him.

Three weeks later, on March 28, 1905 in San Francisco, in what was advertised as an elimination bout for the right to challenge for the world heavyweight championship, 28-year-old Marvin Hart won a close and somewhat controversial 20-round decision over 26-year-old colored heavyweight champion Jack Johnson. Both fighters weighed around 195 pounds.

In explaining his decision, local newspapers quoted Referee Alex Greggains, a former fighter, as saying that he awarded Hart the decision because he was the game aggressor throughout the contest, forcing the fight at all times. "Johnson, in my opinion, dogged it. He held at all times in the clinches. ... I believe Hart won and I believe that he won all the way. It was a good fight to look at, but Hart did the work, and he properly received the decision."

The *San Francisco Examiner*'s W.W. Naughton said Hart's pluck and awkwardness were better than Johnson's mixture of cleverness and cowardice. Hart had won the decision by being persistently aggressive and steadfastly game, never faltering for an instant, constantly pressing towards his opponent. "Johnson simply fought when he felt like it. ... Johnson beyond a doubt showed that he lacks that essential fighting qualification – grit."

---

191 *Seattle Star*, March 8, 1905.

The *San Francisco Chronicle* said Johnson was strong on points, but not as active as Hart, and that cost him. Hart was aggressive at all times. Johnson was "clever but unwilling." The decision was very popular with the crowd. However, racial prejudice was a factor in the crowd's favoritism.

Johnson's clean hitting, his cleverness at blocking and his work all through was allowed to pass with scarcely a murmur, while every blow landed by the white man was cheered to the echo. This blinded the judgment of many, beyond a doubt. But, even then, casting aside all favoritism, a big majority of the people present felt that Hart had won and was justly entitled to the decision. ...

Those who did not agree with Greggains last night based their argument on the assertion that Johnson had shown pronounced superiority over Hart at all stages: that, if there was nothing else, his clean hitting should have entitled him to the verdict. The Hart faction answered this with the statement that Hart had forced the fighting all the way, and that if he had not done this there would have been no fighting to speak of. ...

To put the thing briefly the way it appeared to a man who had no interest one way or the other – only a desire to see fair play and to have the better fighter win – on the score of aggressiveness Hart was entitled to the verdict. On any other score Johnson should have been the favored one.

The *San Francisco Call* said the busier Hart matched his gameness with Johnson's cleverness. "Hart was ready for a severe contest, as the farther it went the better he seemed to get. He began to show a slight lead when half the route had been traversed, and did much the best work in the last ten rounds." It opined, "Referee Alex Greggains gave an entirely just decision in favor of Hart." Johnson had shown his usual lack of aggressiveness, did not take advantage of many openings, and would not follow up even when he did land. His punches lacked power.

The *San Francisco Evening Post* said Hart put up a gritty fight against Johnson, who lost "because he would not fight." Hart fought hard all the time, whereas Johnson only opened up in spots, showing flashes of offensive brilliance, followed by long periods of defensiveness, cautiousness, and clinching. Johnson had "failed to carry home the victory just because he would not fight." He had the superior ability, but Hart had the superior gameness.

The *San Francisco Bulletin* felt that Johnson should have at least received a draw, if not a victory, owing to his decided lead on points and scientific cleverness from start to finish, even though Hart did all of the forcing and was always on the aggressive. "What Johnson should have done was to have waded in and forced his adversary ... but like all clever men, he deemed discretion was the better part of valor and laid back with the expectation of getting the decision. This proved to be a fatal mistake." It too noted that the house was with Hart because he was the underdog and because of racial prejudice.[192]

On the East Coast, it was reported, "The spectators were wholly of the opinion that Johnson was suffering from a streak of bright yellow. Whenever he did fight, he made Hart look like an amateur. The Louisville man's aggressiveness seemed to rattle Johnson and his courage would ooze."[193]

Next up for Tommy Burns was another bout in Tacoma, Washington, just under two months after the Sullivan fight. Tommy was scheduled to box San Francisco's Irish Dave Barry at catchweights. The fight would be held at the Germania Hall, under the auspices of the Tacoma Athletic Club.

A local newspaper noted that Barry had 23 fights under his belt. He had avenged a loss to Harry Foley with a 7th round knockout. Amongst their common opponents, the hard-punching Barry had knocked out Cyclone Kelly twice, in 1 round and 4 rounds, respectively. He had won a 4-round decision over Billy Woods. However, he had lost a 20-round decision to Jack "Twin" Sullivan in 1904. Barry sparred with Marvin Hart in March 1905, before Marvin took on Jack Johnson. Dave was listed as being 23 years old.

Barry was not concerned by what he had heard regarding Burns' cleverness and good left jab. Dave said, "He may be shifty all right, but then there are others, you know. I didn't come all the way up here to get licked." Both were said to be in perfect condition. "Barry can punch, of which a visit to the pavilion will convince anyone."

Oddly enough, despite previously having been quoted as saying that he would never again accept Jimmy Carroll as a referee for his bouts as a result of the Sullivan decision, Burns accepted the hosting Tacoma Athletic Club's manager Jimmy Carroll as the referee. Perhaps Jimmy had made it up to Tommy. After all, he was offering him another fight and keeping him active.

San Francisco fight promoter Alex Greggains, who had refereed Johnson-Hart, managed Dave Barry, and would be in Barry's corner. There was talk of having the winner face Jack O'Brien to determine the world middleweight champion.[194]

Barry was said to be the larger man and to have the superior punching power. One paper described Dave as wonderfully clever and carrying knockout punches in either hand. Another paper said Barry was not a fancy boxer but hit like a blacksmith.

Straight Queensberry rules were to govern the 20-round contest, meaning that both men were to take care of themselves in the clinches and

---

192 *San Francisco Examiner, Chronicle, Call, Evening Post, Bulletin*, March 29, 1905.
193 *Newark Evening News, Trenton Times*, March 29, 1905.
194 *Tacoma Daily, News*, April 28, May 1, 1905.

on the breakaways. "Tommy is a swell boxer, but it remains to be seen how well he will do with a rugged man like Barry in a fight where the men can punch with one arm free."[195]

DAVE BARRY.

TOMMY BURNS.

The fight was expected to attract fans from San Francisco, Portland, Seattle, Vancouver, and nearly every city in the Northwest. Several well-known sporting men from San Francisco were expected to wager their money on Barry, who was a great favorite in that town. Seattle sports fans could take a special train to the fight.

On the eve of the bout, Burns said that he was never stronger or faster in his life. The little roll of fat near his waist that was noticeable when he fought Sullivan had disappeared. Burns knew that Barry was one of the toughest customers in the business, and therefore he expected to have the hardest fight of his career. "Tommy has had some hard fights, too, and he has proved that he can take as well as administer terrible punishment."

195 *Seattle Post-Intelligencer, Seattle Daily Times*, May 2, 1905.

Barry was very confident and highly motivated. "I have never been in better shape during my career in the ring. ... This man Burns may be a clever fighter, but then you must remember that I have gone some myself. You can say for me that this referee in this fight will have nothing to do but count ten when I get ready to land the sleep producer." He realized that victory could lead to a fight for the world's championship, but if he lost, it would financially break the 'Frisco sports who had bet on him.

The local press noted that Barry would be about 12 pounds heavier than Burns, have a 2-inch height advantage (5'9" vs. 5'7"), and a 2.5 inch reach advantage. However, Burns had the speed and cleverness to offset those advantages. Both were considered to be hard punchers who could also take punishment without wincing.[196]

Barry was a 10 to 9 favorite, with considerable wagering taking place. Burns' manager Larry McKenna was said to be betting a lot on his fighter.[197]

On May 2, 1905 at Tacoma's Germania Hall, Tommy Burns fought Dave Barry for the Pacific Coast Middleweight Championship (although it is doubtful that they weighed in at the middleweight limit). It was witnessed by what was called the largest and most enthusiastic crowd that ever saw a fight in Tacoma. The admirers of both principals were in evidence.

When the boxers entered the ring at about 10:30 p.m., one reporter said it was apparent that Barry weighed about 15 pounds more than Burns did. Barry sat in his corner, awaiting the first bell, telling his friends what he was going to do to Burns. Tommy had little to say, other than bowing to the crowd upon his ring entry.

1 – Both sparred. Burns landed a left to the face and Barry countered with a right to the jaw. They clinched and Barry landed his right to the kidneys. Burns sent quick lefts to the face and missed a hard swing to the head. Even round.

2 – Burns twice jabbed Barry's face and they clinched. On the break, Barry landed a right to the head. Burns landed a left to the face, and Barry planted the same and followed with a right to body. Honors even.

3 – Barry rushed wildly and Burns jabbed his face and ducked hard swings. They clinched, and Barry had the best of the infighting. Burns landed a left to the face and right to the head. It was a standoff.

4 – Barry forced the fighting but received hard lefts and rights to the face. Barry planted a left to the face and they clinched. On the break, Burns landed a hard right cross to the head and followed with a left to the jaw. Burns' round.

196 *Tacoma Daily, News*, May 2, 1905.
197 *Seattle Star*, May 2, 1905.

5 – Burns landed his left to the face and Barry clinched. Barry landed a hard right on the body and sent his left to the face. The lights went out, and there was some delay before the lights came back on and the round was resumed. Barry got soaked by four hard lefts to the head and appeared momentarily weak. Burns tried for the knockout but the fast pace took steam out of his blows. Barry recovered and landed a light left at the gong. This was Burns' round by a wide margin.

6 – Most of the fighting was done in clinches, with Burns having all the best of it. He landed lefts and rights to the body, and on the breaks, crossed hard with his right. Barry landed a right to the body and left to the face. Burns' round.

7 – They mixed it up fast at the start, exchanging lefts and rights to the face and body. Barry landed hard on Tommy's mouth and nose. Burns sent a left to the face and they clinched. On the break, Burns landed a hard right, and then Barry rushed in, landing lefts to the face and a hard right to the body. Barry's round.

8 – Both landed to the face. Burns planted two left jabs to the mouth and sent a right to the body. They clinched, and on the break Burns landed a hard right to the jaw. Barry rushed in to clinch and received a hard uppercut to the jaw. Barry landed a hard left to the head and right to the jaw. The round ended with the men clinched and Burns landing rights and lefts to the body. Burns' round.

9 – Barry forced the fighting and landed a left to the head and right to the body. Burns landed his left to the face and followed with a hard right to same place. They clinched repeatedly, but Burns had all the best of the infighting. Burns' round.

10 – Barry started with a fast left to the face and hard right to the heart, but Burns slowed him up with a left and right to the jaw. They clinched and Burns uppercut his jaw. Barry landed a light left to the face and Burns countered with a hard right to the same place, following it up with a left jab to the jaw. They clinched and Burns landed rights and lefts to the body when the bell rang. This was Burns' round by a good margin.

11 - Burns landed his right to the body and Barry countered with the same. Barry made a vicious swing but was short. Barry landed a hard left to the face. Burns sent in a left to the face and right to the body. Barry landed hard lefts and rights to the head and body. This was Barry's round by a narrow margin.

12 – Burns sent in a left to the face. Barry landed a hard right and left to the mouth. They clinched and Barry landed a left to the face and right to the body. Burns struck a left to the jaw, but Barry countered with his right to the head and left to the body. Barry's round.

13 – Barry rushed and landed rights and lefts to the head. They clinched and Burns did some fierce infighting. Barry landed a hard left to the head but Burns countered with the same. They clinched and Barry landed a hard right to the head. Burns showed a burst of speed and landed hard rights and lefts to the face. He cut Barry's eye with a terrific right hook. Burns' round.

14 – Burns resorted to jabbing tactics, keeping his left in Barry's face for most of the round. Barry landed three blows to the head but they lacked steam. Burns' round.

15 – Burns landed rights and lefts to the face at will. He sent a hard straight right to the stomach and followed it up with a hard right to the face. Tommy sent in three quick lefts to the face and Barry hung on. Burns uppercut the jaw on the break and Barry landed lightly to the head and body. Burns' round.

16 – Burns landed several left jabs to the nose and eye and sent in two hard rights to the body. Barry landed three hard lefts to the face. Burns ducked into a right swing. Barry rushed wildly and Burns landed lefts to the head and rights to the body. Burns had a shade the best of the round.

17 – Barry led wildly and received a blow on the mouth. Dave landed a left on the face. Burns sent one to the nose and Barry countered with a right to the head and followed with a left to the face. Burns sent three left jabs to the face but received a hard one in the same place. Dave landed hard on the stomach and Tommy planted his left on the mouth. Barry sent a left to the body. Barry's round.

18 – Barry came up strong and led wildly. He sent a hard left to the face. Burns landed a left to the face and rushed into a clinch. Barry landed to the body and sent a left to the face. Burns landed light left jabs on the face and clinched. Barry's round.

19 – The pace in this round was terrific and Burns fought like a demon. He landed a hard right to the jaw. Barry planted two lefts to the jaw but received a hard one in return. Burns forced matters and sent in hard lefts and rights to the jaw. Barry was almost in, but Burns did not have the strength to put him out. The bell saved Barry, who was hanging on to avoid punishment. It was Tommy's round by a large margin.

20 – Barry came up strong but Burns stopped him with a left jolt to the jaw. They clinched and Barry received a hard uppercut on the jaw. Barry landed a light right to the face but received a hard left in return. Barry rushed but was stopped by hard lefts to his face. He hung on and Burns sent his left to the face. Barry landed a right to the head but Burns forced him to the ropes with terrific lefts and rights to the jaw. After the referee broke them, Burns tried for a knockout. He landed on the jaw repeatedly, but Barry did not wince, and the gong sounded ending the fight. Both men were eager and willing to continue at the end of the bout.

Referee Jimmy Carroll awarded Burns the decision. The local round-by-round account scored it 12 rounds Burns, 5 rounds Barry, and 3 rounds even. The referee's decision was applauded and cheered by the entire house and by the press, even though Barry's admirers were in attendance. Carroll was called as good a referee as anyone in the game.

The *Tacoma Daily News* said it was a great battle, "not record breaking in science," but a terrific fight from start to finish, the best one ever seen in Tacoma. The bruising engagement had tried Tommy's mettle and gameness to the utmost. The fight could not be criticized in any way, for every man present got his money's worth. "The men were evenly matched, in splendid physical condition, and as game as pebbles."

Summarizing, it said that from the 1st round, while sparring at long range, Barry found that he could not keep away from Tommy's long left. Therefore, Barry's seconds called for him to rough it, but to the surprise of many, when he did so, Burns demonstrated that he was adept at infighting as well, and was superior to Barry at his own game. Burns had "outmaneuvered his hard-hitting opponent at all stages, and surprised the crowds with his superior ability at infighting." He had also displayed splendid footwork. Still, Barry had wonderful nerve and a hard wallop. "He did most of the leading last night, but was unable to land often enough on his wily opponent."

However, one writer said that Burns was not clever in terms of setting up a knockout blow, although this perception might have been owing to Barry's toughness as much as anything. Barry was not a boxer but a big, sturdy, strong Irishman, full of fight, and would be dangerous for any man living in a London prize ring rule engagement. He administered some punishment of his own, and took enough punishment to knock out a dozen men, but Burns could not take him out.

Another writer from the same newspaper said, "If Burns had been against most any other fighter than Barry he would have won by the knockout route. He landed often and hard, but the big Irishman proved himself a glutton for punishment." Although Burns received some hard blows and was slowed up a few times, he finished strong, and there was not a mark on him. Barry, on the other hand, showed the effects of the punishment. His body was bruised considerably, and the left side of his face was badly beaten.

Tommy's stock went up. "Tommy Burns has become quite a popular idol. He is certainly a sturdy young boxer. He is built on the Jeffries plan, and in every fight in which he has appeared in Tacoma, has had at least a little the better of it." Another writer said, "Burns showed up better than ever before. He was cool and confident and showed remarkable speed. His footwork was perfect and was the means of saving him from a lot of punishment." He was now the Pacific coast middleweight champion.

The total gate receipts were $1,354. The fighters earned 60% and the club 40%. Burns won a 65% share of the fighter's end, which was $528.06, and Barry 35%, or $284.34.[198]

The nearby *Seattle Post-Intelligencer* called it the best fight seen in Tacoma in years. It was full of action that kept the crowd excited. "Throughout Burns proved the quicker on his feet, did more clever dodging, and excelled in infighting. Barry showed a great capacity for taking punishment, and…rushed his man." Burns landed effectively and was able to land his right in the clinches and on the breakaways. Barry was slow in his defensive work, but took his punishment gamely and was badly marked at the end. The faster Burns fairly won the 20-round decision.[199]

The *Seattle Daily Times* said Burns was too clever for Barry. Tommy's left jab snapped in like the crack of a whip. "Tommy Burns, skipping about like a dancing master, beat a tattoo upon the countenance of Dave Barry." Tommy punished him, but could not drop Barry.

Dave made his strongest showing in the 17th round, but could not land a knockout punch. "Burns was going in and out like a shadow, and in some of the rounds Dave simply stopped bewildered, for he was not quite sure how many men were in front of him." Still, he kept coming in for more punishment in each round.

In the 19th round, some wondered what was holding Barry up. In that round, Burns hit him with everything, the punches so fast that they could not be counted. Dave was wobbly, but weathered the storm. It "seemed impossible for a man to stand up under such a hail of blows, but the ruddy-faced Irishman took everything sent his way without a flinch, and he was boring in for more at the clang of the bell." Burns led all the way, but only really cut loose in the 8th and 19th rounds. Throughout, he peppered Barry, who "assimilated enough punishment last night to whip two or three men." It was a clear victory for Burns.[200]

Shortly thereafter, in early May 1905, undefeated world heavyweight champion James J. Jeffries announced his retirement from boxing. Tommy Burns was still a middleweight.

Subsequent to his victory over Dave Barry, Tommy Burns returned to his original boxing hometown of Detroit, for his first bout there in well over a year, against highly touted Chicago Italian Hugo Kelly (whose original name was Ugo Micheli, but he took on an Irish name). Champion Tommy Ryan was training and grooming Kelly to be his successor as world middleweight champion, given that Ryan wanted to retire. Kelly's career included: 1902 D6 and L6 (twice) Mike Schreck; 1903 W15 and D20 Schreck, and D10 Philadelphia Jack O'Brien; 1904 W6 Jack "Twin" Sullivan, W6 O'Brien, L20 and D10 Sullivan, ND6 O'Brien, and D10

198 *Tacoma Daily News*, May 3, 1905.
199 *Seattle Post-Intelligencer*, May 3, 1905.
200 *Seattle Daily Times*, May 3, 1905.

Schreck; and 1905 W10 O'Brien. Victories of any kind against Schreck, Sullivan, and O'Brien stamped Kelly as a top-notcher.[201]

At that time, Hugo Kelly, Noah Brusso, and Jack O'Brien were considered to be the best three active middleweights in the world.[202] "On the Pacific coast they concede that Noah Brusso is the best man at 158 pounds. In the central section Hugo Kelly enjoys the same distinction." Kelly was said to be of the race-horse type, long and rangy, easily making 158 pounds. He had an abundance of quality experience.

Jack O'Brien had been claiming the world middleweight championship, although most considered Tommy Ryan to be the champion. O'Brien had been considered to be the only formidable challenger to

Hugo Kelly

Ryan, until Kelly defeated O'Brien. Kelly's recent big win over O'Brien essentially made him the top dog at 158 pounds, other than Ryan, who would be Kelly's second for the bout.

"Brusso-Burns" worked out daily at the Detroit Athletic Club. Brusso trained faithfully, realizing that victory would force Jack O'Brien into another match, the Philadelphian allegedly having gained a very close decision over Tommy in Milwaukee.

Those who saw Brusso in training felt that he was faster and cleverer than Kelly. The local press noted that Brusso had changed his tactics from the days in Detroit when he was a knockout artist. Currently, he was more inclined to rely on speed, cleverness and cautious boxing, rather than utilizing his old-time punching power and knockout blows. Some believed that if Burns chose to box instead of punch that he would have his hands full with the elusive Kelly, who also had a punch in either hand hard enough to drop a man.

---

201 Boxrec.com.
202 The local Detroit papers were well aware that Burns was Noah Brusso, and called him such.

However, Brusso claimed that he still had his punch. He explained his recent distance bouts by saying that the men he had been fighting were just plain tough and amongst the best in the business. It wasn't always easy to knock out such men.[203]

Kelly insisted that they weigh in at ringside, just before the fight-card started, at 158 pounds. Although he was struggling to make weight, eventually, Brusso reluctantly consented. For two days prior to the fight, Tommy ate nothing but a couple of poached eggs and a little toast. He took three long runs.

Just one month after his victory over Dave Barry, on June 7, 1905 at Detroit's Light Infantry Armory, Tommy Burns fought Hugo Kelly. The bout was scheduled for 10 rounds; the maximum distance allowed in Michigan.

The afternoon of the fight, Brusso took a long run, and afterwards still weighed a shade over 160 pounds. He had to keep working out. When he stepped on the scales again and weighed an ounce or two over 158 pounds, Kelly wanted to claim the forfeit, and would have done so, had it not been for Tommy Ryan's intervention.[204]

Brusso was weakened by having to make the 158-pound weight limit, by all the hard work he had to do to lose the weight, combined with barely eating or drinking in the days leading up to the fight, plus working out on the day of the fight, and then not having much time to eat, drink, or rest after weighing in to sufficiently re-energize or re-hydrate. As a result, Kelly planned to target Brusso's stomach.

The Brusso-Kelly fight did not get started until quite late in the evening, owing to a delay caused by a police official who said that a permit had not been obtained. He wanted to stop the show. After some frantic telephone calls, the commissioner and superintendent of police said that boxing exhibitions could be allowed, but not fights. This meant that the police were to step in and prevent knockouts. The show went on, and the bouts technically were called exhibitions, with a wink. Eddie Ryan refereed.

---

203 *Detroit News, Detroit Times,* June 6, 1905; *Detroit Free Press, Detroit News,* June 7, 1905.
204 *Detroit News,* June 7, 1905; *Detroit Times,* June 8, 1905.

The three local papers, *Detroit Free Press*, *Detroit Evening News*, and *Detroit Times* mostly agreed on what happened, and the following is an amalgamation of their reports.

In the 1st and 2nd rounds, Brusso jabbed Kelly at will. Brusso showed his good speed and improvement as a boxer. His work was showy, but his punch was not that hard, for several times he landed his right without hurting Kelly. Still, Brusso effectively controlled the first 2 rounds with his jab.

In the 3rd round, the fight got rougher. Despite being outboxed early on, Kelly listened to Tommy Ryan and started boring in and roughing it. He was at his best at the inside short-arm game. Brusso was the fast and clever man, while Kelly was the slugger. Kelly got the worst of it when he attempted to box. They mixed it up, "and Brusso a little better than held his own, thanks to Kelly's habit of dropping back to boxing at times." Brusso's superior long range boxing still edged him the 3rd round. For 3 rounds, Brusso had out-boxed and jabbed Kelly at will, winding him up into knots by his clever footwork, and out-landing him 10 to 1.

Still, in the 4th round, the Italian Kelly really got going and began hitting his stride, having gauged his man. Kelly started battering the wind, knowing that Brusso had taken off at least seven pounds in two days and had only eaten canary bird seed during the day so as not to be overweight. The pace began to tell on Brusso, and the style better suited Kelly. There was no beauty to it, but rather lunge, clinch, work both hands until pried off, and then lunge in again. Clinches and breaks were frequent. This style predominated for the rest of the bout. During this round, Kelly landed an uppercut coming out of a clinch that "started Brusso on the downward path." Brusso weakened under the strain. For several rounds thereafter, it was Kelly's fight.

The 5th round was battled in the same way, with the same result. Referee Ed Ryan perspired as he labored to split the fighters apart. He had removed his coat, vest, collar and tie. Kelly stayed in close and worked both hands, devoting especial attention to the body, but switching often enough to the head to start a gory trickle from Noah's lips and nose.

The 6th round was more of the same. Kelly beat his man around the ring. The bombardment had fatigued Brusso.

In the 7th round, Kelly shook Brusso with a jolt that made the Frenchman wince. It looked to be Kelly's fight at that point. One writer even opined that it appeared as if "the Detroiter" was all gone. Another said that Kelly apparently had Brusso ready for the finishing touch, "Brusso being very weak and weary."

Opinions were mixed regarding the 8th round. One paper said Kelly was again better for most of the round. However, another said that the pendulum swung again in this round, for Brusso seemed to recuperate. He kept matters even, and hooked in one or two hard rights, in addition to his straight lefts. Another reporter said that in the last part of the round, Brusso shot over a fast right that caught Kelly on the jaw. Kelly tottered and Brusso went after him, the bell finding the Chicago man quite weary.

In the 9th round, Tommy Ryan sent Kelly in hard. In the corner, he told Hugo, "Quit boxing and keep fighting." As a result, Kelly bore in like a fighting machine, but the revived Brusso met him half-way. They fought every inch of the way, walloping whenever they could in the clinches, never loafing for an instant.

However, Brusso again shifted the tide to his favor when his right thumped home to the jaw and the iron Italian was "jarred until he blinked." Kelly staggered and his speed left him. Brusso followed up and planted several telling punches. "Whizz! Biff!" Brusso landed a left swing and the right again. Kelly was going. The crowd yelled like mad. The police stood up. They wanted to make sure that only scientific principles were employed and that nobody was seeking a knockout blow. Brusso showered in a rain of punches to the face and body. Kelly grabbed on hard. Referee Ed Ryan had even more trouble in prying him off. He lasted to the gong. That was a very big round for Brusso.

By the 10th round, Kelly was still somewhat slowed. Brusso was a bit tired from his sprint in the previous round. Neither did much effective work, but Brusso forced matters and tried to get him.

Referee Ed Ryan called it a 10-round draw. "His start and his finish were sufficient to secure Brusso the draw." Brusso had won the first three rounds and the last two. The entertainment ended at 11:30 p.m. It was the last scheduled boxing show in Detroit until the late fall.

One paper opined that the right wallop that Brusso landed on Kelly at the end of the 8th round turned potential defeat into a draw. Another said the punch that hurt Kelly in the 9th round was good enough "to change the tide of battle, so that what looked like a decision against him was turned to a drawn contest."

The *Detroit Free Press* said it was the best fight of the season. It was full of action and the spectators sat straight up throughout. The 10-round draw decision "was as good a verdict as it was a popular one." Noah's performance had been good enough to win back many of his old local admirers.[205]

The *Detroit Evening News* said that although the bout was fought with clean break rules, both men were well acquainted with straight Queensberry rules and often fought in the clinches before Referee Eddie Ryan broke them. The men clinched quite often. Referee Ryan was dripping wet and had to employ all he had ever learned in football to break up the clinches. He probably had to break up about 200 clinches in the 10 rounds.

205 *Detroit Free Press*, June 8, 1905.

Kelly was considered to be the best middleweight in the central states, if not the country, so Brusso's performance earned him credit. The thing that struck the crowd most forcibly was the improvement that Brusso displayed. He had been known as the Delray walloper, but demonstrated his boxing skill as well as power.

This paper also agreed that the draw decision was very popular. "Kelly may have had a shade the better of a majority of rounds, but not enough to entitle him to a decision." It had been the best bout of the season held in Detroit.[206]

The *Detroit Times* was even higher on Burns/Brusso, who had to fight both Kelly and starvation. It was a great battle to a draw, but it proved that "Noah Brusso, well trained and in condition to make the weight without resorting to starvation, can lick Hugo Kelly in a ten-round battle." It felt that this was demonstrated just as conclusively as it would have been had Brusso earned the decision instead of the draw.[207]

Despite what the local press said, the *National Police Gazette* reported that Kelly was the better man.

> Kelly was Burns' superior throughout, except in the ninth round, when the latter caught the Chicago man on the jaw with a vicious left and rocked his head into a dazed condition…. During the entire contest Kelly outboxed and outfought Burns. In the seventh, he was nearly out from swings to the jaw, but was saved by the bell.[208]

206 *Detroit Evening News*, June 8, 1905.
207 *Detroit Times*, June 8, 1905.
208 *National Police Gazette*, June 24, 1905.

CHAPTER 5

The Rematches

Following James J. Jeffries' retirement in May 1905, it was unclear who would be heavyweight champion in his absence. The top contenders were men such as Marvin Hart, Jack Johnson, Jack Root, Philadelphia Jack O'Brien, Bob Fitzsimmons, John "Sandy" Ferguson, and Gus Ruhlin.

In late March 1905, the exciting Marvin Hart had defeated colored heavyweight champion and then acknowledged top contender Jack Johnson, albeit in a close and controversial 20-round decision.

The respected Jack Root, a skilled boxer-puncher who had only lost twice in over fifty fights, held a 1902 W6 over Hart. Promoters put up the money for a Hart-Root championship fight to fill the vacant title.

On July 3, 1905 in Reno, Nevada, in a fight to the finish advertised as being for the vacant world heavyweight championship and refereed by James J. Jeffries, Marvin Hart scored a 12th round knockout over Jack Root. It was said that Hart had great strength, stamina, punching power, dogged persistence, and ability to absorb punishment, but knew little of the art of self-defense.

Some thought that Hart needed to defeat more contenders to further prove his right to the championship. However, they at least considered him to be the tentative champion. Others recognized Hart as the champion and the best man in the world other than Jeffries, as long as Jeff was retired. "Hart is the heavyweight champion as long as Jeffries is out of the ring." Still others refused to recognize him, feeling that Jeffries was champion for as long as he was alive, even though he was retired. Jeffries said that only the press and the public could confer the title. "I hope the victor will fight his way to that point where no one can dispute his title." Jeff said Hart was champion "pro tem," and that a number of battles would establish his right to championship honors beyond a doubt.

W.W. Naughton noted that Hart had dubbed himself the champion, "and the conditions are such that he is perfectly justified in doing so." However, he also said that Hart was on probation as a result of the fact that he had not licked the linear champion, the man who had licked everybody else. Therefore, it would be a while, and potentially some "sifting and shifting before a heavyweight looms up who will command the respect that a world's championship should command." Even if Hart came to be hailed as champion or someone was to defeat him and establish a better right to the distinction, "what will it all amount to anyhow, as long as Jeff is alive and enjoys good health?" Essentially, this would be the conundrum for anyone who followed in the wake of the undefeated Jeffries.[209]

The *Los Angeles Herald* said,

> Hart will probably become the acknowledged champion despite his numerous shortcomings. Tom Sharkey is out of it. Jack Monroe was never in it. Jack Johnson has demonstrated that he won't do and Bob Fitzsimmons has about passed the century mark. Not for many years has there been such a dearth of heavyweight material in the prize ring.[210]

In the meantime, as of July 1905, Tommy Burns was still a top middleweight. Given how close and competitive their first bout had been, in order to settle matters between them, Hugo Kelly and Tommy Burns agreed to fight again, this time on the West Coast, in Los Angeles, California, just under two months after their 10-round draw. This time the bout was scheduled for 20 rounds. It would be Tommy's first fight in the Los Angeles area.

The Burns-Kelly fight was advertised and accepted by the local media as being for the world middleweight title. Tommy Ryan had retired and given the title to Kelly. Since Kelly had defeated Jack O'Brien, the claim was justified.[211]

Tommy Burns, Who Fights Hugo Kelly Friday Night.

On July 23, Jack Root joined Kelly's training camp in San Pedro, California. Root had seen both men in action, and although he credited Burns with being faster on his feet, he thought that Kelly would win. He would be Kelly's trainer, and also spar with him.[212]

Burns trained at the North Beach bath house in Santa Monica, sparring with Warren Zubrick. Spider Kelly would be the chief advisor in Burns' corner, along with Professor Frank Lewis, Tommy's trainer.

---

209 *Los Angeles Examiner*, July 16, 1905.
210 *Los Angeles Herald*, July 19, 1905.
211 Tommy Ryan was actually Jewish. His original name was Joseph Youngs, but he changed it to an Irish name for business purposes, feeling that a Jewish name would be a handicap. "But from the first Ryan proved good enough to have fought under any name he chose." *Los Angeles Times*, July 23, 1905.
212 *Los Angeles Herald*, July 23, 1905.

HAS A NEW TRAINING STUNT!

LIKES THAT DASH IN THE SURF

BURNS SPARRING ON THE SAND

One paper noted that there was a "slight hitch in the weight question. Kelly insists that the match was made for 158 pounds, while Burns is holding off for 160." It was anticipated that they would work it out.[213]

A few days before the fight, on July 25, after finishing his swimming in the surf, Burns allegedly weighed 158 ½ pounds. They were to weigh in at 3 p.m. on the day of the fight. Some said they were required to make 158 pounds, while others said the fight would be fought at 160 pounds, technically above the middleweight limit at that time.[214]

Speaking of his chances in the bout, Burns said he was never better in his life and that Kelly would meet a much different man than the one that he had met in Detroit.

> Oh, yes, I know all about Kelly being a dead tough guy. I fought him before, but he made me do a bad weight then and I was just off the train. I'm right now, and I think I will be a good bet. I came near getting him, weak as I was, in the eighth round that time. He won't find the same proposition when we meet next time.[215]

Burns had none of the marks of the game, and "his grin is boyish and engaging." He attacked his training "with a vim and a dash that is good to see."

---

213 *Los Angeles Examiner*, July 25, 1905.
214 *Los Angeles Herald*, July 15, 26, 1905.
215 *San Francisco Evening Post*, July 25, 1905.

BURNS TEACHING TRICKS

Except for the roof, the new pavilion was almost entirely completed. It was thought that Pacific Athletic Club manager Tom McCarey intended to leave the roof off until the end of the hot summer months.[216]

Two days before the fight, on July 26, Burns ran 8 miles, hit the punching bag, skipped rope, and did floor work to strengthen his muscles. He and Warren Zubrick went at it hard in their 3 rounds of sparring. Tom ended the day with a swim.[217]

HUGO KELLY

That same day, Kelly did 6 rounds of bag punching and then sparred with Dick and Jack Sullivan, and "both boys were ready to quit after three rounds."[218]

Kelly was the betting favorite at about 5 to 4 or 10 to 8, but Burns money was plentiful. The fact that both Root and Ryan thought highly of Kelly, and that Hugo had defeated O'Brien, helped boost Kelly and make him the public choice.[219]

The *Los Angeles Examiner* said the weight issue allegedly had been settled. "Burns will try to make 158 pounds, so the middleweight championship will go with the victory." Still, others said that Burns was holding out for 160

216 *Los Angeles Examiner*, July 25, 1905.
217 *Los Angeles Express, Los Angeles Examiner*, July 27, 1905.
218 *San Francisco Evening Post*, July 27, 1905.
219 *Los Angeles Herald*, July 27, 1905.

pounds, while Kelly insisted that the match was made at 158 pounds. The fighters assured McCarey that the weight debate would not stop the fight.

Advance ticket sales had been brisk, with over $1,000 sold two days before the fight.[220]

Burns, who called Kelly the middleweight champion, said, "When I fought with him in Detroit a few weeks ago I was weak. … It was necessary for me to cut off ten pounds in three days." He felt that his performance would be better this time.[221]

Hugo Kelly, Who Meets Burns Friday Night.

220 *Los Angeles Examiner,* July 27, 1905.
221 *Los Angeles Express,* July 28, 1905; *San Francisco Evening Post,* July 27, 1905.

As the fight approached, each local paper scouted the bout. According to the *Los Angeles Times*, Hugo Kelly was a sturdy fighter who liked to bore in and hit with punishing force. He was a fighter rather than a boxer, but had learned many of Tommy Ryan's tricks. His style was likely to earn him a decision if both fighters were on their feet at the end of the fight, which in this case, seemed probable, given the well-known toughness of both.

Burns was described as a strong fellow and a hard nut to crack. "He, too, has a rushing style and mixes up plenty of haymakers with his short arm jolts."[222]

The *Los Angeles Examiner* said that Kelly, champion since Ryan's retirement, would defend his honors against one of the toughest propositions in the fight game. It also said, "Burns is down to weight and will try to weigh in at 158 at 3 o'clock. There will be no hitch on this question."[223]

BOXING CONTEST   **Tomorrow Night**
AT PACIFIC ATHLETIC CLUB PAVILION.

Hugo Kelly vs. Tommy Burns

20 rounds for middleweight championship of the world. Two good 10-round preliminaries. Prices—$1, $2, $3, $5. On sale at Greenwald's cigar store, 107 So. Spring street. Take Eastlake or Downey avenue cars north to Naud Junction. Doors open 6:45; enter ring 8:00.

Up north, the *San Francisco Evening Post* said, "Kelly has the call from some of the wise men for his clever foot work and spectacular dash, while others favor the ever aggressive, bore-in, pile-driving smash of his sturdy opponent."[224]

Both fighters declared that they were in the best condition of their ring careers. Kelly continued to be the 10 to 8 odds favorite.

This would be the Pacific Athletic Club's first ever card, held at its brand new pavilion at Macy and Coreleana Streets, also known as Naud Junction in Los Angeles. The club was destined to be the major hub for big boxing in Southern California. Downey Avenue and Eastlake rail cars going north on Spring Street and stopping at Naud Station would take the patrons a block from the venue. The doors would open at 6:45 p.m. and the bouts would start at 8 p.m.[225]

Tommy Burns and Hugo Kelly fought their rematch in Los Angeles on July 28, 1905.[226] "Fat Al" made the announcements, but the acoustic properties of the roofless pavilion made it difficult for him to be heard. In

---

222 *Los Angeles Times*, July 28, 1905.
223 *Los Angeles Examiner*, July 28, 1905.
224 *San Francisco Evening Post*, July 28, 1905.
225 *Los Angeles Herald*, July 28, 1905.
226 The following account and post-fight discussion is based on the July 29, 1905 reports from the *Los Angeles Herald*, *Los Angeles Examiner*, and *Los Angeles Times*, as well as the *San Francisco Evening Post*, which printed Harry Stuart's ringside report. *The Los Angeles Express* also provided post-fight analysis.

the preliminary, Burns sparring partner Warren Zurbrick scored a KO7 over Kelly sparring partner Dick Sullivan.

4,000 or 5,000 spectators (estimates vary) witnessed the 20-round bout advertised as being for the world middleweight championship. Recently retired heavyweight champion James J. Jeffries was seated at ringside, and the crowd wailed for him. Jeff hid behind a post and appeared to be shy, but was finally prevailed upon to make his appearance. He stepped up and received wild applause and an ovation. Jeff said, "Thank you very much for this applause, but you see, I'm a dead one now, and you might as well cut me out." A man seated near the roof yelled, "You're the huskiest dead one I ever saw!" Jeff returned to his seat, grinning.

Kelly, whom the *Times* said was an Italian "Dago" with an Irish name, entered the ring first, followed by Jack Root, Jim Hickey, Aurelio Herrera and Bill Sullivan. Burns followed just a few seconds later.

Root examined Tommy's bandages and objected to the plaster of Paris on them. Eventually, after a lengthy debate, Burns agreed to remove the plaster. He re-entered the ring at 9:50 p.m. Tommy was seconded by Warren Zurbrick, Professor Frank Lewis, and someone named "McDonald," possibly Jim or Frank McDonald.

The fighters were introduced and referee Charlie Eyton entered the ring wearing a white shirt.

Tommy Burns on left faces off with Hugo Kelly

Referee Eyton announced that owing to a disagreement regarding the weight, the two men had agreed to a draw if they were both on their feet at the end of 20 rounds. However, one local source said that Burns had weighed in at 158 pounds, while Kelly was overweight. It made no sense not to allow Burns to be eligible to win the title via decision as a result of the champion's failure to make weight. Some said that actually, the two had made the agreement because neither wanted to lose unless there was a decisive knockout. Another source said Kelly and his manager had pushed for the agreement, and that Burns, thinking that he would win by knockout, finally accepted. There were some later indications that Burns did not want to make 158 pounds, and that Kelly agreed to an over-the-weight limit if Burns would agree to a draw if they were both on their feet at the end. A report printed a week after the fight said neither man had actually posted a forfeit guaranteeing their weights, despite representations that each had posted $500. It said Burns weighed 161 at 4 p.m., and Kelly used that to leverage the agreement for a draw if both were on their feet at the end. No one knew for sure what the true reason was.

The bell rang to start the fight at 9:54 p.m.

In the first 2 rounds, the men were cautious, trying to size up one another. They felt each other out with light left leads, fiddling and moving around. They clinched often, and did not attempt big punches that might leave them open for counters. Both fired some short blows to the body and head. Another account said they pegged away on the inside with the full assortment of every known punch. On the outside, Burns showed his "lightning foot work." No hard blows were landed, though, for each man was fighting carefully.

In the 3rd round, they got busy and picked up the pace. Kelly was the aggressor and initiated a series of fierce rushes. He rushed Burns about the ring, mostly landing to the body. "Burns was busier than a flea-bitten dog, and waltzed around Kelly like a cake-walk champ, cutting loose with an occasional left lead which was usually slipped aside or smothered by the elusive Italian who vanished like a shadow." Burns was a bit puzzled by the rain of body blows. Kelly rushed in and scored well, moving with lightning speed and irresistible force. He distressed Tommy with straight punches to the body.

However, Burns was able to fight on the inside as well, and was right at home. He fought back hard and came in for more as if he liked the game. Quite often, Kelly landed good uppercuts on the inside. Tommy landed his right to the head, a blow he liked to use frequently. Kelly then landed several blows to the ribs. Each time, the plucky Burns took the blows and fired right back. Both landed several wicked uppercuts in the clinches.

Perspectives differed. One said that Kelly obtained the honors of the round. However, another said Tom had obtained a commanding lead with a further display of marvelous fleetness of foot combined with vicious, sweeping leads.

Burns picked it up and did well in the 4th round, landing jabs and uppercuts. He grazed a right chop for the jaw, timed Kelly with a straight left to the face, swapped rights, and then worked his uppercut to advantage, for one solid jolt rocked Kelly's head noticeably. Tommy landed a stiff left hook to the ear which Kelly countered with a right to the ribs. Kelly also landed a hard right uppercut and followed with his usual rain of body blows. Burns came back more fiercely and landed terrific uppercuts with both hands.

Burns landed a right chop on the back of the head and Kelly went to the floor on his knees, but rose in a flash. It was not a clean knockdown, but it encouraged Burns and he tore into Kelly, ripping both hands to the head and body. Kelly was cool, though, and covered well with his forearms. Burns snuck in some hard body shots. Kelly fought back with body smashes and mixed it up. Burns landed a stiff left on the head, and Kelly stalled for time, sparring and clinching. Burns landed a number of left and right jolts to the stomach, and Kelly seemed to be in bad shape. However, he got out of trouble by using head movement and blocking. Burns had all the best of the round.

The *Herald* said the 5th was a round of light punches to the face and body, with Kelly having a slight advantage. The *Times* said Burns continued his lead during the first two minutes of the 5th, until Kelly rallied and landed many blows to the body with considerable force. The *Examiner* said Kelly landed several hard body shots that could be heard all over the house.

Honors were even in the 6th round, and both looked fresh, despite the back and forth exchanging of blows. Kelly's right on the jaw had little effect.

Burns began reaching the stomach with regularity in the 7th round. They wrestled about the ring, both trying for the body before breaking.

In the 8th round, they clinched repeatedly and Eyton pried them apart. In one clinch, Burns landed two stingers over the kidneys and appeared to have the best of the milling.

Others said that both landed well in the 7th and 8th rounds, and each took turns stinging the other with kidney blows. These rounds were fairly even.

In the 9th round, Burns opened with his favorite right to the jaw and followed with the right to the ribs. Kelly landed his jab, but Burns landed his right to the stomach. Burns pumped his jab to the face several times. Kelly hit the kidneys with his left, but Burns stunned him with a right hook to the jaw and followed it with a right and left to the jaw. Kelly jabbed, and Tommy sent his left to the face and right to the body. Burns was dancing about in a lively fashion. Honors of this round were with Burns.

In the 10th round, Burns was still lively on his feet and apparently as strong as at the start. He reached Kelly's jaw repeatedly. Burns drew first blood with a hard jab to the nose followed by another jolt to the jaw. Kelly's nose began bleeding freely. Both continued hitting the body and head, and they engaged in some fierce exchanges. Kelly's seconds urged him to watch out for the rights. Burns landed his right to the head and then shifted it to the body.

Burns started the 11th round with a confident smile. The *Herald* said Burns was still dancing about, firing punches off of his footwork. On the inside, Tommy landed several uppercuts as well. Burns had much the better of it at the end of the round, and Kelly was still bleeding from his nose. The *Times* said Burns was very aggressive during the round, and took a slight lead, though both seemed to be in good shape. The *Examiner* said Burns landed several rapid uppercuts to the chin, and Kelly looked worried and was trying to protect himself.

In the 12th round, they continued exchanging an assortment of hard blows to the body and head. They clinched, broke, and clinched repeatedly. Kelly kept in close most of the time. Burns occasionally danced about his man. Kelly landed some terrific right jolts on the body. Burns landed a hard left to Kelly's eye, and it began closing. Tommy also threw uppercuts. Coming into a clinch, Burns drove his terrific right smash to the heart. A right reached Kelly's nose and it started bleeding again. Tommy bombarded him with blows, landing two uppercuts to the sore nose. However, Tommy's own left eye was beginning to look red.

The 13th round featured many hooks and uppercuts to the body and head. Kelly's left eye was swelling. He began infighting again and they roughed it. Eyton separated them. One said that Kelly had a shade the better of the round.

A series of hard mix-ups characterized the 14th round. Kelly appeared to be growing stronger with his infighting tactics, while Burns showed some signs of fatigue. However, another reporter said that in a clinch, Burns uppercut Kelly three times in the mouth. A right cross wagged Hugo's head and another right to the nose started the blood again.

The *Herald* said honors were even in the 15th round, with both men landing a couple of good wallops. The *Examiner* said they were in and out of clinches, but they were always working, and some of the most effective blows were landed in the clinches. The *Times* said Kelly had kept up his infighting from the 13th through the 15th rounds, giving him a slight lead in those rounds, as Burns slowed up.

The 16th round once again featured a series of hard blows on both sides. Burns livened up and repeatedly landed rights to the head and lefts to the body. In a fierce mix-up, both landed hard to the body. Hugo landed particularly well to the body, striking several stingers on the ribs. However, Tom landed a wicked left shift and followed with a right wallop to the pit of the stomach. There was much clinching and many even exchanges. After the bell, in his corner, Root gave Kelly smelling salts.

At the start of the 17th round, Burns got busy and forced the fighting in lively fashion, landing two rights to the face. Kelly landed a left but Burns landed his right to the jaw. There was a fierce mix-up with exchanges of rights and lefts to the body and face. Burns kept his arms working. They clinched and fought at close quarters. Kelly landed his right uppercut. Burns stung him to the kidneys. Burns landed a hard right to the jaw. Kelly landed a left to the jaw.

Burns was reaching the face repeatedly, and had Kelly's lips swelling. Another said that Burns appeared to be getting stronger. However, yet another paper said the round ended with honors even.

In the 18th round, they roughed it in the clinches and exchanged hard blows, hammering one another in the body. A flag belt bothered Burns, so the referee pulled it off. Burns forced the fighting and rushed Kelly hard, though Hugo landed well to the mouth. They were in and out of clinches, with both fighting like demons.

The 19th round was another series of clinches, and with every clinch there was a siege of terrific infighting. They rammed rights and lefts to the body. Root had urged Kelly to be aggressive. Hugo responded and did some telling work. Kelly got the better of a fierce mix-up. Burns uppercut him. Kelly landed right and left to the face. Burns landed a left to the face and a right to the kidneys, and also a right to the jaw. Kelly landed two jabs and Burns landed to the face and body.

Kelly landed an uppercut to the nose. Burns bled freely from his nose, the first time in the fight that he bled, but he showed no signs of weakening.

In the 20th round, both men forced the fighting and there was a series of hot mix-ups, but Burns had all the best of it. Burns landed left and right to the jaw. He drove Kelly to the ropes and jolted him with right and left to the body. The hurt Hugo covered up. He fought back desperately. Burns ripped a hard right to the jaw and they clinched. Burns fought furiously during the last half of the round. At the gong, both were fighting fiercely, with Kelly bleeding freely from the nose and mouth.

Referee Eyton technically ruled the fight a draw because of the pre-fight agreement to do so if both fighters were standing at the end. However, he also said that he thought Burns had slightly the better of the fight, and he would have awarded him the bout had he been allowed to do so. Referee Eyton said that by making the pre-fight agreement, "Burns robbed himself of the decision, but there was nothing I could do."

All of the local papers agreed that Burns deserved the win, and had robbed himself of the victory by his pre-fight agreement. The *Los Angeles Times* said Burns' strong and impressive rally in the final round had left Kelly "considerably the worse for wear. Burns forced the pace, and profited by taking it easy in the preceding rounds, finishing like a whirlwind, and dazing his opponent with a shower of blows." This finish would have earned him the bout, but Burns had foolishly cheated himself out of the victory he had rightfully earned.

The rattling bout had been a pretty exhibition of the fine art of boxing, of hitting and getting away. "Burns's agility particularly in the matter of footwork was impressive." As for the blows that did land on him, Tommy's great endurance stood him in good stead and enabled him to weather a storm of smashes that would have put out an ordinary man. Burns made Kelly "look like a last year's punching bag in the twentieth round, and had a comfortable lead on points previously."

Burns looked like a white version of Joe Walcott, which led to his being called "Tubby" Burns.

> Favored in physique, built like a barrel, deep of chest, broad of back and short of waist, Tubby Burns is the style of man that might be built to order for pugilistic championships. Nothing short of a landslip could shock his rugged body.... If he hadn't been of high proof, some of Kelly's piston-rod punches would have put the finishing touch upon Burns's aspirations long before ten rounds had been told off.

> Both knew how to rough it on the Tom Sharkey order. No love was lost from the beginning of the fight, and Kelly was on his trail from the start.

The *Los Angeles Herald* reported that Kelly was still middleweight champion, but only on a technicality. Ring followers "will not be inclined to regard his claim seriously in the future."

> As far as clean hitting and scientific work was concerned the general opinion was that Burns had a shade the best of the fight, Tommy being better liked because of his aggressive work throughout, his ability to secure an even break in the infighting and clearly outpointing the Italian boy in the long range work.

> Neither Burns or Kelly had any decided advantage in any of the rounds, but taken as a whole Burns showed to better advantage in landing damaging wallops, was eager to carry the fight to the Italian and while Kelly was always there to meet him, Tommy's clean cut work earned him the decision if a decision was to be rendered.

Burns' footwork was a "revelation," for he danced in and away from many vicious swings and jabs and bewildered Kelly with his speedy action. Kelly was a trifle slower than was expected, but showed his willingness to go in and hammer away, as well as assimilate the punishment that Burns handed out.

The fight was tame up to the 10th round, with an occasional rally by both. In the 10th, Burns landed a succession of jabs to Kelly's sore nose, which had been damaged in the earlier rounds. Kelly was bleeding profusely when he returned to his corner. Burns' most effective blow was a right and left uppercut, which he worked continually in the clinches, jarring Kelly severely. Hugo seemed weak in protecting himself in the infighting. Burns took much of the ginger out of Kelly in the earlier rounds with a succession of short arm uppercuts.

Kelly looked for a lucky punch, and hoped to wear down Burns, discounting Tommy's superior ring generalship and science. However, Burns was always there, holding Kelly back with right and left jabs, and when it came to infighting, Kelly did not have things all his own way, either.

When it was over, Burns made no mention of the disagreement over the weight question as the referee had announced. He said that he didn't want a hairline decision, and Kelly had also agreed that they would play for a knockout or nothing. However, Tommy thought he had won the fight by a mile. Regardless, the decision was well received by the house. Kelly was satisfied with a draw. His left eye was closed and his face badly puffed, while Burns showed little if any marks of the fierce milling.

The *Los Angeles Examiner* also said Burns had a shade the better of the 20 fast rounds held before a surprisingly good house. The fight was about even up to the 9th round, with the fighting in the clinches the fiercest ever seen in Los Angeles. From the 10th round on, Tommy began to draw away, and after that, Kelly never had a decisive round at any stage. In the last half of the fight, the crowd began rooting for Burns. However, it was evident that both would be strong at the finish. "The story of the rounds was much the same. Burns would jab a few times, dance away, feint a couple of times and then rush in close with a right swing to the head or a left to the body." Half of the time, they fought themselves out of the clinches, and the other half, Referee Eyton went between them. After the 15th round, Burns showed signs of the hard fight, but so did Kelly, though the punishment did not show on his dark skin as it did with Burns' lighter-colored face and body. The 20th round was a whirlwind affair, with Burns hammering away with both hands. Kelly hung on to protect himself from the steady rain of punches. Kelly was bleeding badly, though he was not distressed, and he still seemed able to continue for many more rounds if he had to do so.

When the fight was over, as Tommy left the ring, the crowd repeatedly cheered him, treating him as the winner. "If a decision had been rendered, the fight should have gone to Burns on his clean work, his aggressiveness and his big share of the leading. But Kelly was a long way from a beaten man at the end. Both men took a world of punishment and weathered it well." The *Examiner* also said that Burns "certainly had a shade throughout the fight, at times increasing his lead when it seemed that he had the Italian in trouble, but as Hugo always came back strong it is doubtful if he was ever very near Queer street in all the twenty rounds."

Another *Examiner* writer said, "If ever a man won a decision, Tommy Burns did last night. Taken round by round, he had the best of it in a majority of the rounds." Kelly held his own in the first quarter of the fight, as well as during the 14th through 16th rounds, but the rest of the bout was Burns'. Kelly had the best of several terrific rallies in the early part of the bout, but after the first 5 rounds, Burns succeeded in smothering many of the pile drives to the stomach. Tommy's most effective blows were right crosses to the side of the face and lefts to the stomach.

According to the *Los Angeles Express*, Burns did the better work in the bout which featured fast fighting and a display of the art of hit and get away. Kelly was game and took his punishment, but was not the master of fine footwork that Tommy was, and was a little slow in following his leads. Burns hit frequently, and although not strong enough to knock out Kelly, wore him down and several times made Hugo look sick.

It said that the only knockdown was in the 4th round, when Burns floored Kelly with a sharp right to the head. Burns then went after Kelly hard. The *Examiner* noted this knockdown as well, although neither the *Herald* nor the *Times* mentioned a knockdown.

Up until the 10th round, the fight was about even. From then on, Burns had the best of the fight. "Burns would jump in, jab a few to Kelly's stomach, uppercut him and dance away with Kelly treading on his toes."

Burns showed no signs of punishment until the 15th round. His nose and mouth bled, but Kelly's nose and mouth had been doing so for quite some time. Both tried for a knockout in the last round, which was fierce. They could have fought longer if they had to.

Afterwards, Burns said, "I thought several times I was going to land a knockout, but did not succeed. I am sorry I agreed to the proposition of Kelly and Root to call the fight a draw, as I would have got the decision had I not done so." Kelly said, "Burns did good work…. He is a better man in a long fight than I thought."

Up the coast, the *San Francisco Chronicle* and *San Francisco Evening Post* both said that Burns had robbed himself of victory with the pre-fight agreement, "for he had a sufficient advantage throughout the mill to be characterized as the cleverer man. It was a good, live, clean scrap and was witnessed by a large crowd."[227]

Harry Stuart, who saw the fight, said Tommy won by a block, but was snared by the wily Hugo, who got him to agree to the knockout or draw proposition. Stuart felt that Kelly became nervous after he learned that Burns had bet $500 on himself to win. Kelly's "defensive tactics, pursued all through the mill, was a glowing tribute to his opponent's prowess."[228]

227 *San Francisco Chronicle, San Francisco Evening Post*, July 29, 1905.
228 *San Francisco Evening Post*, July 31, 1905.

Several days later, Stuart said Burns could have been champion had he made weight. Throughout the 20 rounds, Burns waged a spirited, aggressive fight, seemingly immune from Kelly's frequent rasping clips shot across in the rallies. In the final round, Tommy was still slashing away with undiminished vim. He was a very different fighter than the one seen against Kelly in Detroit. However, the true point to be deduced from this analysis is that Burns was a much better fighter when he did not have to kill himself to make weight.

The bettors who took a chance on the underdog Burns were upset, and felt that they had been milked of their winnings. They were upset at Tommy for not making the weight, the club for making a loose agreement, and the referee for "lending color to the scene."[229]

The *National Police Gazette* reported, "Tommy used a right cross with telling effect and had Kelly's eye, nose and mouth in a badly swollen condition. In the closing rounds Burns came up as strong as a bull, and forced the fighting throughout, Kelly hanging on to avoid punishment." There was terrific infighting due to the fact that they had used straight Queensberry rules.

> Kelly planted some awful wallops, but Burns always came back, and in most of the rounds had the better of it. In the fourteenth Kelly was badly dazed and Burns tried his best to score a knockout, but the Italian successfully covered... Kelly's best blow was a right to the ribs, and he stuck many in the stomach which would have been good night with many a man not in the perfect condition of Burns. Tommy was fresh and fighting like a whirlwind at the end of the bout.[230]

Hence, once again, Burns' stock went up with a draw decision, and he was treated as the bout's victor.

The Kelly fight made Burns a hot middleweight. He was receiving a fair amount of ink, particularly on the West Coast. Tom posted a $1,000 forfeit to meet Tommy Ryan. In addition, Pacific Athletic Club manager Tom McCarey said that he would give out a championship belt worth $1,000. "Burns is in dead earnest and believes he can best the clever Ryan." Apparently, the Pacific Athletic Club was also offering Bob Fitzsimmons $5,000 to fight Burns. McCarey said that if such bouts could not be made, he would look to finalize a fight between Burns and Jack Sullivan, which should be a good one, given their previous encounter.[231]

Just as a side note regarding the ongoing battle for boxing's legality, it was reported that two boxers in Montreal, Canada were each sentenced to three months in jail for prize fighting. Boxing's illegality in most of Canada partially explains why a Canadian would be fighting his entire boxing career

---

229 *San Francisco Evening Post*, August 3, 1905.
230 *National Police Gazette*, August 19, 1905.
231 *San Francisco Evening Post*, August 3, 1905.

up to that point in the United States. Also, boxing was more popular and financially lucrative in the U.S.[232]

Following the Kelly bout, Burns took a one-week vacation in Ventura, California, doing some hiking and hunting in that area.

Just one month after the Kelly bout, in late August, Burns would fight a rematch bout in San Francisco against San Francisco's Irish Dave Barry. Despite the emergence of Los Angeles boxing, San Francisco was the biggest California fight town, and it had a great deal of boxing history. James Jeffries' last four championship fights had been held in San Francisco. It would be Tommy's first fight in that city, which was the most populous in the state.

The Barry bout was scheduled for 20 rounds at 158 pounds, the weights to be taken at 3 p.m. on the day of the fight. Tommy said, "I'm after the middleweight championship, and if I win and everything that goes with the title is complied with at San Francisco, the bout's result will compel my recognition as champion all over the country."[233]

Since losing a May 1905 20-round decision to Burns, in early July 1905 Barry was stopped in the 20th round by the well-respected light-heavyweight Mike Schreck in what was called a great and even fight up until the knockout.

Burns and his sparring partner Warren Zubrick arrived in the San Francisco area on August 11. They took up training quarters at Billy Shannon's San Rafael resort.[234]

The powerful San Francisco press got behind the bout and hyped it up. It was said that Barry was a much better scrapper than when he last appeared locally more than two years ago. His great battle with Schreck proved it.

Dave was training at Croll's Gardens with sparring partners Dick Hyland, Harry Foley, and Alex Greggains. Barry said that he never felt better in his life and was morally certain that he would win.

The *San Francisco Evening Post* expected their bout to be "chock full of ginger." "Burns is a fast, clever fellow and is decidedly aggressive and is possessed of a fairly good punch. He is rated the best man to fill the position as middleweight champion."[235]

Tom's performance against Hugo Kelly, wherein allegedly he had won every round, earned him many wealthy admirers in Los Angeles. They were willing to back him for $5,000 against Tommy Ryan or anyone else. "This will be Burns' first appearance in a San Francisco ring and there will be much curiosity to see the fellow who many say is the most legitimate candidate to fill Tommy Ryan's place at the top of the middleweight class."

---

232 *National Police Gazette*, August 19, 1905. However, some boxing bouts did take place in Canada.
233 *San Francisco Evening Post*, August 11, 1905.
234 *San Francisco Evening Post*, August 14, 1905.
235 *San Francisco Evening Post*, August 15, 1905.

Burns' 15-round draw with Woods had put him before the sporting public as an important factor in the division, "and ever since then he has been treated with a degree of seriousness." Although Jack O'Brien had outpointed Burns, that fight was discounted by the fact that O'Brien "usually outpoints his opponents in short fights so this contest should be stricken out altogether." The point being that a real fighter was judged based on what he did in a long fight, not a short bout. Regarding the Twin Sullivan fight, "although Tommy had a big lead all during the fight he was given a draw for his pains." He had won a decision from Barry in a great battle, though Barry complained repeatedly that the referee showed him no favors.[236]

On August 20, Burns entertained a large crowd of visitors at his training quarters, "and every one who watched him work was impressed with the idea that he is a classy fighter who is bound to make his mark in the pugilistic world."

Tommy's weight had been the theme of discussion amongst the followers of the game. They were aware of the fact that he struggled to make weight. Tommy said,

> I will not say what I weigh just now, but I will be there when the weighing-in time comes. … I have placed a forfeit of $500 to guarantee that I will be at 158 pounds at 3 o'clock on the 31st. … I have been after Ryan a long while, but I doubt that he will ever meet me. He saw me fight Hugo Kelly once, and I don't think he would care to take a chance with me.

That same day, fans watched Barry spar 3 rounds with Tommy Sullivan, 3 with Alex Greggains, and 3 more with Dick Hyland. He then swung a big sledge-hammer for 14 minutes, and also engaged in wrestling and shadow boxing.[237]

Barry was the local favorite. He had narrowly lost a 20-round decision to Jack "Twin" Sullivan and had put up a whirlwind contest against Schreck. The *San Francisco Call* did not think it necessarily followed that Burns would repeat his victory over Barry, who was in better shape than ever before. "If Burns wins from him the Irishman will not be subdued without a struggle, as no gamer boxer lived than Dave Barry."

Just over a week before the fight, Barry was weighing 163 pounds. Burns said that he was about that as well, but was not willing to prove it.[238]

Responding to the ongoing concern regarding whether Burns would make weight, at his San Rafael training quarters, after an 8-mile run, Tommy said, "Dave Barry need not worry about me not doing 158 pounds. I will be

236 *San Francisco Evening Post*, August 16, 1905.
237 *San Francisco Evening Post*, August 21, 1905.
238 *San Francisco Call*, August 22, 1905.

at weight all right, no matter what they say about me having lots of trouble in doing it."[239]

Burns said that he was not in the game for honor, glory, or pleasure, but wanted the good money associated with the sport. He realized that a boxer could only make an ordinary living unless he was a champion, so his ambition was to become a recognized champion.

> Most champions draw good, big houses and they can demand a good percentage, but still there are some champions who have not made good money for the reason that they have been poorly handled. I've only made about $4,000 this year, and I haven't got one-quarter of it left. If I win my coming battle with Dave Barry I'll win $1,250. ... Do I bet on myself? Yes; I always place a bet on Burns. When I boxed Billy Woods in Seattle I won a nice chunk that I'd stay the limit. I will bet $500 on myself in this contest with Barry, and then if I win, and I feel confident I will, I want to meet Tommy Ryan for the championship. ...
>
> Fighting men as a rule certainly like to live high. ... I don't go in for that kind of pleasure. I spend a good deal of money for clothes and jewelry, but the most of my money gets away from me through little pleasure trips through the country, vacations, hunting and fishing trips and such sport. Fellows who are successful in this business have to spend lots of money, and I dare say it costs a good fighter $20 a day for his living and other incidental expenses. I like the game only for what money I can make out of it and not for the honor or glory of being a successful boxer.

Burns was very systematic in his training, insisting on everything being in order, with meals and training having a regular routine and set time. Tommy was training with Warren Zubrick, who said that Burns was one of the most particular fellows with whom he had ever worked.

On August 22 at Croll's Gardens, Dave Barry ran 8 miles, and looked impressive in his boxing with Alex Greggains, Dick Hyland and Tommy Sullivan. His gym work occupied more than an hour. "Those who have not seen him box in several months can hardly believe he is the same Dave Barry."[240]

Both Barry and Burns were confident of victory, feeling that the referee would only be a figurehead, because each boxer believed that he would win by knockout.

There was some animosity between the two, because Barry continually claimed that he was kept from knocking out Burns in their first fight when the lights went out in the 5th round, a round in which he claimed to have

---

239 *San Francisco Call*, August 23, 1905.
240 *San Francisco Evening Post*, August 23, 1905.

had Burns at his mercy. An angered Burns said the result of their upcoming fight would prove that Barry's statements were false.[241]

Burns had to work unusually hard to reduce his weight. Lately, Tommy had been struggling to remain a middleweight. The boxers were supposed to weigh in on the afternoon of the fight, at 3 p.m. at Alex Greggains' sporting headquarters on Ellis Street. It was thought that Tom might ask for permission to come in a couple pounds heavy, "a thing that Dave would surely have objected to since there is so much bad blood between the two."

Burns was keeping his weight a secret, and would not step on the scales for the press. "Men very seldom refuse to weigh publicly unless they are heavier than they are expected to be. ... Fighters are as ticklish about their weight as a woman is about her age." Unlike Burns, on the 23rd, Dave Barry was willing to step on the scales, and he weighed 162 pounds.[242]

BUSHNELL PHOTO

THIS PAIR WILL SWAP WALLOPS AT WOODWARD'S THURSDAY NIGHT.

The *San Francisco Evening Post* said it was truly a fight between a boxer (Burns) and a fighter (Barry). Burns had marked cleverness. He could utilize every punch in the book and land anywhere at any time. "Tommy is also a smart one in the matter of foot work and he is fast as a streak of light when it comes to stepping in or out or to the side of an opponent." He was "the embodiment of all that is perfect in the manly art."

Barry was a rugged, aggressive fighter who enjoyed infighting. Dave had willingness, grit, and punching power in both hands. He had a good knowledge of the finer points of the game, a fair amount of speed, and wonderful gameness and strength in abundance. He

---

241 *San Francisco Call*, August 24, 1905. In fact, the lights did go out in the 5th round of Burns-Barry I, but Burns was doing well and won that round.
242 *San Francisco Evening Post*, August 24, 1905.

had always been a good hitter, but had improved in cleverness, and was regarded as one of the best infighters around. He would most likely attempt to wear down his clever opponent with vicious punches. Dave had a particularly good, well-timed right for the head. "Barry has a knack of whipping his right to the jaw just as the other fellow starts to come in, and if Burns holds his head low to avoid Dave's favorite wallop, he will find that Barry is quite tricky in hooking it under with a short jolt that may prove the undoing of the Detroit middleweight." He would likely be after Burns from the start and make Tommy extend himself and show his vast cleverness. Both were in excellent condition and confident of victory, though it was rumored that Burns was having trouble making weight.[243]

Barry said he would surely defeat Burns. He claimed that he was handicapped in Tacoma when the lights were turned off, but no such thing would happen this time. "I am in better shape than ever before, the weight is easy for me, and with no handicaps like I had in Tacoma I'll canter home in a gallop. ... [P]lace a bet on me. I'm the candy in this scrap."

Barry opined that the modern fighter was far superior to the old-timers (something which every generation wants to claim, forgetting about the skills of yesteryear).

> You see, these old-timers weren't in it with us fellows. Now I'm speaking of the present-day fighters as compared with men who were fighting forty years ago. ... The old-time fighters didn't know anything about footwork at all. Their headwork was good enough; they could duck some, all right, but they never made scientific use of their feet. ... Nowadays footwork is one of the most important features of a fight. No matter how hard you can hit or how clever you may be with your head, it won't do you much good if your opponent can dance all around you or rush in and deliver a punch and then skip away before you can make a return.[244]

A judge who saw Barry in training commented, "He's a remarkably strong fellow, isn't he? And how fast he is for a big man. Why, Barry is a much improved boxer since I saw him some two years ago. ... Barry defeated Woods quite handily while Burns, I believe, could only get a draw in fifteen rounds." A local attorney said, "I do believe that Dave Barry is one of the best, if not the best, middleweights in the country, and I have never in all my experience seen a fellow who hits so hard as Barry does, especially with his right hand." Eastern lightweight boxer Eddie Burns said,

> Barry is one of the gamest fellows I have ever seen, and he is strong and hits much better than Tommy. I believe he will beat Burns by reason of his rough aggressive tactics. ... Burns is more of a boxer,

243 *San Francisco Evening Post*, August 25, 1905.
244 *San Francisco Evening Post*, August 26, 1905.

and as the men are fighting straight rules Dave will be able to wear him down with heavy infighting. Barry has improved wonderfully.

Both Burns and Barry had made many friends by their determined clashes, and the winner would be "looked upon as the rightful holder of the championship." It was opined that Tommy probably would be installed as a slight favorite with the betting public as a result of his remarkable showing against Hugo Kelly.

In his attempt to make weight, Burns started drying out on August 28, four days before the fight. Consider the impact that dehydration over several days might have, in addition to the fact that they had to weigh in at 3 p.m. on the same day of the fight, and then have to box that night for 20 rounds, and not just 12 rounds with a day before weigh-in as they do today.[245]

As the rematch approached, Barry had all sorts of excuses for his loss to Burns the first time. Often, Burns was called a classy French-Canadian who was fast and clever, and right after his man all the time. However, Barry said Burns made him do a foot race in Tacoma. He claimed that Burns was permitted to wear heavy plaster bandages on his hands, which made the blows harder. He also charged that in the 5th round, someone intentionally turned out the electric lights to save Tommy from a knockout, as Barry had him on Queer Street at the time (which the local reports did not support). Barry also claimed that the referee, Jim Carroll, was Burns' manager at that time and was getting a percentage of Tommy's earnings, which explained why he gave the decision to Burns.

As of the 29th, Dave was on weight. "Barry never looked so well trained in his life and he is as sure that he is going to beat Burns as he is that he is alive. Dave has unlimited confidence in himself."

On August 29, Burns ran 6 miles and did light work in the gymnasium for 45 minutes. He abstained from drinking any liquids at meal time. He said that he was weighing 160 pounds and would be able to make 158 by the 31st, the day of the fight.[246]

Most thought it was a very even match-up. Many favored Burns because of his speed, clever tactics, variety of blows, and fast and clever footwork. Those who favored Barry cited his rough infighting abilities, very hard wallop with both hands, great condition, game qualities, and ability to absorb punishment. Burns was a slight betting favorite at 10 to 9 odds. Both were in the best of shape, having gone through a thorough course of training.[247]

The day of the fight, boxing expert Harry Stuart picked Barry to win. Words used to describe Barry included "boring-in," "stout-hearted,"

245 *San Francisco Evening Post*, August 28, 1905.
246 *San Francisco Evening Post*, August 30, 1905.
247 *San Francisco Chronicle*, August 30, 31, 1905; *San Francisco Call, San Francisco Examiner, San Francisco Evening Post*, August 31, 1905.

"fighting grit and stalwart nerve." He said Barry's greatly improved knowledge of the game would be a revelation to those who had not seen him in action in a while. Barry held a KO7 over Harry Foley, a well-timed right putting him to sleep for two minutes. In defeating a man who had previously defeated him, Barry had shown that he could improve in return matches. Barry's close decision loss to Twin Sullivan, a bout which many thought should have been a draw, also proved his merit. Barry had Jack O'Brien in a bad way at the end of their 15-round bout. Although stopped in the final minute of his bout with Mike Schreck, many said it was a lucky punch, and that in another 30 seconds, the fight would have been a 20-round draw.

Although Barry would have height and reach advantages, Burns said, "I can lick that fellow sure." Because he was the outsider, fighting Barry in his home territory, "in the Greggains castle," Tommy felt compelled to go for the knockout in order to win the bout. That said, no one could think of an instance where Barry had received a gift decision. Concluding, Stuart felt that either Hugo Kelly had been greatly over-rated or Burns was "a most dangerous factor in the field. Tonight will tell the tale."[248]

The Burns-Barry rematch took place on August 31, 1905 at San Francisco's Woodward's Pavilion, under the auspices of the San Francisco Athletic Club.

The local papers described the bout as slow, dull, tame, wearisome, unsatisfactory, and uninteresting.

The *San Francisco Chronicle* said the "dancing kid" Burns was clever at footwork, but his punches were not very effective. Barry's performance did not arouse much enthusiasm either.

The *San Francisco Examiner* said they spent most of the fight clinched in each other's arms. Burns was a careful, systematic workman, while Barry relied on landing a chance hard blow. "Burns, when not clinching, was dancing a jig in front of the strapping Irishman." Tommy occasionally sent in lefts and rights, but not with much force. Due to Tommy's penchant for clinching, Barry was not able to land very often. Barry landed a good right in the 9th round, and did well exchanging lefts for a few rounds after that, but mostly it was a clinch-fest.

The *San Francisco Bulletin* said Barry was slow and cumbersome, while Burns was much lighter on his feet and had enough science to hold Barry at bay, though without fighting energy. Dave stopped most of the wallops with his jaw and stomach, and through the first 14 rounds, appeared to assimilate them well.

Like the other local reports, the *San Francisco Call* said there was very little fighting for the first 14 rounds.

---

248 *San Francisco Evening Post*, August 31, 1905.

However, the 15th round featured some real excitement. According to the *Call*, Burns started landing straight rights and lefts to the jaw so hard that Barry's head began snapping back. As they were coming out of a clinch, Burns whipped in his left and Barry wobbled. Tommy saw his chance and brought the haymaker right over to the jaw and Barry went down and closed his eyes. It looked like the end, but upon the count of nine he rose to his feet. However, instead of finishing him, it appeared that Burns allowed Dave to stall around; perhaps concerned that Barry might still possess a hard wallop.

The *Chronicle* and *Examiner* saw the 15th round knockdown sequence a bit differently. According to the *Chronicle*, while Tommy was holding Barry's head with his right, Burns landed a stomach punch with his left. After wrestling out of the clinch, Burns landed a short right to the jaw that dropped Barry. The *Examiner* version of the knockdown sequence said Burns held Barry around the neck with his left and pummeled him with the right until Barry dropped. The referee did not do anything to prevent the holding and hitting. Barry recovered and kept fighting.

All of the newsmen agreed that after the 15th round, the fight became dull again. Tommy had been very cautious throughout, and he simply returned to his careful tactics, taking no chances, although most felt that he could do away with Barry if he would just go at him. *The Bulletin* said that like Jack Johnson, Burns "was content to jab and prance around and await the termination of the bout in order to receive the verdict." The spectators jeered the fight and whistled. "There wasn't one decent rally in the whole twenty rounds."

Tommy ran around the ring and jabbed both hands to Barry's jaw, making a getaway before Dave could do anything in return. Barry was groggy several times, but managed to come in after Burns in his awkward style and land a punch now and then that warned Burns that he should not be too rash. Hence, Tommy remained respectful.

According to the *Call*, because of Tommy's style in the bout, most expected a decision victory for him, but when the 20th and final round began, Burns began rushing Barry. Dave could not stop Tommy's left, which kept landing on the sore nose. Suddenly Barry began to weaken, and Burns waded in with more strength. He landed his right a couple times, and when he saw that Barry could no longer raise his hands, Burns clouted him with a right swing to the jaw and Barry went down and out, his head striking the floor and rebounding a couple of times, with just 42 seconds remaining in the final round. He rolled his eyes and tried to rise, but could not.

The *Evening Post* said the knockout came with only 30 seconds left in the fight. Burns landed a right to the jaw that ended "one of the tamest battles ever fought in this city." Alex Greggains, who seconded Barry, jumped into the ring to stop the bout before Referee Mark Shaughnessey finished the count.

The *Chronicle* agreed that Tommy's right hand brought the tame battle to an end. "Barry fell backward and his head hit the canvas with a bump." It too said that Alex Greggains threw in the towel before the count was over.

The *Examiner's* version of the knockout sequence said, "Burns then landed one hard right-hander on the jaw and followed it up with a shower of rights until Barry went down and out." The *Bulletin* said Burns had "demonstrated that he possessed a pretty fair sized kick in his right mitt."

The *Call* summarized that Barry was not fast enough to get to Burns, who showed that he was a clever fellow who had a punch if and when he chose to use it. However, Burns was loath to take chances, mostly preferring to outbox his man in cautious fashion. "He prefers to fiddle around and keep the public in agony till he has a dead one on his hands. Then, when he is sure his opponent is not capable of raising his mitts, he will go in and do the best he can." Still, Tommy had dominated a respected opponent and knocked him out, improving on his prior result, although by using a less entertaining style.

The *Bulletin* noted that the lights were on during the entire bout, so Barry had no excuse. It doubted his earlier claims, feeling that Barry could not hit Burns *unless* the lights went out.

Despite all of its pre-fight hype, perhaps in a backlash for their failure to live up to expectations, the *San Francisco Evening Post* was quite harsh. It said that it was the type of fight that you would rather read about than see. It called Burns "the poorest apology for a fighter that ever danced around the roped arena." Still, Tommy "whipped Barry to a frazzle and at no stage of the bout was there a doubt as to the outcome. He walloped the Irish champion all over the ring." In conclusion, despite the knockout victory, the *Post* said Burns "is one of the best fellows you ever met, but he will never do as a prize fighter. Last night he had one of the slowest men in the business to dispose of and it took him twenty rounds to do it." So, even though he won via knockout over the highly touted local man, demonstrating skill, power, and conditioning, Burns had not exactly raised his standing with the San Francisco fight community, owing to his cautious style. Hence, he shared something in common with Jack Johnson.[249]

At that time, heavyweight champion Marvin Hart was looking to make a title defense. He wanted full recognition as champion. Marvin said,

> On July 3, when I knocked out Jack Root, James J. Jeffries, in awarding the decision, announced his retirement and announced that I was able to defend the title.

249 *San Francisco Call, San Francisco Chronicle, San Francisco Examiner, San Francisco Bulletin, San Francisco Evening Post,* September 1, 1905.

> I am ready to fight any white man in the world. I do not think any man now in the ring can defeat me. When I am beaten it will be recorded that it was a fight from first to last and that the victor was punished within an inch of his life.

Hart said he could whip Gus Ruhlin, Bob Fitzsimmons, and Mike Schreck. He was willing to fight Jeffries. He would not fight Jack Johnson again.

> What I have said heretofore about fighting negroes goes for all time. I am a Southerner, and do not like them. I was forced to fight Jack Johnson in San Francisco, and I beat him. Had the fight been to a finish I would have knocked him out. Toward the last he quit like a cur, and I demonstrated that I am a better fighter than he is – I say fighter – boxers seldom win fights.[250]

Eventually, the *Police Gazette* begrudgingly recognized Hart as the present champion. "Hart has more claim upon [the championship] than anyone else just now."[251]

Owing to his dull performance against Dave Barry, Tommy Burns was not going to be a star in the San Francisco area. However, the Los Angeles sports very much admired and appreciated Burns. They wanted to see him fight again.

It was reported that Tommy Ryan had allegedly (or at least tentatively) accepted a Burns challenge to meet him in a 20-round bout. However, another match first awaited Burns, which, in its own way, helped change the course of his life.[252]

A month and a half after the Barry rematch, in his third rematch bout in a row, Burns once again took on Jack "Twin" Sullivan. The fight was arranged by Tom McCarey for the Los Angeles-based Pacific Athletic Club. Burns had impressed the Los Angeles fans earlier that year at that same club with his entertaining performance against Hugo Kelly. Burns was in demand. Both the Twin and Tommy agreed to make 158 pounds at 3 p.m. on the day of the fight.

Since boxing Burns to a March 1905 20-round draw, Sullivan had scored a KO11 Nick Burley and fought Philadelphia Jack O'Brien to a 20-round draw. Sullivan was one of the era's elite middleweights. "The men in the main event are too well known to need any introduction and both have fought in this city. Twin Sullivan is admitted to be one of the hardest middleweights in the business for any man to tackle." Burns also had a very good reputation as a fighter, particularly on the West Coast.

---

250 *San Francisco Evening Post*, September 13, 1905.
251 *Police Gazette*, September 16, 1905.
252 *National Police Gazette*, September 9, 1905.

Tommy set up his training camp at the North Beach bath-house at Santa Monica. With him were Warren Zubrick and husky football coach Jim Hutch, who would be in charge of the strength and conditioning work.

Jack Sullivan trained at the Pacific Athletic Club pavilion with his twin brother Mike Sullivan. Mike was a lightweight who had fought both Jack Blackburn and Joe Gans to 15-round draws. Jack also trained with Rube Jeffries, a boxer named Daniher, and even heavyweight Jack Johnson.[253]

On October 13, 500 fans watched Jack spar with his brother Mike, who was a shade taller but about 20 pounds lighter. Jack was in excellent condition and as fast as lightning. It was said that he would be several pounds smaller than Burns, but Sullivan did not believe that giving up four or less pounds would be a factor.

MIKE AND JACK, SULLIVAN TWINS, TO MEET ALL COMERS

The Fighting Twins—Jack is at the left

---

253 *Los Angeles Times*, October 13, 1905.

One local writer felt that it was a fairly even match-up. They were equal in cleverness, punching power, and ability to take a punch. However, Sullivan was probably faster, had the more extended ring experience, and was said to have met better men in his time. In 102 battles, Sullivan had lost only to Jack O'Brien, Kid McCoy, and Hugo Kelly. He held decision victories over George Cole, Mike Schreck, George Byers, Dave Barry, and Hugo Kelly. He had made an excellent showing against O'Brien in their recent draw, better than Burns' 6-round performance in a loss to O'Brien, which was said to tip the scales slightly in Jack's favor. "Sullivan will doubtless rule favorite for the fight, although this is not belittling Burns' chances in the least, as Tommy is probably the best match for Sullivan that could have been made."[254]

Tommy Ryan said he would soon be ready to defend the middleweight championship, and might fight the winner.

Two days before the big middleweight fight, on October 15, Burns and Zubrick did their roadwork and then treated spectators to 3 rounds of sparring which showed both to be in the best condition, with speed to spare. Tom McCarey was complimented for being astute in matching scrappers for his events.[255]

The Sullivan brothers were said to use pure English, instead of the usual bowery slang that fighters often used, and expressed themselves in a refined and gentlemanly manner. Both were remarkable pugilists who were popular with the fans. Other than their weight, the only other way to distinguish the twins was that Jack's left ear had been mangled in the ring and had healed imperfectly.

---

254 *Los Angeles Herald*, October 14, 1905.
255 *Los Angeles Herald*, October 15, 1905.

Both fighters were confident and ready for a hard battle. Sullivan said, "I will win without much difficulty, although I do not underrate my opponent, whom I recognize is one of the gamest fighters in the middleweight division." Sullivan was in the best of condition, strong as a bull, stout in wind, quick on his feet, and had developed his punch "until it has become the wonder of all who have watched it go into execution."

Burns said, "I have experienced less difficulty in getting into condition than I expected and am fit to fight the battle of my life. I want to settle the question of who is the best man of the two, and believe I'll get the decision." Burns was said to be in fine shape, and had lost his superfluous flesh to make weight without as much difficulty as expected. However, despite these claims, it was later said that Burns had indeed struggled to make weight, and had lost the weight too quickly.

PACIFIC ATHLETIC CLUB PAVILION

TUESDAY, OCTOBER 17, LOS ANGELES.

20 Round Boxing Contest

TOMMY BURNS of Detroit vs. JACK ("TWIN") SULLIVAN of Boston. Two preliminaries. Seats on sale at Greenewald's Cigar Store, 107 S. Spring st. Reserved seats, $2, $3 and $5. General admission, $1. Take Downey or East-lake cars north on Spring st. to Naud Junction.

Because of his vast experience, Sullivan was the slight favorite at 10 to 9 odds. Still, few wagers had been recorded, because fight fans were unable to form an opinion of the outcome with sufficient confidence to induce the placing of any significant sums. "The bout is sure to be one of the best ever pulled off in Los Angeles. Both are evenly matched in all the essential points, neither having much the advantage of the other."

Ticket sales were remarkable. 1,500 tickets had been sold on the Saturday before the fight, which broke the previous record for opening day ticket sales, and the demand had been steady thereafter. Tommy Burns was a hot ticket seller in Los Angeles. This is something of which promoters take note.[256]

Although Sullivan had been a slight betting favorite, on the day of the fight, late Burns money came in and the odds became even.[257]

On October 17, 1905 at the Pacific Athletic Club's pavilion at Naud Junction in Los Angeles, Tommy Burns fought a rematch with Jack "Twin" Sullivan. One local source said both men made the required weight of 158 pounds at 3 p.m. on the day of the fight. Another said Sullivan weighed in at 153 ½, while Burns weighed 159 ¼. There was some suggestion that there was a two-pound weight allowance. It was opined that by fight time, the smaller Sullivan was probably only about 153-155 pounds, while Burns was estimated to be at least 163 pounds. However, "Twin was as hard as

256 *Los Angeles Herald*, October 17, 1905.
257 *Los Angeles Express*, October 17, 1905.

whipcord while Burns showed the effect of too speedy a reduction in weight."

4,000 fans were present to witness the fight, the biggest crowd ever seen in the new pavilion. In the preliminary, Warren Zubrick knocked out Rube Jeffries in the 2nd round. Former heavyweight champion James Jeffries, who had been living on his Burbank farm, was present. He was introduced to the audience, although he declined to speak. Charlie Eyton refereed.

Flashlight Photograph of Sullivan and Burns in the Ring, Made at the Fight Pavilion Last Night by an "Examiner" Staff Photographer.

The following summary of the main event is taken from the *Los Angeles Herald* and *Los Angeles Examiner*.

1 – They fiddled and danced about. In order to obtain an opening, Burns moved slowly and tried to feint Sullivan into opening up, but Jack was too wise to fall into any traps. Sullivan missed a couple lefts but landed a heavy left to the stomach. He landed a left uppercut and they clinched. Twin missed a left and they clinched again. Sullivan landed two lefts to the stomach and a clinch followed. Twin landed a left and Burns a right to the stomach and they clinched. They exchanged rights and lefts and fell into another clinch. Sullivan landed a right to the stomach, and as they danced out of a clinch he crossed Tommy with his right. Sullivan landed two light

120

lefts and followed with a right and left to the head. They clinched at the gong. The round ended without any decisive blows landed.

2 – Burns started the round with his dancing act, but was still slow. They soon were going in and out of clinches. Twin seemed to have him worried with his awkward style of dropping in his overhand right. In the clinches, Twin used his pet punch, the uppercut. He kept Tommy busy trying to block it. Twin particularly kept his left working on the stomach, but also his right.

They roughed it in a clinch, landing lefts and rights to the head and body. Sullivan landed a left to the head, and as they broke, put a heavy right to the jaw. He also landed a left, while Burns landed a right to the head as they closed in. Sullivan fell to the floor as Burns missed a right. Sullivan landed a right and left and they clinched. Twin uppercut him. He also landed a left to the mouth and a right to the jaw. In a clinch, Tommy went to his knee. After an exchange of rights and lefts to the face and body, they clinched and the gong sounded.

3 – Uncharacteristically, Tommy remained slow. At the times where he should have forced the lighter man off his balance and kept him going, he allowed the Twin time to set himself carefully for every punch, and Sullivan overlooked no opportunity. He landed several overhand chops to the head, left rips to the body, and jarring short-arm blows at close quarters. Sullivan was using his elbows in the clinches as well, and Referee Eyton cautioned him. Tommy mostly used his overhand right for the head, but the Twin took the blows on his ear and smiled. "The story of this round might be the story of the whole fight."

Burns landed a left to the body. He landed a left to the head and Sullivan responded in kind. Clinches followed in rapid succession. Burns landed a left and right to the stomach and Sullivan returned with both hands to the head. Sullivan landed vicious lefts to the face and stomach, staggering Burns. The smack of his left to the pit of the stomach could be heard all over the house. They mixed it with lefts and rights to the body and clinched. Sullivan landed three lefts and a right to the jaw and ran into a clinch. He eluded a left and sent a left and right to the body. At the gong, Jack drove a left hook to the stomach.

4 – On a breakaway from a clinch, Sullivan landed a heavy left. Burns landed a left to the stomach and missed a right for the head and then fell into a clinch. Sullivan landed rights and lefts to the head and they clinched. Occasionally Tommy's head would shoot back as if it was on a hinge, and the Twin's elbow just happened to be under his chin at the time. Twin landed rights and lefts to the head but Burns came back with a left to the body which staggered Sullivan. The Twin landed a heavy left to the face and uppercut with his right. Burns landed a right to the head and the round ended in a clinch.

5 – Burns landed lefts to the face and uppercut furiously in the clinches. They would exchange left and right and then clinch after landing. They engaged in hard infighting. Burns uppercut with his right and Sullivan swung his left to the stomach. Tommy's nose was bleeding a little.

6 – The round was a series of clinches, fighting in and out of the hugging. Sullivan threw a hard left to the stomach and followed with three lefts to the head. Burns sent a right to the body and they clinched. Sullivan landed another left to the head and delivered a vicious uppercut in the clinches. Twin landed rights and lefts to the head and Burns landed his right to the face. They continued exchanging to the body and head and clinching in between.

7 – They were soon clinching and Sullivan was shooting his lefts to the stomach, while Burns was trying his right wallop for the side and top of the head. Burns fought harder. He forced the fighting and rushed Sullivan to the ropes, causing him to clinch. Sully had some blood on top of his head, a glancing blow having made a small cut. Tommy landed his right swing to the ear. He bore in with a right to the body. Sullivan tore in with a terrific left rip in the pit of the stomach and repeated the blow. He landed lefts to the face and stomach in rapid succession and they fell into another clinch. Burns swung heavily, landing to the jaw twice with his right and left and then sent in an awful wallop under the heart.

8 – The men continued clinching after every exchange. Burns landed two lefts and a right to the head and they clinched. Sullivan landed his left. Burns landed a left to the stomach and head. Sullivan landed his lefts. Burns clinched and landed his left to the head. Sullivan did the same and they clinched. Burns placed a heavy right to the head and another to the stomach. Burns sent rights and lefts to the body. Sullivan landed a vicious left to the mouth and right to the kidneys. He sent a left to the stomach and uppercut in the clinch. They exchanged several blows. Sullivan finished with his left to the head.

9 – They continued exchanging and clinching. However, the Twin was landing twice as many blows as Burns, and the left kept reaching its mark. A straight left sent Tommy's head back. Blood trickled from his nose, the effect of the left jabs. The end of the round found Jack landing his left and right at will.

10 – Twin hit the body with his left and a clinch followed. In the clinches, Sullivan was shooting lefts and rights up across Tommy's face in a manner that worried him. Sullivan's rain of straight rights and lefts led to several clinches. Both uppercut as the referee pulled them apart. The ripping lefts continued landing on Tom's stomach. Occasionally Burns would land his right swing to the side of the Twin's head. Sullivan landed a wicked left to the face. They exchanged lefts and rights. Sullivan landed two more lefts to

the battered stomach. Burns appeared to be clinching to save himself as the gong sounded.

11 – This round was largely a repetition of the previous round. Sullivan did the most landing, but Burns was full of fight and kept coming, giving the Twin no time to rest. However, Sullivan kept working and landing.

Burns landed a right to the head but Twin landed two lefts to the stomach and a right to the head. Burns landed hard to the head but Sully came back with his left to the face. Tom landed his right again and Twin landed his left. The round ended with Sullivan hooking in a hard left to the face.

12 – They exchanged lefts and clinched. Burns landed a left to the stomach and Sullivan swung a left to the kidneys. Burns landed his left to the body and right to the head. Twin sent three lefts to the face and fought into a clinch. Both sent lefts to the head and then Burns placed a punch in the lower stomach. Burns landed a smacking right to the side of the head and also landed a pair of stingers on the body. He was apparently growing stronger and fighting like a bull. They ended with an exchange of lefts to the face.

13 – Sullivan landed lefts to the face and Burns returned in like fashion. Burns hit the body with both hands and Sullivan landed an awful left wallop to the stomach, which he repeated. They exchanged blows to the head and clinched. They kept working on the inside. Sullivan landed three straight lefts to the face and closed the round with a terrific left to the head which had the crowd in an uproar.

14 – Burns came up fighting, landing his left to the body and right to the side of the head. Sullivan responded to a Burns right to the ear with a hard left in the stomach. Twin hit the body with the left and sent in two more to the head. They clinched, and as they drew away, Twin put a vicious one to the stomach. Burns landed a heavy right to the kidneys and they clinched. Burns threw another to the head, and in the exchange, Sullivan landed hard to the head. The gong sounded with the Twin landing a left over the eye which drew blood.

15 – Burns opened the round like a whirlwind and backed Sullivan all over the ring, fighting him along the ropes like a wild man. He forced Sullivan to clinch several times between exchanges. However, after the two-minute mark, the Twin brightened up and did some damage at the infighting. He rushed and pushed Burns partially through the ropes, but pulled him back in. The ripping, tearing round set the big crowd crazy. Tommy's eye was beginning to swell, and occasionally his nose would bleed. However, at the round's conclusion, neither man was hurt.

16 – This was another round of hard work by both fighters, but the Twin did more of the rushing and Burns was missing more. The usual exchanges

and clinches were continued. Sullivan forced the fighting, but fell to the floor as he missed a left to the body. He rose with a laugh. Burns finally landed several solid rights to the head, finding a home for his right.

17 – When he came up to start the round, Tommy's right eye was half closed. He was puffing like an engine and seemed very tired, while the Twin kept right on with his good work, using every punch in the book. Burns would dance in and out, and the instant he started a punch the Twin was there with the antidote, well ahead of Tommy. However, there was little clean punching. It was rush, smother, wallop in the clinch, and then Eyton tearing them apart.

The Twin twice landed hard to the stomach but Burns rushed him to the ropes. Tom put a right to the head as usual and Sullivan came back with his left. Burns fought viciously. The end of the round found them fighting hard.

18 – They engaged in a vicious exchange of rights and lefts. Sullivan landed a hard one but then clinched. Burns sent two on the jaw and Sullivan returned with a stinging smash to the stomach. They clinched and exchanged blows with both hands. At the gong, Sully landed a left.

19 – Burns hustled and forced matters, but the Twin was right with him at every stage. Tom landed his left jab, and was successful with two out of three leads. They exchanged rights to the face. Burns landed hard on the neck. He rushed the fighting but Sullivan cleverly protected himself. As they broke from a clinch, Sully landed hard to the stomach.

Sullivan's body blows were effective, and turned the tide in the last half of the round. He landed repeatedly on the face as well. Burns put one to the head and followed with a smash to the stomach. Towards the end of the round, Jack tore in with left rips to the stomach which sounded like a drum, and Tommy doubled up like a jack-knife as each landed. A left to Tom's nose drew blood from it again. It was a hot round, but it was the Twin's.

20 – They shook hands and each landed lightly and ran into a clinch. They went at it. As hard as he had been fighting, the Twin was far from extended. Tommy tried his best to stem the tide with one mighty punch to the body or jaw, continually forcing matters, but the Twin met him at his own game and gave better than he received.

Burns put a right to the head and Sully returned the same. They engaged in furious infighting as Referee Eyton pulled them apart. Sullivan put a right to the head and they clinched. Burns landed a wallop to the stomach and they clinched. Twin landed a right uppercut. Burns rushed him to the ropes and a rapid exchange of body punches followed. Sully landed three hard lefts and a right to the face and Burns clinched. Sully rushed Burns to the ropes but Tom came back with a right and left swing to the body.

Toward the end of the round, Sullivan smashed a hard left to the jaw and Burns reeled. Tom quickly went back at him. However, the Twin landed another clean swinging left to the jaw and Burns went down to the floor. He immediately rose to his feet in an instant, just as the bell rang.

Raising his glove up, referee Charlie Eyton awarded the 20-round decision to Sullivan. The cheering and ovation began. According to the *Los Angeles Examiner,* there was not a dissenting voice. It was clearly Sullivan's fight. Burns stared for a few seconds and then turned away and hurried out of the ring.

The *Los Angeles Examiner* said Sullivan had outpointed Burns all the way, scoring a clean-cut victory. It felt that Sullivan had practically won every round. Burns had "made the mistake of fiddling long enough between exchanges to let Twin set himself and shoot his blows in and every one of them hurt. He had Tommy's nose bleeding from the fifth round on, and he never lost an opportunity to put in a punch. Twin is certainly a wise old owl."[258]

The *Los Angeles Times* saw it as a close and exciting fight. They went at it nonstop with no rest, engaging in the hardest kind of boxing. Burns was "strong as a bull, full of fight on the aggressive from start to finish." Sullivan kept busy and held his own though. He bloodied Burns' nose several times, puffed his right eye, and had him groggy with stomach punches in the last round. Sullivan had an abrasion on his head and was reddened around the neck from Tommy's overhand swings. It was the best fight local sports had seen in quite some time. Hence, even though Burns lost, his stock did not drop. He was the type of fighter the local fans wanted to see again.

The larger Burns was quick and active and in fine condition, opening every round by rushing and leading. He continually attacked in every round, but usually ran into a left or right counter, though they did not stop him. The pace was quite fast. "Both men are good boxers, and the little superiority that Sullivan has was somewhat overcome by Burns's rushes. He hardly ever let Twin settle himself until he was at him and thus they fought back and forth through twenty long rounds."

Sullivan hit low three or four times early on and Referee Charlie Eyton warned him. Tommy came back strong, though, rushing every time.

They really got going in the 3rd round, which was fierce and grueling. They exchanged heavy smashes to the face with both hands.

There was considerable clinching throughout the fight; for Sullivan generally stood his ground before Tommy's rushes and fought back. Sullivan's head was skinned by a glancing blow and Burns' nose bled from repeated lefts in the face.

The 6th and 7th rounds belonged to Burns, who was working at high speed. Tommy went at him well again in the 12th, but in the 13th round, Sullivan slowed him up with some stinging lefts and rights. Burns had the

258 *Los Angeles Examiner,* October 18, 1905.

best of the 14th, but after that, Sullivan had the edge because Burns could not land effectively and Sullivan landed some hard blows.

They engaged in hot exchanges of slugging in the 18th round, but in the 19th round, Sullivan took Tommy's steam with body blows. Sullivan had much the better of it in the 20th round as well, which earned him the decision. "The crowd seemed to be with Burns, and yet the decision was well received, for the sports had their fill of good hard fighting for twenty fast rounds." The impression given by this article was that it had been a closely contested, competitive bout.[259]

The *Los Angeles Express* said Sullivan had outclassed Burns. Jack's science had been put in opposition to Tommy's remarkable strength. The packed pavilion went wild with delight over the fight. However, "There was no doubt as to where the bird of victory was perching during the battle, and only once did it leave the Sullivan corner."

Burns had set a great pace. In the 7th round, some felt that his pace was wearing on Sullivan, but Jack came out the next round cool and ready to meet Tommy's rushes with a stream of good blows that would have finished a lesser man.

Overall though, Sullivan was on the defensive, except on the break, when he would shoot in a blow and then clinch again. Sullivan would give ground against his aggressive foe, but met his rushes with clean getaways or quick falling into clinches. Sullivan was better on the inside. He was also not loath to sneak in foul blows. "Time after time Tommy Burns' head would fly back as Sullivan 'accidentally' touched his chin with his elbow." The referee cautioned Sullivan, but Jack would do the same thing again.

The 19th and 20th rounds were "violently scientific." They both tried to finish each other. Burns was as strong as an ox, but of a cool demeanor. They went back and forth, but at the close of the 19th, Sullivan landed a stinging left to the nose.

They fought hard in the 20th round, with Burns boring in and throwing with all the power he had in his body. Sullivan though was able to catch and elude the blows. He then attacked Burns and had Tommy hanging on after he was hit by a right hook to the jaw and left to the heart. They wrestled, and after a break, Sullivan went in with a right to the chest and left to the face which staggered Burns. Another left "raised him an inch from the ground and landed him – a clean knockdown – onto the mat. The gong sounded at once, but Burns was up like a flash." The referee raised Sullivan's arm.[260]

The *Los Angeles Herald* said it was one of the prettiest fights ever seen at the Pacific Athletic Club pavilion. The fight was on the savage give-and-take pounding order. Sullivan had slightly the better of the first 10 rounds. "He

259 *Los Angeles Daily Times*, October 18, 1905.
260 *Los Angeles Express*, October 18, 1905.

was better able to guard himself from Burns' vicious swings and uppercuts and demonstrated better ability as an infighter."

In the early stages, both played for the head and landed some hard wallops, with Burns scratching the Twin's head in the 3rd round, but the injury was slight. Sullivan landed his left to the head almost at will. During the latter stages of the fight, the Twin played for the wind and landed some terrific stomach punches.

The fighting was so fierce that after almost every exchange of blows they would go into clinches, and while in these positions, they would do their most effective work with uppercuts and body shots. At infighting, the Twin had all the best of it. He landed numerous vicious stabs. It was generally give and take throughout the fight, though Sullivan managed to get in the most effective blows, and eluded more than his opponent did.

Several times the Twin rushed Burns to the ropes, and in the mix-ups, landed some telling body blows, which were his most effective punches. Burns landed several hard wallops to the head, but they did not daze the Twin.

They fought in the roughest possible manner and Referee Eyton warned them repeatedly against fouling. Burns made a claim of foul early on, but it was not allowed. Both were equally guilty of fouling, though the low punches did not appear to have any effect on the final result.

Burns was disappointed, but had no excuses to offer, at least not immediately after the bout. He felt that the fight should have been ruled a draw, but was not insistent upon the point.

> Burns is not satisfied with the decision and says that the worst he should have received was a draw. Fight experts, and even some of those who were backing Tommy to win, say that the decision was eminently fair and correct.

> Twin was much the cleverer and exhibited better judgment and superior generalship. He repeatedly landed his mighty left on the head and face of his opponent and whenever he put the left to Tommy's stomach the 'smack' made the audience groan.[261]

The *National Police Gazette* reported that it was one of the hardest fights ever seen in Los Angeles, but that Burns could not have fought another round.[262]

Regardless of the result, it had been an exciting, fan-friendly fight and a financially lucrative endeavor for Tom McCarey. He wanted to see both Sullivan and Burns fight at his club in the future.

---

261 *Los Angeles Herald*, October 18, 1905.
262 *National Police Gazette*, November 4, 1905.

CHAPTER 6

The Underestimated Phoenix

By mid-October 1905, Marvin Hart was still looking to make a heavyweight championship title defense. He was willing to fight any white man, including James Jeffries.

> I am willing, and what is more, anxious to meet any man in the world in the ring in a finish fight. I mean just what I say. This challenge doesn't apply to colored people. ...
>
> [I]f Jeffries should ever re-enter the ring I stand ready to meet him and believe that I am big enough and strong enough to give a good account of myself. ...
>
> Fitz has been a great fighter, but he has long since seen his best days and no one knows this better than Bob. I will wager money that I can knock Fitzsimmons out in fifteen rounds or less. ...
>
> I do not mind what Johnson says. I was forced into fighting him once, but I will not do so again. I am not side-stepping him, but it is against my principles to fight a negro.[263]

During October, Hart hired former world middleweight champion Tommy Ryan to be his new trainer and co-manager.[264]

Following his October 17, 1905 20-round decision victory over Tommy Burns, Jack "Twin" Sullivan wanted to fight "Philadelphia" Jack O'Brien again. However, O'Brien had a scheduled heavyweight bout with hot up-and-comer Al Kaufman (sometimes spelled Kaufmann). The 19-year-old Kaufman weighed 190 pounds and stood 6'1". He learned to box at San Francisco's Olympic Club. He had sparred with Marvin Hart before Hart fought Jack Johnson. The big and powerful Kaufman had won all six of his battles via 1st round knockout. The San Francisco press considered him to be the best young prospect in the heavyweight division.[265]

On October 27, 1905 in San Francisco, Philadelphia Jack O'Brien scored a KO17 over Al Kaufman. Despite being a 10 to 7 underdog, the "smooth, slippery, eel-like" 165-pound O'Brien outboxed the larger 190-pound man, puffed him up, bloodied his mouth and nose, and knocked him out with a right to the jaw. O'Brien established himself as a formidable heavyweight.[266]

---

263 *Los Angeles Examiner*, October 15, 1905.
264 *Police Gazette*, October 28, 1905.
265 *Los Angeles Herald*, October 11, 1905.
266 *San Francisco Call*, October 28, 1905.

On November 28, 1905 at the Naud Junction Pavilion in Los Angeles, Jack "Twin" Sullivan won a 20-round decision over light heavyweight Mike Schreck.

Mike Schreck at the Left and Twin Sullivan

In the winter's biggest fight, on December 20, 1905 in San Francisco before a huge crowd of 8,000 fight fans, 28-year-old Jack O'Brien scored a KO13 over 42-year-old Bob Fitzsimmons to win the world light heavyweight championship; although some even said that the bout was for the heavyweight championship. It was a bloody battle, but O'Brien was in control all the way, outboxing Fitzsimmons with his fast footwork and quick punches, dropping him in the 3rd and 8th rounds, until Bob retired after the 13th round.

Subsequently, O'Brien began claiming the heavyweight championship. He believed the championship reverted back to the previous title holder, Fitzsimmons, when Jeffries retired. "That makes me champion." The victory certainly made O'Brien a very big name on the boxing scene, although he had been quite prominent even before the victory. He was the first man to defeat Fitzsimmons, other than Jeffries.

O'Brien was cut from the cloth of James Corbett. He was handsome, well dressed, intelligent, well spoken, had a sharp tongue, and could play hardball in negotiations. Even their styles were similar. O'Brien was fast with his hands and feet. The press loved him.[267]

"Philadelphia" Jack O'Brien and Bob Fitzsimmons

Promoters and the press wanted O'Brien to fight Marvin Hart to settle the issue regarding the heavyweight championship. However, O'Brien wanted to fight as a middleweight and take on Tommy Ryan first, before fighting Hart. He wasn't overly eager to get back into the ring with Hart, probably given that Hart had badly hurt O'Brien in both of their 6-round bouts.[268]

Tommy Ryan, who was training and co-managing Hart, said O'Brien's victory over Fitzsimmons meant little, because Bob was actually defeated by old age.[269]

In general, Marvin Hart was accorded greater recognition as champion than was O'Brien, although most still considered Jeffries the champion, despite his retirement. Still, the press wanted to see the highly respected O'Brien in the mix in a title fight, and their recognition of Hart as champion was begrudging at best.

---

267 *Police Gazette*, January 13, 1906.
268 *Police Gazette*, February 3, 1906.
269 *Los Angeles Express*, February 16, 1906.

Jack Johnson was looking for recognition as a top contender to the crown, but he had to deal with the color line clearly drawn by Hart. Also, many reporters simply did not feel he had done enough to earn a title shot. "Jack Johnson might have forced a fight had he been willing to do his best against other heavyweights, but by his fights with Sandy Ferguson and Marvin Hart he lost all chance to be considered a coming champion in his class."[270]

In late 1905 and early 1906, Tommy Burns wanted in on a potential payday fight with the best men around, either as a middleweight or a heavyweight. He wanted a rubber match with Jack "Twin" Sullivan, but was also willing to fight Jack O'Brien or Tommy Ryan. He issued challenges to all three of them.

In particular, Burns made repeated attempts to get Sullivan to agree to fight him again. Tom said that he had been weakened by the process of a hasty weight reduction before the Sullivan bout, which explained why he had done much better with Sullivan the first time that they had fought. Burns even offered Sullivan a guarantee of a $5,500 house and a $1,000 side bet. However, Sullivan refused to entertain a third match.

Burns said that he would also be willing to take on top heavyweights, including "Philadelphia" Jack O'Brien, because he would not have to make weight, and felt stronger at a higher weight anyhow. Tommy felt as strong as a bull at 165 pounds or more. He said, "If Sullivan is good enough to fight O'Brien twenty rounds to a draw I can defeat the Philadelphian in the same length of time. I am better at 165 pounds and over than at a less weight and in my challenge to O'Brien I offer a side bet of $1,000 that I will win." O'Brien had defeated him in a 6-round bout, but Burns felt confident that he would turn the tables in a bout of greater length. "I am no exhibition battler, but when it comes to going the route I bar none of them in my class." However, O'Brien had other things in mind.[271]

Pacific Athletic Club manager/promoter/matchmaker Tom McCarey wanted to make a match between Burns and another name fighter. He tried matching Burns with either Tommy Ryan or with heavyweight champion Marvin Hart, whom Ryan co-managed with Jack Curley. "Ryan and Burns probably will fill any house in Los Angeles, and at a good price."[272]

The Ryan-Burns middleweight championship fight at 158 pounds was tentatively scheduled, but the match fell through when Ryan insisted that Burns weigh in at ringside immediately before the fight. Burns said that he could make weight at 3 p.m. on the day of the fight, but would need time to eat and drink before the fight. He could not make 158 pounds at ringside without seriously draining himself. Ryan knew that Burns struggled to make weight. He did not want to give up the competitive edge. Neither man

270 *Los Angeles Examiner*, February 7, 1906.
271 *Los Angeles Herald*, January 1, 1906.
272 *Los Angeles Times*, January 4, 1906.

would compromise. Today's fighters often struggle to make weight the day *before* the fight, let alone at ringside or on the afternoon of the fight.[273]

It is possible that Ryan played hardball with Burns because he thought there might be more lucrative alternative bouts available. He also began negotiations with Jack O'Brien, who had made a big name for himself with his recent victories over Al Kaufman and Bob Fitzsimmons. However, O'Brien was noncommittal, and was talking with George Gardner and others as well. Regardless, O'Brien said that he was not able to have a big fight until April on account of his current lucrative theatrical engagement. It is also possible that Ryan simply wanted to remain retired for the time being. In fact, he did not fight again until 1907.[274]

Burns told McCarey that he would be willing to take on new heavyweight champion Marvin Hart. McCarey was impressed with Burns' fighting abilities, and likely noted that Tommy had been a big gate draw in Los Angeles, so he tried to make that match instead.

Hart co-manager/trainer Tommy Ryan later said that he had held out with Burns regarding the weight issue, but received a telegram from McCarey saying, "If you're afraid, match Burns with Hart." Ryan's reply was that it would be "Easy money! Marvin does the work and I get the money – at least, my share of it."

So, just like that, by mid-January 1906, a title fight was made between Burns and Hart, set to take place on February 23 in Los Angeles, California. Clearly, the Hart faction saw this as an easy fight for a payday against a much smaller man, and an opportunity for Marvin to show his stuff. After all, Burns was just a middleweight, and was coming off a loss. Hart was not considered the most skilled boxer, but he had very good conditioning, solid punching power in both hands, the ability to absorb punishment, and was 20-30 pounds bigger than Burns. He had defeated both Jack Johnson and Jack Root within the previous year. In fact, Ryan thought very highly of Marvin Hart. He said, "Hart will be the pugilistic idol, and will be champion of the world for many years."[275]

However, what Ryan had discounted was the fact that Burns was a clever boxer with good footwork and solid punching power, who had put up an exciting battle in his last fight against a high class fighter (albeit in a loss), that he had plenty of experience in lengthy fights, could fight on the inside or outside, and had never been knocked out. Burns had essentially defeated Hugo Kelly, who had victories over Schreck, O'Brien, and Sullivan. Furthermore, he would not have to kill himself to make weight at 3 p.m. on the day of the fight. Burns had been struggling to make weight for quite some time, which could explain some lackluster performances. He

273 *Los Angeles Express,* January 5, 1906.
274 *Los Angeles Times,* January 6, 7, 1906.
275 *Los Angeles Express,* February 16, 1906; *Butte Miner,* January 11, 14, 1906.

could eat and hydrate to his heart's content, and not be over-trained or drained at all.[276]

Hart and Ryan were on a sparring exhibition tour. During that tour, on January 15, 1906 in Butte, Montana, a 200-pound Marvin Hart scored a KO2 over the unknown Pat Callahan in a 4-round exhibition bout. Also sparring with Hart at that time was Jack "Twin" Sullivan, which perhaps was no coincidence.

Marvin Hart.

276 *National Police Gazette*, February 3, 1906.

Burns started training immediately, anxious to redeem himself for the "rather weak showing" against Sullivan. Tommy anticipated that it would be easier to go against a heavier man than a lighter man in view of the fact that he had grown so large that weight reduction would be disastrous. He asserted that the effort to make 158 pounds had detracted considerably from his strength. It was thought that he would weigh around 175 pounds against Hart. "Burns without doubt possesses a hard wallop, the effect of which will not be weakened by grueling training in order to meet a weight out of keeping with his naturally heavy build."

Regardless of the upcoming fight's result, the press often harped on the belief that James Jeffries would be the real champion for as long as he was alive, even though he had retired.

> Hart is technically champion by reason of the fact that Jeff awarded him the laurel after Hart's defeat of Root. The big Californian is, however, the legitimate champion and will remain so unless someone gets him into the ring and wrests the crown from him. This is a very unlikely possibility, as the farmer pugilist appears to be a man of his word and to all intent has forever retired from the ring.[277]

Another paper said there were a number of good men that the winner would have to beat before the majority of sports would recognize him as the real champion.[278]

Tommy Ryan told Jack O'Brien that he would fight him, but would not concede an ounce beyond the middleweight limit. If O'Brien preferred, Jack could fight Hart instead, after Marvin took care of Burns. Ryan felt that the 29-year-old 200-pound Hart would be too much for Burns. Ryan did not think Burns ranked with Jack Johnson, whom Hart had defeated, and therefore looked for a Hart victory, "though there are conflicting reports out about the real outcome of that Johnson-Hart battle." Hart arrived in Los Angeles on January 18.[279]

In preparation, Burns was sparring the 6'1" 190-pound Al Kaufman, who was getting ready for a bout with Dave Barry. "Kaufmann and Burns are profiting by their training together, as both are heavy and able to rough it in fast style around the gym." Although Kaufman was the favorite to defeat Barry, Burns anticipated a competitive and entertaining fight. He said, "Kaufmann surely has a wallop, but Barry is a good hand to take punishment and has been known to hit some himself." Subsequent to his 20th round knockout loss to Burns, Dave Barry's results had included: 1905 KO18 Jim Tremble, D20 Billy Woods, and D20 Mike Schreck, which proved that Barry was a good fighter.

---

277 *Los Angeles Herald*, January 15, 1906.
278 *Los Angeles Times*, January 24, 1906.
279 *Los Angeles Times*, January 19, 1906.

Burns anticipated that he would win a decision over Hart. Despite the fact that many believed the fight would be a mismatch in Hart's favor, Burns had his supporters, particularly from the local press, which had seen him in action. The *Los Angeles Herald* said, "The chances are that Burns will be in the fastest form of his life, and unless Hart can land a dream drop the Detroit boy has all of an even show to take the money."[280]

On January 26, 1906 at the Pacific Athletic Club's Naud Junction pavilion in Los Angeles, Al Kaufman scored a KO14 over Dave Barry. In attendance at the fight were Tommy Burns, Jack Sullivan, James J. Jeffries, and Marvin Hart.

Burns and Sullivan, who for a time had no love for each other owing to Sullivan's refusal to meet Tommy again, hobnobbed together like the best of friends. Eventually, Sullivan would spar and train with Burns to assist in his preparations for the Hart bout.

Al Kaufman

Unlike the Burns-Sullivan warm display towards one another, when Jeffries appeared in the ring and Hart was leaning against the ropes, Jeff totally ignored his presence. Marvin worked Barry's corner. Following this fight, Barry would become a Hart sparring partner.

Speaking of the upcoming Hart-Burns fight, the *Los Angeles Herald* said,

> Hart and Burns are both of the same fighting type, though the Kentuckian has the advantage in weight. Both can take punishment and neither are overly clever at the hitting game. Burns perhaps has the shade on footwork and his best chance appears to lie in ability to dodge the southerner's blows and land sufficiently to gain a decision.[281]

Hart wanted full recognition as champion, and was upset that Jeffries was still regarded as the champion even though Jeff had said that he was

280 *Los Angeles Herald*, January 24, 1906.
281 *Los Angeles Herald*, January 27, 28, 1906.

through with fighting. Although Hart was not formally challenging the retired Jeffries, Marvin wanted the first chance to fight Jeffries if Jeff renounced his retirement. Hart argued, "Immediately after Jeffries retired, the title was vacant and it remained for any two heavyweights to fight for it, a club standing to offer the purse, advertise the contest for the title, and the winner must be the new champion." Hart defeated Root in that way. Jeffries was announced at Reno as the retired champion, and refereed the bout for the vacant title, essentially putting his stamp of approval upon the bout. Hart argued that Jeffries did not give him the title, but rather he earned it through his victory over Root in a fight for the vacant title. If Jeffries would not fight him, there was nothing more for him to do.[282]

In early February, Burns was looking good in training, and was "surprising his friends the way he is shaping up." When sizing up the fight, the *National Police Gazette* said, "In fact had it not been for his bout with Twin Sullivan, in which he was outboxed and outfought, Brusso's chances would look pretty fair, at that." The *Los Angeles Examiner* said, "He is big and strong and may surprise many of the Easterners who had expected it would be a giant against a pigmy." Tommy was being trained by the wise and experienced Jack "Twin" Sullivan. Therefore, "the fight begins to look a whole lot better than it did." Sullivan had recently been sparring with Hart, so he would be able to give Tommy tips.[283]

The *Los Angeles Times* opined that Burns had always reduced himself too much in weight to be at his best, which in the past had left him weakened, and therefore it predicted that he would do better against Hart. Still, "Hart is a tough customer, and is a cracking good one." There was a feeling around town that the smaller Burns had a lot of nerve to go up against a heavy man like Hart. However, the *Times* felt there would not be that much of a weight difference. Hart would likely weigh about 190 pounds, while Burns would weigh around 180 pounds. At that time, Burns was weighing 183 pounds, and looked strong and rugged.

> He won't be weak this time, for he will not be forced to reduce himself, and those who see the scrap will see a very different Burns from the one they saw go against Twin Sullivan. He is training at Lewis's place on South Spring Street, and the best evidence that he thinks he will win from Hart is that he will bet his own money on himself. ... Burns thinks he has a very good chance to get the long end of the purse, and there are other experts who think the same way.[284]

282 *Los Angeles Times*, January 31, 1906.
283 *National Police Gazette*, February 3, 1906; *Los Angeles Examiner*, February 11, 1906.
284 *Los Angeles Times*, February 12, 1906.

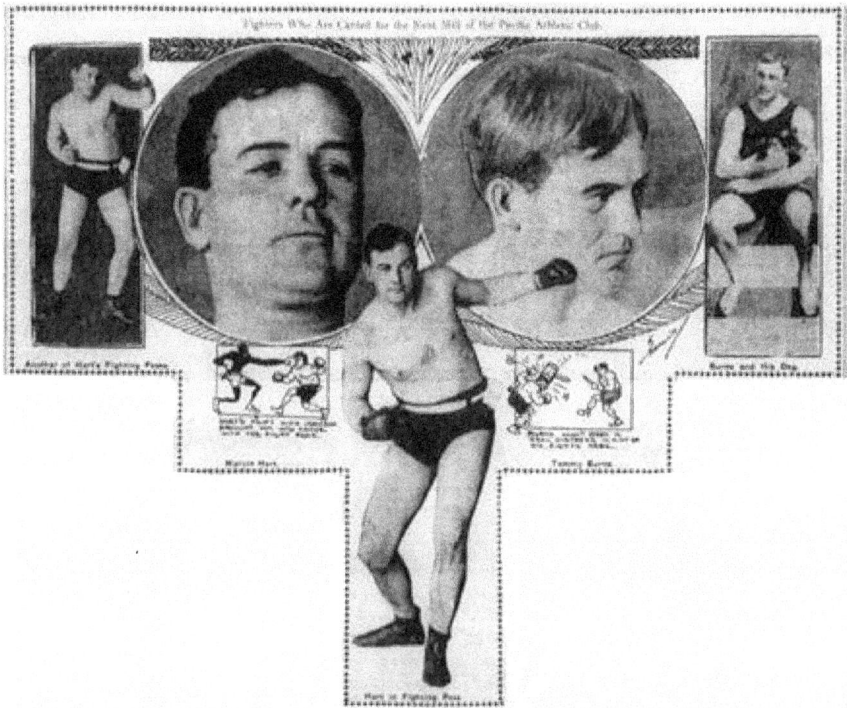

Fighters Who Are Carded for the Next Mill of the Pacific Athletic Club.

Hart was being trained by Tommy Ryan at Santa Monica, and was also sparring with Dave Barry. Each afternoon, Barry sparred from 4 to 8 rounds with Hart.[285]

As of mid-February, Burns said he was weighing 180 pounds. He did not look fat in the least. He said that he was correcting the mistake he had made all along of trying to make too low of a weight. He had been forced to diet on the lightest of food and run many miles on the road to make weight, which took the fight out of him before he entered the ring.[286]

Just under a week from the fight, both men were training hard, and enjoyed the strenuous work. "No more conscientious trainer than Burns has worked in a local gymnasium." He had wonderful stamina. Burns was growing larger almost on a daily basis, but wearing the weight well, looking strong of build. Tommy said making 158 pounds would be an utter impossibility at this point in his career. He would fight Hart at a favorable weight.

However, another paper that same day said Burns had taken off weight during the last week and currently weighed just over 170 pounds, and would probably fight at about 172. Tommy was boxing with the foxy Jack "Twin" Sullivan.

285 *Los Angeles Examiner*, February 13, 1906.
286 *San Francisco Bulletin*, February 15, 1906.

Marvin Hart

Tommy Burns

They will fight here Friday night.

Hart was also training diligently, looking big, ominous, and strong as a bull. He was said to be benefitting from Ryan's experience, improving the manner in which he handled himself. He was still sparring with Dave Barry as well. After a long run in the morning, in the afternoon, Hart weighed 195 pounds. He had the height and weight advantage (5'7" Burns to Hart's 6'), though Tommy had the slight ½ inch reach advantage.[287]

Despite the fact that the local papers thought Burns had a good chance to win, and were hyping up the fight, as of February 18, the betting odds had Hart as the heavy 2 to 1 favorite. The gamblers simply did not see how Burns could withstand the larger Hart's strength, size, powerful blows, aggressiveness, dogged tenacity, durability, and condition. However, there was plenty of Burns money in sight at those odds. Nearly all of Tommy's supporters were betting that the fight would go the 20-round limit. After all, he had never been knocked out.[288]

The 29-year-old Hart had begun his professional career in 1900, having had two more years of experience than the 24-year-old Burns, who had been boxing as a pro since 1902. Like Burns, Hart had begun his career as a middleweight. However, he quickly grew into a light heavyweight and eventually a full-fledged heavyweight. Hart had wins such as 1901 KO11 Al Weinig, KO7 Jimmy Ryan, KO16 Tommy West, KO6 Dan Creedon, and KO10 Jack Beauscholte; and 1902 KO3 and W6 Billy Stift, and KO9 Kid Carter. He fought Jack O'Brien to two 6-round no-decision "draws" in 1902 and 1903, but decked O'Brien late both times and nearly had him out. O'Brien was their only common opponent. Also in 1903, Hart had fought Joe Choynski to a 6-round no-decision "draw" and scored a KO15 over

---

287 *Los Angeles Herald, Los Angeles Examiner,* February 18, 1906.
288 *Los Angeles Times,* February 19, 1906.

138

Kid Carter. In 1904, Hart fought former world light heavyweight champion George Gardner to a 15-round draw that everyone except for the referee considered to have been a Hart victory. Heavyweight bouts that year included a D6 John Willie, W20 John Sandy Ferguson (which most thought should have been a draw), and WND6 and D12 Gus Ruhlin. In 1905, Hart won a very close and competitive 20-round decision over Jack Johnson. Marvin avenged a 1902 6-round decision loss to Jack Root by stopping him in the 12th round to win the vacant world heavyweight title.

Marvin Hart Wrestling With One of His Trainers.

Hart said Burns would not last more than 10 rounds.

> Burns may be fast, but he will have to be a ten-second man to get away from me. This hot foot game won't count for anything. I am going right after my man from the minute the referee turns us loose and there won't be a long story. There is nothing much for me to gain by whipping Burns and I must do it in quick order to benefit my reputation.

When told of Hart's prediction that he would knock him out within 10 rounds, Burns said he did not think any man alive could whip him in 10 rounds. He promised to show Hart a good time.

Each morning, Tommy was running 8 miles over the hills back of Elysian Park. He was sparring with Jack Sullivan, but was also training with Terry Davis and Kid Kelsey.

Tommy Burns Boxing With Twin Sullivan Before One of Burns' Female Admirers.

Sullivan.

Burns.

Marvin Hart.

A few days before the fight, the betting had livened up. As more wagers on Burns came in, the odds shifted to 10 to 8, although still in Hart's favor. Some bet that Hart would win inside of 15 rounds. Many felt that Burns was much the cleverer fighter and if Hart failed to put him away inside of 15 rounds that Tommy had a good chance of earning the decision. However, Hart's trainers said Marvin would prove a surprise from the standpoint of cleverness.[289]

---

289 *Los Angeles Examiner*, February 21, 1906.

Hart was anxious to show that he was a true champion, despite the refusal of many to recognize him. Marvin said, "If this fellow lasts twelve rounds it will be a long time before he's fit to fight anybody else." Despite his talk, "Hart realizes that Burns is no third-rater, nor anything other than a first-class man, and is going at his training with the knowledge that he has his work cut out for him." Still, Marvin was confident, assuming that he would knock out Burns, and was discussing his future plans. Hart said that he would be glad to take on Kaufman next, but it was Jeffries whom he really wanted to fight. He felt that if Jeff would not consent to a match then the public would have to grant that Marvin was the true champion.

The next day, the odds again shifted, with Hart as the 10 to 6 favorite. "Hart looks all over a winner. He is strong as an ox and in a rushing fight will make things decidedly interesting for his smaller opponent." In his training, he had been a glutton for work. Each day, he took a long 11-mile run along the beach. He would spar 7 rounds with Dave Barry and then take on a heavyweight fighter named Young John L. Sullivan for 3 more. Occasionally, he also sparred Tommy Ryan. "Hart was never better and hardly a man has seen him work who has not left the training camp convinced that the big Kentuckian would get the long end of the purse."

The fact that the 6'-tall nearly-200-pound Hart had the height and weight advantages did not affect Tommy Burns' confidence at all. Tom said that he would rely upon his speed to keep away and cut Hart to pieces.

Hart said that he expected to weigh 190 pounds for the fight. Burns expected to weigh 176 pounds.

Advance interest in the fight was quite high, for ticket sales had already reached $4,000 a couple days before the contest.

Although Hart was the strong betting favorite, Burns was said to be heavier, stronger, and faster than ever. The local press harped upon the point that it would be the first time in a long time that Burns would not have to kill himself to make weight. "According to the Burns dope, O'Brien is as good as Hart, Hugo Kelly is better than O'Brien and Burns is better than Kelly."[290]

When Burns was told of the current odds heavy in Hart's favor, he simply smiled and called attention to the fact that Jim Corbett was not considered in it for a moment before his fight with the much larger John L. Sullivan, but had proven the odds-makers wrong. The *Times* opined, "The man who attempted to prophesy on the outcome of the mill would be rash, indeed. … One thing is certain; the fight will be contested bravely on the part of both men."[291]

The *Los Angeles Examiner* noted that Hart had whipped top heavyweights, whereas Burns had made his record in the middleweight division. "Form followers would hardly play Burns to beat a man like Jack

290 *Los Angeles Examiner, Los Angeles Express,* February 22, 1906.
291 *Los Angeles Times,* February 22, 1906.

Johnson, yet Hart beat the negro giant in twenty rounds of hard fighting, proving his gameness beyond question in that encounter."

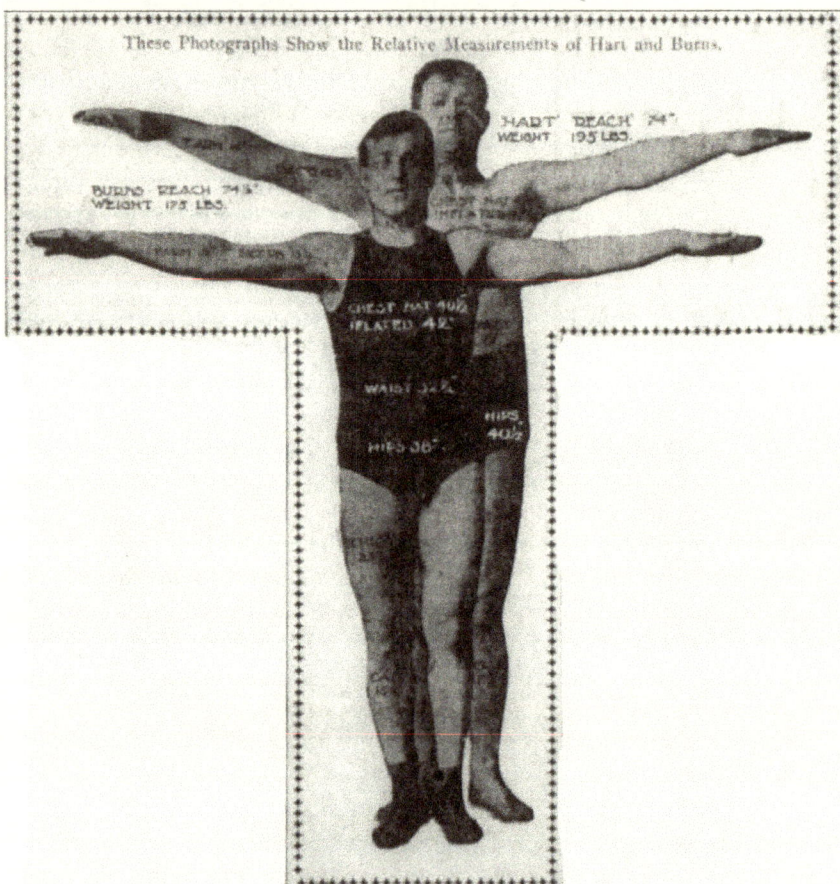

These Photographs Show the Relative Measurements of Hart and Burns.

In an interview the night before the fight, Tommy Ryan said Hart fought only one way, "slam bang all the time."

> He's as tough as a young grizzly bear and he does damage when he lands that right hand of his. I expect him to walk in any time around the ten round mark. I hear that Burns thinks Hart's stomach is his weak point. Tommy has noticed that Marvin looks high in flesh. He always looks that way. … I look for a hard fast fight but the big man should win any time he cuts loose.

Hart said, "I do not claim to be a butterfly boxer; I am a fighter and I don't believe in wasting a thousand punches that do no harm. I work for results and I can't figure out that Tommy Burns has a chance with me."

Burns remained confident. He expected to outbox Hart and focus on the body. He said,

Do you think I'd be going into the ring with a man that I didn't figure I had a chance with? Nay, nay. I've seen this big fellow fight and he is made to order for me to lick. … Everybody he ever fought hit him on the jaw and didn't hurt him. Downstairs for mine. I'm going to see whether that washboard thing is on the level or not. If he whips me he will have to be better than he has been in the past.[292]

It was Burns' first heavyweight fight. "Burns says he will box the big fellow from start to finish…. Hart has the advantage in everything except reach and cleverness."[293]

The *San Francisco Bulletin* said the battle was important because it would show just how serious a claim Hart had to the title. It said that he was vastly improved, and had gained in strength, speed and cleverness under the tutelage of Tommy Ryan, who said that Hart could beat anyone in the world. Ryan was thought to be a good judge, because he had trained Jeffries. Hart expected to win easily.[294]

PACIFIC ATHLETIC CLUB PAVILION   FRIDAY NIGHT, FEB. 23.

GRAND BOXING CONTEST
MARVIN HART   vs.   TOMMY BURNS
of Kentucky   of Canada.
Prices $1.50, $3.00, $5.00, $10.00. Take Downey Avenue and Eastlake Park cars to Naud Junction.

The Marvin Hart-Tommy Burns heavyweight championship bout took place on February 23, 1906 at Tom McCarey's Pacific Athletic Club pavilion at Naud Junction, in Los Angeles. A large crowd of about 5,000 was in attendance. At ringside, Hart remained the 2 to 1 favorite. Charlie Eyton refereed.

The local *Express* and *Herald* said Burns weighed 175 pounds, 17 pounds above his previous fighting weight. Hart tipped the beam at 195 pounds, 20 pounds bigger than Tommy. The *Los Angeles Times* said the weights on the night of the fight were Burns 175 pounds and Hart 192 ½ pounds.

Tommy Ryan objected to Burns' bandages. Tommy had several layers of black adhesive tape over his knuckles and wrist. "Tommy, evidently in a very ugly mood, sent back a warm reply." Referee Eyton ordered Burns to remove part of the bandages, but Tommy refused. He simply sat in his corner. After a long, tiresome wait, Hart gave in and the gloves were put on.

When they came to ring center, Hart wanted to fight straight Queensberry rules, but Burns would not agree. After some hot words, Tom refused to shake hands with Marvin, and he stood in the center of the ring arguing with the referee. Eyton read Tommy the riot act and sent him back

292 *Los Angeles Examiner*, February 23, 1906.
293 *Los Angeles Express*, February 23, 1906.
294 *San Francisco Bulletin*, February 23, 1906.

to his corner with the understanding that he was to break at the referee's command.

The following is a summary of the local *Herald*, *Times*, and *Examiner* accounts.

1 – Burns danced around Hart and kept rushing into clinches every time Marvin tried to lead with his right. Hart swung his right and Burns tripped, falling part way through the ropes. They clinched. Hart led with his right and another clinch followed. Tom landed a jab and clinched. The round was a succession of clinches, with Hart missing right swings as Burns glided in and out of his reach. On the inside, Tom landed a couple rights to the body. Generally though, Burns did no aggressive work, satisfied to keep out of harm's way. In one clinch, Hart landed a right to the kidneys. They were clinching at the end of the round. "Neither landed a hard blow during the round and at times Hart appeared awkward while Burns was not over anxious to mix it."

2 – This round was more of the same, although Burns opened up more. He landed a left to the stomach and Hart came back with a right to the face. They clinched often. Each snuck in blows on the inside, with Hart trying harder to work. Tom complained that Marvin was using his elbows in the clinches. Hart endeavored to land his right and Burns jabbed his left to the face. During the infighting, both men hammered at the ribs. Burns was able to land his left at will, and taunted Hart as the latter swung wildly with his right. Hart became excited by the punches that he was receiving, but could not land effectively in return. For the most part, Burns either kept away from him at long range, or closed in and clinched, being very cautious.

3 – They clinched. After breaking, Burns put his left to the face. Hart tried but failed to land his wallops. Burns grew more confident and danced around and hammered Marvin with several hard jabs to the nose that started it bleeding. Marvin's right eye also began closing. Those jabs eventually closed Marvin's right eye and made it black and blue. Still, true to form, Hart kept coming. Marvin was furious, and like a mad bull, tried to tear Tommy out of the clinches so he could beat him with sheer strength. Tommy jabbed the stomach and face and ducked and clinched. Blood was streaming down Hart's face. The crowd cheered for Burns because he was the much smaller man, the short-ender who lived in Los Angeles, and also because he was the better boxer.

4 – Hart led with his right and Burns landed his left to the jaw. Hart landed a right over the heart. Tommy ducked a vicious right. Burns rammed his left to the face repeatedly, landing at will. The crowd went wild for him. Hart could not land his wallops because Tom either danced around and jabbed at long range or clinched. Hart was hopelessly outclassed at boxing, and he fought as though he knew that his only chance was to land a hard swing. Burns landed three hard blows to the nose and eyes, cutting Marvin's right

eye, and he also landed a hard left to the stomach. Marvin's eye was badly cut from the effects of the straight left jabs, and the blood flowed from the nasty cut. Hart's features were nearly unrecognizable at the end. Tommy had a slight cut over his left eye as well.

5 – Burns again started at the sore nose, and three successive clinches followed. Hart was trying to land his right, but he could not get set. Burns landed his jab and then jumped away, and then shot in another and clinched. Tommy sent lefts and rights to the face and body, and Hart's hard right swing caught Burns in the back. Burns kept jabbing the sore spots and ducked Hart's hard blows. They were clinched at the gong.

6 – Tommy kept landing his usual left to the face. Hart tried to work him to the ropes, but Tommy was too shifty for him. Following the usual clinch, Tom ripped a left to the stomach. He sent another low one to the stomach and they clinched. Both worked uppercuts and body shots. Hart held his arms high for the break and Burns pushed him away. Hart landed several hard smashes to the right side. In another clinch, Hart drove his left to the jaw and right uppercut to the body. Burns reached the head with several hard drives and then shifted to the body. Hart's nose was bleeding again.

7 – Burns drove his left to the face but received two rights on the head. Tom ripped a vicious left to the stomach. Marvin focused on the body. Eyton was forced to part them from several clinches. Tommy would punch to the body and head and then clinch. They worked on the inside in between holds.

Tommy enticed Hart to his own corner, and as Marvin swung hard with his right, Hart slipped to the floor with the gong. Another version said Burns rushed Hart and wrestled him to the floor, to the cheers of thousands who admired the smaller man's strength. A third version said Tom had landed a left, but that Hart's awkwardness caused the fall more than the effect of the blow.

8 - Burns led for the face and Hart sent his right to the body as they clinched. Both were willing to clinch often. In one clinch, Tom pushed Marvin across the ring. Hart rushed Burns to the ropes, but Tom ducked under a lead, hugged him and laughed. The only effective blow of the round was a jarring right which Tommy hooked to the head. Tom jabbed and clinched. Marvin hit the body and Tom hung on. Hart threw his right to the body and neck at the gong.

9 – Hart came up strong and forced Burns into a clinch. He was rushing but failing to land. Much clinching was indulged in, with Hart striking with his right during the infighting, mostly to the body. Burns was able to reach Marvin's nose repeatedly, drawing the blood, while Hart landed but one successful blow, his right to the kidneys. Tom worked the body as well. Hart landed a right uppercut to the chin, but coming out of the clinch that

followed, Burns responded with a right to the jaw. "Hart is badly battered about the face but is apparently strong."

10 – By this round, the fight had settled down to the same old thing. Burns would feint, jab, and then clinch. Tommy began by stinging Marvin with a left jab to the nose. Hart landed his right to the stomach. While clinching, both momentarily turned at the sound of a disturbance in the pavilion. Two patrons were fighting. Hart resumed and sent a right to the neck. He landed several times during the round, particularly hard to the body, causing Tom to clinch. Tommy would not break at the referee's order, and so Referee Eyton had to go between them. Hart was angered by these tactics, and did his best to tear Burns away from him. However, Burns was working his plan to perfection. His continual tantalizing pokes to Hart's face made the blood flow in torrents. The red flood streamed over Burns' shoulders and spattered the referee as he struggled to make them break.

11 – Under orders from Tommy Ryan, who recognized the gravity of the situation, Hart increased the pace. Hart opened with a right to the body and they went to the ropes clinching. The round was a repetition of the preceding ones, with Tommy hammering Hart's face repeatedly with right and left as Hart attacked the body. Hart slugged Burns on the side and back, but the blows did little damage. Hart's open-armed advance was perfect for Burns, who found no trouble in delivering his one punch and slipping between the widespread gloves to smother Marvin. Tom would also land and dance away from returns. Burns landed an effective jab to the pit of the stomach and then shot his right to the ribs. Hart endeavored to rough it in the clinches. Tommy only laughed and kept jabbing his straight right and left blows to the face or body. The men rushed time after time to a clinch and were struggling when the gong rang.

12 – Burns jabbed away and landed a right to the head. Marvin also landed a right to the same place. Burns clinched, ducked, and jabbed. Hart was earnest and landed some, but was ineffective. Tom landed some short shots to the head and body. The round concluded with Burns landing a right to the head and then holding on in a clinch, pushing Hart to the ropes in the wrestling.

13 – Hart came in crouching, but Burns jabbed a couple lefts into his stomach. Tom danced away from Marvin's leads and returned with a hard right to the body. Tom would fire a shot and then jump away. If Hart landed, Tom would fall in and clinch. Hart landed a couple hard rights to the body. Tom landed a left to the nose that started the blood afresh. After the men rushed to a clinch, the pavilion electricity died out for a moment, and the boxers were hugging each other as the illumination was resumed. Hart was not able to do anything with Burns, who danced away from every vicious lead, only to come back and whirl his left to the sore face.

14 – Burns was back at it with his jab to the bleeding face. In a clinch, Hart fell to the floor in the wrestling match. He was up immediately and landed a left to the head. They exchanged rights and lefts to the body. Clinch followed clinch. Hart fought hard, but Burns easily took care of himself.

Towards the end of the round, Hart forced Burns across the ring and planted a hard right to the face. However, Burns replied with a right on the jaw and left in the body that dazed Hart. Burns went after Hart in furious fashion, landing hard swings with both hands, rocking Marvin. One source said Burns drove eleven rights and one left to the head. Others said Burns slugged him with both hands on the jaw. The blows were at short range and the house went wild with excitement. Burns slugged Hart hard and often and had him staggering, apparently at his mercy.

One writer said Burns slugged Hart for about fifteen seconds, but could not finish him. Another thought that Burns was well aware of Hart's reputation for strong recuperative ability and big power. Therefore, Tommy did not want to take any chances of fighting himself out, and did not attempt to finish him.

Hart collected himself and held on. The crowd hissed Hart for wrestling and hitting in the clinches. Tommy grabbed Hart around the head with his left and beat him in the face with his right. Hart rallied and landed three hard rights, but Burns came back strong and was fighting hard at the close of the round. It was the most exciting round of the fight.

15 – This round was a resumption of the earlier part of the contest. Hart missed and they clinched. He hit the kidneys with his right. Tom landed two jabs to the body and Marvin hit the jaw with a right uppercut. They went out of a clinch and into another. Tom hit the eye with a right and then sent a left to the bleeding nose. He ducked a right swing. In a clinch, Tom blocked a left to the body. Hart landed a hard right to the body. He poked a jab to the face and they clinched again. After the break, Hart feinted his left and sent a hard right to the stomach.

Throughout the round, Hart attempted without success to land his right to the head. He could find no openings. Tommy rapped his left to the face and jaw.

16 – Hart worked his right, but Tommy danced out of danger. The round was vicious, with much clinching and usage of rough tactics. Honors were nearly even, with very few blows landing.

17 – They started fast, and after the opening clinch, Hart drove his right to the head. Burns landed his piston rods to the stomach. Marvin failed to reach his shifty opponent, missing the majority of his leads by a wide margin. Tom landed his right to the head and right to the wind. In a clinch, Hart stung him in the body. Coming out of the clinch, Burns shot a hard uppercut to the mouth, jabbed two lefts to the face, and blocked a return.

Tom landed right and left to the head and they clinched. Tom ran away from a right swing and ducked under a left lead.

18 – They clinched and broke repeatedly. In one clinch, Hart almost threw Burns off his feet. Tom kept dancing away from the right. When against the ropes, he ran into a clinch. Tom shot his left to the face. In the middle of the round, Burns uppercut viciously with his right, and followed with left jabs to the face. Burns landed many blows and further swelled Hart's puffy and bleeding lips "in an astonishing manner."

Hart's right eye was closed, his lips were badly swollen, and blood was streaming from his nose. Tom landed a hard right to the body and hard left to the face. Marvin shot in his right to the body. As they came to a clinch, Burns uppercut Hart with both hands. Tom sent several lefts to the nose. Marvin landed a right to the body. The gong found them wrestling, with Referee Eyton struggling to separate them.

19 – Both appeared determined to end the bout, and following a wild rush to a clinch, Tommy slammed rights and lefts to the face until they clinched again. Hart tried with his right and a long clinch ensued. Tommy whipped a vicious right and left to the head and danced away from Marvin's leads. Hart landed a right to the body and Burns sent his left to the face, drawing a fresh torrent of blood from Marvin's face. Tom feinted his left and landed a right to the stomach. He missed a left for the head and they clinched. Hart landed two smacking rights to the stomach and they clinched. Misses and clinches predominated.

20 – They shook hands for the final round. Realizing that his only hope was to land a knockout blow, in a desperate effort, Hart lunged with every ounce of strength at Burns, who heeded the cries of his seconds and fought cautiously. Hart twice landed his right to the body. Tom danced away and poked his jab to the face. He side-stepped a left and then clinched. Tom landed a right to the body but took one in return. They fought viciously in a clinch. They were in and out of clinches. The majority of the round featured continual clinching. Hart vainly tried to land a decisive right.

Eventually, Tommy landed an uppercut. He sent a terrific right wallop to the side and followed it with a left uppercut to the jaw that disconcerted Hart. They struggled in a clinch. Hart landed a right uppercut to the face and they clinched. Hart landed another right uppercut to the mouth and missed another. Tom sent rights to the body. The bout ended with the men clinching.

Burns had suffered little to no damage, while Hart had a cut, swollen, and bleeding face, and "he spit blood from the bruises on his lips."

Referee Charlie Eyton took Burns' arm and held it aloft, showing that the underdog Tommy Burns had earned the 20-round decision victory and won the heavyweight championship. The big crowd voiced its approval with a great chorus of cheers.

According to the *Los Angeles Express*, Hart, the "so called heavyweight champion," made a "wretched showing." Burns used straight lefts to the face and bore into repeated clinches. He "stepped in and out at will, sending lefts to the big fellow's nose, eyes and jaw and he hugged his way into the clinches, danced tantalizingly before the helpless bulk in front of him and grinned at his seconds."

Until the 13th round, Hart did not land an effective blow. "As far as the fight went there was nothing to it until the thirteenth, when Hart did enough hitting to break even on the round." Hart followed him around with his arms spread wide, and Burns would shoot punches between them and then back away, keeping far from Hart's right. When Hart grew angry at his inability to land, he started rushing, but Burns was able to run away or clinch.

Hart came in crouching, trying to protect his battered face, but Burns shifted to the body, doubling up Hart. Tommy also hooked to the neck and sent in right uppercuts to the face that rocked Marvin. Hart rushed and Burns held his ground, taking a few hard blows. However, Tommy was beating Marvin savagely.

The 14th round was similar, but Hart was not as busy, and he was trying to avoid the stinging rights Burns used to stop Marvin's rushes.

A couple times in the fight, when Marvin rushed him, Tommy threw him to the ground, showing his strength. At the end of the fight, it was obvious that Burns had won, and there was no doubt about the decision even before the referee raised his arm.[295]

The *Los Angeles Times* harshly called Hart a "monumental dub" and a "big stiff." On the other hand, Burns was "quick, active, strong, confident and courageous." Before the fight, it was even money that Burns would not last 15 rounds. However, "if they saw the fight…it was even money that Hart would not last twenty rounds from the beating the little man gave him from the third round to the finish."

Burns would duck, sting and pound Hart on his sore and bleeding face, and then either dance away and elude his haymaker swings, or step inside of his blows and grab his arms. "It was like a fox fighting a dog. It was a battle of a big man against a little one who jumped in and jabbed and then jumped away or hugged himself safe into a clinch." Hart tried to wrestle, elbow, and hold and hit, but it was to no avail. "It was science and quickness against bull strength."

Burns rattled him with left jabs to the nose and eyes that brought blood and puffed up Marvin's face. "It was practically Burns all the way, and only in the twelfth and thirteenth rounds did Hart make any kind of a showing." The 12th was about even, and in the 13th, Hart landed some hard rights to the body that must have hurt. "Ten of the previous rounds had been in

295 *Los Angeles Express*, February 24, 1906.

favor of Burns, with the exception of the ninth, wherein Hart hammered Burns on the back in some of the clinches and again as he ran away." The only real damage Hart inflicted was in the clinches, "where he wrestled Burns and beat him in the head and back and shouldered him in the effort to shake him loose. It is hard to believe, but Burns threw Hart down once or twice in their rushing clinches."[296]

Unlike the other local papers, the *Los Angeles Examiner* provided mixed reviews of the fight and Tommy's performance. One reporter said Hart was not hurt, but only wearied by 20 rounds of fruitless efforts. Hart, "the man they were wanting to call champion and who was a foolish favorite in the betting," was compared with a big, awkward Newfoundland dog, while Burns was like a quick and alert fox terrier.

> You could not call it a good fight by any stretch of your imagination. … Hart was too mushy, too loose in his method, too everything that lacked fighting class for any word of commendation. Burns is a quick, shifty fellow, who can hit and go away or hit and go in as suits his pleasure. If he had something of that quality in his blows which sporting men call steam, he might knock somebody down and out one of these days. … He could hit Hart wherever and whenever he pleased. But aside from bringing the superficial blood from a cut eye and a bruised nose, he made no impression on the mistaken Kentuckian. Hart was merely tired at the end of the twenty rounds of futile efforts. He wasn't hurt, notwithstanding the blood that flowed from his skin-deep wounds. One could not help thinking as he watched the one-sided contest that if a less aggressive man than Burns were in the ring with Hart there would be no battle at all. It would be a walking argument, with Hart looking vicious and doing nothing at all.

This reporter said Burns was there all the time, sending in light blows on a coat of mail that would not dent. It was like shooting bullets at a big hulking ship. Sinking Hart was "entirely beyond the capacity of his batteries." However, Burns was both game and smart. "He went in and fought, and when fighting seemed to him too hazardous, he grappled and ducked. … It was hit and hug with Burns through the long, dreary twenty rounds." Because Burns was so much smaller, the crowd supported him. "Plainly, too, it was because whatever else he did he would fight some." Hart looked to land a single hard knockout blow, but his efforts were futile. Burns would smash him and then go to him or away from him as the circumstances warranted.

Hart was a bloody mess. His blood dripped off his cheek and over Tommy's back in the clinches. He even wiped his bloody nose on the

---

296 *Los Angeles Daily Times,* February 24, 1906.

referee's shirt. The blood stained the floor. In the last few rounds, the crowd called for Burns to keep away, given that he had the contest won. However, Burns kept bringing more blood. The "pang, pang of the Burns blows went right on to the end, ruining a budding reputation and building up a new one."

Another *Examiner* reporter harshly called the fight a sad spectacle and a wretched exhibition. A "second-rate" middleweight had made the heavyweight title claimant look like an amateur. "The reign of the Pretender is over. If Marvin Hart ever had the slightest claim on the heavyweight title, he lost it last night."

> For twenty rounds Tommy Burns made Hart look like the rawest kind of an amateur, feinting him into knots, jabbing him dizzy with straight lefts and wrestling him fairly off his feet the rest of the time. Burns fought a great defensive fight. He took no chances. It was jab and clinch, jab and clinch, and Referee Eyton wore himself out tearing Burns away from his victim.

> The only thing which can be said in Hart's favor is that he was willing. He knew what he wanted to do, but he didn't know how to do it, and the crowd laughed at his awkwardness. … Hart would rush out, crouched double, with both arms spread out… Burns would skip in and out, feinting until Hart tied himself into a knot, then dart into a clinch, landing a stinging left to the face as he did so. … Hart tried to fight himself out of the clinches, but Tommy hung on until Eyton was forced to go between the men. Then it would begin all over again – feint, jab and clinch; feint, jab and clinch, in a wearying monotony.

> There was only one spot in the whole affair which closely resembled a real fight. It came in the fourteenth round. Burns stood up and began to slug and for fifteen seconds he rocked the big fellow with rights and lefts to the jaw. It was plain fighting, but Hart seemed unable to block any of the blows and Burns battered him dizzy before he backed away.

W.W. Naughton, who tended to make extravagant statements, was even more critical of the fight. His statements bordered on the cruel. He said that although Burns deserved the verdict as far as blows and blocks count, "it looked as though both men should have been locked up for gaining money under false pretenses."

> Burns didn't prove that he was a fighter. He simply proved that the other man was no fighter. He prevented Hart from fighting. … Mr. Hart of Kentucky didn't place one good wallop.

> Burns had a trick of rasping his forearm against Hart's nose before diving into a clinch, and he made the clinches so frequent that the bout resembled a wrestling match more than a scrap with gloves.

At no time was there a good, honest exchange of blows. Burns acted like a man who was there to stay the twenty rounds and to do just enough to keep in favor with the referee. ... Hart...was very willing. He slugged and cuffed, but he failed to accomplish anything. There was never a time when there was an air of despondency about the big Kentuckian. He seemed to be thoroughly imbued with pride and self-reliance; but his failure to accomplish things was piteous. The man he had before him is not a fighter and never will be. ...

In Hart's corner was Tommy Ryan. ... The fight had not gone two rounds before Tommy seemed to see that he was behind a lobster.

Before the fight was three rounds old it was patent to all the watchers that it was to be an uninteresting affair.

Like the other *Examiner* reporters, Naughton noted that it was mostly a hugging match, with Hart trying to do something in close, and Burns baffling him. Burns was quite adept at side-stepping and clinching. "The only telling blows delivered were those lefts of Burns' in diving into a clinch." In around the 15th round, Burns gained confidence and started landing rights as Hart came in, but Tom did not hurt him, and he was so intent on clinching that he did not put any real force into his blows.

As a rule, the winner of any kind of athletic event is cheered and his victory carries with it a certain degree of credit and glory. About the only thing accomplished was to show that Marvin Hart is a poor apology as a world's champion.

When Tommy Ryan took hold of the Kentuckian it was supposed that he would show improvement. As a matter of fact, there was a falling off. ...

Burns is built on the Sharkey order. ... He is very quick on his feet and very tricky. As shown by his fight with Hart, his aim appears to be to prevent himself being hurt rather than to hurt his opponent. ...

The contest exploits the hopelessness of the heavyweight situation. ... Hart has little to commend him apart from his willingness, while Burns is simply a catch-as-can artist.

Jack O'Brien is easily the master of either of the participants in last night's battle. As for Jim Jeffries, it would be downright cruelty to send him into the ring with either man.

The gist of the whole story is that the only heavyweights in sight are Jack O'Brien, Al Kauffmann and Sam Berger. O'Brien has already won from Kauffmann, but if the San Francisco promoters can bring about a match between Kauffmann and Berger the winner will be a worthy opponent of the gentleman from Philadelphia.[297]

Hence, some local reporters were quite high on Burns' performance, while others did not want to give him much credit at all, although they were not loath to use his dominance as fuel to criticize Hart.

The *Los Angeles Herald* was extremely high on Burns' performance. It said Burns outpointed, outfought, and outgeneraled Hart in every round to earn a decisive victory. It called him the new heavyweight champion of the world. Burns "won all the way, having a distinct advantage in every round." Despite the fact that Hart outweighed him by 20 pounds, he was no match for his clever opponent. Burns carried the fight to Hart, but when the champion attempted to force matters and hit him, Tommy was not there. "His footwork and speed surprised everybody in the audience of 5,000 persons." Burns landed many more blows, and his stabs were more effective.

From the 4th round until the end of the 20th round, Hart's face was covered with blood as a result of the constant left jabs sent to his face. By the end, Marvin's left eye was closed, his right eye was dimmed, his nose was bruised, his mouth was bleeding, and his lips were so swollen that he could scarcely talk afterwards except in pain.

Burns was too fast for Hart. He repeatedly stepped in and landed effective blows to the head, and then moved away before Hart could make a return. Tommy's footwork was a "revelation," and he gave the "prettiest exhibition ever seen in Los Angeles." The fight clearly proved that Burns was too heavy to battle in the middleweight class, and that he could only be at his best when not burdened with the necessity of making weight.

What Burns lacked in weight and height he made up for in "gameness, boxing ability, and effectiveness." Hart was too slow and swung wildly, seldom landing. Burns would duck his mighty rights and then jump in and land counters. He was far superior in his ability as a boxer, in ring generalship, and ability to land effectively. "It was a pretty battle and the best man won. The audience was wild with enthusiasm."

Burns said that he was certain of victory from the 4th round until the end. He had felt out Hart in the first few rounds, and ascertained that the champion could not hit him effectively. Thereafter, Tommy stepped in and delivered rights and lefts whenever the opportunity offered, and got away before Hart could return the blows.

Prior to the fight, Burns had signed a lucrative contract to do a vaudeville tour, conditioned upon his winning the Hart fight. Hence, like

---

297 *Los Angeles Examiner*, February 24, 1906. Comparing Burns with a catch-as-can artist meant that he was someone who took advantage of any opportunity that came, by using or making do with whatever means or methods that are available to him. Naughton was implying that Burns was simply concerned with winning the fight, regardless of the style employed.

other champions before him, Burns would seek to capitalize on his new-found status before engaging in serious title defenses. However, Tommy would be a fighting champion.[298]

The *San Francisco Bulletin* reported that Hart's nose and rib were broken and his face resembled a sponge soaked in blood. After the 1st round, Burns was heard to tell his corner, "I'll lick that big duffer sure." Hart made himself unpopular with the crowd by trying to use his weight in the clinches and by using his elbows. The 10th was the only round which Hart made any semblance of a showing, for some of his hard kidney wallops temporarily affected Burns, but Tommy came back fresh and strong in the next round.

After the fight, the *Bulletin* representative visited the dressing rooms. Burns "looked in condition to go to a pink tea," while Hart's face was "receiving the attention of a staff of dermatologists."

Burns said,

> Everyone figured me to lose, and I guess I surprised them. At no time during the fight did Hart hit me a blow that bothered me. I am willing to fight any man in the world, bar Jim Jeffries, and just say for me I think Jeff is a class by himself. I do not draw the color line. If Jack Johnson, Jack O'Brien or any other fighter in the world wants to meet me I will be ready to talk business in a couple weeks. Heretofore I have gone out of my class and weakened myself fighting at the middleweight limit. I was twenty pounds heavier tonight and fought stronger than ever before. I attribute my good showing to Twin Jack Sullivan and Professor F. L. Lewis.

The *Bulletin* opined that Hart had proven himself a worse fighter than the San Francisco public thought, even though San Franciscans had not rated him a world-beater. They had been unable to forget his bout with Jack Johnson, who "outpointed him," despite the referee's decision. "That one fight cooked Hart's goose with local fight fans as far as taking him seriously as a champion."[299]

Hart told the *Bulletin* representative, "I think I was entitled to the decision, as I was the aggressor throughout the fight. Burns broke my nose by butting me. He also fouled me repeatedly and I appealed to the referee on numerous occasions." He displayed a broken rib which he said had been damaged in the Jack Johnson fight and was reinjured against Burns.

The *San Francisco Examiner* reported that Hart claimed that Burns butted, hit low, thumbed him and continuously held and refused to break, all of which were against the rules. Marvin felt that without the use of such tactics by Burns that he would have won.[300]

298 *Los Angeles Herald*, February 24, 1906.
299 *San Francisco Bulletin*, February 24, 1906.
300 *San Francisco Examiner*, February 25, 1906.

Like Bob Fitzsimmons, the former middleweight Tommy Burns had become a heavyweight champion. Defying the odds, a smaller but cleverer man had defeated a larger, stronger man. As such, Burns can be seen as being part of the line of Corbett over Sullivan and Fitzsimmons over Corbett - smaller fighters defeating larger ones. Unlike the others, Burns had not caught Hart after a lengthy period of inactivity (although Hart had not been as active since winning the title in July 1905 as he had been as a contender).

Philadelphia Jack O'Brien was one of the most surprised men in the world at Burns' victory. He had fought both, and thought much more highly of Hart. "I thought Hart would have no trouble in beating Burns as I beat him easily in a 6-round bout. ... I could not see where Burns had a possible chance of winning from Hart. ... I think that Burns is now entitled to a fight with me for the heavyweight championship title as he beat Hart so easily that the public demands that I fight him."[301]

Some folks around the country did not want to give Burns credit for his victory, or accept him as champion, in part because they never accepted Hart's claim to the championship. Therefore, they belittled Burns' claim. Unlike the Los Angelinos, the San Franciscans were not as kind. The *San Francisco Bulletin* called Hart a joke of a fighter and champion. "People will be very loth to grant the title to Burns." It said Jack O'Brien came closest to having the right to being called champion.[302]

JEFF APPRECIATES THE JOKE

However, in the days subsequent to the bout, the *Los Angeles Herald* fully supported Tommy, saying,

301 *San Francisco Bulletin*, February 25, 1906.
302 *San Francisco Bulletin*, February 25, 1906.

Some disappointed fans are prone to scoff at the new heavyweight champion, Tommy Burns, and belittle his claims upon the title, yet his claim is ten times stronger than was that of Marvin Hart. ... If Hart was entitled to make the claim, Burns has demonstrated that he is more entitled to the honor, as he clearly outfought, outpointed and outgeneraled Hart at every point of their battle Friday night, unmercifully whipped the Kentuckian and emerged from the battle with not a scar or bruise. ... Burns was a revelation to the fans who have made the same mistake all along that the former champion made, that of holding him too cheaply and belittling his abilities as a battler.

Throughout the twenty rounds of grueling, Burns was ever cool and collected in his conduct, quick to take advantage of an opening, effective when he landed and so speedy on his feet that he could rush in and lam-lam Hart and get away before the slow-moving and desperate Kentuckian could make any return.

Burns fought Hart in much the same manner that Jack O'Brien fought Bob Fitzsimmons. Criticism of Burns' tactics is, therefore, criticism of O'Brien's methods. O'Brien, however, was much sung about for his speedy footwork and cleverness in avoiding punishment, while Burns is roundly criticized by a few who are, probably, incited by the pangs of disappointment.

Hart was made to look like an amateur overgrown boy fighter because Burns clearly outclassed him at every point. Because Hart was so greatly outclassed, it cheapened the victory of Burns in some minds and robs him of much of the glory of the battle.[303]

The ironic point was that Burns had been too dominant to receive credit from some. Instead of lauding him, they denigrated Hart. Others wanted to see Burns stand toe to toe and score a decisive knockout, rather than just clearly outbox Hart. They did not care for the style that he had employed. Regardless, no writer or expert who had seen the fight disputed Burns' victory.

The *Herald* opined, "Those who accepted Hart as champion must also accept Burns as the new champion." It noted that both Fitzsimmons and O'Brien, believed to be the top contenders to the title, had sidestepped Hart. Burns had met and defeated him in a one-sided affair when others had been reluctant to get into the ring with Marvin after he had knocked out the respected Root. "By defeating Hart, Burns becomes champion of the world in the heavyweight division, and none can gainsay his claim upon the title since Jeffries has retired and refuses to further defend his claim."

---

303 *Los Angeles Herald*, February 25, 1906.

Although Burns did not look the part of champion, "what he lacks in weight he makes up for in cleverness, speed and ability as a fighter." Even his most ardent supporters and admirers were amazed by the great improvement shown since his defeat by Jack Sullivan. The battle he put up had demonstrated the truth of Tommy's claims that he had been weight drained when he went up against Sullivan. Against Hart, he was "hard as steel, faster than ever before and had developed a punch which brought to him the title of heavyweight champion of the world."

The fact was that very few had given Burns a chance to defeat Hart, "just as they now hoot at his claims and scout the ability of the new champion to defend his title. Burns announces that he will defend the title against all comers." Tom said that he was willing to fight Al Kaufman or Sam Berger, "both of whom have been suggested by the wiseacres of the game as more entitled to fight for the title than Burns, and Burns says he will fight both of them ten rounds on the same night if allowed thirty minutes between battles." Burns was also confident that he could defeat Jack O'Brien.

The *Herald* said Burns would take some time to appear on the stage, but noted that Tommy was willing to defend his claim to the title. "Tommy Burns will presume to wear the laurels he fairly, cleanly and decisively won by whipping to a standstill the man whom the same fight experts have previously and at all times heretofore acknowledged as the successor to Jeffries as the world's champion."[304]

HEAVYWEIGHT CHAMPION OF WORLD WILL DEFEND TITLE

Tommy Burns

Marvin Hart and Jack Curley, Hart's manager, said Burns' victory entitled him to wear the world title. Curley said, "All this criticism of Burns and attempts at arguing him out of the full right of wearing the heavyweight championship honors is bosh. Burns is the real heavyweight champion and I predict that he will surprise even his friends by the manner in which he defends the title." Curley said Hart had won the title relinquished by Jeffries, by defeating Root. Burns defeated Hart, and therefore succeeded to the title. "That is all there is to it in fairness and justice."

Curley was very high on Burns, and felt that he was underrated. He opined that Tommy would easily defeat Al Kaufman or Sam Berger. He

---

304 *Los Angeles Herald*, February 25, 1906.

said Jack O'Brien would be the hardest game for Burns, but still believed that Tommy would win. He also said that Gus Ruhlin would have no chance with Burns, for he was too big and bulky to deal with a man as speedy as Burns.

When interviewed, Burns said, "Yes, I appreciate the fact that I am champion. … I propose to defend my title as long as worthy opponents are in existence." He would soon take up a vaudeville tour for fifteen weeks and then take a vacation. After that, he would give attention to any challengers in waiting, and would give all the heavies a chance at his scalp. Tommy wanted to show the world that he was worthy to wear the crown. He most wanted to take on Jack O'Brien.

> I saw the bout between Hart and O'Brien in Philadelphia and am sincere in the statement that O'Brien was very fortunate to stay the limit. O'Brien cannot, in my opinion, take the punishment Hart stood for Friday night and I know that O'Brien's tender spot is his stomach. He cannot fight the battle put up by Hart and stand for the stomach lacing the Kentuckian took.

Tommy said that he was a different fighter at 175 pounds than he was at 158 pounds. Against Hart, "after the third round I felt absolutely certain that I would win. After the fourteenth round I knew that I had such a big lead over Hart that it was not necessary for me to take any great chances, and I did not afterwards try to win on a knockout."[305]

The *Los Angeles Times* echoed the *Herald's* sentiments. It said that several newspapers failed to give Burns any credit for easily defeating Hart. However, it credited Tommy for defeating a larger, taller, and stronger fighter. It had confidence that he would do well against other top contenders.[306]

In subsequent days, the *Herald* again noted that the fight was supposed to be Hart's opportunity to show how much he had improved under Tommy Ryan's tutelage during the past few months. Burns was just supposed to be a body for Hart to give a demonstration upon. Yet,

> Tommy sprung the greatest surprise in recent years…and did it in such a decisive manner that no legitimate reason exists for the criticisms which have been passed upon him by many of the critics. When Jack O'Brien glided in and out between the long arms of Bob Fitzsimmons and eventually wore the old boxer down he was greeted as a great general. Burns fought along the same lines, and yet some of the credit due him is begrudged.[307]

---

305 *Los Angeles Herald*, February 26, 1906.
306 *Los Angeles Times*, February 26, 1906.
307 *Los Angeles Herald*, February 28, 1906.

The *National Police Gazette* reported that it had been a vicious and bloody fight, but that Hart was "well walloped" and clearly beaten all the way. His face "presented a terrible sight, being a mass of blood, both eyes practically closed and his lips so swollen that he could scarcely speak." Burns fought cautiously and exhibited remarkable speed in outgeneraling and outclassing Hart. Marvin's left eye began closing in the 4th, his right eye and mouth swelling in the 10th, and in the 14th round, Burns landed eleven rights to the head and Hart only saved himself by clinching. In the 18th, Hart was again wobbly, but clinched. "Burns was fast and cool. Hart was wild and desperate." The fight was not in doubt after the 5th round. Hart led with vicious rights, but could not land, while Burns ducked and countered with rights and lefts to the body or head. The victory was popular, as it was clear and decisive.

The *Gazette* provided further thoughts and critiques. As a boxer, Burns was known as "a willing worker, with much strength and ability to take punishment, but he has not been regarded as a candidate for championship honors, and it follows that he has either improved very remarkably or that Hart has deteriorated." That said, "Hart's championship claim was never seriously considered because of his mediocre pugilistic ability."[308]

The following week's report said that the comparative novice Burns "with extreme cleverness and considerable punching power proceeded to make the would-be champion look like a novice. ... Hart's friends declared that he had been drugged, for they could not account in any other way for his ridiculously weak performance." Apparently, the result "caused Jeffries, who sat at the ring side, much amusement."[309]

Over a year later, when analyzing Burns' career, one writer said,

> Burns was never reckoned as a heavyweight of real class until after his battle with Marvin Hart. Tommy, who had been weakening himself to make a low weight for middleweight fighters, came into the ring against Hart weighing in the neighborhood of 180 pounds. ... [N]ot once did Marvin get anywhere near Tommy's jaw with that dangerous right hand. Burns did not stay on the defensive in this fight. He was in and out and all over Hart like a lightweight. For twenty rounds Tommy lashed away with a straight left, occasionally stepping in with a right swing and at the end of the fight Hart was a badly beaten man.[310]

Hart and Ryan had made a huge miscalculation. They had lost the championship, and had not made much money for it. Apparently, only $4,800 had been taken in, (or so the promoter claimed). The fighters' purse

---

308 *National Police Gazette*, March 10, 1906. It also said, "Tommy Burns is the fighting name of a native of Detroit, Mich., named Noah Brusso. His first incursion into athletics was as a lacrosse player."
309 *National Police Gazette*, March 17, 1906.
310 *San Francisco Examiner*, July 4, 1907.

was one-half, or only $2,400, of which Burns received $1,650 and Hart $750, which was likely the cost of Marvin's training expenses. Because Hart had held Burns too cheap and thought it would be a cinch to beat him, he had insisted that the money be divided 70% to the winner and 30% to the loser. Ultimately, that deal worked much to Tommy's favor and to Hart's detriment.[311]

Burns wanted to take on Jack O'Brien next. "However, I will consider all challenges directed at me and will endeavor to show to the world that I am worthy to wear the honors I have won."

Initially, the *Police Gazette* did not want to recognize Burns as champion. "Brusso-Burns claims he is the champion." There had been some dispute about whether Jeffries had the power to name those who would fight for his vacant title, and therefore some had not accepted Hart as champion. It said Burns' claim to the championship "is baseless. To begin with, Hart was not champion." Of course, one of its writers had previously said that Hart had greater claims to the championship than anyone else.[312]

The bottom line is that several newsmen would not grant that anyone was heavyweight champion other than James J. Jeffries, despite the fact that he was retired. In their estimation, the undefeated champion would be such for as long as he was alive. It would take Burns some time to obtain full recognition as champion.

Regardless, Burns had quite easily defeated the man who had defeated Jack Johnson, who had been considered Jeffries' strongest potential challenger. True, many felt that Johnson deserved the victory over Hart. However, Burns had clearly defeated Hart in a dominant performance, whereas the Johnson-Hart bout had at least been close and competitive. Burns had handled Hart and unquestionably defeated him. At least, that was the perception. One can debate to what extent race played a role in that perception. Either way, no one questioned Burns' victory over Hart, and many had recognized Hart as the champion before Tommy defeated him.

After he returned home to Louisville, Hart offered a number of excuses for his loss, including that "he was robbed by the referee, jobbed by the club, fouled by his opponent and abused by the press." A more interesting excuse was his statement, "It was a deliberate frame-up. Ryan only boxed with me three times. He spent all his time with McCarey, who is a sort of manager for Burns." The suggestion was that the fight had been fixed for Burns by not properly preparing Hart.

---

311 *San Francisco Bulletin*, February 27, 1906; *National Police Gazette*, March 24, 1906. The claimed relatively small amount taken in seems to contradict the prior claims that there were 5,000 persons present in the house. If those numbers were even close to being true, then much more money would have been taken in, given that the ticket prices were $1.50, $3, $5, and $10. Someone was not telling the truth. Either there were far fewer folks present or the promotion took in much more money than it claimed.
312 *National Police Gazette*, March 24, 31, 1906.

The *Los Angeles Herald* noted that before Hart had left Los Angeles, he acknowledged that Burns had defeated him honorably and was the best man. Marvin's opposite statements about the fight led the *Herald* to opine that Hart was attempting to garner interest in a potential rematch, but such was not probable, because Hart would have "no chance" with Burns. "The speed, footwork, generalship in the ring and cool-headed boxing exhibited by him when he whipped Hart to a standstill was a distinct and startling revelation to the fans who have witnessed Burns in battle when half dead from training to make weight." The *Herald* said the decision for Tommy was "eminently fair," for Burns was Hart's absolute master every minute of the battle, and every one of the 5,000 fans who witnessed the battle would agree. It opined that Hart was whimpering and trying to save face with his hometown fans, but his claims were laughable.

Burns said that if Hart would put up a $5,000 side bet, he would grant him a rematch and do the fight in Hart's hometown of Louisville, considering it easy money.[313]

313 *Los Angeles Herald*, March 6, 1906; *National Police Gazette*, March 31, 1906.

CHAPTER 7

The Fighting Champion

As heavyweight champion, Tommy Burns would prove himself worthy by fighting or attempting to fight often, in part as a result of his desire to gain respect as champion and to solidify his claim to that status. He also liked earning the money that fighting brought him.

Immediately after winning the title on February 23, returning the favor for having trained him for Hart, Burns trained Jack "Twin" Sullivan for an upcoming middleweight title bout with Hugo Kelly. Tommy and Jack boxed and wrestled on a daily basis.[314] On March 9, 1906 at the Pacific Athletic Club pavilion, Jack Sullivan fought Hugo Kelly to a 20-round draw.

Tom McCarey most wanted to match Burns with Jack O'Brien, and preliminary negotiations began. However, O'Brien had an inflated view of his worth, and wanted two-thirds of the gross receipts. The local press called O'Brien arrogant. Big fights usually took a while to get made.[315]

There were ongoing negotiations for potential Burns title fights with O'Brien, Kaufman, Root, and others. Hart had defeated Root, and O'Brien held a victory over Kaufman, so the press most wanted to see Burns fight O'Brien. However, O'Brien wanted the lion's share of the purse, continually pricing himself out of the market. Perhaps to goad him into changing his demands, the press called O'Brien's claim to the championship "ridiculously laughable." Beating an over-the-hill Bob Fitzsimmons was insufficient to legitimize O'Brien as champion. Still, while acknowledging that Burns was the real champion, the press also said, "If Burns meets and defeats O'Brien he will have a clear and undisputed right to the title."[316]

Just over one month after winning the championship, in late March 1906, Burns decided to take on two men on the same night and attempt to stop both within 20 rounds. The bouts would be held at the National Athletic Club in San Diego, California. Tommy would fight Jim O'Brien of Philadelphia or Pittsburg (depending on the source) and James Walker of Battle Creek, Michigan.

Burns worked out every afternoon in San Diego from 3 to 4:30 p.m. at the club pavilion on First Street, between avenues G and H.[317]

Both James Walker and Jim O'Brien trained at Tommy Ryan's gymnasium. Walker cited the fact that the great Tommy Ryan could not

---

314 *Los Angeles Herald*, March 1, 7, 1906.
315 *Los Angeles Herald*, March 20, 22, 1906.
316 *Los Angeles Herald*, March 25, 27, 1906.
317 *San Diego Union*, March 25, 1906.

dispose of him in 6 rounds, so he felt confident that he could make a good showing, as he had done in a number of other battles. "If Tommy Ryan could not put me out in six rounds – Burns cannot turn the trick."[318]

Burns was weighing 175 pounds. Jim O'Brien weighed 190 pounds, while James Walker weighed 180 pounds. Despite being smaller, Burns was confident that he would put both men out in less than 15 total rounds. However, "A great many of the sporting fraternity say that Burns in making such an agreement to put these two heavyweights out in twenty rounds, has bit off a great deal more than he will be able to chew." They had a point. In 1903, Jim O'Brien had gone the full 10-round distance with a middleweight-sized Burns and lost a decision.[319]

At that time, there were still those who remained staunchly opposed to boxing, especially from the religious community. In the *San Diegan-Sun*, a reverend said, "The man whose chief asset is ability to put another man to sleep by brute force is not of the highest type of manhood, and there are few attainments beneath his, or less noble."

Tommy Burns felt that a man could be religious and a fighter at the same time. He responded,

> I have not missed a Sunday at church for over a year. I do not think that pugilism interferes with a man's religion at all – at least I know it never did with mine. ... The public does not seem to designate between those prize fighters who conduct themselves in a proper way and those who want to bully over the average man who is not trained for a fighter.
>
> Take, for instance, a football game. Arms and legs are broken and men are killed, still the mothers and sisters of the players go to see the game and enjoy it. People talk about the brutality of the ring, but they seem to forget that we are trained for just that kind of thing. There are very few ministers who will condemn football because it corrupts the morals, then why should they condemn prize fighting?
>
> I was brought up in the Roman Catholic church, and when I was small and at home attended Sunday school regularly. ... Prize fighting does not corrupt the morals or destroy the religion of any man who is desirous of living the right kind of a life.[320]

The night before the bouts, Burns and National Club manager Roche encountered a pair of robbers. As they were walking down Third Street, one of the men asked Tommy for a match. As he reached into his pocket, the robber snatched a pin from Tommy's tie and ran. Tommy gave chase,

318 *San Diego Union*, March 27, 1906; *San Diego Evening Tribune*, March 29, 1906.
319 *San Diego Union*, March 28, 1906; *Los Angeles Herald*, March 29, 1906. Secondary sources indicate that Walker had results such as: 1890 LKOby1 Peter Jackson, 1893 LKOby3 Frank Childs, 1893 LKOby15 Charles Turner, 1899 LKOby4 Joe Kennedy, and 1903 LKOby5 Tommy Ryan. Boxrec.com.
320 *San Diegan-Sun*, March 28, 1906.

caught up with him, and knocked him down. He recovered his pin, although the thief managed to get up and run away, as did his companion. Boxing had its benefits in more ways than one.[321]

The doubleheader took place the next night, on March 28, 1906 at the National Athletic Club pavilion in San Diego, California, before a large crowd, one of the largest that town had seen in some time. The ring was only 18-square-feet. Billy McMahon refereed the main bouts. Many present thought that Burns had undertaken a herculean task.

Jim O'Brien was up first. He had advantages in height and weight. Despite seeming nervous, he immediately went after the champion and managed to land several blows which had no apparent effect. Burns was more than willing to swap punches. Within the first 30 seconds of the 1st round, Burns landed a swift blow to O'Brien's jaw, following it up with several in the body. Another punch to the jaw sent O'Brien down for three or four seconds.

O'Brien rose and landed a punch to Tommy's short ribs, but it had no apparent effect. They mixed it up. O'Brien was caught off his balance and went to the floor again. He rose and kept fighting gamely. Soon thereafter, Burns came in with a terrific heavy left hook and possibly a follow-up right to the jaw in quick succession and O'Brien went down and out, only 2 minutes and 18 seconds into the 1st round. He had been down three times.

After an interval of only two minutes, James Walker was second up. Walker immediately forced the fighting, demonstrating his confidence, having said before the fight that he would last at least 10 rounds. He was faster and cleverer than O'Brien, which gave Burns a chance to show some of his clever footwork for a while. Walker bore in as if he was going to win. He gave Burns two or three fast ones on the head, and then a strong left in the wind. However, the blows had no effect. Tommy just smiled.

Burns landed a hard left to the jaw that made Walker a bit dizzy. However, Walker was game and would not concede an inch, continuing his attack. Burns came back with another hard left to the head and Walker stumbled to his knees, his nose bleeding.

When he rose, Walker landed a punch to the chest. Burns then ducked between his arms and landed a terrible short right on the point of the chin. Walker whirled almost completely around, his arms dropped and he went down flat on his face like a log, landing with a resounding thud. He lay on the mat motionless, with blood running from his nose and mouth. A concerned Burns rolled him over onto his back before the count had concluded.

Burns had put Walker out at 2 minutes and 55 seconds into the 1st round, just before the end of the round. It took Walker more than five minutes to recover. "The knockout was one of the cleanest and most

---

321 *Los Angeles Herald*, March 28, 1906.

complete that has ever been seen in this city." Many spectators said it was the prettiest knockout they had ever witnessed.

Two impressed local papers agreed that Burns had proven his right to championship honors. There had been just five minutes and thirteen seconds of fighting, but there had been no play about it. The *San Diego Union* said, "Burns had shown to the satisfaction of the large audience that he was a fighter in every sense of the word." The *San Diego Evening Tribune* said Burns was fast on his feet, clever, hit a good blow, and had a cool head. "He is a dangerous man and it would seem should be able to hold his own with any man in the ring today." He was willing to fight 20 rounds against two separate fighters, no easy task, but had quickly shown his heavyweight knockout power.

Another local paper opined that O'Brien and Walker could have lasted several rounds more had they played more defense and fought to survive rather than to win. However, neither man ran away, but instead took it to the champion. "This was exactly what Burns wanted, for it gave him an opportunity to exchange wallops and to win in much less time than he could possibly do were he compelled to chase his men about the ring."[322]

Tommy took the morning train back to Los Angeles.

Burns would be out of the ring for a while with his vaudeville tour. In the meantime, it was up to the top aspirants to the crown to justify a title shot. The press and Burns most wanted a Jack O'Brien bout, but O'Brien was reticent to take the fight until he obtained the terms that he wanted.

On March 23, 1906, Mike Schreck had stopped Dave Barry in the 8th round, when his manager threw up the sponge.[323] However in late April, the referee stopped a bout between Schreck and George Gardner in the 2nd round when it appeared that Schreck was carrying Gardner and that they were faking. It was declared a no-contest.[324]

On April 18, 1906, Tommy Burns married his girlfriend of one year, a Catholic woman named Julia Keating. Tommy called her Jewel. The ceremony was held in Long Beach, California, the city where Tommy was living, just south of Los Angeles. Burns had met her a year ago in Portland, while he was training for the Sullivan fight.[325]

Also on April 18, 1906, massive and devastating earthquakes and resulting fires hit San Francisco and nearly destroyed the entire city. At least 3,000 were killed and hundreds of thousands were left homeless. That city, which was the most populous in the state, had been the center of big boxing for quite a while. The tragedy would help Los Angeles gain a further hold on big boxing in California.

---

322 *San Diego Union, San Diegan-Sun, San Diego Evening Tribune*, March 29, 1906.
323 *National Police Gazette*, April 7, 1906.
324 *Boston Globe*, April 20, 1906; *Boston Herald*, April 20, 1906.
325 *Los Angeles Herald*, April 19, May 4, 1906.

On April 24, 1906 at the Naud Junction Pavilion where had had won the title, Burns took part in an exhibition benefit to raise funds to help the victims of the San Francisco earthquakes and fires. In attendance at the exhibition were high society men and women.

Amongst the exhibitions, Burns boxed 4 rounds with George Blake, a clever boxing instructor, exhibiting his speed. The final exhibitor was retired champion James J. Jeffries, the "Burbank farmer," who wore red tights and an American flag belt. He first boxed with Jack Root. "He handled Root like a puppet. ... Jeff did not endeavor to hit and contented himself with receiving the hardest wallops that Root could send in. The last event was a two-round go between Jeffries and a husky young man named Long." This was likely Dan Long, an ex-Jeffries opponent.[326]

Apparently there had been a rematch scheduled between Jack O'Brien and Bob Fitzsimmons, but O'Brien "flunked out." Burns said that he was willing to take his place.[327]

Burns agreed to fight Bob Fitzsimmons in Philadelphia for a $15,000 purse. The *Los Angeles Herald* opined, "Of course Burns will win, and win easily. It is no trouble to whip Ruby Robert now." It also said, "There are none of the present day heavies, barring Jeffries, who seem to have more than a passing chance with the improving Canadian. There is a vast difference between the 158-pound Burns and the 180-pound Burns."[328]

DOE HUMPHREYS   SCHRECK   TIM HURST   MARVIN HART

---

326 *Los Angeles Herald*, April 24, 25, 1906.
327 *National Police Gazette*, May 12, 1906.
328 *Los Angeles Herald*, April 29, 30, 1906.

On May 3, 1906 in New York, which had recently legalized limited-round no-decision bouts, 175-pound Mike Schreck fought 195-pound Marvin Hart to a 4-round no-decision in a slugfest that was considered a victory for Schreck. However, New York fans were not necessarily impressed with either man.[329]

In late May in New York, Gus Ruhlin and Sandy Ferguson knocked each other down and almost out en-route to a 6-round no-decision that the newspapers called a draw.

Despite the earthquakes and fires, boxing was not dead in San Francisco. On May 31, 1906 at Woodward's Pavilion in San Francisco, Al Kaufman scored an impressive KO1 over Jack "Twin" Sullivan. This was significant, given that Sullivan held 20-round decision victories over Burns and Schreck. This victory served to boost Kaufman, but it boomed Jack O'Brien even further, given that he held a dominant knockout victory over Kaufman.

Jack Johnson mostly fought other black fighters, because most of the top white contenders drew the color line. In March, he won a 15-round decision over Joe Jeannette. In April, he scored a KO7 over Black Bill and won a 15-round decision over Sam Langford.

The Burns-Fitzsimmons bout was eventually called off in July, when the Pennsylvania governor put a stop to it.[330]

A Burns-Gus Ruhlin match was arranged, but it fell through. Tom also agreed to meet Mike Schreck, but the club that was going to host the bout withdrew its offer.[331]

On July 12, 1906 in Colorado, "Fireman" Jim Flynn fought Jack "Twin" Sullivan to a 15-round draw. Sullivan was the better boxer, but Flynn was more aggressive and carried the fight to Sullivan in every round.[332]

On July 16, 1906 in Philadelphia, 175-pound Jack O'Brien fought 200-pound Sam Berger in a competitive 6-round no-decision bout. The *National Police Gazette* and several other papers reported that Berger had defeated O'Brien. However, there appears to be a split in news reports regarding who won or whether it was really a draw. Berger was an ex-amateur who had just begun his pro career. He had won a gold medal as a heavyweight at the 1904 Olympics. Certainly, Berger's stock went up as a result of his strong performance against O'Brien.

Burns said that he was willing to fight Berger. He even offered to stop Sam within 20 rounds or forfeit his end of the purse. However, Berger was relatively green in the pro game and had not yet fought past 6 rounds. It was not clear how he would do with Burns or O'Brien in a lengthy bout.[333]

---

329 *New York Sun, New York World*, May 4, 1906; *National Police Gazette*, May 19, 1906.
330 *Los Angeles Herald*, July 12, 13, 1906; *National Police Gazette*, July 21, 1906.
331 *National Police Gazette*, July 21, 1906.
332 *National Police Gazette*, July 28, 1906.
333 *National Police Gazette*, August 4, 1906; *Los Angeles Herald*, July 17, 18, 25, 1906.

There was talk of Burns being matched with Hugo Kelly for a fight to be held in late August or September, but Kelly wanted the fight to be held at a 165-pound catch-weight, which was not acceptable.[334]

On August 7, 1906 at the Pacific Athletic Club pavilion at Naud Junction in Los Angeles, Burns refereed the Harry Baker-Frankie O'Neil bout, awarding the 20-round decision to Baker. Burns also refereed several bouts at a show held there on August 17, 1906.

As of August 1906, a match was arranged between Burns and Al Kaufman, who was considered to be the best of the young rising heavyweights. Kaufman had a 1905 LKOby17 Jack O'Brien but a 1906 KO14 Dave Barry and KO1 Jack "Twin" Sullivan.[335]

Burns and Kaufman had sparred earlier in the year, when Tommy was preparing for Hart and Al was preparing for Barry. "According to Tommy Burns, what he did to Kaufmann during the training times would be a shame to relate." Burns claimed to have easily handled Kaufman.[336]

The champion might have had a point regarding his superiority over Kaufman, because Billy Delaney, Kaufman's manager, declared that the bout was off, giving the excuse that Al had theatrical engagements. The press did not buy it. Many called Kaufman afraid of Tommy. "Poor Tommy Burns is again wondering whether or not he is doomed to retire because no one will agree to meet him in the ring."[337]

Burns claimed that Berger and O'Brien were out for easy money and were fakers. Tom alleged that the Berger-O'Brien bout was a fake, claiming that O'Brien had agreed to go easy so that they could obtain even more money for a rematch. He said that both men were afraid of him. Tom offered to give Sam Berger $1,000 of his own money if he could merely last 20 rounds with him.[338]

Perhaps trying to save face, Kaufman came out and said that he would fight Burns after all. Tommy said that he would put him away in short order, and then go after O'Brien and Berger. "Those fellows have got to meet me sooner or later and the quicker it is over the better."[339]

On August 22, 1906, Burns took part in a matinee exhibition at Arcadia, California, sparring 3 rounds with Abdul "The Terrible Turk" Malgan. "Tommy Burns clipped Abdul Malgan with a twelve-ounce glove that all but sent the big oriental to the mat." They were sparring at a fast rate when Tommy accidentally landed a hard right. "The Turk stopped and staggered about the ring, bleeding profusely from the mouth." However, Malgan's powerful physique "stood him in good stead, and after a short respite Abdul

---

334 *Los Angeles Herald*, July 27, 28, 1906.
335 *Los Angeles Herald*, August 12, 1906; *National Police Gazette*, September 8, 1906.
336 *Los Angeles Herald*, August 12, 1906.
337 *Los Angeles Herald*, August 15, 1906; *National Police Gazette*, September 8, 1906.
338 *Los Angeles Herald*, August 16, 1906.
339 *Los Angeles Herald*, August 17, 1906.

insisted upon continuing and Tommy withheld his hurricane right for the remainder of the bout."[340]

Abdul Malgan continued exhibition sparring with Burns on a daily basis, although some were wondering how long he could last as Tommy's sparring partner.[341]

Since stating that he was willing to fight Burns, Al Kaufman had not been heard from. The press felt that he was side-stepping and insincere like O'Brien.[342]

A frustrated Burns stated,

> I will defend my title as heavyweight champion of the world against all comers, none barred. By this I mean white, black, Mexican, Indian or any other nationality without regard to color, size or nativity. I propose to be the champion of the world, not the white or the Canadian or the American or any other limited degree of champion. If I am not the best man in the heavyweight division I don't want to hold the title.

Burns was increasingly gaining respect and recognition. The *National Police Gazette* changed its position in regard to Burns and started recognizing him as champion. It said,

> It has been the custom in the past…for the big fellows who have no shadow of a claim upon the title, among them Berger, Kaufman and O'Brien, to sneer at the claims of Burns, but it is notably true that Tommy has offered this trio every reasonable inducement to get them in a ring for a fight and has signally failed. Now Burns proposes to put it up to them in such a manner that they must fight or take off their hats to him as their master. Talk will not go with the public any longer, especially since Burns has issued this remarkable defi to the world. It is a case of fight or shut up.[343]

"Fireman" Jim Flynn of Pueblo, Colorado, said that he was anxious to meet Burns. Flynn had recently secured a 15-round draw against the respected Jack "Twin" Sullivan, and was considered to be an entertaining and improving up-and-comer by those who had seen him in action. He had also fought George Gardner to a 1904 10-round draw and Joe Cotton to a 1902 20-round draw. His most notable loss was a knockout in 8 rounds to Jack Root back in 1903. Flynn also had a 1904 W20 Cyclone Kelly and D10 Harry Peppers, two fighters whom Burns had knocked out, and a KO9 Fred Cooley. Flynn, who was of Irish-Italian heritage, had changed his name from Andrew Schreiglione. He was a former locomotive fireman.

---

340 *Los Angeles Herald*, August 23, 1906.
341 *Los Angeles Herald*, August 25, 1906.
342 *Los Angeles Herald*, August 30, 1906.
343 *National Police Gazette*, September 22, 1906.

Burns, Flynn, and the Pacific Athletic Club engaged in negotiations. As of September 6, Pacific Club manager Tom McCarey announced that Burns and Flynn would fight at Naud Junction in late September. The local *Los Angeles Herald* said Flynn possessed a far better record than "runaway" Kaufman anyhow, so the bout would be as good or better with Flynn.[344]

While Burns was training to fight Flynn, negotiations for a subsequent bout with Jack O'Brien were ongoing, should Burns emerge victorious. There was an offer out of Los Angeles for a guaranteed $20,000 purse, which was agreeable to O'Brien. Things were looking up.

Burns said that he would fight O'Brien differently than he did Hart, because he respected Marvin's knockout punching power, while he did not feel the same way about Jack's punch. He recognized that O'Brien was the cleverest and shiftiest man in the ring, but felt that he could go after him with no fear of receiving a knockout blow. The press thought that such a bout would be the fastest seen in years.[345]

JACK O'BRIEN

As of mid-September, O'Brien continued playing some negotiating games, while Burns and Flynn continued training for their bout, now set for October 2. Jim Flynn claimed to be 23 years old, and "undoubtedly he is a hard nut to crack."[346]

McCarey did not want to offer a purse guarantee to O'Brien or Burns, but agreed to split the gate receipts evenly with them, 50/50. The proposed date for the fight was Thanksgiving Day.[347]

Since Burns accused O'Brien of picking dubs and fixing his fights, O'Brien, when talking about who his next opponent might be, sarcastically said, "Of course I will fight the easiest man I can find." When asked about Burns, O'Brien said, "Had the honor of securing a decision over him one night in Milwaukee. Why haven't I met him again? Well, to tell the truth, I have been afraid of him and when I do meet him it must be for something remunerative."

344 *Los Angeles Herald*, August 30, September 7, 1906.
345 *Los Angeles Herald*, September 14, 1906; *National Police Gazette*, September 29, 1906.
346 *Los Angeles Herald*, September 16, 17, 1906.
347 *Los Angeles Times*, September 18, 1906.

Jim Flynn looked good in his training at the East Side Athletic Club. On September 18, he took a long 10-mile run, had a rub down and meal, took a walk through Eastlake Park, and at 3 p.m. did his gym work. First, Flynn worked the pulleys, punching bag, and shadow boxed.

Following his preliminary work, Flynn sparred with Arthur Collins and Kid Dewey, both black heavyweights, and lightweight Frank Sheedy. Flynn was always in range, sailing in. He took his sparring partners' hard blows without flinching and rocked their heads with short-arm jolts. There was no telegraphing of his blows. Flynn also demonstrated some fancy blocking skills, and was always ready to fire back a hard jab or hook. Afterwards, Collins said, "I'm sorry for Burns. If Flynn cuts loose with either hand at close quarters there will be some counting."

The 170-pound Dewey was fast, but not fast enough to handle Flynn, who proved that "even the fastest man must step lively to escape that boring in style and close quarter work Flynn dishes up." Flynn was "never off his feet going backward or forward and works either hand with ease."[348]

On the 19th, Flynn and Dewey sparred 2 fast rounds, mixing it up in lively style, both throwing hard blows. Lightweight Billy Walsh was up next for another 2 rounds, and then Arthur Collins went 4 hard rounds. Flynn was showing up well in his work, which was observed by a large crowd that included Jack O'Brien and Tom McCarey. O'Brien remarked that Flynn was one of the toughest boys he had seen in the ring.

---

348 *Los Angeles Herald, Los Angeles Times*, September 19, 1906.

O'Brien, on left, shakes Flynn's hand. Photos of Flynn follow on right.

The very confident Burns again said that he would post $1,000 guaranteeing that he would knock out Sam Berger in 20 rounds. He also said that he would fight Jack O'Brien for a $5,000 side bet. The *Los Angeles Times* felt that Burns should be cautious about making such speeches, for both Berger and O'Brien were a lot better than men like Billy Woods, Mike Schreck, and Jack Sullivan.[349]

Both Flynn and Burns were training faithfully. Both had posted their $250 forfeit money guaranteeing their appearances. On September 22, Flynn accidentally knocked out lightweight sparring partner Eddie Webster.

Burns met with O'Brien and McCarey to further discuss a potential fight. When Tommy offered to shake hands, O'Brien drew back and remarked, "Gentlemen never shake hands with fakers, and that is what you call me, I see from the papers." Burns grew angry and said, "Yes, of all the fakers and fixers, you are the limit. You never fought in your life without having it fixed beforehand." O'Brien replied, "I am a faker. I let you stay with me six rounds in Milwaukee when you begged me not to knock you out. I could have put you away then and I believe I can do it again. It is such dubs as you that ruin a fighting man's reputation. Yes, I faked once." Burns flew off the handle and "let go with a list of adjectives anything but complimentary," and wanted to fight right then and there, but O'Brien

---

349 *Los Angeles Herald, Los Angeles Times*, September 20, 1906.

refused, saying that he was no barroom fighter, but would be content to take his chances in the ring and give Tommy a thrashing there. The war of words continued. Burns accused O'Brien of being yellow. O'Brien called Burns the greatest dub ever. Those present in the room finally pulled Tommy away.[350]

The press continued scouting the combatants for the upcoming championship bout. Flynn was a called a natural fighter whose methods were to wade in on top of his man and punch to hurt. "Flynn is surely rugged and, what is more, he is dangerous." It was hard for him to find sparring partners. In one session, Flynn went after Kid Dewey and Arthur Collins, his two black sparring partners, knocking them both out, despite the fact that "an ordinary fighter would have had his hands full with Dewey alone."[351]

On September 23 in sparring, Flynn knocked out Al Godfrey. Flynn also sparred 4 rounds each with Kid Webster, Kid Dalton, and Arthur Collins.[352]

The newsmen said Flynn had a natural ruggedness, and his condition was superb. He was working on his speed, the mantra from his manager Jack Linke, who said that Hart was too slow for Burns. Every morning, six chickens were let loose, and Flynn was set to catching them. The manner in which he was handling his sparring partners was causing many to become imbued with respect for Flynn.

George Memsic, Tommy Burns, Billy Woods

350 *Los Angeles Herald, Los Angeles Times*, September 23, 1906.
351 *Los Angeles Examiner*, September 23, 1906.
352 *Los Angeles Examiner*, September 24, 1906.

Burns was training hard at Arcadia. He said, "I am taking no chances with this fellow, and I am going to be in the best possible shape."[353]

On September 25, in the morning, Burns took a 12-mile run. He later took a 10-mile horseback ride. Tommy sparred 3 rounds at a hammer and tongs pace with former foe Billy Woods. He then sparred 3 rounds with lightweight George Memsic, also known as Tommy's so-called "cousin" Jimmy Burns. Tom finished with 2 rounds of shadow sparring and a couple rounds at the bags and with the rope. After his day's work, Burns tipped the scales at 169 ¾ pounds.

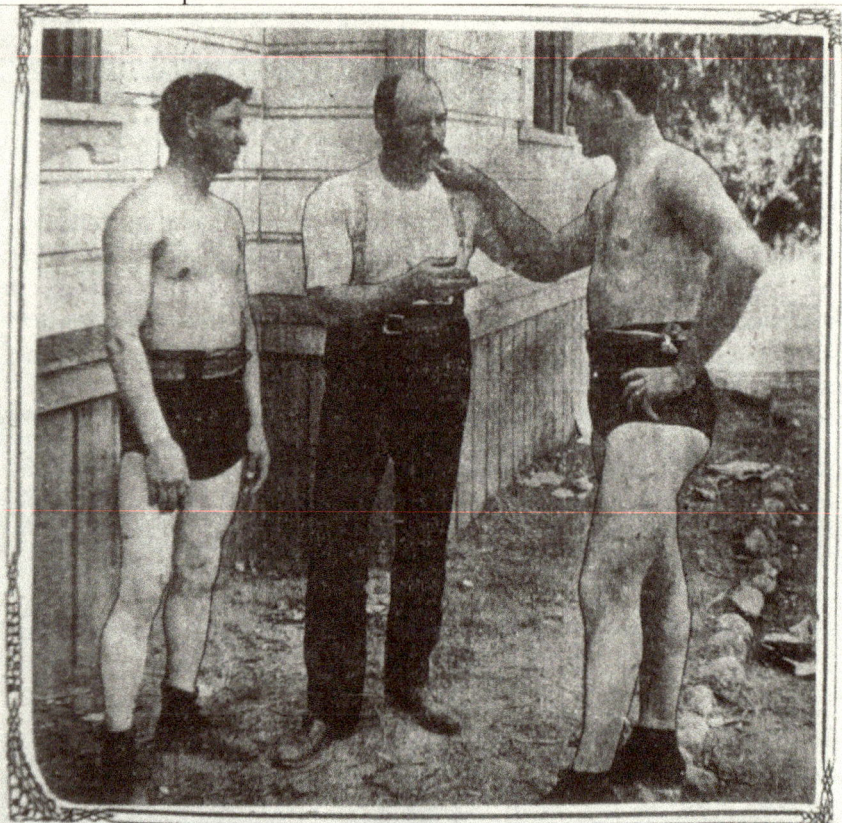

Trainer Lewis giving Burns instructions about his work at the Arcadia camp. At the left is Jimmy Burns, and at the right the "real thing."

That day, Flynn went 4 rounds with his heavy sparring partners and 3 rounds with Kid Dalton and Kid Webster. Flynn weighed about two pounds less than Burns.[354]

On the 26th, Flynn sparred 3 rounds each with lightweights Kid Ramer and Frank Sheek, and also regular sparring partner Arthur Collins.

353 *Los Angeles Herald, Los Angeles Times,* September 26, 1906.
354 *Los Angeles Examiner,* September 26, 1906.

Both fighters had wives who were supportive of their training endeavors.[355]

On September 27, Flynn dropped Kid Williams to the mat several times and caused him to quit sparring after 2 rounds. It was said that Burns, who was quite confident of victory, might be underrating his opponent.[356]

A writer for the *Los Angeles Examiner* noted that promoters were constantly trying to get James J. Jeffries to come out of retirement, to no avail. This reporter felt that none of the contenders stood a chance with him anyhow. Sam Berger had nothing but a 6-round bout with O'Brien. Al Kaufman did not have enough class, for O'Brien beat him for 17 rounds and then knocked him out. "Jack Johnson?

Principals in the heavyweight battle Tuesday night.

They cannot build a fence high enough to keep the black-and-tan champion from climbing over and taking to the woods. Johnson is the best fighter in the bunch, but he has a yellow streak a foot wide." O'Brien could not run fast enough to get away from Jeffries, who sooner or later would corner him, land his mighty left, and end matters.[357]

There was talk of Jack O'Brien possibly fighting Fred Cooley. Earlier in the year, Cooley had been O'Brien's sparring partner, but in one of their sparring bouts, Cooley had landed a punch that dropped O'Brien and possibly even knocked him out. O'Brien said that he would fight both Cooley and another man on the same night. There were also discussions of a potential O'Brien bout with Sam Berger in San Francisco.[358]

---

355 *Los Angeles Examiner*, September 27, 1906.
356 *Los Angeles Herald*, September 28, 1906.
357 *Los Angeles Examiner*, September 28, 1906.
358 *Los Angeles Times*, September 29, 1906.

Burns Surrounded by His Colored Supporters.

Those who watched Jim Flynn train on September 29 were impressed. "The consensus of opinion is that Flynn has a decidedly wicked punch, and is quick at delivering it." Flynn said, "If Burns stands up and fights, I will guarantee I will not take one step backward. ... I have had some pretty hard knocks in my days and can stand a few more." Flynn said that his chances to win were lessened if Burns took to his bicycle and ran away.

At that point, Burns was a 10 to 8 and 10 to 7 betting favorite. However, Flynn had shown so well in his training that generally, sentiment was about evenly divided as to who would emerge victorious.

Burns said that he never felt better in his life. He gave Flynn credit for being a good man, but expected to defeat him in a decisive manner. "I have no fear for the outcome of the fight."

They were fighting for 50% of the gate, to be divided 60% to the winner and 40% to the loser. Burns would receive a 5-10% bonus depending upon the size of the house.

A couple days before the fight, Flynn was listed as weighing about 169 pounds and standing 5'9 ½" to Burns' 170 pounds and 5'7". Although allegedly Flynn was 22 or 23 years old, secondary sources indicate that he was really age 26. Burns was 25 years old.

The press said the match was about the best balanced made in a long time. Although they weighed the same, Flynn appeared to be the more muscular. Burns had the longer reach. "The dopesters will have a hard time figuring out the result."

The *Times* opined that Burns would probably win a 20-round decision. "Very few believe that Burns can knock Flynn out." Many believed that if Tommy mixed it with Flynn that Burns might be knocked out.

The *Herald* said the question surrounding the bout was whether Flynn could weather the storm of blows that Burns would rain upon him, and whether Tommy had the punch to put away such a tough customer.

The *Examiner* opined that on form, Burns should win easily. "He knows how to jab and get away again, and though he has not shown us punch enough to stop a good lightweight, Thomas is there with the ringcraft that wins decisions." Burns had defeated Hart "systematically and thoroughly" in "the worst fight ever seen." However, it thought that if Flynn fought as he trained, Burns would have no chance to dance, fiddle and feint, but would have to fight. "There is only one way to handle a rough chap who comes at you like a bear, and that is to stand up and fight him back. Running may go for a time, but sooner or later the aggressor corners the sprinter and it becomes a stand-up fight." If Flynn tried to box with Burns, Tommy would "outpoint him to a moral certainty." Both fighters were in top condition. Burns looked fat, but that was only because he was a naturally chunky fellow. Ultimately, it thought that Burns would win a decision. If Flynn won, it would have to be via a knockout.[359]

Two days before the fight, on September 30, Burns boxed with Billy Woods for the last time. After his workout, he weighed 170 pounds. Flynn claimed to weigh one pound less. In his corner, Tommy would have

---

359 *Los Angeles Herald, Los Angeles Times, Los Angeles Examiner,* September 30, 1906. Boxrec.com.

Professor Lewis, who was known as a wrestler, while Flynn would have manager Jack Linke and De Witt Van Court.[360]

The day before the fight, it was said that the "sports who have seen Flynn have an idea that he will give Burns a tough battle and probably a beating, for he is a husky young giant and has had considerable experience. He has trained hard." One reporter even said, "A look at the records of both men would lead to a belief that Flynn has something of a margin on Burns." The local press certainly got behind the bout.[361]

Flynn was not as wide or as thick, but he was noted for his iron jaw and corrugated front. "He does not mind punishment; he likes it." He could dish it and take it.

It was thought that the weather could be a factor in the fight. It had been very hot during the last few days, and was likely to hit well over 100 degrees. "It is hard to go twenty rounds under the most favorable condition, but to fight a full hour in an oven is enough to put a crimp in the most enthusiastic nature."[362]

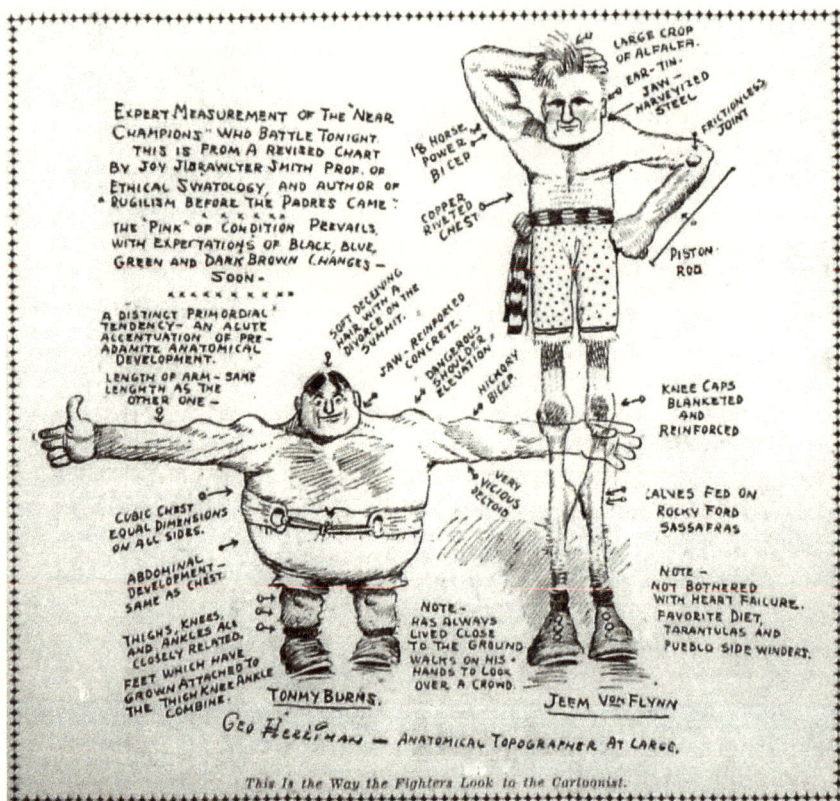

This Is the Way the Fighters Look to the Cartoonist.

360 *Los Angeles Examiner*, October 1, 1906.
361 *Los Angeles Herald, Los Angeles Times*, October 1, 1906.
362 *Los Angeles Examiner*, October 2, 1906.

Tommy Burns and "Fireman" Jim Flynn fought in Los Angeles on Tuesday October 2, 1906 at the Pacific Athletic Club's Naud Junction Pavilion. Eddie Robinson refereed. The main fight was set to begin around 9 p.m.

A vast throng of thousands crowded into the pavilion. Seating capacity was sorely taxed. More interest attended the bout than any other ring contest in Los Angeles.

Before the fight, both Jack O'Brien and Jim Jeffries were introduced to the crowd, and they got into the ring and shook hands. Announcer Cook introduced O'Brien, who received a deafening cheer. O'Brien said that Los Angeles was a lovely town with lovely people. He concluded by saying, "The newspapers of the country have said that I am anxious to meet Mr. Jeffries in the ring. Gentlemen, at last I have met Mr. Jeffries in the ring, and wish to state that this is the only way I wish to meet him." The crowd admired his humble words and his popularity was enhanced many times over. Jeffries, who wasn't much for talking or speeches, said, "All I can say is that I wish to thank the gentleman for his compliment."

Burns was first into the ring, followed shortly thereafter by Flynn. Tom sat in his corner looking splendid and extremely confident. Both threw off their robes and readied themselves for the bout. Flynn's muscles stood out all over his body, especially his abdomen. He appeared to be a well-trained athlete.

The round-by-round account is an amalgamation of the *Los Angeles Herald*, *Los Angeles Times*, and *Los Angeles Examiner* accounts. Jack O'Brien wrote the *Examiner* round-by-round account.[363]

1 – Burns led with his left and Flynn gave him no time to fiddle. They rushed into a clinch, with Burns uppercutting. They roughed it in the clinches from the start. Burns hit the stomach and ribs and uppercut the jaw. As they broke, Flynn landed a right and left to the face. Burns danced away and landed a light right on the head and left to the face. They clinched and fought fiercely. On the breakaway, Burns landed a right to the head. Burns forced matters, but Flynn was cool and calm. The pace was fast, which was kept up for the whole fight. They were clinched at the gong and the sports cheered loudly.

Jack O'Brien said Burns showed good judgment in his outside fiddling and feinting, and demonstrated superior generalship in doing splendid work in the clinches with telling short shots on Flynn's body while ducking Jim's blows. Burns' short build was a big advantage to him on the inside. "Burns looks very superior in this round."

2 – Burns landed a light left and they clinched. Flynn hit the body with his left. Flynn did the showier work and sent Burns back with a right to the ear.

363 *Los Angeles Daily Times, Los Angeles Herald, Los Angeles Examiner*, October 3, 1906.

He scored again to the face, while Burns threw his head onto Flynn's shoulder and bore into the body. As they came to another clinch and Burns missed a left lead, Flynn landed his left to the body. On the break, Flynn landed a right to the head. They wrestled about the ring with their heads close together. As they broke, Flynn landed a hard left to Tommy's eye. The crowd cheered Flynn for the fast battle that he was putting up.

O'Brien said they were fighting like demons. Burns was still acting cool, and took advantage of the clinches, working well on the inside. He blocked most of Flynn's leads and crossed inside onto Jim's jaw. He repeatedly landed his right to the body. A small mouse appeared on Flynn's right eye. As Tommy returned to his corner, a small black swelling could be seen on his right eye. It was Tom's round by a slight margin.

3 – As they rushed to a clinch, Flynn landed a right to the body. Both fought savagely on the inside. As they parted, Burns sent a right to the face. Flynn came in close and landed a hard right hook to the face. Burns landed a left to the face and used both hands in the clinch. As they broke, there was an exchange of lefts to the face. Burns landed hard rights to the body and face. O'Brien said Flynn had settled down and was doing better work. Burns took his time and was very cool.

Burns demonstrated his good footwork. After fiddling and dancing, Tommy put in a hard right and left to the mouth and nose, bringing blood for the first time in the fight. Bloody Flynn dashed in like a whirlwind, but Burns stopped him with a hard right to the jaw. As the gong rang, Burns landed a right to the head. Burns won the round by a good margin. Tom hopped to his corner, while Flynn went slowly and was met with a splash of water from one of his seconds.

4 – Burns had the decided advantage in this round as well. He made Flynn miss his hard swings. Tom would feint and make Jim try to block imagined blows, and then hit him with straight lefts and follow with right swings.

They rushed to a clinch and Flynn put a right to the body, while Burns uppercut viciously to the jaw and stomach. They exchanged heavy blows to the body and head. The crowd cheered their work. Flynn led and forced Tommy against the ropes, but Burns bore Flynn down with his weight. O'Brien observed that Burns was holding the neck with his left and hitting with his right, doing so on a couple of occasions. Tom liked to hold and hit. Flynn landed a hard right to the heart and the crowd cheered. Burns jabbed as they came to a clinch, and then landed a hard right and left to the head. As they broke, Burns shot in a hard right to the face. O'Brien said that Burns' superior work was telling. He showed class, and was a "much improved boxer since I saw him last in 1904."

5 – Tommy opened with a right to the ribs and attempted to force the fighting, thinking that Jim was weakening. However, Flynn was still strong and carried the fight right back and kept it even. Flynn landed a left to the

face and uppercut his right to the jaw. Burns danced away, and as they met again, Tom hooked a right to the head. They fought all over the ring, and the crowd went wild. Flynn landed a right and left to the head, but Burns countered with a right to the jaw. They clinched and Burns used both hands during the infighting. Jabs again stopped Flynn and Tommy landed under his guard with hard rights. At the gong, he sent a left to the face.

O'Brien, who seemed to view the fight a bit differently than the newsmen, said Flynn was making a splendid fight of it, but the odds were against him, for he was being "completely outclassed by a more finished boxer and fighter combined." Flynn's leads were too amateurish and his blows ineffective. Burns' class was showing to superior advantage. Regardless of the punishment, Flynn was still continually forcing matters. Burns feinted and countered with rights and lefts. Jack actually opined that it would be better to stop the contest and declare Burns the winner in order to save the overmatched Flynn from a terrible beating. "There is no doubt that Flynn is game."

6 – The newspapers said it was another even round with fast work. Flynn landed a left to the head but Burns landed a right to the jaw. Tom repeated the dose to the head. Burns feinted, jabbed and swung in succession, his usual course of action. "He drew Flynn open and then landed hard. Flynn got in close and chopped high left swings which put Burns's right eye to the bad and opened up a cut." The pace was beginning to tell, and Burns showed the first signs of fatigue. When Flynn swung and missed and went to the floor, Tommy stepped back and got a rest. They rushed to a clinch and the referee was forced to break them. The crowd was cheering and enjoying the fight.

O'Brien said Flynn was still leading and forced Burns around the ring. Burns danced around as usual, jabbing right and left to the face with telling effect. In the clinches, Tom illegally held with his left and punched with his right, but the referee either didn't notice or didn't care. Flynn landed several punches, but O'Brien felt they had little effect on Burns.

7 – The newspapers said Flynn had an advantage in this round. He landed hard blows with both hands. He forced matters and had Tommy on the ropes. However, Burns kept cool. Tom sent a right to the face at the gong.

O'Brien saw things differently. He said Burns did more good work with both hands to the body. He was able to duck Flynn's leads. Tom landed a telling right cross. Flynn was still forcing but invariably clinching when they came close. "I cannot understand why Flynn does so, as he is positively at sea in a clinch." He also opined that De Witt Van Court was the only member of Flynn's corner who was helping him much.

8 – Flynn continued his good work and kept it even. They fought to a clinch and Flynn landed a left to the face, driving Burns back to the ropes. They squared off again and Flynn landed a vicious right to the head. They

clinched. Burns performed some of his dancing antics and led with an effective right and left. After some more fiddling, Burns shifted and shot in a hard left to the stomach, although O'Brien felt that it missed. Burns showed signs of recovering and landed hard to the face and ribs. They were clinched at the gong. O'Brien felt that Burns seemed a bit more fatigued and noted that the mouse under his right eye was growing larger. Still, Tom sat in his corner peacefully, with the same confident air.

9 – At first, they started their clinching tactics again. When they broke, Flynn landed two lefts to the head. Burns rushed Flynn against the ropes with several heavy body blows, and in the clinch, uppercut his right to the face and body. Tommy was trying hard to knock him down. However, Flynn did the same, and they exchanged blow for blow. At the break, they exchanged rights and lefts to the face and body.

Flynn again sent a right and left to the body and rushed Burns to the ropes. While Burns was against the ropes, Flynn landed several telling blows with both hands to the head. Burns circled and backed out of the corner and then landed left and right to the body in hurricane fashion. Flynn landed a right uppercut as Tom ducked. The crowd cheered, but no harm was done.

Although his own mouth and nose were badly banged up, Flynn was doing good work, ducking several blows and landing to the face and body. He was still strong at the close of the round. Flynn staggered Burns with a hard right to the jaw, the best punch that he had landed in the fight thus far. On a break, Flynn landed another right to the head. They were clinched at the gong. Flynn's spurt in this round, which was the best of the fight thus far, earned it for him. O'Brien agreed that Flynn was much improved and apparently stronger than Burns in this round.

10 – Flynn began the round with a confident air and led and landed a left hook on the jaw. They resumed the same terrific pace. Burns landed a heavy left to the face and used his right in the clinch, resting his head against Flynn. They exchanged several lefts to the face and body. Flynn landed a hook to the stomach and jaw. Both were doing effective work, and O'Brien even noted that Flynn's form was improving.

However, one writer opined that Flynn began tiring, and was worried about the jabs and rights to the face that Burns was landing. O'Brien said Tom landed a left hook to the jaw. He then landed a right lead to the jaw and followed it with a jab and two more straight rights. Flynn hung on in a clinch and showed signs of weakness. Despite this, the newsmen said that at the round's conclusion, Jim made a stand and fought back toe to toe until they clinched. At the gong, Burns landed a hard left to the face. O'Brien said a cut showed on Burns' right eye.

11 – Burns began coming after Flynn. He attacked, jabbing and clinching, looking for an opening for a hard swing. O'Brien said Burns was

outgeneraling Flynn, who in return was trying to beat Tommy with gameness. Burns landed a light left and they clinched. Referee Robinson was forced to part them. Burns sent a left to the head and a heavy right to the face. They exchanged vicious blows at short range. Flynn landed right and left to the heart. Burns landed rights to the jaw and Flynn hung on in the clinches, which allowed Burns to do effective body work. Flynn rushed and landed a hard right to the ear. They continued exchanging. O'Brien opined, "Burns realizes that he cannot outgame Flynn and is taking to leading and jabbing the face constantly, easily stepping back from Flynn's leads." Flynn landed two lefts to the head, but they seemed to have no effect. Burns jabbed Flynn's face repeatedly, and they stood glaring at each other at the gong. Flynn returned to his corner bleeding from his nose and mouth. O'Brien said, "Burns seems worried a bit but still wears that supremely confident air."

12 – Burns came up fresh, dancing about. They mixed it frequently. Flynn landed his left uppercut and they fiddled and clinched. They exchanged rights and lefts to the head and wrestled about the ring. On the inside, Burns landed uppercuts to the chin. Flynn fought back gamely, and had the crowd with him.

13 – The crowd cheered Flynn at the start of the round, and he responded with his best effort, leading and landing effectively to the body. They rushed to a clinch and Burns got in a left to the face. The referee separated them. They again clinched. Flynn rushed Burns against the ropes but tripped and fell backwards to the ground, rising immediately. O'Brien said it was a half slip and half push. Burns attacked with rights and lefts to the head, and in the clinch, uppercut with his right, causing Flynn to twist and try to break. Burns landed two hard rights which made Flynn appear groggy. Flynn hung on to save himself. At the bell, Burns was the stronger of the two.

14 – According to one *Examiner* writer, with about 30 seconds left in the round, a Burns right caught Flynn on the jaw, Jim's knees sagged, and he went down to the ground on his hands. For the first time in the fight, he was really hurt. When he rose, Burns whipped another right over. Flynn staggered but remained upright. Burns bombarded his chin with punches for the next 20 seconds, but the bell ended the "punching bag work."

The *Times'* version of the 14th round said that Burns, who was very strong, immediately rushed and showered blows upon Flynn, who was very groggy. Burns landed four rights to the jaw in succession, but Flynn took them and came back for more. However, "It was more than human power could stand, and Flynn went down twice for the count, at one time being nearly out." He recovered sufficiently to fight back gamely, roughing it to protect himself, but grew tired quickly. Flynn was hammered into a groggy state and only saved by the bell.

The *Herald* and O'Brien accounts did not mention any knockdown. According to the *Herald's* version of this round, Flynn sent a right to the body and they clinched. Burns landed a heavy right and left to the face. As they came to a clinch, Burns sent a hard right uppercut to the jaw. Flynn threw a hard right to the body, but Burns didn't mind it and shot a heavy right to the face that staggered Flynn. Burns followed his advantage. Flynn hung on. Burns shot in five hard rights to the face in succession and Flynn was saved by the gong.

O'Brien said Flynn came up smiling and led, though without effect. Burns landed repeatedly with left and right to the stomach and right to the jaw. Flynn landed to the body with both hands. Tom would land on the jaw and Flynn would respond with body punches. Burns landed three jabs to the face in succession. Flynn was fighting desperately, but Burns was backing him all around the ring, trying to place a right swing. Tom landed five effective rights to the jaw and the bell rang.

15 – A *Herald* version said the boxers met in the middle of the ring and Burns landed a heavy right to the jaw that sent Flynn down for a three-count. Burns rushed and landed several right hooks to the face and jaw. Flynn went down again on his back, and just at the count of ten rose from his knees. Burns went in and hammered him mercilessly on the jaw. Jim rallied and shot a right to Tom's jaw. Tommy rushed again and peppered his face and jaw with several rights and lefts until Flynn dropped for the final time.

The *Times'* version of the round said Flynn came up weak, and was an easy mark. He received awful punishment from Burns, who rushed him like a tiger and forced the fighting. He simply battered Flynn down and out, dropping him three times in all. Flynn barely beat the count after the first knockdown of the round, rising just as the referee was counting 'ten.' Burns inflicted terrific punishment and dropped him again. Flynn was groggy and grappled to save himself. When Flynn made his last desperate rush, Tommy sent over the finishing right swing to the jaw and Flynn fell back and rolled over in agony for the third and final knockdown of the round. He was counted out and remained unconscious.

An *Examiner* version said Flynn was still dazed when he started the round. Burns rushed him into a corner and landed a right cross to the chin and Flynn went down on his back. After five seconds, he dragged himself to his knees, and in that position was counted out. He rose after the tenth second. Referee Robinson made a move to catch Burns' elbow and stop the fight, but changed his mind, and, stepping aside, allowed the fight to continue. Tom soon had him down again. Flynn rolled over and rose to his feet, staggering. Burns looked at the referee as if to question the advisability of continuing with the slaughter, but Robinson said nothing and allowed it to continue. Though ready to fall again, Flynn was still game, and he threw some wild swings until he dropped without being hit. Robinson had him get up again and Burns tore in, landing a punch high up on the side of the head which sent Flynn to the floor face down. Van Court jumped through the ropes and the fight was over.

Jack O'Brien said Flynn came out of his corner in a dazed condition. After a clinch, Burns went after him. He hit Flynn repeatedly with rights to the face, staggering him. He set himself for a right swing which caught Flynn on the jaw and he went to the floor. Flynn rose on the count of ten and then went to the mat again without being hit. The referee warned him not to do it again or he would be disqualified. Flynn rushed at Burns and in an exchange of wallops Burns landed a left to the head, putting him down and out. Referee Robinson raised Burns' arm and declared him the winner.

The police found it difficult to prevent spectators from entering the ring to catch a glimpse at the man who lay unconscious, stretched out on the ring floor as his seconds tried desperately to revive him.

Flynn was out cold for ten minutes. De Witt Van Court objected to Councilman Doc Houghton's attempt to assume charge of Flynn while he was unconscious, and there was a minor disturbance. Jim was finally revived by vigorous fanning, and helped to the dressing room by his seconds.

Afterwards, in the dressing room, Flynn claimed that his supporter slipped down off his body, thus allowing Burns' low blows to weaken him. He attributed his knockout loss to this fact.

Burns claimed to have hurt or broken his left hand in the 3rd round. After the battle, he was unable to close it. His right thumb was sprained as well. However, he was still able to use his hands to administer punishment when he needed to do so.

Flynn's game effort made Tommy's victory over him even more impressive. Burns had demonstrated skill, strength, toughness, coolness, endurance, and power in defeating a good opponent.

Jack O'Brien said Flynn was a very game man, but Burns was a clever and experienced boxer, fully capable of being classed with the best men in the world. Burns showed his superiority in maintaining a cool head throughout the contest, never allowing Flynn to land an effective punch.

The *Los Angeles Times* said Flynn fought as game a battle as any man had ever fought. Up until the 14th round, he stood toe to toe with Burns and returned punch for punch, and was just as strong as Tommy, although Tom was outboxing him.

Despite his game effort, in only two rounds did Flynn have the best of it, although in several rounds he kept matters even. For all his effort, Flynn was not able to hurt Burns. Tommy was considerably battered up though, and had been given one of the hardest battles of his career. His right eye was nearly closed and there was a long cut above it, and his mouth bled through the latter part of the fight. Yet, Flynn seemed unable to inflict serious punishment.

Burns had put up a great fight, one of the best of his career. Combining science with hard hitting, he outgeneraled Flynn. He feinted frequently and jabbed Flynn's mouth and nose until they streamed blood in every round after the 3rd. He would then follow with his long right swing to the jaw or ear, which rocked Flynn's head.

Burns was clearly better at long range, so throughout, Flynn would rush into close quarters and throw short hooks and uppercuts. Flynn was better on the inside than the outside, and the crowd backed him, but he landed only occasionally, and was not able to inflict serious punishment.

Half of the time they were locked in a clinch, where Burns was good at roughing it. Sometimes Burns would shove his left glove into Flynn's face and then swing or hook his right across. Tom drew some hisses for some head butts. Burns was never seriously hurt, and assimilated what punishment he did receive. "In return for the roughing Flynn carried to him, he hammered a tattoo on the stomach and short ribs, with occasional uppercuts to the chin, which sent Flynn's head back every time they landed."

Both men were in excellent condition. Whenever Flynn looked like he might weaken, he came up strong and showed wonderful vitality under the punishment. However, in the 14th and 15th rounds, Flynn endured an awful beating, and was hurt and dropped several times.

The *Los Angeles Express* called it a very good fight. Flynn was game and constantly rushing, but eventually he was worn out by his own hard pace and Burns' body punches. Burns hit well in the clinches and landed body shots quite often, sometimes straying below the belt. Flynn exhibited remarkable endurance, but was eventually knocked out cold in the 15th round. "Burns is a fast fighter and will make a showing against any of the heavyweights." Flynn "went down and out, but not disgraced, for never did a fighter show better mettle."[364]

The *Los Angeles Herald* said it had been a grueling battle, one of the most thrilling heavyweight contests ever seen. Both men gave and received punishment. Flynn proved that he was game to the core, and when he left the ring, he was the center of an admiring outburst.

Throughout, Burns went at Flynn in a cool, calculating way, and despite the fact that Jim was a mixer from the start; Tommy outpointed him and won without appearing to have exerted himself to any great extent. Still, Burns came on with a terrific onslaught in the last few rounds.

As Flynn had promised, from the start, he proceeded to mix things at a lively rate and there was scarcely a moment during the contest that they were separated to any extent. They engaged in considerable clinching following short rushes, each man battling savagely during the infighting.

---

364 *Los Angeles Express*, October 3, 1906.

Flynn was a surprise during the early rounds, and had Tommy guessing. He was strong as a bull and appeared anxious to have Burns remain at close quarters. Flynn discolored Tommy's right eye in the 2nd round. Jim showed more cleverness than he had been given credit for, but still, Tommy proved his superior when it came to ring science.

Flynn's best showing came in the 9th round, when he forced Burns to the ropes with a series of rights and lefts to the body, and Tommy appeared to weaken for a moment. Flynn's supporters went wild with delight. However, there was no limit to Tommy's endurance, and he withstood Flynn's body attack and stinging wallops to the face with a cast-iron stand.

Just before the end of the 14th round, Burns peppered Flynn with heavy rights to the head, and Jim was saved by the gong.

One version said that early in the 15th round, Burns sent a heavy right to the jaw and Flynn went down for several seconds. As Flynn came up, Burns rushed him and Flynn dropped, apparently exhausted. Robinson counted off ten seconds and called Flynn out as Jim rose and immediately went for Burns. Robinson allowed it to continue. Tommy dropped him again, but Flynn came back with a final rally until he was sent down for good for the fourth and final time.

According to another summary, after the initial knockdown in the 15th round, Burns had him helpless, and Flynn dropped to the floor not as a result of any particular blow. Referee Robinson cautioned him to rise or be disqualified, perhaps feeling that he had gone down without being hit. Burns sent him down once more, this time for good. Flynn was carried from the ring in a semi-conscious state nine minutes after he was dropped for the final time.

The *Herald* felt that Flynn had indeed been counted out on the first (or second) knockdown in the 15th round, but the referee improperly decided to allow him to continue. Flynn got to his feet just as the referee was counting ten and calling him out, but he immediately attacked, and so he was allowed to continue. Some felt that Robinson should have called the fight at that point, for it would have saved Flynn from further debilitating punishment. However, Robinson said, "The count was so close that I feared an uproar from the house, which might not understand that I had made the count."

An *Examiner* writer, C.E. Van Loan, agreed that Flynn had been knocked out twice, thanks to a blunder on Referee Robinson's part. It quoted Robinson as saying, "It is said that I counted Flynn out in the fifteenth round and then allowed the fight to go on. Just as I finished counting in the fifteenth Flynn's knee left the floor and he started for his opponent."

Summarizing the fight, Van Loan said Flynn was slow and awkward, leaving himself open to hundreds of punches, while missing most of his own. Burns had fought a fast, rough fight, eliminating a great deal of his fancy footwork and instead tearing into the infighting. He continually rocked Flynn's head with jolting right uppercuts. Tom also timed him with full arm swings. Flynn locked his left arm around Tom's neck in the clinches and hung on until the referee tore them apart. The real end of the fight came in the 14th round, when Flynn was pummeled into a dazed condition, functionally ending matters.

Both men were marked up. Flynn had split Tom's right eyebrow, blackened his right eye, and kept him bleeding from the mouth. Burns had hammered Flynn's nose out of shape and cut him about the mouth. The crowd had received full value for their money and had thoroughly enjoyed the fight.

One source said the receipts of the best house that ever packed the pavilion netted $6,500. Burns received about $2,000 and Flynn about $1,000. The following day, it was said that the bout had generated $6,938.25. Half of that, or $3,469.12 went to the fighters. Burns received 60% of the fighters' share, plus a 5% cut of the grand total receipts as the champion's guarantee. This made his share $2,428.38. Flynn earned $1,040.74.

Afterwards, Jack O'Brien, who witnessed the fight along with Jim Jeffries, again repeated, "I have met Jim Jeffries in the ring tonight and I want to say to you, reports to the contrary notwithstanding, that is the only way I do want to meet him." That was O'Brien's way of saying that he did not want to fight him. The result of that comment was that the sports applauded for several minutes. Previously, O'Brien had said that he wanted to fight Jeffries, which practically was seen as sacrilege.

The day after the fight, Flynn's seconds claimed they told Jim to keep away after the 11th round, but he would not do it. This was possibly because the difference between the two was even more marked from the outside, so Flynn thought his best chance to win was in close.[365]

Despite the accolades for Burns, no one thought that any of the present-day fighters had any chance with Jeffries, who was seen as the greatest heavyweight champion of all time, and to challenge him was seen as ridiculous. Some thought that Jack Johnson was the only one with the size and skill to be able to compete with Jeffries, but the *Herald* said, "Johnson has never shown anything that would entitle him to the slightest consideration as an opponent of Jeff. Jeff would make him jump out of the ring inside of two rounds." Jeffries had been built up to such mythical proportions that the press could not conceive of anyone even giving him a test. All championships fought in his absence essentially had an asterisk to them – *champion as long as Jeff was retired. Hence, Burns had an uphill battle to gain full recognition and respect as champion. However, his knockouts of two men in one night and his impressive performance against

---

a worthy contender in Flynn in an exciting fight had served to boost his growing reputation.[366]

Burns returned to his home in Long Beach, California. Tom was confident that he was the master of every fighter in the ring, with the exception of Jeffries. Jim Flynn received nothing but praise for his game performance. He had only gained esteem, even in a knockout loss.[367]

Jack O'Brien was scheduled to fight both Fred Cooley and Jim Tremble on the same night, on October 16, two weeks after Burns-Flynn. Tremble had just scored a KO5 over 217-pound Indian Joe Schildt on the Burns-Flynn undercard, after Joe had first taken on Abdul the Turk for 5 rounds.

It was anticipated that if he was successful in defeating the two men in one night, Jack O'Brien would be Tommy's next opponent. This was the fight that the press most wanted to see.

366 *Los Angeles Herald*, April 2, 1906.
367 *Los Angeles Herald, Los Angeles Examiner*, October 4, 1906.

CHAPTER 8

A Questionable Decision

Tommy Burns and Jack O'Brien were without question the most advertised heavyweights in the business, and therefore, a fight between them would be the biggest drawing card. Only lightweights Joe Gans and Jimmy Britt compared with the amount of ink and press attention. Even those who thought Jack Johnson had defeated Marvin Hart agreed that Burns had defeated him much more convincingly. Therefore, in their minds, the one man who stood before Burns for undisputed supremacy was O'Brien, the man who had defeated Fitzsimmons, the last champion before Jeffries. Some thought the crown reverted back to Fitz when Jeff retired, and so when O'Brien defeated Bob, that gave him a claim to the championship. Therefore, Tom McCarey had been continually negotiating for a Burns-O'Brien fight for undisputed supremacy in Jeff's absence.[368]

Burns said that he was willing to fight O'Brien winner-take-all, as long as it was a fight to the finish. O'Brien wanted a guarantee of the larger end of the purse, which naturally was not acceptable to Burns.[369]

They finally agreed to a 75/25% division of the purse based on winner/loser, with O'Brien to receive a 10% bonus regardless of the result. Wanting the fight badly, Burns agreed to waive his objection to the bonus issue. It was reported that Tom also consented to clean breaks at the referee's order, giving in to O'Brien's demands on this point as well, although apparently this later changed.[370]

On October 11, 1906, the two fighters signed articles of agreement for a 20-round bout before the Pacific Athletic Club at 9:30 p.m. on November 29, Thanksgiving Day. Despite prior reports to the contrary, the articles said the men agreed to fight according to straight Marquis of Queensberry rules. However, neither man would be allowed to hold and hit, or risk disqualification upon the third offense. Both were to break upon the referee's order. O'Brien wanted George Siler to referee, but Burns wanted the club to make the choice. The articles stated that if they could not agree upon a referee by November 22, the club would choose the referee.

The articles further stated that they would fight for a $12,000 purse. O'Brien would receive a 10% bonus of $1,200, with the remainder of the $10,800 to be divided 75% to the winner and 25% to the loser. Each party would post a $2,500 forfeit guaranteeing their performance. They were to

---

368 *Los Angeles Herald*, October 6, 1906.
369 *Los Angeles Herald*, October 8, 1906.
370 *Los Angeles Herald*, October 10, 1906.

wear brand new 5-ounce fingerless kid gloves without bandages, to be put on in the ring. The moving picture receipts were to be divided 1/3 to each party, O'Brien, Burns, and Tom McCarey, on behalf of the club.[371]

Despite all of the attention that O'Brien and Burns were receiving, one *National Police Gazette* writer opined that the only fighter who would really have a chance against Jeffries was Jack Johnson, for O'Brien and Burns were too small to handle Jeff's bulk. It felt that Jeff might return to the ring if he was provided a sufficient financial incentive. Regardless, that was merely a hypothetical fight. Burns-O'Brien was the talk of the boxing world.[372]

On October 16, 1906 at the Naud Junction Pavilion, fulfilling his previously signed contract, Jack O'Brien took on two solid men during the same night - Fred Cooley and Jim Tremble, endeavoring to knock them out within 20 rounds.[373]

---

371 *Los Angeles Herald*, October 12, 1906.
372 *Police Gazette*, October 13, 1906.
373 Fred Cooley's record included: 1904 L6 George Gardner, LKOby9 Jim Flynn, and KO1 Peter Maher, amongst the more notable names on his record. Although Cooley was often a knockout victim,

O'Brien skipped about the ring with lightning speed, his footwork remarkable in the extreme, smiling and feinting, making each man miss, toying with them until he decided to unleash his quick and dazzling blows to take them out.

The confident O'Brien had predicted that he would stop Fred Cooley in the 3rd round, and he accomplished it. He predicted an 8th round knockout over Jim Tremble, and narrowly missed it, scoring four knockdowns in that round before ending matters in the 9th round.

O'Brien was rated as a marvel, but Burns had his supporters too. It was noted that Tommy had vastly improved in science, and had never been stopped.[374]

Burns planned to do some light training and exhibiting at Long Beach until November 1, when he would begin hard training.[375]

On October 26, 1906 in Los Angeles, at a benefit for the police, Burns boxed 3 rounds with police officer and former Jeffries opponent Dan Long. The exhibition was well received, and repeated on the afternoon and evening of the 27th.[376]

On Halloween, October 31, 1906 in San Francisco, Al Kaufman scored a KO10 over Sam Berger. O'Brien had fought a 6-round no-decision with Berger, and had stopped Kaufman in the 17th round of their bout.

On November 4, 700 people gathered at the Long Beach bath house to watch Burns box with regular sparring partners Billy Woods and Jimmy

he had gained some notoriety by dropping O'Brien in an exhibition sparring session in January. Jim Tremble's record included a 1902 D20 Billy Woods and 1905 LKOby18 Dave Barry.

374 *Los Angeles Herald*, October 17, 1906.
375 *Los Angeles Herald*, October 20, 1906.
376 *Los Angeles Herald*, October 27, 1906.

Burns (a.k.a. George Memsic). Tommy looked fast and shifty. He later engaged in a swimming race with Memsic, and won.[377]

The principals agreed to change the fight date to Wednesday, November 28, Thanksgiving eve, instead of the 29th. O'Brien would train at Venice.[378]

Tom McCarey sent a $2,500 check to the Miles Brothers in San Francisco, which would be in charge of the films. It was estimated that the picture venture would entail an investment of $11,000 to $12,000, to be divided one-third each between McCarey and the two fighters.

Burns was regularly sparring with George Memsic, and likely Billy Woods as well. It was anticipated that Jim Tremble would also assist Tommy.[379]

On November 8, Burns sparred with Abdul "the Turk" Malgan.[380]

Former champion James Jeffries was asked to render his opinion regarding the probable outcome of the fight. He said it was a hard one to guess, but felt that O'Brien should win if they had to break clean, for he was the better boxer. Burns had a better chance if he could work on the inside and hit the stomach. "It should be a good fight, but O'Brien has no cinch, for Burns is a hard little man to thrash."[381]

On November 13 at the Naud Junction Pavilion, Tommy Burns was in Jimmy Burns/George Memsic's corner for his bout with Charlie Neary, which Memsic won via KO2.

Fight fans were excited about the upcoming title bout. "Consensus of opinion has decided that barring Jim Jeffries there are no two boxers as worthy of claiming the active title as are O'Brien and Burns."

In his training on the 14th, O'Brien punched a heavy sand bag for 30 minutes. He worked with the light bag for a bit, as well as weights and pulleys. He then sparred several alternating rounds with Abdul Malgan, Bob Ward, the amateur coast champion, and Mortimer Swanson. O'Brien demonstrated blazing speed, lightning-like precision, and excellent defense. It was estimated that Jack weighed about 168 pounds. O'Brien was quite the attraction at the Venice Auditorium. Even the ladies came to watch him box.

Abdul "the Terrible Turk" Malgan, who had recently boxed with Burns, said O'Brien could not only hit hard, but in several places at once. He opined that O'Brien was better than Burns.

Tom McCarey convinced James Jeffries to referee the bout, offering him a very large $1,500 to do so. The sports had confidence in Jeff's integrity, and it was also believed that his involvement might stimulate the subsequent motion picture receipts.

---

377 *Los Angeles Herald,* November 5, 1906; *Los Angeles Times,* November 6, 1906.

378 *Los Angeles Herald,* November 5, 1906.

379 *Los Angeles Herald,* November 8, 1906. Some thought that Jack Sullivan would again work with Burns, but it appears that he did not do so.

380 *Los Angeles Herald,* November 9, 1906.

381 *Los Angeles Times,* November 11, 1906.

Jeffries said the fight might go to a decision, and no matter which way he would decide, there would be roars of disapproval from the audience, and such was what any man disliked. Of course, if he was concerned about that, then perhaps he should not have taken up the role of referee.[382]

More than 500 persons watched Burns work out at the Long Beach bath house on the 15th, despite the wind and fog. He ran 6 miles in the morning and sparred in the afternoon.

Regarding the newly named referee, Burns said, "I am glad that Jeffries will be the third man in the ring, for he will let us fight from the tap of the gong. He wants no sparring exhibition, and there will be nothing in my way. I can go in all I please with Jeffries." Tom also said that Jeff had no sympathy for a boxer and would see to it that O'Brien fought.

The *Examiner* thought O'Brien would fight hard, owing to the fact that they were fighting for an unclouded right to the title of world champion.[383]

The O'Brien-Burns championship contest was the principal talk of the sporting world. O'Brien would be the favorite, owing to the fact that he had a vast amount of science, speed, craftiness, generalship, and experience. Jack had a "string of victories over good men as long as your arm, and has won the most of his battles on ring generalship." O'Brien had defeated Joe Choynski, Mike Schreck, Jack "Twin" Sullivan, Bob Fitzsimmons, Al Kaufman, and also held a victory over Burns. Secondary sources say he had at least 89 known victories to his credit, and only 4 official losses, including: 1902 WND6 Joe Walcott, WND6 Young Peter Jackson, KO6 George Cole, W6 Billy Stift, W6 Joe Choynski, WND6 and DND6 Peter Maher, and DND6 Marvin Hart; 1903 WND6 Joe Choynski, D10 Joe Walcott, DND6 Marvin Hart, WND6 George Byers, WND6 Jack Sullivan, W6 Mike Schreck, W15 Jack Sullivan, and D10 Hugo Kelly; 1904 WND6 Tommy Ryan, W15 Mike Schreck, L6 Hugo Kelly, KO3 Jack Sullivan, KO3 Kid Carter, DND6 Kid McCoy, DND6 Bob Fitzsimmons, WND6 Hugo Kelly, KO2 Billy Stift, KO1 Joe Butler, W6 Tommy Burns, KO3 Jim Jeffords, and WND6 John Willie; 1905 WND6 John Willie, WDQ2 and W10 Young Peter Jackson, L10 Hugo Kelly, D20 Jack Sullivan, KO17 Al Kaufman, and KO13 Bob Fitzsimmons; and 1906 DND6 Sam Berger, in addition to his recent KO victories over Cooley and Tremble on the same day. Some primary sources said he had over 150 fights.

O'Brien's original name was Joseph Hagan or O'Hagan, but for whatever reason, a fellow thought that Jack O'Brien would be easier to pronounce, so the name was changed. Like actors, fighters often had stage names.

The *Examiner* said a remarkable amount of interest was being shown in the bout, for very good reason, because "the man who wins will have a real excuse for calling himself the heavyweight champion of the world."

382 *Los Angeles Herald, Los Angeles Times, Los Angeles Examiner*, November 15, 16, 1906.
383 *Los Angeles Examiner*, November 16, 17, 1906.

In spite of the hysterical statements of several Northern and Eastern sporting writers, big Jim Jeffries shows no signs of coming out of his retirement. If he stays out of the game, the heavyweight title must go to the next best man. This fight will develop that man.

Burns said, "I want to clinch my right to call myself a real heavyweight champion and I think by defeating O'Brien, I can do this."

It was well known that the men had almost come to blows on two of the occasions that they had met. "Burns, the aggressor in this sort of fighting, cannot bear the sight of Philadelphia Jack and this is no idle press agent story either. No man who witnessed the clash in McCarey's office can ever doubt that the antipathy is deep seated." On that day, Burns had said to Jack, "Yes, you dancing master, I'll make you hop around the ring; I'll make you tin-can every minute of the fight, and you can bet on it."

Analyzing their styles and abilities, the *Examiner* said O'Brien was a fighter who danced in and out and used his jabs until he had a man blinded and ready to fall victim to a short cross or hook. O'Brien had more fights than anyone else in the heavyweight class. He was never out of training, and did not dissipate in any way, never touching an intoxicant and never smoking. He was 28 years old.

The 25-year-old Burns was a tough, well-seasoned young man with immense natural strength and endurance. Although not thought of as a big heavyweight puncher, his persistence with jarring rights and lefts had worn down Flynn. He too was an abstainer and took the best care of himself.

O'Brien's boxing prowess was undisputed, and therefore he opened as the strong 10 to 6 betting favorite. It was unheard of for a heavyweight champion to be installed as the betting underdog, let alone such a big underdog, but such was the case here. O'Brien had the edge in experience, speed, and ring generalship. Strength and weight would favor Burns.[384]

Despite the odds, Burns was confident of victory, and said that he would bet a pot of money on himself. A number of local sports fancied Burns on account of his ability as a boxer and his hitting powers combined. These two fighters did not like each other, and they knew that victory would place them on top of the fighting game, so fans expected a very good fight.[385]

Jewish world featherweight champion Abe Attell, who had been working with Burns, said,

> I cannot see how O'Brien will be able to beat Burns. In the first place, Tommy is young and strong as a bull. He has never been hurt in his life. … He is a man who takes on flesh very rapidly. While he was fighting at 158 pounds he was doing himself just such an injustice…he was tampering with his fighting strength. When he let

---

384 *Los Angeles Examiner*, November 18, 1906.
385 *Los Angeles Times*, November 19, 1906.

that weight business go, you saw a new fighter. Tommy Burns has just begun to make his reputation and I expect to see him establish himself as the best heavyweight in the business by beating Jack O'Brien. Burns' only chance lies in going in like a wild man. O'Brien is too clever for him, just as he is too clever for most fighters. Burns cannot hope to get anything by standing away and letting O'Brien jab and escape. O'Brien can do that all night without tiring himself out. Burns figures to go to O'Brien so fast right from the start that Jack will never have a chance to do any of that monkey work. I don't care how clever a fighter is, there are some fellows fast enough to make them fight and I think Burns will prove himself in that class. He will be all over O'Brien like a lunatic and the only thing Jack can do is to fight back to protect himself.

Burns badly wanted to whip O'Brien, and while he had never said that he wanted to meet Jeffries, and was not claiming to be a match for the big fellow, he thought that he could defeat every other heavyweight. The *Examiner* concluded, "Well, Tommy, if you trim this Philadelphia boy, they will simply HAVE to listen to you. There won't be any getting away from it."[386]

Burns said there were a lot of folks who did not give him credit for what he had done in his career, but that his showing against O'Brien would surprise them. He had surprised the experts by defeating the strongest and most aggressive fighter in Hart, and would do the same thing by defeating the quickest and most elusive boxer in O'Brien. He admitted that O'Brien was fast and clever, but said that he was a clever and fast fighter himself, and stronger than Jack. He would be after O'Brien from the start, and if he did not get him, it would be because O'Brien ran away. If Jack tried to fight, Burns was confident that he would knock him out.[387]

---

386 *Los Angeles Examiner*, November 20, 1906.
387 *Los Angeles Herald*, November 21, 1906.

O'Brien was training like a fiend. He was said to be one of only a half dozen fighters who never got out of condition, so he was practically ready to fight even without the training that he was doing.[388]

C.E. Van Loan said the fight was so big that men who had never discussed boxing were arguing over the probable outcome of this bout. Those who had never spent any money on a fight would be in the gallery for this one. "There has been so much talk about it."

Van Loan said Burns was a good, dashing fighter, but no one knew just how good he was, for he had never been fully extended as a heavyweight.

> In Jack O'Brien, Tommy meets more class than he has ever met in his life. It is Tommy's chance to set the stamp on his class as a heavyweight fighter. If he disposes of Jack O'Brien there is no man in the country who will have the right to dispute Burns' claim to the championship.
>
> Jack Johnson still lingers about the scene and every little while he emits a small yellow growl, but Jack deserves his fate. He might have been a top-notch fighter, but he was cursed with a great display of citrus fruit and every time he got in a pinch he showed the lemon color. The championship lies between Burns and O'Brien, and by this time next week it is hoped that one man will have a clear title to Jeff's cast-off shoes.[389]

Both Burns and O'Brien were said to be in the best condition of their lives. O'Brien was as fast as a flash. On the 21st, he worked the punching bag, snapping punches with both hands with a rapidity that drew bursts of applause. He boxed with 200-pound Bob Ward, the Terrible Turk, and Battling Swanson. He wrestled and worked his forearms and shoulders in a manner which made it clear that he expected a rough fight. Jack said he had never trained harder for a fight.

> I was never more confident of winning a battle, though I know that Tommy Burns is a tough, hard fellow to whip. ... I have done everything to insure my success. I am going into the ring in great condition and I feel that my experience and my cleverness will carry me through a winner."[390]

O'Brien was a unique individual. He liked to give lectures and speeches on boxing, to dance, and he even had an English tutor. He was a talkative self-promoter.

When a photographer took photos of Burns, the champ said, "Take one of me as I will look after the fight." When the photographer said that he

---

388 *Los Angeles Examiner*, November 21, 1906.
389 *Los Angeles Examiner*, November 22, 1906.
390 *Los Angeles Examiner*, November 22, 1906.

might have a black eye or two afterwards, the confident Tommy replied, "Don't you worry, friend. I won't look much different than I am now."

Tommy said that when he wasn't training, he enjoyed the quiet home life on East Adams Street with his wife.[391]

Tommy Burns doing road work behind an auto. From left to right—Arthur Collins, Tommy Burns, Kid McClung, Trainer McDonald, chauffeur, and Jimmy Burns.

Frank McDonald, who trained Joe Gans, and was said to be perhaps the best trainer in the country, was also working with Burns. Tommy gave him no lip, and was a conscientious trainer.

Tommy's current manager, C.A. O'Connor, said Burns was willing to bet $5,000 on himself. Burns had posted that wager for O'Brien to cover, and they took Jack's refusal to do so as a sign of who actually had the confidence.[392]

Burns said he was not muscle bound, and noted that he kept his muscles loose and relaxed and ready for action on the instant. There was a time in his career when he was too tense with his muscles. Back when he had sparred Jim Corbett, Jim told him that he held his arms too tensely. "After that I boxed several times with Corbett and each time learned more about handling myself."[393]

At Venice, O'Brien was doing some training under yellow and blue lights in order to become accustomed to the effect which would be produced in the ring when the Cooper-Hewitt lights were turned on for the motion picture machine. In training, Jack sparred, worked with the medicine ball and weights, shadow boxed, and ran 5 miles.

At Long Beach, Burns sparred with Arthur Collins and Jimmy Burns. He remained the 2 to 1 underdog, but several wise ones were betting on him.[394]

---

391 *Los Angeles Times*, November 22, 1906.
392 *Los Angeles Herald*, November 22, 1906.
393 *Los Angeles Herald*, November 23, 1906.
394 *Los Angeles Examiner*, November 24, 1906.

On the 24th, Jeffries and McCarey visited O'Brien's training camp to discuss the rules with him. They would visit Burns for the same purpose on the 25th.[395]

O'Brien harped on one major point. Although they were fighting according to straight Queensbury rules, each to protect himself at all times, O'Brien wanted Jeff to ensure that there would be no holding and hitting allowed. Jeffries replied, "Of course not. That is one of the rankest fouls a man can commit. The only way a man can do anything like that is to lose his head entirely, and a man who loses his head while in the ring is not a good fighter." O'Brien told him that they had agreed not to wear bandages, but only fingerless kid gloves under the mitts. Jeff said, "That's a good scheme. I never hurt my hands until I began to wear those bandages and when I did I broke bones right away. After that I fought without bandages or kid gloves underneath."

The subject switched to championship fights of the past. The slick O'Brien, probably trying to ingratiate himself with Jeffries, called attention to Jeff's famous body blows that he had used to defeat Ruhlin and Corbett, amongst others. During the conversation, Jack said, "Then was it true that they had to take you to the Receiving Hospital after that fight with Corbett?" Jeff replied, "Me? To the hospital? What for?" Smiling, O'Brien responded, "I understood they had to take you there to cut your fist out of Corbett's stomach."

Regarding whether Jeffries had donated his championship to the winner of the Hart-Root battle, Jeff said that he had no right to give the championship away. "I am out of the game now and the championship must go to the next best man – whoever he is."

Leaving O'Brien's training quarters, Jeff said, "Jack is in great shape, and he has to be. Burns will give him a hard fast fight. All I hope is that it ends in a decisive manner, one way or the other."[396]

395 *Los Angeles Herald*, November 25, 1906.
396 *Los Angeles Examiner*, November 25, 1906.

According to the *Los Angeles Times*, not in years had a prize fight caused so much interest and speculation as to the result. Both fighters were in their prime. Burns was a natural, a fighter more so than a boxer, but he had developed his boxing skills as well, as demonstrated in his battle with Hart. He could box or fight, combining the two. He had free action of limb and body, and despite his short stature, had long arms and wonderful quickness for a man of his proportions. He was more of a fighter than O'Brien, but then he was not the boxer that O'Brien was.

O'Brien was not as strong, but had proven that he had lightning fast hands and some pop as well. "Burns will be up against both a fine defense and a great offense." Jack was smart and extremely quick; dazzling his opponents with the rapidity of his blows, and was just as active in avoiding punches. He proved that he could do damage in his bouts with Kaufman and Fitzsimmons, two big, sturdy, and strong men.

O'Brien said his form was all that could be desired, and he was as quick as or quicker than he had ever been with his hands and feet. "My nimble athleticism, my speed and ring experience will stand me in good stead in the coming contest."[397]

The advance ticket sales were the biggest in the history of the game in Southern California. After all, "The battle is for the heavyweight championship of the world."

This would be the first time in the history of fight films that Cooper-Hewitt lights would be used to film a fight. The Miles Brothers were in charge of the process, and had five experts preparing things. Ninety lights would be used. Each light was valued at $40, which made them worth $3,600 even before one was turned on. They were said to provide better illumination than sunlight, and would prevent shadows.

Sizing up the men, Burns would probably weigh around 175 pounds, while most thought that O'Brien would weigh 165-170 pounds. Jack stood 5'10 ½" to Tommy's 5'7". O'Brien had been fighting for ten years, while Burns had been boxing for about five years. "Burns has fought forty-two battles; O'Brien has fought 155 contests." Jack was faster on his feet, had many more years of experience, and was considered to be the better ring general.

Burns claimed the heavyweight championship as a result of his victory over Hart. O'Brien claimed the middleweight and light heavyweight championships, as well as the English heavyweight championship, which he won from George Crisp in 11 rounds in 1901.

Despite having fought for a decade, O'Brien "shows fewer signs of it than most fighters who have been in the business for two years. Add to this that O'Brien is the busiest fighter in the business and you have some idea of the fine physical condition of the Philadelphia boy." Jack said that he had

397 *Los Angeles Times*, November 25, 1906.

averaged about 18 bouts a year, and one year even had 33 fights. "You see, I look at it like this; I am in the fighting business and I regard it as a business… [and] therefore I like to do as much business as possible." Although 28 years old, given his fitness, Jack thought that he would be able to fight past age 35. O'Brien was so confident that he was already making arrangements to fight England's current champion, Gunner Moir.[398]

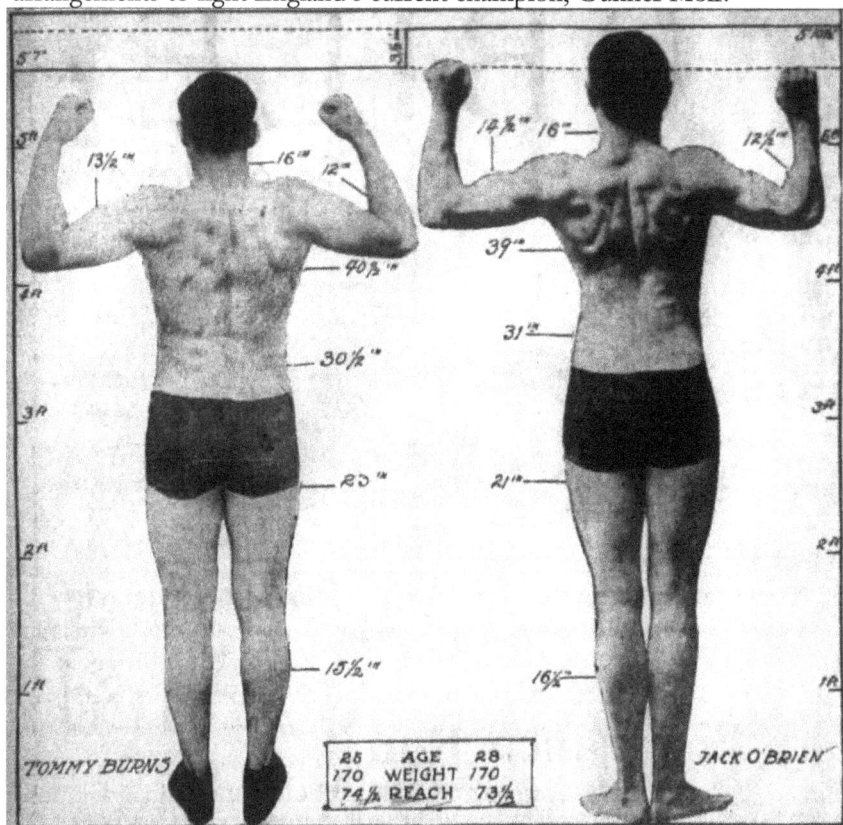

W.W. Naughton noted that O'Brien was a top-heavy choice in Los Angeles, and rightfully so. "It doesn't follow, however, that because O'Brien is favorite that O'Brien will win. Burns is a sturdy fellow and should be able to stand lots of wear and tear. The Canadian chunk is built for heavy weather and he is as shifty as…a flea." Tom was trained to perfection and built for going the distance. However, O'Brien was taller, faster, and cleverer. Jack was wiry and agile, and "in the matter of endurance can keep step for step with Burns through an extended bout."[399]

Both parties agreed to remove from the contract the clause which said that three fouls would lead to a disqualification. They were willing to rely on Jeffries' judgment.

---

398 *Los Angeles Examiner*, November 25, 1906.
399 *Los Angeles Examiner*, November 25, 1906.

Three days before the fight, on the 25th, Jeffries visited Burns' training camp at Long Beach. He watched Burns hit the bag for 15 minutes. Jeff said, "The boy is in fine condition. This should be the fastest heavyweight battle which has occurred in years and I look for one of the two to put over a knockout blow." Tommy looked very fit, with no superfluous flesh.[400]

Burns was satisfied with the terms of the battle, and was ready for a tough fight. He said,

> I expect to take a hard beating in the ring, for O'Brien is a good man. More than one battle has been lost by underestimating an opponent, and I do not want to suffer from this condition. If O'Brien considers me easy money so much the better. … I expect to come out of the ring with the title I won from Hart still in my possession.

Although the odds had been 2 to 1 in O'Brien's favor, there was a slight shift to 10 to 6, given the wonderful condition which Burns was showing. Although neither would give out his weight, or prove it, most estimated that Burns outweighed O'Brien.[401]

PACIFIC ATHLETIC CLUB PAVILION

Wednesday Night, November 28th.

Twenty Round Boxing Contest for the Heavyweight Championship of the World. James J. Jeffries will Referee. $12,000 Purse $12,000.

Tommy Burns vs. Philadelphia Jack O'Brien

Moving Pictures will be taken. General Admission $3. Reserved Seats $5, $10 and $20. Tickets on sale at A. B. Greenewald's Cigar Store, 107 S. Spring street.

Two days before the fight, on the 26th, both fighters were given the opportunity to see the Cooper-Hewitt lights tested in the arena. The lights emitted an intense bluish glare, although not accompanied by the agonizing heat that was associated with Jeffries-Sharkey II. The light played strange tricks with ordinary colors. Faces looked blue, while everything red appeared dark purple. Blue eyes became deep violet and eyes of other colors turned yellow. Jack O'Brien said, "Wonder what Jack Johnson would look like under this light? Well, there's one thing sure, there will be no color line drawn under this light. We'll all be the same color!" Burns said nothing, but he entered the ring and occasionally sent a baleful glare towards O'Brien. Both fighters agreed that the lights would not interfere with their vision.[402]

Famous sportswriter William Walter Naughton, who had seen all of the champions in action starting with Sullivan in 1886 against Paddy Ryan, would give his fight report for the *Examiner*. Naughton was born in New Zealand, but was of Irish heritage. He had watched Jeffries "develop from an awkward, clumsy fellow into the greatest champion the game has ever produced." Jeff "was of the improving kind." Although Naughton said sportsmen tended to give too much credit to past heroes, nevertheless he

---

400 *Los Angeles Herald*, November 26, 1906.
401 *Los Angeles Examiner*, November 26, 1906.
402 *Los Angeles Examiner*, November 27, 1906.

agreed that the higher ranked men of the present time did not compare with the top notchers of ten years ago like Jackson, Corbett, Jeffries, Sharkey, Ruhlin, and Choynski.

Naughton called Burns a roly poly fellow resembling a heavyweight cupid shorn of wings. No one had seen him weigh, and he was not required to do so for a heavyweight bout, though his weight was given out at 168 pounds. O'Brien thought Tommy was a good deal larger than that. O'Brien weighed for Naughton in his street clothes and tipped the scales at 172 pounds. Naughton thought Burns was about that *without* clothes. He noted that the bad blood between the two fighters seemed to be genuine, despite the fact that often such differences were a promotional "trick to stimulate interest and increase the sale of tickets."[403]

The day before the fight, both fighters did some work in front of the moving picture camera. Tom punched the bag, did a little sparring, and skipped rope, showing the types of things that he did in training.

> Tommy did not enter into the work with much abandon. Tommy is of the old school. For him, the fight is the main thing. He does not care for the sideshow privileges. He would rather be known as a fighter than a speechmaker, but he did everything the moving picture people asked of him.

The *Examiner* opined that Burns knew that by defeating O'Brien, he would clinch his claim to the championship, "making even his enemies respect him as the best man in the heavyweight bunch."

Tom told C.E. Van Loan that by whipping O'Brien, he would put an end to any talk about the "bunk" champion. "It has been a long time since O'Brien has had a sound drubbing, but it is coming to him Wednesday night, and don't you forget it." He said the animosity between them would not have arisen had O'Brien treated him fairly. Jack had tried to belittle him, and make him look like a sucker and take a back seat.

> There never would have been any personal collision if it had not been for O'Brien's habit of trying to Buffalo me. He began it that day in McCarey's office and I jumped in and roasted him just to make him see that he did not have me scared. I regret this business just as much as anybody, but show me another fighter that I ever had any trouble with. O'Brien began it and I am going to end it tomorrow night.

Burns had placed a $1,100 bet on himself at 10 to 6 odds.

After watching his green eyes under the glare of the film lights, W.W. Naughton also chatted with Burns. The only thing that worried Tommy was the O'Brien publicity and promotion bureau. Tom argued that the public and press erroneously gave O'Brien more credit for defeating the decrepit, all-in Fitzsimmons than he received for defeating a young, strong Hart, the

---

403 *Los Angeles Examiner*, November 27, 1906.

man destined to fill Jeffries' shoes, who had dropped O'Brien and had him all but out in their two bouts.

> He defeated Fitzsimmons, yes, but was it the Fitzsimmons that used to be? No sir! There was as much difference as there is between a living breathing man and one of your ancient Egyptian mummies. He defeated Kauffman. Well, Al is a nice fellow and I don't want to become entangled in outside arguments but Kauffman and myself had many little spars in private and Delaney, if he speaks the truth, can tell whether I have Kauffman's measure or not.

> O'Brien says he gained a decision over me. He did, by courtesy of the referee. I travelled four days and nights from Seattle to Milwaukee without training and not knowing whom I was to meet. ... I have improved 100 per cent since I met him before and I don't think he has improved a bit. For the sake of argument, I will concede that he is a bit cleverer than I am with his hands. He is no better on his feet and no shiftier. I will bet if there is any way of measuring the films it will be found that he has covered fifty miles by the time this fight is over. But that won't save him. I am going to carry the fight to him – make no mistake about that. He won't be able to keep out of my way and when it is all over I will be recognized as his master.

Naughton noted that the greatest number of wagers were on the probable length of the contest. More wagers had been placed on Burns' ability to stay 20 rounds than on any other betting proposition.

Philadelphia Jack O'Brien, the "spectacular one," welcomed the film folks with open arms. "Jack knows the value of advertising; he works the press agent end of the game to the last notch." He sparred three one-minute rounds with Ward, Malgan, and Swanson. He also tossed the big ball, worked the wall machine, and punched the bag and shadow boxed.

O'Brien said fighting was a business, and he tried to keep the personal side out of it. He did not understand why Burns had made charges against him. "Such squabbling is childish and does not lend any dignity to the profession." Jack said he was in great condition and that Burns could not fight too fast a fight for him.

> I am going into the ring with Mr. Burns, the present claimant to the title, fit to fight for my life. If Mr. Burns beats me, he will beat me the best day I ever saw and I will take my hat off to him. ... May the best man win, and, of course I think I know who the best man is.

Tom McCarey said the house would be sold out. He expected a terrific fight.

> While I cannot express an opinion on the outcome, I may say that Tommy Burns is a much underrated man. It took the public a long time to acknowledge that Jim Jeffries was anything but a big fellow

with more luck than skill. It has taken them a long time to see anything in Tommy Burns, but after tomorrow night's fight, however it may end, Tommy Burns will come nearer than ever to filling his proper place in the heavyweight class. O'Brien is a wonderful fighter and his cleverness puts him in a class by himself, but we have never seen Jack O'Brien under a bombardment and we will see it tomorrow night. It will be the kind of a fight that makes a real champion – you can bet on it.[404]

Jack Johnson, "the black and tan champion of the world," wanted to fight the winner. His manager, Sam Fitzpatrick said, "Johnson and the winner coming together would prove a real championship contest." The *Examiner* opined in response, "Yes, if people could forget Jack Johnson's canary streak, he might make a good match with the winner. But so long as the memory of his orange stripe lingers Jack Johnson will be a beggar for matches. That is where he figures." Many in the press thought Johnson lacked gameness inside the ring.[405]

The day of the fight, Burns remained the heavy 10 to 6 underdog, despite the fact that the majority of opinion on the street seemed to be with Tommy. That wasn't how the coin was being bet. Most were wagering on the vaunted O'Brien. O'Brien had shown his class against Fitzsimmons and Kaufman. He had proven that he could defeat boxers and punchers, both big and small. He held the previous decision victory over Burns. The betting was 10 to 7 ½ that Burns would stay the full 20 rounds. "This is probably the heaviest betting fight ever pulled off in the South."

Jack Sullivan, who had fought both men, picked O'Brien, and bet Tommy's manager $600 at the prevailing odds. Still, Burns had improved wonderfully since he had fought Sullivan, and it was said that Tom would be the favorite were he and Sullivan to meet again.

The house was practically sold out the night before the contest. The advance ticket sales were slightly over $10,000.

The *Times* and *Express* estimated that both boxers would weigh about 170 pounds. The *Herald* anticipated that O'Brien would weigh about 163 pounds to Burns' 174 pounds. A couple days before the fight, O'Brien had taken the scale in his street clothes and weighed 172 pounds. Burns' weight was given out as 168, but he had not yet taken the scale for public benefit. He likely weighed more than that. Neither man weighed in on the day of the fight, for they were not required to do so for a heavyweight bout.

Reflecting the feeling of real enmity between the two, Burns said, "I've got it on that big bluffer." O'Brien retorted, "Burns will wake up to the fact

404 *Los Angeles Examiner*, November 28, 1906.
405 *Los Angeles Examiner*, November 28, 1906.

that he doesn't know even a little thing about fighting when I get him in the ring."[406]

It was anticipated that in Burns' corner would be Frank McDonald, Professor Frank Lewis, Jimmy Burns/George Memsic, and possibly George Brown and world featherweight champion Abe Attell.

O'Brien's seconds would probably be Bob Ward, Abdul "the Terrible Turk" Malgan, Mortimer "Battling" Swanson, Jack "Twin" Sullivan, and Spider Kelly.

The main event fighters were scheduled to enter the ring at approximately 9 p.m.

The much awaited, anticipated, and hyped Burns-O'Brien championship fight took place on Thanksgiving Eve, November 28, 1906 in Los Angeles, at the Pacific Athletic Club's pavilion at Naud Junction.

The fact that James J. Jeffries was brought in to referee the bout further brought the battle into the limelight, because there was as much interest in seeing him as the principals, although the interest was already very high.

The fight was "of supreme importance to the sporting world" because it was to settle who had the right to the championship. O'Brien had been occasionally claiming the championship since his victory over Fitzsimmons, though most recognized Burns as the real champion.

O'Brien was the favorite at 10 to 6 and 10 to 7 odds, but the experts wondered if he would lose his active footwork after Tommy broke down

---

406 *Los Angeles Herald, Los Angeles Daily Times, Los Angeles Express, Los Angeles Examiner,* November 28, 1906; *Philadelphia Inquirer,* November 28, 1906, from a November 27th Los Angeles dispatch.

his body. "O'Brien has the experience and the boxing ability and Burns the punch and the grit, and both are about equal in footwork."

The purse was $12,000, of which $1,200 (10%) was to go to O'Brien and the remainder ($10,800) divided 75% to the winner and 25% to the loser. Straight Queensberry rules were to apply, with the men to protect themselves on the breakaway, but they were required to break upon the referee's order.

The movie camera would take about 1,700 photos per minute (about 28 frames per second), which are actually more than the present day standard 24 frames per second (1,440 per minute). No smoking would be allowed in the arena, so as not to interfere with the filming of the motion pictures.[407]

The gathering was called the greatest ever assembled at the arena or in Southern California. The attendance was all that McCarey could have hoped for. Many hundreds were turned away from the sold-out house. Fully 6,500 persons packed the building.

One said that the Cooper-Hewitt lights sent a bluish shadowless glare over the vast throng. Another said the moving picture lights gave off an odd violet hue that made the natural colors seem oddly purple, gray, and black. Even blood looked black.

Burns entered the ring first, chewing gum, wearing a long gray bathrobe. The *Police Gazette* said Tom selected the corner that offered the best protection from the motion picture lights.[408]

O'Brien entered a minute later and walked over to Burns, who shook his hand in a chilly manner.

At first, there was some dispute about whether Burns could wear an inflated padded rubber belt under his trunks. Tom said it protected against low blows. "Burns contended that he has as much right to wear the belt as he had to wear the customary aluminum cup." A lengthy talk ensued. O'Brien refused to fight unless Tommy removed it. Burns allowed Referee Jeffries to examine it, and Jeff told O'Brien that he saw no reason why Burns should not wear it. It did not cover the legal scoring area. However, Jack refused to fight if Tom wore the belt. The crowd hissed O'Brien, who just grinned and bowed. They blamed him for the long delay that the debate had caused.

Tom McCarey finally talked with Burns and asked him to remove the foul protector. Tommy decided to abide by McCarey's request. So, Burns returned to the dressing room and removed the pad. This was ironic because it was later said that O'Brien was wearing plaster on his back. Plus, it appears as if Jack's trunks were high. When Tom returned, an upset Burns decided to inspect O'Brien's trunks, and grabbed his beltline and gave it a rough tug. O'Brien carefully examined the standard 5-ounce gloves, but they met with his approval.

---

407 *Los Angeles Express*, November 29, 1906.
408 *Police Gazette*, December 15, 1906.

Before the fight, it was announced that Hugo Kelly, George Gardner, Jack Sullivan, Jim Flynn and Al Kaufman all challenged the winner.

The round-by-round account is an amalgamation of the *Los Angeles Herald*, *Los Angeles Times*, and *Los Angeles Examiner*.

1 – At first, both were cautious. Burns was crouching low and O'Brien dancing away. Jack snapped Tom's head back with a jab. Burns rushed in and his shoulder butted Jack under the chin. After O'Brien clinched, he protested when Burns kept both hands working. Jack whipped in a terrific right uppercut which started the blood from Tom's nose. Jeffries had difficulties parting them from clinches. Burns tried to work on the inside. O'Brien jolted Burns with a right and left hook and they clinched. In another clinch, Jack effectively blocked Tom's attempts at infighting. At the gong, O'Brien whipped up another uppercut, drawing more blood from the nose. One writer said the rather tame round ended with neither man having an advantage. W.W. Naughton said it was a very fast round with no advantage on either side. ,

2 – O'Brien danced around and Burns chased him. On the inside, Burns hit savagely, and effectively worked the ribs. He protested Jeffries' separating them. The crowd hissed Burns for hitting in the clinches, despite the fact that it was perfectly legal. O'Brien complained about one punch that landed

low. Jack missed many jabs. Tom landed a stiff right to the jaw, his first effective blow. Jack danced away with marvelous footwork, tapping Burns at will as the latter rushed. As Tom rushed in, Jack whipped up a terrific right and left to the face, causing Burns to drop forward into a clinch. O'Brien landed many more punches, including jabs, rights, hooks, and uppercuts. Tom kept trying to rough it in the clinches, but Jeff kept breaking them. One writer said, "The round was strongly O'Brien's, who appeared to have taken the measure of his opponent and seemed very confident." W.W. Naughton agreed that it was O'Brien's round.

3 – Burns led with hard punches and O'Brien either countered or would lead as Tommy advanced. Burns continued to hit in the clinches and on the breakaways, particularly focusing on the body. O'Brien smiled as Tommy clinched. Tom landed a stiff right to the heart and worked well in a clinch. He chopped a right and left to the head and rushed in but was stopped by a vicious right uppercut. O'Brien made him miss a right and came back with a whipping right to the face and left to the body and followed with a right uppercut to the jaw. Jack was freely landing his right uppercut. Tom landed a left to the face but Jack came back with right and left to the head and body and clinched. Naughton said, "It was hard, fast and rough work and O'Brien's lips were parted as if the exertion was telling on him. It was O'Brien's round by a small margin."

4 – O'Brien danced in and out with superb footwork. He hit Tommy's face with ease. Burns landed a left to the head and muttered to O'Brien, "Why don't you stand and fight?" Jack skipped away from Tommy's savage rushes. Jack would land and then clinch. Burns continued hitting in the clinches. Jeff had trouble breaking them. Jack rushed into a clinch and roughed it. Burns engaged in vicious infighting that caused O'Brien to break. Tommy kept advancing and ducking, trying to work in close and corner O'Brien. Burns hit the body. Both shot across some hard lefts and rights, and Jack followed with a left uppercut. O'Brien's most effective blow was his right uppercut, which was used by him throughout the fight. Naughton said, "The pace and rough usage seem to be telling on Jack." Overall, though, the reporters agreed that the round was rather even, with a great deal of clinching.

5 – Burns tried to work him into a corner, but O'Brien dashed in and out and teased his opponent. Burns landed a right to the body. He took time to strip off his silk belt, and took a left to the stomach. Inside, Tom landed several lefts to the body.

As O'Brien was stepping in to punch with his right, like a flash Burns whipped across a terrific well-timed right to the nose that landed with double impact. It caused O'Brien to bleed horribly. The shower of blood spurted in a stream. The dazed O'Brien staggered to a clinch, and after breaking, he ran away. Burns attacked, smashing in rights and lefts, most of which O'Brien blocked or avoided, but he was in a bad way and had to stall out the round, ducking, dodging and quickly moving all over the ring.

Burns whipped across another vicious right that caught Jack over the right eye and cut a one-inch gash. O'Brien was blinded by his own blood while pursued by a bull-like demon that rushed at him. Jack was groggy, and the picture machine lights made the blood appear black, giving him a terrible appearance. However, he managed to stay away in marvelous fashion. When Tom got him to the ropes several times, O'Brien would duck, twist and turn, or move away. Jack did not throw a punch for fully a minute.

Jack's broken nose was sunken, his eye terribly swollen and his lips badly bruised. Jack Sullivan told O'Brien to throw the right uppercut, and he responded by landing a couple right uppercuts, but they were weak and did no damage. Burns landed a right to the chin. O'Brien was hurt and kept running away. The crowd went wild at the bell. The round was decidedly Tommy's. O'Brien's cornermen administered him smelling salts.

6 – Burns rushed while O'Brien sparred cautiously, trying to kill time and recover. Burns followed him around the ring. Eventually, Tommy taunted O'Brien, asking him to fight. However, Jack kept away, clearly afraid to mix it. Jack trotted around and would clinch whenever Tommy drew close. Burns continued talking to him in a clinch. The crowd grew disappointed and urged O'Brien to fight. Jack finally whipped in a vicious right uppercut. He landed several right uppercuts and got some respect. Burns finally landed a right to the jaw. The left jab was O'Brien's favorite blow, but Burns showed remarkable cleverness in ducking Jack's jabs. Tom hammered the body in the clinches. One reporter said, "A decision at this stage would have given the fight to Burns on aggressiveness. O'Brien ran away all this round and stalled." Naughton said the round was even.

7 – Burns attacked savagely and punched in the clinches. He landed some rights. Jack landed his hard right uppercut. They wrestled. O'Brien landed some hard right and left hooks. Burns showed his ability to duck left leads.

Tom again invited Jack to fight as O'Brien ran away. Once inside, Burns worked hard in the clinches and hit the kidneys. The crowd did not approve of Tommy's kidney blows. As usual, O'Brien waltzed away. He landed several blows. He particularly liked uppercuts, landing them with both hands, but they had no effect. O'Brien seemed worried, and one reporter said that "the effect of the blows landed throughout the round were rather in Burns's favor. He pounded hard on O'Brien's kidneys." Naughton said, "It was an even round so far as the work done went, though Burns deserves all kinds of credit for his aggressiveness."

8 – Tom rushed and hit the body and kidneys. Jack landed the right uppercut and right hook. Burns rushed to a clinch and started O'Brien's nose bleeding again with a hook. Both were covered in Jack's blood. Tom did almost all of the infighting. A Burns left and right to the jaw almost dropped O'Brien. Burns chased him around and rushed like a bulldog. He would fairly leap at O'Brien. Jack landed a stiff right and wrestled. He was bleeding freely from his eye, mouth, and nose. Tommy cleverly ducked a left swing. They clinched for a long while, to prolonged hisses. O'Brien was inclined to hold on. O'Brien landed an uppercut but kept away as much as possible. Burns finally just stood still with his arms at his sides and waited for him to come into range. "Burns displayed unexpected agility in slipping under O'Brien's leads. Burns was the aggressor, O'Brien making a poor showing. Jeffries shook his head in disapproval of his chances." Naughton agreed that it was Burns' round.

9 – Burns tore after him like a tiger and landed a right to the jaw before they clinched. O'Brien kept away. Jack stopped a rush with a stiff left and clinched. Burns worked hard. When close, O'Brien would clinch tightly, and Jeff had trouble breaking them. Tom whipped in an overhand right to the face and opened a gash above the eye. O'Brien's face was covered in blood, and his blows had lost their steam. Burns tried hard to land a knockout blow. Every time Burns would land O'Brien would clinch. At the gong, Jack landed two stiff right uppercuts, causing Tom to grab. "The round, through Burns's eagerness to attack, was his. O'Brien appeared somewhat disturbed when the gong sounded. O'Brien's eye was badly cut." Naughton also said that it was Burns' round.

10 – Burns continued rushing and hitting hard in the clinches. He dashed at O'Brien like a fiend, hitting wildly and chasing him to a corner. Almost the entire round was spent in the clinches, both holding a great deal, with Burns having a slight edge in the infighting. Tom would hit the body and then send in overhand jolts. Tom even hit the back, where pink plaster protected Jack. O'Brien seemed groggy and tired, leaning on Tom's shoulder. He straightened Tommy up with a right uppercut but took hard rights on the kidneys. Jack landed some jabs that had no effect, for he was moving backwards when he landed them. As O'Brien incessantly moved about,

Burns "stood disgustedly in the center of the ring" and teased him about being afraid to mix it. Naughton called the round for Burns.

11 – Burns rushed and swung wildly and fell into a clinch. He broke and snapped in a vicious left to the face. He also landed a right and followed with swings with both hands. They clinched as usual.

Burns used his hands whenever an opportunity afforded. He continued rushing and firing on the way in and on the inside. O'Brien danced, punched, and clinched. Tom landed a hard right and Jack countered with a right to the body and left to the head and clinched. "Under the glaring blue of the light O'Brien's visage is a ghastly sight. Jeffries' pink shirt is bloodied from shoulder to cuffs, owing to his interference in the clinches." Burns landed several jabs and a hook to the head. They both landed rights to the body in a rush. Jack managed to land a left hook to the body and a stiff right uppercut. He also landed a stiff jab at the gong. Naughton called the round even.

12 – Burns pursued him around the ring until O'Brien grabbed. Tom asked him to break. Again Burns advanced and Jack gave him an elbow as they clinched and Tommy protested. Tommy landed a left to the ribs and right to the face. He also landed a hook to the head. He ducked a left and chased O'Brien around the ring. Tom whipped a right to the head but O'Brien rallied with a hard right and left uppercut and then shot into a clinch. They wrestled. Tom worked the body in the clinches.

Burns was compelled to do by far the most leading. He landed several lefts, but did little damage. Jack used his right hook effectively. Both men were wrestling, and Jeff parted them with difficulty. There was a great deal of clinching. "Burns swung O'Brien from him with apparent disgust at his tactics." Naughton: Round about even.

13 – Burns was eager to get close, but O'Brien evaded him. They rushed to a clinch and Burns sent a hard right and left to the head, punishing him. They hugged and wrestled for fully a minute. Jeff struggled hard to break them. Jack broke and shot across a right and left to the face. Burns measured the distance and whipped across a stiff right and then two more. Jack clinched. Burns landed two lefts that renewed the stream of blood from the mouth and nose. Jack used his right uppercut twice in rapid succession. He appeared more willing to come to close quarters. Burns landed a left to the ear and O'Brien countered as they clinched. He spit blood and held on tightly. They were clinched at the gong. The press agreed that the round was fairly even, and O'Brien seemed to be growing a little bolder, not running away quite as much.

14 – Burns began the round by rushing until O'Brien clinched. Tom bore in again and landed a hard right hook to the head and several body blows at close range. He also assaulted the kidneys. Tom chopped a stiff right to the

jaw and followed with left and right to face and head. They clinched and wrestled, with Jeff struggling to part them.

O'Brien whipped in a hard left hook. Tommy's left eye appeared to be closing slightly. "Fight, you dog," said Burns as Jack danced away. Tommy landed a clean left to the chin before another clinch. Burns led with a left hook to the stomach. O'Brien responded with the same. They exchanged rights and hooks. Tommy shot a right hook to the jaw and they clinched. O'Brien was punching and firing back more. One reporter said, "O'Brien is making a much better showing than he did earlier in the fight. The crowd sarcastically called on O'Brien for a speech." Naughton said, "Burns seems to be as strong as when he started, while O'Brien has a bedraggled look. Even round."

15 – O'Brien landed a left uppercut and Burns responded with a right hook. He pursued O'Brien. In a clinch, Tom landed a short uppercut just above the belt. Both seemed loath to break from the clinch. Jack shot in a hard right to the head and followed with an uppercut to the jaw, but Tommy did not stop. Tom countered a right with a harder one of his own. O'Brien snapped in two left jabs and they clinched. He landed a left jab to the mouth and a tap to the head. Jack again landed his jab, and appeared to be in better shape than before. Tommy's left eye was closing. They tugged savagely in a clinch. Burns did all of the work in the clinches. One writer said Burns had all the best of the infighting and hit the ribs at the gong. However, Naughton and another writer said it was O'Brien's round.

16 – Burns landed a left hook to the jaw and clinched. They wrestled. As they broke, Tom whipped in a hard left to the head. Jack jabbed and clinched. On the break, Tommy jabbed twice. During another clinch, Burns' seconds protested O'Brien's holding Tommy's right glove. Tom hooked the body. As they broke, O'Brien landed a right hook and Burns countered with a left jab. Jeff worked hard to separate them. Jack landed a stiff right to the ear. Burns was roughing it considerably in a clinch at the gong.

One source said the round slightly favored O'Brien. Both were tired and clinching, though Tommy was still the most aggressive. Naughton said it was Burns' round. "O'Brien imprisoned Burns' arm frequently in the clinches and seemed anxious to prolong the holding as much as possible."

17 – Burns rushed and shot in a hard right to the face and light left to the ribs. They clinched, and were too tough to part. O'Brien landed a stiff right uppercut and clinched. He landed a left hook. Tom came back with a hard left hook of his own. O'Brien landed a number of effective blows between the usual clinches, including a right uppercut, left hook to the body, and some left jabs. It was punch and clinch. One right uppercut caused Tom's left eye to tighten. They mixed it fiercely at the gong. After the bell, Burns

shoved him with his left, which brought hisses from the crowd. Naughton said it was O'Brien's round.

18 – O'Brien started quickly and mixed it up, using both hands effectively. Both were fast, and apparently not tired. They clinched and wrestled for a minute. Burns landed three left jabs, while O'Brien worked his left jabs and right uppercuts to good effect. Jack rocked his head with a stiff left. Tommy landed two leads. Jack jabbed him several times, dancing nimbly out of the way of the vicious right swings. Burns was still aggressive and landed a stiff left jab to the stomach. Honors were about even, but O'Brien was using his left to some advantage.

19 – Though viciously aggressive, Burns was tiring. O'Brien gained speed and landed lefts to the face and danced away easily. O'Brien then wrapped Burns in an embrace that required Jeff to break them. Jack stood toe to toe and landed a left and right to the face with no return. Burns clinched and did some effective work inside. Jack used his left jabs to keep Tom at a distance. O'Brien blocked a hook but took a right to the chin. Burns slipped under a left and sent a right to the body hard. O'Brien landed his right uppercut. They clinched most of the time. Both men blocked well. Tom worked his left in the clinches. Both slowed up at the gong. One reporter said the round closed without either having an advantage, but Tommy's left eye was almost entirely closed. Naughton said Burns did not seem to be quite as strong as he was a few rounds earlier. He called the round for O'Brien.

20 – Tommy seemed tired. Jack circled him, teasing him into a rush and clinch. Jack missed a jab and Tom's return caused the blood to start again from the nose. They wrestled and then sparred, boxing prettily until Burns whipped across a stiff left hook to the face, opening the tender spots. That was the only clean blow of the round. A light tap from Jack's right shut Tommy's left eye tight. Both butted and shoved about the ring like bulls, locked in an embrace that even Jeffries failed to break, but doing little damage. Finally, Jeff had to use his strength to break them apart. Jack landed a right uppercut to the mouth and Tom landed rights to the body. "Burns appeared somewhat less vigorous and weakened when O'Brien planted a hard left to the jaw. In the clinch that followed Burns's head seemed to wobble and he was not so vicious. He clung fully twenty seconds to avoid punishment and Jeffries used his shoulders to push Burns away." Jack used his right uppercut again and they did their usual rough work. They were clinched again at the gong. Jeffries raised both men's hands, signifying that he had ruled it a draw.

At the decision, "O'Brien's ghastly wreck of a face managed to distort itself into a smile and he held out his hand to shake. Burns turned away like a naughty little boy, and wouldn't be polite." Tommy was not happy. "Burns was stunned by the decision, and went to his corner all broken up…. However, there were plenty who openly acknowledged that Burns had the best of the argument, and if the two fight again Burns will be the favorite."

One *Los Angeles Times* writer said, "The greater part of those who saw the battle believed Tommy Burns had all the best of the milling, but Jeffries was of the opinion that the difference between the men was not sufficient to entitle either one to claim the championship." Although most felt that Burns deserved the decision; some writers said the decision was just.

The *Times* said Burns rushed throughout and gave O'Brien his toughest fight. O'Brien used jabs and uppercuts, but either failed to land or did no damage. Burns was not concerned at all by Jack's blows and mostly only crouched to protect himself.

O'Brien began the fight with considerable speed, winning the early rounds, but a terrific right in the 5th round flattened Jack's nose and sent the blood pouring in streams. "That blow put O'Brien in a bad way and he never recovered from it, for he had to stall throughout the battle and immediately after it landed he was groggy and held on for dear life." Thereafter, Jack was mostly on the defensive. Another writer said, "O'Brien simply ran away. No other name for it. He ducked and dodged like a chicken."

Burns tapped the nose frequently and brought blood each time. O'Brien held in the clinches while Tom hit his body. Burns constantly bore into him like a madman, giving Jack little opportunity to demonstrate his science. O'Brien did all he could do to escape by using his superb footwork. However, O'Brien's "vaunted cleverness and punishing powers amounted to little against Burns's bull-like rushes and boring in tactics." Therefore, when his footwork did not work, Jack held in the clinches until Jeffries had to tear them apart. Burns did his best to fight on the inside, but O'Brien just held. O'Brien's strength left him and his blows grew weaker.

As the fight progressed, the odds on O'Brien kept going down. Burns tried to get him to fight, but O'Brien had other ideas. Burns hit in the clinches, while O'Brien was mostly defensive there. Jeff had to work hard to break them. Tommy often spoke and cursed O'Brien when Jack was dancing away. "Burns made fame as a fighter last night, but did not achieve a very heavy reputation as a gentleman." The *Police Gazette* later said, "Burns was most abusive in the ring – so much so that his language disgusted many spectators." He didn't mind taunting O'Brien in order to try to get him to fight.[409] In conclusion, the *Times* said,

> The only thing that earned O'Brien a draw was the fact that toward the close of the fight Burns tired somewhat while O'Brien, by constantly holding on to avoid punishment, recovered much of his strength and seemed to be getting stronger. He stayed with Burns in

409 *Police Gazette*, December 29, 1906.

the last two rounds and by jabbing the latter's bad left eye closed the member completely so that Burns's attack was less accurate.[410]

The *Los Angeles Herald* felt that O'Brien should consider himself fortunate that Jeffries raised his arm along with Burns'. Apparently, the final two rounds helped secure him the draw, as he did not skip about the ring as much, and stood before Burns when Tommy was tired and did not exhibit the same vim and speed that he had throughout the battle. However, Tommy's weariness was from his constant effort to attack, as the ring general O'Brien darted away from him in practically every round from the 5th to the 18th rounds. Still, Tommy had exhibited great strength and stamina throughout the fight.

For the first 4 rounds, O'Brien jabbed Burns as he might a punching bag, feinting and sending in his lightning lefts. Jack literally peppered Burns at will for the first 4 rounds, smiling with supreme confidence. He was at his best in the 3rd round.

However, in the 5th round, maddened by Jack's dazzling jabbing and steel clad defense, Burns rushed like a bull and went at O'Brien in a cyclonic manner. A terrific murderous right drive to the nose almost proved O'Brien's undoing. His legs bent and his eyes grew narrow. He was sorely hurt. Only superb blocking and brain power saved O'Brien. The blood spurted in torrents over his face, and under the film lights, the gore was an inky black. It seemed that Tommy's superior strength and power was better than O'Brien's superior skill and craft. In the corner, the bluish blood could not be stopped. Even Jeff's face was covered with the purplish fluid.

Throughout the fight, Jeffries had to struggle mightily to untangle and break the two. Even his gigantic strength was taxed. Both were guilty of holding, though O'Brien's clutch was the more noticeable.

After the 5th round, Burns fought his man to more than a standstill. He never gave O'Brien a moment to rest, except at times in the clinches. Although O'Brien had the superior skill and might have landed the cleanest blows, it was difficult to figure where Burns did not have the shade when the bout had been completed. O'Brien had clearly received the worst of the argument. Tommy's strength was far superior and Jack danced away a major portion of the time, landing with no effect, so far as Tom's strength was concerned. Tom left the ring with a badly closed eye, but his mouth had begun swelling during the early rounds.

However, O'Brien did not run away in the final two rounds, and since Tommy was tired from all of his efforts and chasing, he did not have a terrific windup, which perhaps secured the draw for O'Brien. "There was no outcry of disapproval but a quiet sentiment prevailed throughout the house that Jack O'Brien was the lad who might give Thanksgiving today."

---

410 *Los Angeles Daily Times*, November 29, 1906.

Burns' great showing was said to be the result of magnificent physical condition. If he had not been in such great shape, O'Brien would have easily outboxed him. That said, O'Brien was in great shape as well, for he had to be in order to be able to move around that much for so long. Tommy mostly had Jack on the defensive from the 5th round on. Burns' eyes burned with bitter wrath as he followed and followed O'Brien around the ring.

Burns said that he had clearly won the fight, for he had O'Brien running around the ring to get away from his punishing blows. "I had him beat a mile. I did all the forcing and had him covering from the blows most of the time. I was robbed."[411]

Burns told the *Examiner*, "I chased O'Brien fifty miles and Jeffries only gave me a draw. I showed the people I could fight and that is all I cared for. If the fight had been to a finish there would have been no doubt as to the outcome. I will fight him again."

Afterwards, O'Brien told the *Herald* that he was happy with the decision, and would not fight again as a heavyweight. "I am very well pleased with the decision. The man was too heavy and strong for me. Tonight I am down to middle weight and was fighting a man much heavier than myself. Hereafter I shall fight in the middleweight division."

O'Brien told the *Examiner*, "I am well satisfied with the result. Early in the battle I found that Burns was stronger than I was and I gave my whole effort to making the fight as scientific as possible. In the early rounds Burns struck me low and that materially injured my chances of winning."

According to the *Herald*, Referee Jeffries said, "I could give no other decision, as there was not enough to choose from at the end." Jeffries offered his analysis of the bout. The *Examiner* quoted him as saying,

> It was a hard battle in which each man did effective work at his own style of fighting. It was a contest without a knockdown and with both men fighting equal at the finish. For this reason I called the Burns-O'Brien fight a draw. Prior to the bout each man had asked that no hair-line decision be given. I acted accordingly.

> But I will make this statement that had it been necessary that some decision be given; I would have given the benefit to Burns. He had a slight shade.

> O'Brien did much running away and holding, but he also landed many a clean punch and improved from the fifteenth round to the finish. O'Brien also had the lead during the early rounds, demonstrating his cleverness at long-range fighting.

> Had the fight terminated at the end of the fifteenth round I would have been forced to have given Burns the decision. He had his

411 *Los Angeles Herald*, November 29, 1906.

opponent in a bad way, but Tommy failed to keep up the pace to the windup.

I must say Tommy Burns fought a surprising battle. He has greatly improved and all but put O'Brien out in the fifth round when he landed a terrific right full on O'Brien's nose. This was the most effective punch in the fight. In getting away and keeping away until he gained the strength to withstand Burns' rushes O'Brien displayed his ring generalship. This blow hurt O'Brien and it was ten rounds before he fully recovered from it. In the clinches, where Burns did his most effective work, O'Brien resorted to holding on and I was forced to pull his arm away many times.

O'Brien's best punch was a right uppercut which he sneaked in many and many a time during the battle. He sent it to the face and body and had Burns' left eye closed tight at the end of the fight. O'Brien missed many straight lefts and landed many, but they did not have great force behind them.

During the early rounds of the fight, Burns stood up under terrific rights which would have put many a poorer man to the bad.

I never saw a fight in which there was such footwork, and on this particular O'Brien did not show up so much better than Burns. Both were clever. To have given a decision would have been a blow to the reputation of one of the men and Burns' shade was so slight that I did not feel like splitting hairs so finely.

In the last two rounds O'Brien began doing some work in the clinches, something he had not done before, and held his own at this game which he had been trying so industriously to avoid during most of the fight.

Analyzing the fight, round by round, you will find O'Brien far in the lead the first few rounds. The long fellow sent in punch after punch which landed cleanly, but not for a second did Burns back up. He kept coming and his determined spirit told in the fifth when the tide of battle turned so suddenly. From the fifth to the fifteenth Burns employed rushing tactics. O'Brien was often on the defensive in the clinches, but often he would stop in his shifting to send in stinging right uppercuts. Burns displayed cleverness in escaping O'Brien's straight lefts.

After the fifteenth Burns let up and O'Brien gradually improved, his work in the concluding rounds saving him.[412]

412 *Los Angeles Examiner*, November 29, 1906.

The *Examiner's* writers, who mostly hailed from San Francisco, an area which tended to laud O'Brien, were more supportive of the decision than most of the local Los Angeles papers. C.E. Van Loan claimed that the draw decision was received with tremendous cheers and there was scarcely a dissenting voice. However, Burns let his hands fall at his sides as if amazed. "And still we have no heavyweight champion!"

It was a fight between a matador and the constantly rushing bull. Jack's jabs did nothing to stop Tom's boring in. Burns almost had him out in the 5th round. Jack skipped, ducked and dodged and every once in a while came in like lightning, planting his stinging darts, but the bull came at him from first to last. Although he took some jabs and right uppercuts that made his head go back, Tom never stopped tearing in. "Tommy Burns fought a great fight."

Through the first 4 rounds, O'Brien sidestepped and nailed Tom's face almost at will, bringing some blood. However, he grew careless and in the 5th round Burns nailed him on the nose. "That one punch changed the whole complexion of the fight. O'Brien stopped trading punches with Burns after the fifth round. He was satisfied to keep out of the way of that right hand and rip in a telling uppercut or a straight left when an opportunity offered." Tom fought harder than ever after the 5th round. He literally ran after O'Brien. Throughout, Tom wanted to hit on the inside, but Jack had his arms locked. Jeffries had to tear them apart, and his white shirt was smeared with blood, and even his face was flecked with O'Brien's blood.

After the 15th round, O'Brien began fighting again. "His face was still covered with blood and there were times when he spat out great mouthfuls of gore, but his head was clear and he devoted himself to outpointing Burns with clean punches, covering and getting out of danger." In the 17th round, Jack landed two wallops to the chin, but the sturdy Burns did not falter for an instant. He was the "living, breathing incarnation of the fighting spirit." At times he dropped his hands and taunted O'Brien, begging him to fight. Jack never accepted, dancing and skipping until he was ready to whip in a clean punch to the face. At the end of the round, Tom threw O'Brien from him and Jack nearly fell. "The last three rounds of the fight were on the same order – Burns doing all the rushing and O'Brien doing three-fourths of the clean hitting." Tom tried to work inside but O'Brien was determined not to let him.

Van Loan opined, "O'Brien's clean hitting in the last five rounds of the fight saved him from defeat." Burns led in terms of damage done and aggressiveness. O'Brien led in terms of pure clean lands without consideration of damaging effect. O'Brien had a broken nose and damaged mouth. Burns had a completely closed eye. "Jeffries split the difference and his decision was a very popular one."

Another *Examiner* writer, Sandy Griswold, said O'Brien would have won had there been clean breaks. He felt that O'Brien was a masterful pugilist who hit easily, cleanly, accurately and with great force and speed with both hands, without giving any indication of where he intended to land. "There is no tell-tale shoulder duck or body swing to telegraph his blows." He felt that Jeff's decision deserved approval.

W.W. Naughton said, "Jack O'Brien is a lucky man." He shared the honors of a draw, but up to the 14th or 15th rounds, he was clearly behind. Burns was as strong as a bull and too strong for O'Brien. His vehemence took all of the starch out of Jack early on, and O'Brien's blows lacked steam. Burns clearly wanted to fight in close. He rushed in whirlwind fashion. Jeff broke them repeatedly, but Tommy would not be denied. "His strength was immense and he was willingness personified and he kept hurling himself at Jack and tearing away with short arm punches, while O'Brien tried to hold him back." Jack's jabs were of little use. After the 5th round, O'Brien's confidence seemed to have been destroyed. He circled the ring with Burns chasing after him. Occasionally Tommy would drop his hands and with a look of derision, exclaim, "Why don't you stand and fight, you cur?" O'Brien made a circuit of the ring many times in every round.

O'Brien picked up points in the 15th round with jabs and right uppercuts, though in the following round Tom again had Jack in a bedraggled condition from his free-arm work. From the 17th round on, O'Brien's confidence returned and he closed Tom's left eye with his right uppercut. Burns continued rushing and trying to tear his arms loose and work on the inside.

Ultimately, Naughton said,

> All things considered, it was a fair decision. If the articles of agreement had stipulated that there must be a winner, Burns would have received the award of honor. Taking the things by and large, O'Brien's cleverness in hitting and cleverness in defensive work offset Burns' aggressiveness. ... The men may and should come together again, next time for a finish fight. If they do, Burns will be the favorite.[413]

Totaling Naughton's own round-by-round report, he scored the fight 5 rounds Burns, 5 rounds O'Brien, and 10 rounds even.

According to the *L.A. Express*, most felt that Burns deserved the decision. O'Brien "had his face beaten into a mess and otherwise was mauled around the ring last night…and it was only the charity of Referee Jeffries that kept the decision from going to Burns." Tommy was "still in possession of an alleged title to the heavyweight championship." The

413 *Los Angeles Examiner*, November 29, 1906.

spectators were of the belief that "Burns would give O'Brien a worse beating should they decide to try the issue again."

Burns was the aggressor throughout the fight, and although he caught a number of uppercuts on his lowered rushing head, O'Brien's blows lacked steam. In the 2nd round, O'Brien hit him with five uppercuts in succession, and after that Tommy took more evasive action. Burns had the best of it after the 2nd round all the way to the end. "A vicious punch by Burns in the fifth is what put Mr. O'Brien's countenance out of recognition. The blow smashed his nose and drew rivulets of claret." After that, O'Brien mostly either ran or clinched. "Jeffries required all of his immense strength to pull apart the combatants as both held on at various stages, though O'Brien was the chief offender in this regard."

In the 14th round, Burns chased him all around the ring, as Jack was clearly distressed and trying to avoid any mix up.

Still, the *Express* attempted to justify Jeffries' decision. O'Brien landed an excellent right in the 17th round and closed Burns' eye such that it disconcerted him for the rest of the fight. Burns eased up a bit and O'Brien came on, though Burns still held his own.

> The pictures will show O'Brien running away from Burns in every round except the seventeenth, nineteenth and twentieth with O'Brien puffing at all stages after the fifth round. ... It was this flash of O'Brien's at the end which caused Jeffries to declare the bout a draw. Had Burns finished the fight as he had carried it on in the middle rounds the referee undoubtedly would have given the decision to Tommy.

Further excuses for the decision were made. "Although Burns forced the fighting throughout there had been a tacit understanding that if the men were on their feet without a decided show on either side, the affair was to be declared a draw." However, most thought that Burns had the decided advantage in the fight.

At the end, O'Brien had a battered face, with a smashed nose, swollen upper lip, bruise over the right eye and abrasion on the left cheek, and was horrid looking.[414]

The gate receipts totaled $25,875, although one source said they totaled $26,500. With the draw decision, O'Brien earned $6,600 as his share (50% of $10,800 plus his $1,200 guarantee), while Burns earned $5,400. The fighters would each also receive one-third of the moving picture receipts.

The next day, it was reported that O'Brien's nose was broken. One reporter said O'Brien had Tommy going in the first few rounds, but the thunderbolt punch to the nose in the 5th round had changed the fight.

---

414 *Los Angeles Express*, November 29, 1906.

O'Brien said the blow to the nose prevented him from defeating Burns, because it affected the optic nerves, so he was unable to see clearly, which explained why he missed so many punches. O'Brien also claimed that his left arm had been useless. His arm was badly swollen, particularly his left elbow. Jack further claimed that his right hand was hurt in the 2nd round. His injured hand and arm had affected his punching ability. He claimed that he could defeat Burns in another meeting. Still, O'Brien gave Burns credit.

> He is a wonderfully improved fighter. He has improved even since he boxed Flynn I think. His strength, too, is prodigious. I made a mistake, though, in not fighting back in the clinches sooner. ... I didn't win and I am not going to rob Burns of any of his credit. He surprised me and showed that he is a dangerous opponent for any man. Yes, I'll fight him again if there is a demand for such a contest, but I don't want any more roughhouse rules. Clean breaks for me next time.[415]

O'Brien intended to go on the road for several months to make money with the films and to give lectures on the physical culture.

Burns wore an eye shield over his injured left eye, which was badly swollen and discolored. His face showed the effects of the left jabs and uppercuts that O'Brien had landed.

Burns "was not loath to say that he should have received the decision, and in this he was backed yesterday by a great majority of those who witnessed the battle."

The main reason why there was not a vigorous general public protest about the decision was because it was rendered by the respected Jim Jeffries. Still, his decision was not to general liking.

It was believed that the films would prove quite lucrative. "Burns is the man who will gain the most renown, once the films are exposed. ... In all probability a general verdict will ensue that Tommy had the best of it."[416]

The *Examiner's* C.E. Van Loan said the fight supported the old saying, "It depends on how you look at it." Two men who had attended the fight, one supporting O'Brien and the other supporting Burns, engaged in debate, each wholeheartedly believing their man had won. During the fight, the Burns man said, "Why Tommy is making him look like a rank sucker! He's doing all the forcing and all the fighting. If O'Brien would only stand up and fight Tommy, it would all be over in about three wallops. I thought O'Brien had some class; he ain't showing it tonight." The O'Brien supporter retorted, "Who's doing all the clean hitting? O'Brien. Who's doing two-thirds of the leading? O'Brien. Why, I tell you, Burns can't lay a glove on O'Brien unless he gets him into a clinch." He said the 5th round punch to the nose was a lucky one. The Burns man again came on, "Who's

415 *Los Angeles Examiner*, November 30, 1906.
416 *Los Angeles Herald, Los Angeles Times*, November 30, 1906; *Police Gazette*, December 29, 1906.

breaking ground and running away? O'Brien! Ain't Burns chasing him all around the ring? Who's holding on? O'Brien! And when it comes to punishment, that one wallop of Burns' did more harm than a thousand of O'Brien's right uppercuts! Skipping around and running away don't get a man anything! O'Brien ought to fight!" The O'Brien supporter retorted, "I suppose when a man gets into the ring he ought to first remove his brains … What do you suppose a man was given a brain for if not to use it?"[417]

Two days after the fight, the confident Burns challenged O'Brien to meet again for a side bet of $5,000. Burns said if they fought again, he wanted the articles of agreement to clearly bar O'Brien from holding his arms again. At that point, the swelling in Tommy's left eye had subsided with the aid of leeches, and but for blackness, his face and eye looked normal.

O'Brien had spent two days in bed recovering from the fight. He had a cut on his forehead. His left arm was badly swollen. He was given credit for putting up the fight that he did after getting badly dazed in the 5th round.

O'Brien did not want to talk fight, but about where the pictures were to be shown and how the expenses were to be borne. The fighters met with McCarey on December 1 to discuss matters.[418]

In subsequent days, Jeff's decision received more criticism, and fewer were attempting to justify it. "Ever since the fight there has been a great undercurrent of dissatisfaction over the decision." Jeffries was respected and his integrity unquestioned, but the majority of those who witnessed the fight did not agree with him. "As a referee, judging a battle on its merits and acting in the capacity of arbiter on the fine points, Jeffries proved himself a failure."[419]

The moving pictures were successfully developed and exhibited for the first time on December 6 at the Lyric Theater. First, the films showed O'Brien training, using pulleys, hitting the punching bag, and sparring with the Terrible Turk, Bob Ward, and Mortimer Swanson. Next, Burns' training and sparring was shown, and Tommy was seen to drop his sparring partners. Then the pre-fight, including the argument about the belt, and the entire main fight was exhibited. The punch that nearly ended the fight in the 5th round was clearly seen. O'Brien's wonderful footwork was on display, but his holding was all too apparent. Time and again, Jeff had to remove his arm. Jack's efforts in the last two rounds were there, but both men showed a desire to give it their last ounce of strength during those rounds.[420]

On December 7, 1906 at the Naud Junction Pavilion, Tommy Burns refereed the Abe Attell-Jimmy Walsh world featherweight title fight, which Attell won by KO9.

417 *Los Angeles Examiner*, November 30, 1906.
418 *Los Angeles Express*, *Los Angeles Herald*, December 1, 1906; *Los Angeles Times*, December 2, 1906.
419 *Los Angeles Times*, December 2, 1906.
420 *Los Angeles Herald*, December 7, 1906.

The Burns-O'Brien motion pictures were again shown at Morlay's South Grand Avenue Skating Rink on the 10th, and would be exhibited there throughout the week every night at 8:15 p.m. The show lasted just under two hours. Admirers of both men saw the films and said things like, "How could Jeffries have given a decision like that after the fight that Tommy put up against the Philadelphian?" Or, "The decision was well rendered and should be well received by true sportsmen." More than half of the spectators in the audience were women.[421]

The East-Coast based *Police Gazette* reported that the fight pictures were the best ever taken of a fistic encounter.

> The fight was anything but an interesting boxing exhibition. Every round was a repetition of Burns tearing out of his corner like a mad bull and the elusive Jack sidestepping and leading, presumably to avoid a mixup at close quarters. Burns showed up like Sharkey's twin brother, but seemed at a loss to know what to do after he had closed in on O'Brien. His only blow seemed to be a right swing, which invariably went wide of the mark....

> O'Brien was a disappointment in that he appeared throughout the fight only to be intent upon getting away and staying the limit. At times Burns got disgusted at Jack's sprinting tactics and dropped his hands to his sides....

> Jeff loomed up like a mountain in the ring and was kept busy throughout the fight prying the men apart. The decision, according to good judges, was the only one that could have been rendered justly.[422]

A substantial portion of the fight films still exist (about 50 minutes total), and they allow independent insight. O'Brien was the taller man, and to say that he used a lot of footwork and clinching in this fight is an understatement. With his hands down, O'Brien moved incessantly. He danced, sidestepped, or literally ran or quickly walked away, not wanting to fight in close. He would circle, feint, occasionally attack with one or two quick punches at the most, and then immediately grab to avoid the counter or move away. His paltry offense also ensured that Burns would have few openings, for by not throwing many punches at a time, he was rarely in one spot or exposed for more than a moment. Once Jeffries managed to break them, and he did have serious difficulties in doing so despite being much bigger than both, O'Brien would move and grab again.

Burns stalked O'Brien with his hands down, but he knew how to lift them up or punch when in range. He constantly kept the pressure on, advancing with his right leg bent and slightly dipping to the right. Tommy would either walk or slide in, looking quite alert and ready to punch. Burns

421 *Los Angeles Herald*, December 10, 1906.
422 *Police Gazette*, December 29, 1906.

could have utilized more lateral footwork to cut him off, but it probably would not have mattered much against O'Brien's constant running around and holding. O'Brien's leg conditioning was absolutely amazing. Usually, fighters who move that much will hit the wall at some point and become exhausted, especially in a lengthy bout.

Burns was ferocious on the inside, hooking to the body and head when O'Brien tied up his right arm, or throwing rights when the left was held. He made a determined effort to work his hands free and punch. Tom did most of his work on the inside with short shots, primarily to the body.

O'Brien clearly did not want to mix it up on the inside, choosing to hold with a practical vice grip. He seemed more interested in moving or grabbing incessantly rather than punching. He would even hold Burns' head down in a vice grip, which Tommy made easy because he had a tendency to lean or dip forward. When O'Brien held Tommy's head down with his left arm, Burns would hit Jack's back or side with his right.

O'Brien was made quite wary by the fact that Burns was always advancing, always eager to mix it up, knew how to punch hard and fast when in range, and could counterpunch as soon as O'Brien let his hands go. This made O'Brien cautious and eager to clinch as soon as either punched so that he could prevent Burns from getting off very much.

At times, Burns seemed perturbed by O'Brien, dropping his hands well below his waist and either standing in ring center and turning to watch Jack's circling, or simply walking to him. He even stared at O'Brien after rounds were over, as if to ask him whether he was going to fight. From the newspaper accounts, it is likely that he did just that. In between rounds, their seconds would wave towels to cool them off.

After 20 rounds, Jeffries called it a draw by raising both fighters' arms, but based on the films, Burns deserved the victory. From the start, O'Brien appeared more interested in survival than fighting. As for O'Brien's good start and Tommy's alleged slowing down and O'Brien's coming on at the end, that was either newspaper spin to justify Jeff's decision, or missing footage. O'Brien did not appear to pick it up all that much in the final rounds, and basically continued his same tactics. If Burns did slow up, it was slight, and he was still more determined to make an offensive effort than was the gripping O'Brien. Tommy Burns was the better fighter throughout, from start to finish, and deserved the decision.

So why did Jeffries call the fight a draw? Was he just a poor judge? Is it that he took a liking to O'Brien? Did he think calling it a draw made himself look better by having no undisputed champion since he retired? Or was there some sort of pre-fight agreement or incentive to do so? Perhaps he felt that without a knockout, it should be a draw. He might have been concerned about upsetting one faction or the other, so he hoped to make everyone happy by calling it a draw. Perhaps it was simply his honest opinion, and there might be missing footage. It is true that Burns was not able to land many clean punches, owing to O'Brien's defensive style. There are no definitive answers, but some of what was revealed after the Burns-O'Brien championship rematch can easily be used to fuel some debate.... To be continued.

CHAPTER 9

Fixing a Wrong

In December 1906, it was reported that promoter Tex Rickard allegedly offered James Jeffries $50,000 to come out of retirement. However, such an offer didn't make sense, because Rickard was also quoted as saying that boxing "is today without a man who could be considered to have a possible chance to whip Jeffries, or even to make him extend himself."[423] The *Police Gazette* said, "Neither O'Brien nor Burns for that matter would have a ghost of a chance with Jeffries, who stands alone as the greatest heavyweight pugilist in the world." James Jeffries was a hard act to follow.[424]

Certainly, Jeffries dwarfed both Burns and O'Brien. He was so much bigger; it looks like he could decapitate both with one punch. A fight between Jeffries and either Burns or O'Brien at least would have been a physical mismatch. However, men like Choynski, Fitzsimmons, Sharkey, and Corbett had proven that a very good fighter, regardless of weight, could give Jeffries a stiff test. O'Brien and Burns might have been quicker than Jeff. Also, Jeffries had been physically inactive and was fat. He had not fought in over two years.

Jack Johnson's manager said that a Philadelphia club had offered 60% of the gate receipts for a 6-round bout between Johnson and Burns. "In fairness to Burns it must be said he has never said anything about drawing the color line, and it may be that he will be willing to meet Johnson."[425]

Regarding the possibility of fighting Johnson, Burns said,

> I wish someone would put an end to these stories that I ever intended meeting Jack Johnson. I am having a hard time with my wife now, as she wants me to cut out this business. I don't know what she would do if she heard I fought a negro. She's a southerner and I guess you know what southern folks think of negroes. They may say I am afraid of Johnson and anything else they want to, but I am never going to fight a negro. I have fought them, but am drawing the line now.[426]

The *Police Gazette* responded, "As was expected, Tommy Burns has drawn the color line in the direction of Jack Johnson."[427]

---

423 *Police Gazette*, December 15, 1906.
424 *Police Gazette*, December 22, 1906.
425 *Police Gazette*, December 22, 1906.
426 *Los Angeles Herald*, December 13, 1906.
427 *Police Gazette*, December 29, 1906.

However, Tommy Burns was not afraid of a stiff test. According to Burns, on December 19, he met and point-blank asked Jeffries for a fight. Jeffries told him that he would come out of retirement and fight him if he was offered a $50,000 purse. Tommy responded, "If I win decisively from O'Brien and someone offers us a purse of $50,000 will you meet me in the ring?" Jeff said, "Yes, I will, kid. Sure if someone gives us that much money." Tom said,

> Jim, I think that you are not as good as you were at one time, and I believe that if anybody would have a show with you I would have the best look-in, that is, if I get O'Brien this time, and I expect to do so. This fellow Johnson who is hollering for a match ought not to be considered so long as I am in the game. Marvin Hart beat him and you know what I did to Marvin.

Tom wasn't calling Jeff out of retirement, but was concerned about rumors that Jeff might meet Johnson for a big payday. Burns wanted to be sure that if Jeffries came out of retirement that he would be given the first opportunity to fight Jeff, not Johnson. However, Jeffries said that he had no intention of fighting a black man.[428]

Tex Rickard issued a statement saying that earlier reports regarding his alleged offer were false.

> The stories printed in the east and all over the country about my offering $50,000 for a fight between Jeffries and Tommy Burns or Jeffries and Jack Johnson are all absolutely untruths. To even think of such a thing would be ridiculous. Sam Fitzpatrick, Johnson's manager, started all this talk and the eastern sporting papers aided him. I would not for a minute consider a match between these men.[429]

On December 21, 1906 at the Naud Junction Pavilion in Los Angeles, Tommy Burns refereed the Al Kaufman-George Gardner bout, won by Kaufman via 14th round knockout. Despite his victory, the local press criticized Kaufman's performance, perhaps unjustly, saying that he lacked class and condition.[430]

Tom McCarey wanted Burns and O'Brien to fight again. Their fight had yielded a very big payday for everyone, and the films would generate even more income. He expected that a rematch would generate another hefty payday for all parties concerned.

On December 22, McCarey secured the Burns-O'Brien rematch for an alleged purse of $30,000. The articles of agreement were between the Pacific Athletic Club, Noah Brusso, and Joseph Hagan. Straight Marquis of

428 *Los Angeles Herald*, December 20, 1906.
429 *Los Angeles Herald*, December 20, 1906.
430 *Los Angeles Herald*, December 22, 1906.

Queensberry rules would govern. The match would take place sometime between May 7 and 14, 1907, otherwise known as Fiesta Week. The purse would be divided 60% to the winner and 40% to the loser. All three parties would pay the referee's fee, divided one-third each. McCarey was authorized to settle all disputes not covered by the Queensberry rules. They would wear 5-ounce fingerless gloves, but this time soft bandages would be allowed. Jeffries would referee, or someone else mutually agreed upon. The two fighters would be allowed to engage in interim matches if they desired, but not after March 18, when the fighters were required to appear in Los Angeles to train. Each fighter allegedly deposited a $2,500 forfeit. Burns left for Philadelphia, where he was opening a theatrical venture.[431]

In January 1907, the *Los Angeles Herald* reported that there were claims on the East Coast that the O'Brien-Burns battle was a fake, that O'Brien allowed Burns to last, and that the two had rehearsed their affair, but that Tommy double-crossed Jack and hit too hard. It was rumored to be the greatest fake of the century, and that they set things up so they could box a rematch and earn more money. However, the *Herald* said that anyone who saw the fight would laugh at such a claim. "A series of such fakes would cram Naud Junction six times a week."[432]

There were some negotiations for a match between James Jeffries and rising Australian star Bill Squires for a $30,000 purse, but Jeff wanted $25,000, win, lose, or draw. Jeffries, who really did not want to come back unless it was an offer too good to refuse, turned down $20,000 guaranteed. The Rhyolite club representative in Nevada said,

> Jeffries' demands are entirely unreasonable. He should understand that this fight will not be a great drawing card compared to a fight with Johnson, and that we cannot afford more than a $30,000 purse. He can pretty nearly name his own purse if he will fight Johnson, but when he refuses to fight the only man for whom there is a really national demand, he cannot expect to get a gold mine for fighting someone else.[433]

On January 4, 1907 at the Naud Junction Pavilion in Los Angeles, "Fireman" Jim Flynn won a 20-round decision over Jack "Twin" Sullivan. One month later, on February 12 at the same venue, Flynn and Sullivan would fight to a 20-round draw. Flynn's performances gained Burns even more credit for his knockout victory over Flynn.

While in Philadelphia, on January 10, 1907 at the Lyceum Theater, Tommy Burns boxed Joe Grim in an exhibition bout. Grim was a very experienced fighter who was known for his durability and ability to take a beating, leading to his nickname, "the Iron Man." He was born in Italy, but

431 *Los Angeles Herald*, December 23, 1906.
432 *Los Angeles Herald*, January 9, 1907.
433 *Philadelphia Inquirer*, January 4, 1907.

lived in Philadelphia. He had results such as: 1903 LND6 Jack O'Brien, LND6 Bob Fitzsimmons, and L6 Hugo Kelly; 1904 LND6 Peter Maher; and 1905 LND6 Jack Johnson. However, despite having signed a contract to box Burns for 3 rounds of three minutes per round, before the bout started, Lyceum manager Miller announced that Grim insisted on boxing only one-minute rounds.

Burns attempted to stop Grim, but the rounds were too short. Grim did everything that he could to survive, including holding and dropping down to recover. In the 1st round, Burns began by feinting and stepping in and out. He landed a right to the jaw and they clinched. Upon breaking, Tom landed another right to the jaw and Grim went down. When he rose, he stuck his left in Tom's face. Burns landed his right to the cheek and Grim went down again. They were clinched at the end of the one-minute round.

In the 2nd round, Burns rushed and Grim backed away. Tom put out his left to measure and tried to land his right, but could not do so owing to all of Joe's footwork.

In the 3rd one-minute round, Grim tried to keep his left in Tom's face to keep him away, while Burns tried to hit him. He was after Grim all the time, but Joe showed a lot of shiftiness. Still, Grim went down three times, twice without being hit, in order to survive.

It was opined that the shortened rounds had saved him, and that Grim could never last 6 regulation rounds with Burns (the maximum distance allowed in Philadelphia). That was a high compliment, given Grim's known ability to take punishment.[434]

During January, Burns received an offer of 2,500 British pounds to fight English champion "Gunner" Moir. The Brits had been trying to make a match with Moir and Jack O'Brien for several months as well. Burns said he would consider such a proposition after he fought O'Brien again.[435]

While on the East Coast, when asked about his plans, Burns said he would defeat O'Brien the next time without question. He was out for all the money that he could get. He was willing to box Fitzsimmons, and also wanted to fight Jeffries. "No man can last forever. Jeffries' time will come, and I may be the man to beat him. I am a better man than Tom Sharkey ever was, and Sharkey gave him a good fight when [Jeffries] was younger and in better shape than he is today." At that time, Burns was doing his vaudeville turn.[436]

Burns, via his manager C.A. O'Connor, cabled to England saying that he would fight Gunner Moir for $7,000 plus $1,000 in expense money.[437]

English middleweight champion Jack Palmer was also asking for a match with Burns.[438]

434 *Philadelphia Record,* January 11, 1907.
435 *Los Angeles Herald,* January 17, 1907; *Los Angeles Times,* November 2, 1906.
436 *Los Angeles Herald,* January 21, 1907.
437 *Los Angeles Herald,* February 3, 1907.

As of February 21, it was said that Tommy had been traveling in the east for the past six weeks with a theatrical company. He had even visited Canada.[439]

On February 22, 1907 at the Naud Junction Pavilion in Los Angeles, in a bout against his sparring partner, Abdul "the Turk" Malgan, Jack O'Brien won via 5th round disqualification when Malgan hit him with a low blow.

TOMMY BURNS

While in St. Louis, Burns spoke with a reporter regarding Jeffries. A year ago, when the same reporter spoke with Jack O'Brien regarding the same topic, Jack said he thought that beating Jeffries would be a cinch. He said Fitzsimmons had nearly blinded Jeffries in 8 rounds. O'Brien was much faster than Fitz, and therefore would close Jeff's eyes within 6 rounds, and therefore be able to knock him out with a punch that Jeff could not see coming. "Biggest snap on earth," he said.

O'Brien was considered very cocky and arrogant for making such a brash statement. At that time, modesty was a valued character trait. Hence, when he met Jeff in the ring before the Burns-Flynn fight and said that he did not want to fight him, it was O'Brien's way of showing Jeff respect and regaining favor.

Tommy Burns was nowhere near as cocky in his answer as O'Brien was. He reiterated that all champions get beat if they keep fighting long enough. Tom did not want to boast, but felt that his chances against Jeffries were fairly good. Burns had been fighting and winning regularly, and was in perfect physical condition. "I know I am fast, and I have some cleverness. Moreover, I am not afraid to fight any man living." He would fight Jeff in the same manner as Corbett did with Sullivan, with footwork, to keep him moving, and to get under his punches and work the body. He said that Jeff was in the same physical condition as Sullivan was when he fought Corbett. "The biggest and toughest man living can't drink raw whisky the way Jeff does and keep his vitality. It didn't hurt Jeffries for a few years, but it has him going now. Jeff is terrible heavy. ... He can't train down the way he used to." Tom said another advantage would be the fact that Jeff would

---

438 *Los Angeles Herald*, February 20, 1907.
439 *Los Angeles Herald*, February 21, 1907.

underestimate him, regarding him as an easy mark that was too small for him, and therefore would not train in the same manner. "And there he'd make a mistake. I look small, but I weigh just what Sharkey weighed at his best. And I'm faster and a more clever boxer."

Burns felt confident enough to match his skill against any man. However, he also said that like the others, he would meet his master one day. If he was beaten once, he would try again. However, if he was beaten twice, he would leave the ring. "I am unlike some other fighters. I don't care for the notoriety. I'd much prefer to be at home living quietly than out with a show." Tom boxed and did the theatrical thing because it made him money. The name of champion had economic value. To him, the business was about maximizing his income. Regardless, "I fight for all I am worth every time I get into a ring."[440]

On March 26, 1907 at Naud Junction, Jack Sullivan stopped Jack Palmer in the 9th round of their bout. Palmer was game and absorbed a lot of punishment, being outclassed and knocked down six times in all throughout the bout until the towel was thrown in. Tommy Burns, who had just arrived in Los Angeles via train, attended the fight.[441]

About that time, the *Herald* said that in order to be a true world champion, a fighter had to defeat the best representatives of America, England, and Australia. Perhaps this gave Tommy some ideas about his future plans.[442]

On April 10, 1907, a judge fined Tommy Burns $5 for committing a battery upon W.F. Gensel, who was said to have jostled Tommy's wife and then made an insulting remark. Tom admitted to striking the man, but asserted that he thought Gensel needed it, and that there were a great many men whose manners would be improved if they were treated likewise.[443]

During April, there was a report that Jack O'Brien was afraid of Burns and might be trying to find a way out of their bout. Jack cited what he claimed was an obligation in the articles for McCarey to post a large sum of money, but all those with a copy of the articles said there was no such thing. Therefore, many suspected that Jack might be having cold feet, and they called him a rank quitter.[444]

O'Brien had been training in San Francisco, and wanted to remain there, but McCarey wanted him to train in the Los Angeles area as the contract required, which would help promote the fight to the local crowds.[445]

McCarey had expected O'Brien several days earlier, so as of April 16, he said if Jack did not show up, he was going to call off the fight. Actually, under the articles, both fighters were supposed to be in Los Angeles as of

440 *Los Angeles Herald*, March 3, 1907.
441 *Los Angeles Herald*, March 27, 1907.
442 *Los Angeles Herald*, April 5, 1907.
443 *Los Angeles Herald*, April 11, 1907.
444 *Los Angeles Herald*, April 11, 1907.
445 *Los Angeles Herald*, April 15, 1907.

March 18, a month earlier, and to remain in the area until the fight. Only Tommy had complied. O'Brien was in breach of the contract, and had not been answering telegrams. Like Corbett, Jack was a pain to deal with.[446]

The next day, O'Brien sent a telegram saying not to worry, that he would be down soon, and was training daily. Burns shifted his training from the East Side Club to Long Beach.[447]

On April 17, 1907 in San Diego, Jim Flynn knocked out former world light heavyweight champion George Gardner in the 18th round. Flynn's recent strong performances against Sullivan and Gardner made Burns' knockout victory over him seem all the more impressive.

A big boxing platform was built in the middle of the Long Beach skating rink, where Burns would complete his training for the O'Brien fight. Tom also secured a large house at 915 East Ocean Avenue for him and his retinue to stay.[448]

In late April, a couple weeks before the fight, O'Brien finally arrived in the Los Angeles area. He trained at Arcadia.[449]

Tommy was training with Frank Lewis, Billy Woods, and Jimmy Burns. On the 25th, more than 200 people, including women, paid a small fee to watch him train. He did calisthenics, punched the bag, and then gracefully jumped rope continuously for 10 minutes. Next, wearing heavily padded gloves, he and Billy Woods, who was a hard hitter and quick as a flash, mixed it up intensely for 3 rounds. Tommy's wind appeared to be in excellent condition.[450]

It was said that Burns and O'Brien were opposites in manner. Tommy was quiet, said little, and seldom smiled. He took life and work very seriously. Burns trained with a solemn, sullen, determined manner.

O'Brien, on the other hand, was jolly, usually smiling, and liked to joke around and josh folks. He was a talker. O'Brien was like an actor who was always on stage, seeking to gain as much publicity as possible. He was very good at keeping his name in the papers. "The real man is hidden beneath a surface layer of pose." O'Brien was said to have an overwhelming faith and confidence in himself, or what some might call a swelled head. He felt that he knew more about boxing than any other man alive.[451]

O'Brien was sparring with Bob Ward, Abdul the Terrible Turk, and Bob Swanson.

Tom McCarey said the pavilion would seat 5,500 persons, and the ticket prices for the big fight would be $30, $20, $10, and $5.[452]

---

446 *Los Angeles Herald*, April 17, 1907.
447 *Los Angeles Herald*, April 18, 1907.
448 *Los Angeles Herald*, April 20, 1907.
449 *Los Angeles Herald*, April 25, 1907.
450 *Los Angeles Herald*, April 26, 1907.
451 *Los Angeles Herald*, April 28, 1907.
452 *Los Angeles Times*, April 28, 1907.

The suburbs of Long Beach advertised that the heavyweight champion of the world was training at the Long Beach Skating Rink. Burns started the morning of April 30 with an 8-mile run and dip in the surf. At 3 p.m., he showed up at the rink to train with Professor Lewis and sparring partners Billy Woods and Jimmy Burns. Tom went about his work in a dogged, sullen way, never resting, never acknowledging the audience. He worked on his abdominal muscles for 8 minutes, and then he skipped rope, an exercise at which he excelled. Next, he hit the punching bag. More rope skipping followed, and then the bag again. Jimmy Burns sparred 4 rounds with the champ. Woods then took his turn, and they engaged in grueling, hard work.

Tommy was confident, saying that no matter how often O'Brien hit him; Jack could not hurt him, which would enable him to go after his foe with a ferocity that O'Brien could not handle. Burns had never been knocked out. Conversely, O'Brien knew what would happen if Tom landed on him.

I am so confident of beating O'Brien that I wish the fight was tonight instead of a week from now.

There is only one way to beat O'Brien; that is to keep right on top of him all the time. ... I honestly don't believe O'Brien could knock me out if I stood up and let him swing on my jaw: I don't think he has the punch. ...

O'Brien has made a great deal ado over the sore condition of his arm the last time we fought. Now let me tell you something; I had a sore arm that night, but no one heard of it, and wouldn't now, only I'm tired of his cry baby talk. I injured my left arm at the elbow when I fought Marvin Hart. ... O'Brien had nothing on me that night: he won't have next Wednesday night.[453]

It was reported that O'Brien was heavier than ever, and had gained eight pounds. He wanted to be bigger and stronger in order to handle Tommy's bulk.

Those who picked O'Brien to win said Burns had landed a lucky punch in the 5th round that would not be repeated again, and the clever O'Brien knew what to do this time in order to defeat him. They alleged that but-for that punch, O'Brien would not have moved and grabbed as much, and would have punched more and landed more blows, as he had done in the first 4 rounds.

Those who were wagering on Burns cited the fact that he had a shade on O'Brien the first time. The first fight had already proven that Burns was the better fighter, but because O'Brien was a media darling and popular with the public, they did not want to accept what the fight had shown.[454]

On the morning of May 1, O'Brien ran 12 miles. In the afternoon, he engaged in 35 minutes of juggling a 10-pound rock to strengthen his hands. He then shadow boxed, skipped rope, punched the ball, worked the pulley and weight machines, and wrestled with sparring partners Bob Ward, Abdul Malgan, and Mortimer Swanson. He said, "I am in better shape today, both physically and mentally, than I have ever been before in my life." He also said that he was several pounds heavier than ever before, his condition near perfect, and he was supremely confident of victory.[455]

Since neither of the fighters had offered the name of a referee, McCarey selected Charlie Eyton, and neither fighter objected. It seemed that both fighters wanted McCarey to choose. "Charlie Eyton has the confidence of the fight fans in general, and it is believed that he will be a good official."

Despite the result of the first fight, the prevailing odds once again had O'Brien as the favorite at 10 to 8 odds. This was thought to be the result of Burns' friends holding back their wagers until the last moment, and also

---

453 *Los Angeles Examiner*, May 1, 1907.
454 *Los Angeles Herald*, May 1, 1907.
455 *Los Angeles Examiner*, May 2, 1907.

because a lot of money from back East, where O'Brien was very popular, had been wagered on Jack.[456]

On May 2, Burns took his usual long morning run of about 8 miles. In the afternoon, he performed abdominal exercises, punched the bag, skipped rope, shadow boxed, and worked with pulley weights for about half an hour. He sparred Jimmy Burns and Billy Woods, 3 rounds each. Burns again expressed absolute confidence.[457]

O'Brien was said to weigh 171 pounds, while Burns was thought to be about 173 pounds, although neither man stepped on the scale. If the weights were accurate, with a victory, Burns could essentially claim the world light heavyweight crown as well. However, no one knew for sure, because fighters tended to under-report their weights and rarely stepped on a scale to prove them. Heavyweights were not required to weigh in.[458]

The press said that not since Corbett-Fitzsimmons or Jeffries-Fitzsimmons had there been such keen interest in a boxing contest. "The fact remains that Burns and O'Brien are the best men in the heavyweight division today."

JACK O'BRIEN, REFEREE CHARLES EYTON, TOMMY BURNS.

Although the fight was scheduled for 20 rounds, it was agreed that if the bout lacked a decisive winner after that distance, the fight would continue for another 5 rounds. There would be no draw this time.

Despite the fact that the betting odds remained in O'Brien's favor, the rank and file were about evenly divided in their opinions regarding who would emerge victorious. According to Burns' supporters, the only thing that saved O'Brien in their former battle was his running away and holding.

456 *Los Angeles Times*, May 2, 1907.
457 *Los Angeles Examiner*, May 3, 1907.
458 *Los Angeles Herald*, May 2, 1907; *Los Angeles Times*, May 5, 1907.

O'Brien's supporters cited his strong start before he was handicapped by the blow to the nose, and the fact that Burns was tired at the end and Jack had closed his eye. The Burns backers retorted that Tommy wore himself out chasing O'Brien and that Jack's finish was "spasmodic," that O'Brien's punches could not have hurt him, and Tommy could have gone on much further.[459]

O'Brien said that his left, which he had always used to jab a rushing fighter into submission, was practically useless in the last fight owing to an injury he carried into the fight. "This time you will not see many left leads go wrong." He would jab away incessantly and then finish Burns with a

---

459 *Los Angeles Times*, May 5, 1907.

right cross or uppercut. He also said that carelessness, owing to the fact that he was paying attention to the picture machine, was why Burns had caught him. "Now, you will remember that, dazed and helpless as I was, he never landed another one like that." He would be nearly as heavy as Burns this time, which would help him with the infighting. "There will be no running away in this fight; the only reason I ran before was because I would have been a fool to do anything else." O'Brien advised all of his friends to bet on him. "I am going to win it."[460]

C.E. Van Loan opined that O'Brien was the betting favorite owing to his added weight and strength, wonderful skill and condition, and the fact that

460 *Los Angeles Examiner*, May 5, 1907.

he was able to make a draw of it even after being badly dazed. He was outpointing Burns up to that point. If O'Brien could do so well in a half-dazed condition and still come on strong at the end, then he would do much better this time, when he would be sure to watch out for Tommy's big right. Supporters also noted that he was practically a one-armed fighter owing to his left elbow injury.

On the other hand, Burns was a strong natural fighter who could fight all night if need be. His supporters argued that he was only outpointed in the early rounds because he was feeling out O'Brien, and that once he gained confidence, he went in and made it a mixing fight. They argued that Jack could never hurt Tommy, and the rushing style would force O'Brien to assume the defensive.

Burns said, "If O'Brien will stand up and fight me and not run away every time he thinks my right hand is coming over, the fight will never pass the ten-round mark. ... It is hard to run a fast man down and knock him out."[461]

In the meantime, San Francisco promoter James Coffroth was negotiating with both O'Brien and Burns, trying to get the winner to agree to fight Australia's Bill Squires. Burns demanded a side bet of $5,000. He also wanted a guarantee and a percentage of the gate. Coffroth told him that he could either have a guarantee or a percentage, but not both. O'Brien wanted a long rest after the Burns fight, and said that he might go to England to fight Gunner Moir. Eventually, Burns agreed to fight Squires for the side bet and a guarantee of $8,000.

Coffroth also visited Jeffries on his alfalfa ranch and asked if he would be willing to fight Squires if Bill gained the fight public's confidence with a victory over a respected fighter. Jeff said that he would consider the match, but would require seven months to train.[462]

Jack O'Brien's respected trainer/manager Billy Nolan said that should O'Brien defeat Burns, he wanted Jack to fight Jeffries.

> [B]ear in mind that it has been three years since the boilermaker has been in the ring. This fact alone is the greatest detriment to a fighter who wishes to attain success in any walk of athletic life. Inactivity will force a man to the back ranks quicker than anything else, to say nothing of the abuse of strong drink and tobacco. Neither of these vices are strangers to Jim Jeffries....
>
> There is no more disparity as to the relative sizes of Jack O'Brien and Jim Jeffries than there was between Corbett and either Jackson or Sullivan.... This extra poundage will be a detriment to [Jeffries].... Jim Corbett never did anything that Jack O'Brien could not do.... Corbett fought Jeffries when the latter was in his prime.... The

461 *Los Angeles Examiner*, May 5, 1907.
462 *Los Angeles Examiner*, May 3-6, 1907.

former was then a dead one from a pugilistic standpoint.... At that, Corbett made Jeff look pretty cheap. ... In the history of the ring show me a single case where an individual ever returned and amounted to anything after as long a retirement as that of Jeffries.[463]

On May 5, 300 spectators paid 25 cents each to watch Tommy train at Long Beach. Burns did his usual preliminary work and sparred 3 rounds each with Jimmy Burns and Billy Woods. Burns "had Woods out on two different occasions, but held back and allowed the colored man to recuperate." Ten seconds after their bout, Tom's heart rate was back down to 80 beats per minute, as declared by a physician.

Tommy said it was his last day of training at Long Beach, for he would finish up his training at the Naud Junction Pavilion to give the Los Angeles fans a chance to see him and make their wagering decisions, and also so he could become accustomed to the actual fight ring. He would spar for the public there on Monday without charging an admission fee. "This speech was a record breaker for Burns, for it is seldom that the big fellow will condescend to say a dozen words at the same time."

Speaking in a quiet, business-like manner, Burns said,

I don't think any more of meeting O'Brien than I do of my daily workouts with my sparring partners.

The fact that O'Brien is the long-end in the betting doesn't concern me in the least. It only means that I will get a better price for my money.

Did you ever hear of the betting making a man win? No! I could cite you a dozen instances where top-heavy favorites have gone down to defeat, and this will be another case of the same kind.

There won't be any speculation as to which of us is the better man after next Wednesday night.[464]

That same day, 600-700 folks visited O'Brien's Arcadia training camp. He gave a few of his inevitable speeches, and shadow boxed, skipped rope, punched the bag, threw the medicine ball, wrestled, and worked with the pulley machine. He also sparred 3 rounds each with Swanson and Malgan. Jack said that he had run 8 miles in the morning, and would probably do 5-6 miles the following day. He said that his wind was even better than when he met Burns before, and his hands were in good shape. He strongly urged his friends to bet on him.[465]

A couple days before the bout, it was noted that it was strange for the current odds of 10 to 7 to be so much in O'Brien's favor, particularly given

463 *Los Angeles Times*, May 5, 1907.
464 *Los Angeles Examiner*, May 6, 1907.
465 *Los Angeles Examiner*, May 6, 1907.

what happened in the first fight. "[W]hy the odds should be this way, must be difficult for anyone to guess. Burns had the best of their previous fight in the way of damage done." The speculation remained that folks on the East Coast thought so well of O'Brien that they were wagering heavily on him, making Jack the favorite. However, after the fight, further insight into this question would be revealed.[466]

PACIFIC ATHLETIC CLUB   Wednesday, May 8.

Twenty-round Boxing Contest for the WORLD'S HEAVYWEIGHT
CHAMPIONSHIP

TOMMY BURNS vs. PHILA. JACK O'BRIEN

General admission $5. Reserved seats $10 and $20. Box seats $30. Tickets on sale at A. B. Greenewald's Cigar Store, 107 South Spring St. Take Eastlake park or Downey ave. cars north on Spring st. to Naud Junction.

On Monday May 6, 1907 at the Naud Junction Pavilion, just two days before the fight, women were amongst the 1,000 to 1,200 fans who watched Burns train and spar. It was one of the biggest crowds ever just to watch a man train.

Tom jokingly said, "Must be a fight going on this afternoon." He told the newsmen, "Never felt better in my life. I know that's an old chestnut, but it's the truth." He said the only area that did not feel perfect was his left arm, which he was not able to completely straighten out, so it was one inch shorter than his right. The injury was a permanent one, resulting from the Hart fight.

Burns said that he would step on the scales for the newsmen to show them that he was on the square. He tipped the beam at exactly 178 pounds. Tom was a little heavier than he had expected. He thought he was weighing between 171 and 175 pounds. This shows the difference between self-reporting weights, as was often the case, and proving a weight.

First, the crowd watched Tom do abdominal and back exercises, skip rope and shadow box with dumbbells.

Next, using heavy 14-ounce gloves, Burns sparred 2 rounds with lightweight Jimmy Burns, also known as George Memsic in the East. Tommy allowed Jimmy to outbox him in the 1st round, absorbing strong rights and right uppercuts. The champion got going in the 2nd round and slugged hard. A right to the ear stunned Jimmy, and they had to delay the sparring for fifteen seconds to allow him to recover. Jimmy came back and slugged away. As Burns was sliding back, Jimmy "swung a left to the head and partly from the force of the blow and partly from tripping over the matting, Tommy went down full length." It was more of a slip.

Burns then sparred former opponent Billy Woods, the black fighter whom Tom had fought to a 1904 15-round draw. They sparred 3 terrific rounds at top speed. Burns not only dealt out punishment, but took all that Woods had to give. In the 2nd round, they slugged as if it were a real fight,

---

466 *Los Angeles Times, Los Angeles Herald,* May 6, 1907.

and Burns dropped Billy to his knees. Some thought that Burns was insane to go so hard only two days before the fight. Professor Lewis warned Tommy several times to be careful, fearing a head butt or a hand injury. In the 3rd round, Burns again walloped Woods into submission, the end of the round finding Billy hanging on to survive. "Burns showed to be in excellent condition. … He was faster than ever, and mixed it up with his fast but husky opponents."[467]

Tommy Burns, Who Will Meet Jack O'Brien Tomorrow Night, as He Appeared in Go With Woods Yesterday.

That same day, O'Brien took a one-hour hike, worked the pulleys, skipped rope, shadow boxed, and wrestled with Jack and Mike Sullivan. He refused to step on the scales.

> I am heavier now than I ever was in my life. I couldn't be any heavier and retain my cleverness, and I want to tell you right now that foot work is going to have a great deal to do with the result Wednesday night, although I don't intend to make a runaway match of it by any means. …

467 *Los Angeles Times, Los Angeles Herald, Los Angeles Examiner,* May 7, 1907.

It is a matter of history that I had all the better of Burns up to the time that he landed that lucky punch. I have said a hundred times, and I repeat it, that was the hardest punch I ever received in my life. If Tommy couldn't cop me when I was badly hurt and dazed, what can he expect to do when I am at my best? I certainly shall see to it that he doesn't sneak in another such wallop.[468]

Ticket sales were quite brisk. $30 seats were selling as fast as the $20 and $10 chairs.

The night before the fight, Burns said,

Honestly, nothing would please me better than to have O'Brien stand up and fight. I chased him enough in the last battle. Let this fight be a fight, not a foot race.

I will win this fight and then will be ready to meet Bill Squires or any other heavyweight who thinks he can call on the championship title.

I am just as confident that I will win this fight as I am that I deserved the decision the last time we met.

BURNS.	O'BRIEN.
Neck, 16 Inches.	Neck, 17 Inches.
Shoulders, 48½ Inches.	Shoulders, 44 Inches.
Chest, Normal, 40½ Inches.	Chest, Normal, 40½ Inches.
Chest, Inflated, 41¾ Inches.	Chest, Inflated, 45 Inches.
Waist, 33 Inches.	Waist, 33 Inches.
Biceps, Flexed, 14½ Inches.	Biceps, Flexed, 14 Inches.
Lower Arm, 11¾ Inches.	Lower Arm, 11½ Inches.
Wrist, 7½ Inches.	Wrist, 7½ Inches.
Thigh, 22½ Inches.	Thigh, 22½ Inches.
Calf, 15⅝ Inches.	Calf, 16½ Inches.
Ankle, 8½ Inches.	Ankle, 10½ Inches.
Reach, 74½ Inches.	Reach, 73½ Inches.
Height, 5 Feet, 7 Inches.	Height, 5 Feet, 10 Inches.

468 *Los Angeles Examiner*, May 7, 1907.

O'Brien not only expected to defeat Burns, but said that he would also post $5,000 for a match with Jim Jeffries. "If I meet defeat it will be because Tommy Burns is the better man, and I certainly will offer no excuses."[469]

The day of the fight, it was reported that the $30,000 purse was to be split $18,000 to the winner and $12,000 to the loser, "although it has been hinted that the fighters have agreed to split the purse, $15,000 to each." No one knew for sure, for often there were back-room side deals not revealed to the public until much later, different from what was announced before the fight.

O'Brien still remained the odds favorite at 10 to 8. "Although O'Brien is the favorite of the betting men, the common run of fight fans lean toward Burns."[470]

W.W. Naughton noted that despite the rumors that big chunks of money were being bet on Burns, O'Brien remained the favorite. "Considering that the majority thought Burns had a wee shade the better of the milling in the last affair one might be inclined to say that this was peculiar." However, Naughton thought the odds were the product of logic, although it might prove to be false logic. O'Brien entered the ring the last time with a hurt arm, and still Burns could not finish him. This time, Jack had two good arms, more weight, and better knowledge regarding Tom's tactics.

Although there was a rumor that Billy Nolan, O'Brien's manager, might try to cause a hitch at ringside by demanding clean breaks, the articles called for straight Queensberry rules, for each to protect himself at all times.[471]

Both fighters' camps confirmed that they had agreed that if Referee Eyton was not able to render a definitive verdict after 20 rounds, that he would be authorized to have them fight 5 more rounds, so that there would be a clear winner.[472]

The big fight took place on Wednesday May 8, 1907 at Naud Junction in Los Angeles, under the auspices of the Pacific Athletic Club. It was scheduled for 20 rounds (or up to 25), for an alleged $30,000 purse, one of the largest ever offered. The show was to start at 8 p.m., with the main event at 9 p.m. The crowd size was a bit below expectations, but still quite large at close to 4,000.

To the crowd's chagrin, there was a long delay before the main event, for each fighter wanted the other to enter the ring first. Eventually, O'Brien entered first, at about 9:45 p.m. Burns entered the ring at 9:50 p.m. O'Brien walked over to Tommy's corner to shake hands, but Tom remained seated on his stool while he shook, and looked down at Jack's feet.

---

469 *Los Angeles Examiner*, May 8, 1907.
470 *Los Angeles Times*, May 8, 1907.
471 *Los Angeles Examiner*, May 8, 1907.
472 *Los Angeles Herald*, May 8, 1907.

The usual announcements, introductions and preliminary instructions followed. Photographers had the men pose for their cameras.

Just before the fight began, something unusual took place; Referee Charlie Eyton declared all bets off. "Gentlemen, for good and sufficient reasons, I declare off all bets on this contest!" He said Manager McCarey had ordered this action. Eyton refused to give a reason at ringside, but referred all questions to McCarey.[473]

After the bets were declared off, O'Brien looked very concerned, and seemed hesitant to leave his corner after the bell rang to start the fight. O'Brien's seconds had to shove him out of his chair. Then the running match began.

The *Los Angeles Herald* and *Los Angeles Examiner* provided round-by-round accounts. "It's almost a shame to write last night's joke as it came off in three-minute sections, but here goes."

1 - The crowd hooted at O'Brien's immediate incessant dancing and running. Jack even looked back over his shoulder like a scared rabbit. Tired of following him around, Burns stood at ring center, dropped his hands and used some choice language, begging O'Brien to fight. Someone in the gallery shouted, "Get out in a ten-acre lot!" Tom rushed in but Jack clinched. Burns worked the body and kidneys in the clinches. O'Brien threw a right to the body but immediately clinched. After the referee broke them, O'Brien danced away. Jack jabbed but Tom hit him with a right to the head

---

473 *Los Angeles Times*, May 9, 1907.

and O'Brien ran again. "It was a round of running and clinching on O'Brien's part, and he was hooted as he went to his corner."

2 - When Burns threw, they came together in the usual embrace. After Tom landed a left to the head, Jack danced away from further harm. Tom rushed in savagely, and in the wrestling match that followed, he threw Jack to the floor, falling on top of him. After helping O'Brien up, Tom hooked a right to the face, while Jack missed several jabs. Burns used left hooks to the face and ribs. O'Brien clinched repeatedly, drawing a warning from Eyton. "So far O'Brien had made no effort to fight."

3 – Burns tried cutting O'Brien off, but Jack usually turned and ran the other way. After Burns would throw they would clinch. Jack jabbed and Tom landed a hard right to the temple that rattled O'Brien. Burns tore after him like a cyclone, but O'Brien moved, covered and clinched. Tom cut Jack's mouth with a hard jab, but received two hard jabs on the eye. The round ended in another of the innumerable clinches. According to one reporter, this was a livelier round, with honors even.

4 – Tom blocked Jack's jabs. In between clinches, O'Brien jabbed his left to the face several times and then danced away. Two hard lefts made Tom's nose bleed a tiny stream. They followed with more fiddling about. Burns dropped his arms and looked at O'Brien derisively. Honors were about even.

5 – Burns came in fast, but his leads were blocked. He landed a left on the neck but received a left on the nose that started the blood flowing fast. Tom rushed in wildly, receiving a jab for his trouble. He swung his left to the stomach and followed with one to the face. In the frequent clinches, Tom's blood smeared over Jack's body. O'Brien landed his left and Burns came back with a hard left to the ear, but Jack kept away from the savage rushes, twisting, jumping and dancing about until the crowd hissed him.

6 – Burns landed a left to the stomach. He tried to corner O'Brien, but received jabs, none of which hurt. Jack landed a right to the stomach, and just before he clinched, Tom shot his left to the ribs. Burns complained that O'Brien was holding his arms. Eyton broke them. Jack landed a left and right to the head, but Tom responded with a hard right to the ear. Burns forced him to the ropes, but no damage resulted from his savage onslaught.

7 – They exchanged lefts. Jack landed a left on the ribs. In the infighting, Burns landed frequently on the kidneys and then tore in and walloped O'Brien on the head. Eyton broke them and Burns landed his left again. Jack ran away from Tommy's rushes. After one of the numerous clinches, Jack sent a right to the body and then ran away. The crowd called O'Brien several names. "It is a bum round, even for this show." Another writer called the last few rounds "wretched exhibitions on O'Brien's part." A third

said, "Burns was consistently the aggressor, while O'Brien made a runaway fight of it."

8 – Burns landed his left lead to the stomach and O'Brien did a lot of dancing before he clinched. Burns tore loose with a left to the face, but O'Brien then ducked and clinched to escape punishment. O'Brien hung on until Eyton tore him away, and just as he did so, Burns landed a right swing that nailed Jack high on the head. There were frequent clinches, which marked the round as one of "unusual worthlessness." Another said, "O'Brien's style of fighting had the gallery crowd in continued ill-humor, and there was loud hooting after every round."

9 – O'Brien came out crouching, but straightened up when Burns hit him with a left in the stomach. Tom rushed him to a corner, but Jack escaped. O'Brien landed a right uppercut before clinching. His left to the face did no damage, and when Tom started after him like a bull, the crowd hooted at O'Brien's running. Tom tore his arms away in the clinches and punched. A hard left over the eye opened up a cut on O'Brien's face, but Jack's close embrace prevented further damage. He then ran away, as usual. Another writer said Jack's right cheek near the eye was cut.

10 – Burns stood still in the center of the ring with his arms down while O'Brien danced around him. The crowd jeered. When they did get close, it was a clinch-fest again, with Eyton breaking them. O'Brien would run and hug. He refused to break when the referee asked him to do so. Tom hammered a few hard ones on the ribs at close quarters. The crowd again hooted Jack's tactics.

11 – O'Brien started with his dancing exhibition. He landed a left but clinched and hung on until the referee forced him away from Burns. Jack used his elbow and landed a left to the stomach and head. A jab caused Tom's lip to bleed. When Tom tried to hit him, Jack hung on. Jack again jabbed him at range.

12 – O'Brien ran and clinched, but Burns landed a right to the stomach and face. Jack held on. The crowd hooted his sprinting tactics. Tom forced him to the ropes. A hard body shot seemed to unsettle O'Brien. Jack's face was bleeding copiously from a deep cut between the eyebrows, by the bridge of the nose, but he managed to jab several times between clinches. O'Brien also landed some right uppercuts, but mostly got the worst of the infighting. Burns rammed his gloves to the body with spirit. O'Brien's right eye was swollen and his mouth hung open. He moved about again. "The round looked almost like a real fight and the crowd cheered." Another said, "Burns had a good deal the better of this round."

13 – Coming out of a clinch, Tommy swung his right to the head. Burns put the right to the heart and then countered Jack's jab with a right to the sore eye. O'Brien jabbed and clinched. Tom dug into the body. Jack made a face

and said something about being fouled, but Eyton told him to forget it. Left jolts made Jack's head wag. Between clinches, O'Brien landed a few jabs, making it a "fair round." "O'Brien had little difficulty in touching Burns' face with the left, but his anxiety to get out of danger caused him to put very little force into the blows." Eyton cautioned O'Brien about using his elbow in the clinches.

14 – O'Brien sent Tom's head back with a left poke, but danced away and clinched without attempting anything more. Burns worked his right to the body. Tom jabbed his left to the head and O'Brien ran around to the hoots of the crowd. Jack landed a half hook and followed with a left to the stomach, which Burns returned in kind. Four of the arc lights over the ring went out, and so the house was left in a half light. O'Brien remarked, "Maybe the lights were fixed!" By clinching, running away and jabbing at long range, O'Brien managed to escape without injury. Burns seemed to be conserving his energy, as his work rate was slower at this point. The round was very tame.

15 – Jack started with jabs as he moved about. Tom grew sore, standing still and calling him names. He tried to talk O'Brien into making some sort of a fight. Burns landed a right uppercut and left chop that started O'Brien's right eye bleeding in streams again. After clinching tightly and being broken apart, O'Brien ran and the crowd hooted. Tom landed a right to the face and Jack ran, to the hoots. At intervals, O'Brien momentarily stopped his movement to bluff with his left and dive into a clinch. O'Brien jumped high in an attempt to get Burns to land low, but no foul blow was struck. They mixed it in the next clinch. Tom forced Jack to the ropes, where O'Brien protected himself as usual. Burns landed a left to the body and O'Brien crossed his right on the jaw. Jack landed a right uppercut on the heart and Tom returned with a left on the face. It was a good round, and at the end O'Brien was bleeding profusely. Another said it was a lively and even round.

16 – The whole crowd yelled and voiced its support for the Canadian. O'Brien started the round by running, jabbing and clinching. He kept up these tactics, as well as jumping high whenever he thought Tommy was going to the body, hoping to get him to land low so he could win on a foul. Another writer thought Jack jumped in the air to add force to his jab. Tom countered a jab with a right to the chin. Clinches were frequent. O'Brien would either land a jab from the outside, or an uppercut in close, and then he would clinch until Eyton forced him to break. Tom landed a right at the bell. "O'Brien ran away a good deal in this round."

17 – They fiddled and embraced. Jack jumped up and then landed a hard left uppercut. Burns was mad, but O'Brien saved himself by clinching. "O'Brien took to circling the ring again, stopping long enough at times to plant a light harmless left and then running again." Tom kept up his monologue of choice language for O'Brien, who kept jumping in the air as

they came to a clinch. Misses were frequent on both sides, though Tom landed one jarring left jolt to the jaw. The slow round made the crowd sore again. "O'Brien had all the appearance of a very jaded ringster as he went to his corner."

18 – O'Brien started by sprinting and high jumping. Burns called him a few more names while standing still with his arms at his sides at ring center. Whenever Tom did this, Jack would crouch and come in, but when Burns started to advance, O'Brien would turn his back and run away again. While Jack made a quick getaway, Tom hit him in the back. Burns tore loose in a clinch. Jack kept out of harm's way by running and clinching. The past two rounds were very tame.

19 – They fiddled and clinched. O'Brien's punches were weak. Tom shot home a left to the stomach and tore in and forced Jack to the ropes. Burns landed his right on the head, trying for a knockout, but O'Brien's defense was too fast. For the first time, O'Brien became aggressive and forced Burns back a bit. However, neither did much harm in the round. At the bell, Tom landed a good left hook to the head.

20 – They touched gloves and O'Brien immediately hit Burns with a jab. The crowd hissed and Tom made a number of mean motions, but Jack kept away. O'Brien started to "break the hundred-yard dash record." Burns stood in the middle of the ring and shouted to O'Brien, "Why don't you come and fight?" O'Brien walked around and around as the crowd hooted. Tom did not want to chase him though. He landed a good left to the eye and they clinched again. Burns savagely shot home two lefts to the face, but the clutching spoiled further action. Jack landed a right and left to the head. Tom rushed in and Jack uppercut him with the right, though it was smothered by Tom's forearm, and the bell ended matters. "Eyton reached for Burns at once and the joke was over." Tommy Burns had clearly won the 20-round decision.

The *Los Angeles Herald* said O'Brien had disgraced himself and disgusted the immense throng of spectators by refusing to stand before Burns and fight. The fans hooted and hissed his runaway tactics. "So far as the decision was concerned Referee Eyton could not have possibly acted otherwise than raise Burns' hand." Members of the crowd called Jack "yellow."

It was obvious to everyone that O'Brien just wanted to get through the bout. During the fight, he often leapt into the air in an effort to receive a foul low blow, and then acted as if he was in pain. By this incredible action it was obvious he had no belief or hope that he could win in any other way. Eyton paid no attention to his tactics, and waved him to go on.

O'Brien ran so fast and continuously that it seemed almost impossible for Burns to reach him. The entire fight from start to finish was O'Brien on the run. Burns sometimes chased him and sometimes stood like a statue at ring center, waiting. True, O'Brien jabbed often, but his face wore a look of fear as he dashed away. Burns missed time and again as Jack jumped away. If Burns did get close enough to hit him, Jack just grabbed him around the neck, refusing to break until Referee Eyton physically pried them apart.

Every round was a repetition of the former. Jack jabbed him several times, but he was more concerned with running away than hitting. "Burns himself did not appear to be fighting the same battle he did previously, but could scarcely be expected to do so under the circumstances. When it became evident that O'Brien was determined to run away the crowd started hissing and kept at it until the end." Burns did reach the forehead above the nose and had O'Brien bleeding badly. Tom's eyes were slightly cut, but that was all.[474]

The *Los Angeles Times* also called it a very poor fight; so poor that it did not give a round-by-round account. Not surprisingly, it was for the most part a replay of their first fight, with O'Brien running around and grabbing, but even more so than the first time. Oddly enough, the newspapers and fans acted surprised, having expected a good fight, completely having ignored the reality of what the first fight had proved.

> Burns received the decision…but it was through no good work of his, for O'Brien would not fight except in spurts measured by seconds of time, and during the remainder of the three minutes of each round he sped about the ring with Burns alternately chasing him and standing in the center of the ring looking on in disgust; and when O'Brien did make a stand, Burns refused to lead. …

> O'Brien did very little fighting, and Burns did less than in their first contest. Burns was willing enough to mix it up, but when he might have gone in and taken a chance he became cautious and danced about until the opportunity to really mix it was lost.

> Very little punishment was dealt by either man. A real good blow was not struck. Burns inflicted the more punishment, but nearly every blow delivered by him was struck at close range when the men were coming together or glanced off at long range. O'Brien has nothing but a left jab with an occasional right which he failed to deliver often because he was afraid to get in close.

> O'Brien at times ran for dear life never minding the storm of hisses which arose. Then when Burns got in close and mixed it with him he held on desperately, as he did in the first battle. Referee Eyton refused to allow the men to stay together unless they got busy in the infighting, and promptly broke them. Nevertheless, they were locked in each other's embrace for many minutes of the fight. …

---

474 *Los Angeles Herald*, May 9, 1907.

Burns cut O'Brien above the nose and on the left eyelid. He also battered his mouth so that O'Brien was spitting blood throughout most of the fight. O'Brien raised a roof on Burns's right eyelid and puffed his eyes, nose, and mouth with his left jabs. Burns's nose bled considerably, and he also spat blood at times. Otherwise, the men were not injured.[475]

It was clear that Burns had won, so Referee Eyton did not need to demand that they fight 5 more rounds, as he could have done. O'Brien did not protest the decision or even seem to care. The patrons were upset that they had paid such high prices for such a dull fight.

Barney Reynolds, Bill Squires' manager, said, "Burns and Squires will make a highly interesting fight, and I think Squires will win. The men fight alike. … I am satisfied that Burns will take a lot of beating before he will acknowledge defeat."

Jim Jeffries had watched the fight from ringside. He said Burns deserved the honors, as he won by four and a half miles, "actual distance covered." O'Brien refused to fight, making it more of a running match than a fight. He was evidently afraid to let himself loose, so he did little but run, and he even turned his back. At times, Jack would momentarily show fight, but he was always ready to back away again. Jeffries said, "Burns was up against the hard proposition of a clever man who would not fight and he made the best of it." In his opinion, O'Brien might have won the 4th round, and about six rounds were even, but all the rest were for Burns.

Although Burns showed good judgment at first in not running after him, eventually he was driven to it. O'Brien never did make a stand. He devoted himself to blocking, clinching, and running. He simply would not fight. He looked to be in good shape, "even better than Burns, but his every move seemed to show he was afraid of his opponent. He was backward in leading and apparently had no confidence whatsoever." His punches had no effect on Burns.

W.W. Naughton said Burns had fairly earned the decision. There had not been five minutes of real fighting in the sixty-minute bout. "This was because O'Brien chose to make a runaway fight of it. He started out like one whose sole object was to last the full twenty rounds and he accomplished his purpose. He went on the defensive from the first tap of the gong." Early on, the crowd hooted him. There were times when the jeering spurred Jack to engage in more aggressive tactics, but they were few, and usually resulted in a clinch in which O'Brien was walloped around the body, "the kind of treatment the Philadelphian dislikes." Burns kept rushing and chasing and depending on his strength to wrench his arms free in the clinches and work.

---

475 *Los Angeles Times*, May 9, 1907.

O'Brien preferred to jab, although he occasionally threw a right to the body or head. He did not use his jab as freely as he did in other fights. Although his jab had bruised and blinded many opponents' eyes, it had no punishing force against Burns. It did bring some blood from the nose and mouth, "but all and all it was a harmless assault."

The contest was monotonous. It was either clinching, with Burns eager to work as Jack grabbed, or O'Brien skipping around the ring while Burns chased or stood in the ring center as the crowd hooted at O'Brien. After the 10th round, Burns did not over-exert himself. Confident that he had a strong lead, he took things comparatively easy. "The decision was the only one that could have been rendered under the circumstances." Many felt that O'Brien had retrograded in a marked degree and was a back number. Yet, the strange part of it was that Jack looked better physically than he did before the first fight. However, his methods showed plainly that he had very little confidence in himself.

Naughton noted that another strange thing was that the odds were strongly 10 to 6 in O'Brien's favor, and there was practically no money on Burns. He thought Eyton had called off the bets because of the hard-to-explain partiality towards O'Brien by the betting fraternity.[476]

C.E. Van Loan said O'Brien had made a wretched showing. His blows absolutely lacked steam. He had engaged in a running match that disgusted the crowd. Some of the wise ones thought O'Brien was stalling for the first few rounds in order to tire Burns and slow him down. However, he remained defensive for most of the contest. Van Loan opined that as a result of his disgraceful showing, O'Brien was down and out as a top boxer.

O'Brien declined to make a statement afterwards. "No amount of talking will ever square Jack O'Brien with the sporting world." It was apparent that he was not out to win but merely to last the distance and save himself from a knockout. "Had he stood up to fight and been put away inside of ten rounds, his position would have been infinitely superior to the one which he must now occupy." Van Loan said O'Brien had not won a round. The fight had "proved beyond question that Tommy Burns can beat O'Brien any day in the week."

Van Loan said Burns came out of the fight with no marks other than a slight bruise over his right eye. O'Brien's face was slashed, especially about the eyes.

Apparently, the gate receipts were just over $22,000, ordinarily a very good house, but not for a fight in which the promoter had promised so much money to the combatants.

Afterwards, Burns said,

> If O'Brien had stood up and fought like a man, if he had made the least pretense at fighting, I would have whipped him inside of five

476 *Los Angeles Examiner* May 9, 1907.

rounds. Not once during the twenty rounds did O'Brien land a punch that hurt me in the least. It is a fact that my sparring partners extended me more in the three-round daily training bouts than O'Brien did tonight. ... There can be no question in the minds of the public now as to who is the better man.[477]

Burns also said the only reason that he was not able to knock out O'Brien was because Jack was so swift of foot, held so much, and took few chances at punching to win, lest he leave himself open to Tommy's blows. O'Brien had fought to survive.

Although the fight had been poor, the interesting part was just getting started. Naturally, all those who had wagered on Burns demanded an explanation for why Referee Eyton, acting upon Tom McCarey's instructions, had declared the bets off before the fight. Declaring all bets off *before* the fight took place was a very unusual and suspicious event. Usually this occurred when a bout in progress was stopped on suspicion of a fix or if the men were not giving a legitimate effort. The fact that the bets were declared off before the bout even began hinted that something about the fight was "crooked" and that McCarey knew about it beforehand.

Tom McCarey simply said,

> There were enough suspicious circumstances for me to believe that something might be wrong, and to cause my action. I do not consider that anyone was hurt by having the bets declared off, while they might have been wronged if they had been allowed to stand. That is all the reason I will give tonight. I do not care to implicate any one at this time.[478]

However, Tommy Burns was not as shy or guarded with his words, and actually unloaded a huge bombshell. Burns revealed that O'Brien had refused to make the fight unless Burns would agree to throw it. Upset at the previous decision, Burns wanted to fight him again and settle matters. Therefore, he agreed to throw the fight in order to get O'Brien to take the bout. However, he had intended all along to double-cross O'Brien and fight to win.

Burns said,

> The wily Jack O'Brien was caught in one of his own traps last night. He would not enter the arena unless there was a previous agreement as to the outcome in which I was to 'lie down' and let him win. The purpose of this was to win large sums of money by betting on O'Brien...

477 *Los Angeles Examiner* May 9, 1907.
478 *Los Angeles Times*, May 9, 1907.

I at first declined to have anything to do with such a thing, but I soon saw that there was no other way to get O'Brien into the arena. I wanted to show the Los Angeles public that I was the man's master. I always have contended that I won by long odds the last fight with him...

He made the deal without ever intending to follow through. Burns went on to say,

But when Referee Eyton declared all bets off a realization of the true state of affairs came into the O'Brien camp. You saw his condition when this announcement was made. Why, when the gong sounded the first time he did not ever get out of his chair. His seconds pushed and half lifted him out. Then he ran from me all over the ring. I could not catch him....

The reason of the bets being declared off was simply for the protection of the public, who had made wagers on O'Brien in good faith. I was instrumental in that... It cost me just $3,800 to do that, for I stood to win that amount on myself.... They plotted to pull off one on the public and they got fooled.[479]

Reports confirmed that O'Brien sat in his chair for five seconds after the first bell rang, as if he did not want to fight, supporting the claims that Jack was stunned and realized that he was being double-crossed when the bets were called off, and that he was about to be forced to engage in a real fight. Conversely, "Burns stepped promptly forward as if he expected the announcement." O'Brien's ace-in-the-hole confidence immediately left him.

The fight itself was on the square, but was a "rotten" exhibition. Burns tried to fight, but O'Brien, when he found himself double-crossed, made a runaway fight of it to survive and stay the limit, saving himself from being knocked out, rather than try to win. "His wretched runaway tactics are now explained in full."

Referee Eyton said he suspected from the fact of O'Brien's being a 2 to 1 favorite that McCarey had discovered a kink in the situation. "Anyhow, I planned to declare the bets off just as the men were starting to fight. Had I done so sooner O'Brien might have found some excuse for leaving the ring; as it was he was into the swirl of the battle before he had time to think." McCarey planned to have the bets called off right before the fight started, in order to forestall any attempt on O'Brien's part to start an argument over the clean break proposition and give him a chance to leave the ring and refuse to fight.

Burns said O'Brien had agreed to pay him $3,500 to go out, but Jack told Tommy that he could make even more by betting on O'Brien, as well as his share of a big purse, which he would not earn if he did not agree to

---

479 *Los Angeles Express*, May 9, 1907.

throw the fight. O'Brien knew that he was the biggest fight out there for Burns, so he held firm. They made the agreement at a meeting at Tom's house shortly after the first fight, before the champion left on his eastern theatrical trip. "O'Brien was afraid to meet me in a square fight and he suggested that there was a big bunch of coin in sight and it would be a shame to let it get away, meaning that if I did not agree to his plan there would not be any fight." Burns said there was no way to get O'Brien into the ring unless Jack thought he had an ace in the hole. Tom had planned to trap O'Brien by appearing to agree to the scheme. So Burns agreed to lie down in the 11th round.

The *Examiner* called it "the most sensational story of prize ring crookedness unearthed in many years." Burns was not embarrassed by the scheme, but actually "rather proud of the part he played, in fact." O'Brien had been "beaten at his own dirty game."[480]

No wonder the odds had never shifted from being in O'Brien's favor. With so much inside money laid on him to win by the knowing ones, it would have made and kept him the favorite unless others had been as sure of Burns to re-shift the odds. O'Brien clearly had his Philly friends bet a bundle on himself, relying on the fact that Burns would take a dive.

Burns wanted to embarrass O'Brien and show the world that he was a faker and fixer of fights, and had attempted to fix this fight and defraud the betting and paying public.

At first, manager McCarey did not want to speak further, but when told that Burns had made his revelations, McCarey confirmed that Burns had told the truth, corroborating all of his statements. "It was a case of two to one so far as O'Brien is concerned. ... As the lawyers might say, the preponderance of evidence is against O'Brien." McCarey knew that Burns would try to knock out O'Brien despite the agreement to throw the fight. McCarey said,

> When Referee Eyton was told by me to declare all bets off, for good and sufficient reasons, he went into the ring and made the announcement, the effect on O'Brien being apparent to every spectator at the ringside.
>
> After I found out that O'Brien had made this agreement with Burns, I changed the conditions of the match, and the three of us met and agreed that Burns was to receive half of the purse, and that O'Brien was to get 30% of the gross receipts.[481]

In explaining why he had performed the way that he did, O'Brien claimed that his hands were on the bum and he did not care to take chances. McCarey said O'Brien knew that he never stood a chance with

480 *Los Angeles Examiner*, May 10, 1907.
481 *Los Angeles Express*, May 9, 1907.

Burns, which was the real reason why he chose to fight that way. He said Tommy did what he needed to do in order to get O'Brien into the ring.

Initially, O'Brien refused to comment on the fix allegations. A note was sent to him informing him of what McCarey and Burns had said. He remained in his hotel room and would not take calls.

The next day, O'Brien finally agreed to talk. He told one paper that there was an agreement before their *first* championship fight in November that the bout would be declared a draw, on account of the moving pictures. A competitive and even draw would mean greater interest in watching the fight. He told another paper that it was arranged to be a draw so that a rematch could be held and they could make even more money. Jack alleged that it was not an uncommon practice for frame-ups to be pulled off. He said, "I trusted McCarey to see that a draw decision was rendered."

O'Brien also said it was agreed that he would win the second fight by decision, after fighting with clean breaks. He claimed that initially, it was Burns who came to him and asked Jack to take a dive, but it was eventually agreed that Burns would lose. After Burns was defeated, it was planned that Tom would show his true form against Flynn and knock him out, so that another lucrative match between O'Brien and Burns could be arranged to be held in February 1908. "Well boys, the big expose has come. It goes to show that men are not honest. I'm not trying to excuse myself. I was crooked, if you wish, and was handed a nice package Wednesday night. But it takes more than one to frame things and those who double crossed me instigated the proceedings." He admitted that when he realized that he was being double-crossed, he fought to stay the limit.

McCarey responded, "O'Brien is foxy enough to frame up something to take away the sting of exposure from himself…. O'Brien had 24 hours in which to work up something which might reflect off Burns and myself and this was about the only thing he could find." McCarey called O'Brien a liar, saying that the first fight was on the square, but that Jack wanted to try to get revenge by casting aspersions on Burns' and McCarey's integrity, since his own integrity had been ruined. "The statement is a lie pure and simple. The contest was fought and decided upon its merits. O'Brien is trying to malign me and draw attention away from his performance Wednesday night."

O'Brien said it was left up to the fighters to make their first fight a draw, for referee Jeffries was not in on it. However, this claim did not match up with what happened. Burns did try hard to win and was obviously better. If Burns had crossed O'Brien that time, why would Jack believe him the second time? This showed that the first fight was on the square.

However, for conspiracy theorists, perhaps Jeffries was in on it and O'Brien was correct that the first fight was to be a draw, but incorrect in his assertion that Burns knew about it. O'Brien might have fought very defensively because he knew it would be a draw if he just lasted. However, he learned that Burns was not as easily handled as he had expected and took punishment. Therefore, he wanted to bring Tommy in on it the second time around. However, this would have to mean that Jeff was in on it back in November, and no one believed that. Jeff's integrity was thought to be unimpeachable. Others noted that Burns would have been given more money for allowing O'Brien to draw, if such was the case, but that they had split the purse.

Another possibility is that there might have been an agreement the first time that it would be a draw if they remained standing. Recall that the *Express* had said after their first fight, "Although Burns forced the fighting throughout there had been a tacit understanding that if the men were on their feet without a decided show on either side, the affair was to be declared a draw."[482] This certainly jumps off the page in a different way in light of what was said after their second bout. Had Jeffries been told to make it a draw if there was no knockout or dominant winner? It is possible that O'Brien wanted to amend the agreement the second time around so that this time he would not have to take any punishment.

However, many felt that the first fight and its decision were perfectly on the level, but O'Brien had spun stories about it in order to deflect from what he had tried to pull off in their more recent bout, or to try to impugn the integrity of Burns and McCarey as a counterattack for revenge. Some thought he made such claims to deflect from the fact of his poor performance in the first championship fight. Therefore, even after that fight, he had generated rumors on the East Coast that he could have defeated Burns, but carried him to the draw.

The Burns side said the agreement to throw the fight was made in December, when O'Brien called Burns and asked him to take a dive. Burns would not agree at first, but later gave in. "Jack told Burns frankly that he was no match for him because of Tommy's superior weight, strength and hitting powers." He also told Tommy that a loss would not be a big impact upon him because he was still young, while a loss for O'Brien would "put him to the bad." This explains why after their previous fight O'Brien had said that he did not want to fight as a heavyweight again, but then changed his mind after he had gotten Tommy to agree to throw the fight. The first championship bout had already convinced O'Brien that he could not handle Burns, and therefore he was only willing to fight him again if the fight was fixed.

McCarey did not learn of the fix agreement until O'Brien arrived in Los Angeles from San Francisco and Jack had sought confirmation that Burns would throw the fight. O'Brien told him that his hands were very bad and he was taking too much of a chance with Burns. He felt that Burns ought to be willing to "concede something to a man of my wonderful reputation. ..."

482 *Los Angeles Express,* November 29, 1906.

Burns is getting a chance to fight for a lot of money." O'Brien eventually came out and said there would be no fight if Burns would not throw the bout. When contacted, Burns told McCarey, "Agree to anything he asks, and trust me to knock his block off when I get him in the ring." McCarey said, "I was in already with quite a sum in promoting the contest so I thought it over and in the end went out to Arcadia and told O'Brien that everything was all right as far as Burns was concerned."

McCarey and Burns agreed that there was no $30,000 purse as was advertised, although McCarey claimed that it had been genuine until the fix talk arose. An amended agreement was made to give Burns $15,000 cash and O'Brien 30% of the receipts, neither side being aware of what the other was to receive. McCarey was able to convince Jack to take less than the guarantee owing to the fact that he was going to win the bout. O'Brien's real profits were to be from the bets on O'Brien, as well as future economic value as champion, or so Jack thought. Burns had also placed a wager on himself, intending all along to win.

The gross receipts turned out to be $21,503 according to one source, and a trifle over $22,000 according to another. O'Brien's share was about $6,390.60. The referee received $200. McCarey actually lost money on the fight.

McCarey and Burns did not decide to call off the bets until soon before the fight, "because it was thought that there would be too much censure if the bets were allowed to stand and Burns profited by the ruse." O'Brien's version said the bets were called off when bettors on O'Brien found out that Burns planned to pull a double-cross and fight to win. Either way, when the bets were called off, "O'Brien was paralyzed with fear."

The *Examiner* opined, "O'Brien's case is worse than hopeless. There was never such a complete expose of a crooked deal."

O'Brien said that originally it was agreed that Burns was to be knocked out in the 11th round. Burns confirmed this. However, the agreement was later amended to a 20-round decision loss for Burns. The battle was to be fought with clean breaks, which would be used to explain why O'Brien could win a decision.

O'Brien's manager Billy Nolan was eventually told of the agreement. Nolan wanted to call it off, but O'Brien persuaded him that he could legitimately win the decision on the merits with clean breaks. "He said that he believed Burns could beat him if they fought straight rules with hitting in the clinches; whereas, in clean breaks, he could beat Burns."

> McCarey said that the clean break had been agreed upon, and produced a paper showing such an agreement with Burns's signature attached. Nolan demanded a set of articles calling for the clean break, but McCarey would not agree to it, saying that the matter would then become public and spoil the fight. Previously he had refused to make public this feature for the same reason.…

When the referee called the men together in the center of the ring to give instructions, nothing was said about the clean break…. Eyton supposed the original agreement to be in force, and O'Brien thought that the clean break would prevail by tacit agreement when the men began fighting. When the referee made the announcement that all bets were off, O'Brien realized for the first time that he had been double-crossed. He sat in his chair stupefied. He turned to Nolan and remarked that he guessed it would be a real fight. And it was, for the straight rules prevailed and after that O'Brien's sole object was to save himself as much punishment as possible.[483]

All this made what happened and what was said regarding their first bout resonate with a different tone. There it was again - a *tacit* agreement. There may have been some funny business about the breaks and hitting in clinches in their first fight. Burns fought hard on the inside throughout, and one paper noted that this was contrary to agreement. Burns was often hissed by the crowd for doing so, because he was breaking the agreement not to hit in the clinches. That said, when the articles were published before the fight, no such agreement was mentioned. Rather, it was said that straight Queensberry rules were to apply, with the men protecting themselves in the clinches and on the breaks. "That straight Marquis of Queensbury rules are to govern the contest, the men to protect themselves in the breakaway."[484] Compare this to the fight report which said, "Burns was hissed for attempting to hit in the clinch…. Burns continues to hit in the clinches and breakaways without regard to agreement."[485] Why then did some in the press and the crowd believe that they were not supposed to hit in the clinches? O'Brien claimed that McCarey had previously refused to make public the no-hitting-in-the-clinches feature so as not to affect interest in the bout. The public felt that fights were more exciting and legitimate with straight rules. Was this agreement previous to the first championship fight, second, or both? Certainly, some folks were aware of the confusion regarding the rules even during the first fight.

Ultimately, the clean break issue seems more like an attempt at spin. Nolan was trying to minimize O'Brien's attempt to fix the fight by suggesting essentially that the fight wasn't fixed, but that they had agreed to clean breaks. O'Brien felt that he could legitimately win such a fight on the merits, but then when he was double-crossed and the fight was fought with straight rules, he realized that he could not win under such circumstances. In fact, the real agreement had nothing to do with the rules, but the fact that Burns was supposed to allow O'Brien to win. The clean break argument was actually just a ruse used on Nolan to convince him to allow

483 *Los Angeles Times, Los Angeles Herald*, May 10, 1907; *Los Angeles Express*, May 10, 1907, May 11, 1907.
484 *Los Angeles Daily Times*, November 28, 1906.
485 *Los Angeles Daily Times*, November 29, 1906.

the fight to go forward. It was also supposed to be the reason given to the public to explain why Burns might lose a decision.

The other question is why did some reporters try to sell the draw the first time when it was obviously Burns' fight? O'Brien wound up fighting basically the same way the second time and everyone was upset, but the critics were not all that hard on Jack when he did the same thing in the first bout. Perhaps it was a matter of expectations. O'Brien had been the well-respected highly touted media darling throughout the country for years. The *Police Gazette* regularly reported his bouts. Burns had been a relative nobody, who had only recently emerged. It seemed that the experts wanted O'Brien to win; wanted to provide him with an excuse; and wanted to sell the idea that the first fight was close and rightfully a draw so that there could be a rematch, believing that the nose injury was a fluke and that Jack was the better boxer who would fight better the next time without that happening.

Making matters worse for O'Brien's credibility was the fact that the *Los Angeles Examiner* reported that James J. Jeffries claimed O'Brien had offered him $80,000 to lie down to him and take the count in a fight to be held in Nevada. Jeff had not exposed O'Brien previously, but in light of what had just been revealed, he believed the time had come to tell the story and rid the game of him.

> Well, it shouldn't surprise me in the least considering that he tried to do the same thing with me. Jack O'Brien is the first and only man who ever came to me and asked me to do a crooked thing. Of all the fighters and managers I have known, this man is the only one who ever had the gall to ask me to fake a fight. Worse than that, he wanted me to lay down to him.

Jeff laughed at O'Brien and told him that he didn't need money that bad. Jack, seeing that Jeff was not going for it, interrupted and said, "Of course I did not think that you would pay any attention to it and I told the Nevada people so at the time." The *Examiner* said Jeff's exposure "will go far to kill the Philadelphian as a fighter."[486]

In subsequent days, it was opined, "The contradictory stories told by the two parties shows that one side is lying and the other side may not be telling the whole truth. So far, the odds are against O'Brien."[487]

Quite naturally, the fans were very upset that they had paid high ticket prices of $5, $10, $20, and $30 to see the fight. They had been "summoned under false pretenses," and were "milked." Another report said, "Patrons of the sport were fooled into believing that the purse was genuine, and prices of seats were set accordingly." McCarey was blamed for allowing such a fight to proceed, because there was no guarantee that O'Brien would train properly, given that Jack believed that Burns was to lose. When he realized

---

486 *Los Angeles Examiner*, May 10, 1907.
487 *Los Angeles Times*, May 11, 1907.

that he was double-crossed, O'Brien didn't fight to win, but to survive, robbing the paying public of a real fight. The battle had been a farce in which O'Brien simply made it a runaway fight to last the 20 rounds.

At that point, many in the press believed or wanted to believe the worst, even about the first fight, and chose to go with O'Brien's version. "Burns and O'Brien, in the first contest, agreed to box to a draw, and the plans were so carried out." Perhaps such a belief just made for a better story and sold more newspapers.

Regardless, it was opined that what had happened would kill boxing in Los Angeles and that lawmakers would pass legislation. Some said that the sooner boxing was made illegal, the better.[488]

> The expose, taken at whatever angle, is the most surprising pugilistic scandal ever sprung. In other scandals, no one was ever caught 'dead to rights.' Gans confessed to faking, but none corroborated his statement. The San Francisco scandals implicated many, but the expose occurred long after events took place.[489]

Despite the scandal, Burns was already making plans for his next fight. He agreed with promoter James Coffroth to fight Australian champion Bill Squires at the Colma Club, near San Francisco, to be held May 30 or July 4, at the promoter's discretion. Jeffries would referee for $1,000. The agreement was signed on May 9, the day after the O'Brien fight. The bout was scheduled for 45 rounds using straight rules. The boxers would be allowed to wear surgical bandages or fingerless kid gloves under the mitts. Burns would receive $8,000 guaranteed, and Squires 60% of 60% of the gate receipts if he won, or 40% of 60% of the receipts if he lost. The parties posted their $2,500 forfeit money with W.W. Naughton of the *San Francisco Examiner*.

Two days after the fiasco, Jack "Twin" Sullivan and Hugo Kelly fought a 20-round draw at the Naud Junction Pavilion, in a bout advertised as being for the world middleweight crown. Tommy Burns refereed the fight. When his name was announced, Burns was greeted with a mixture of a chorus of cheers, hisses and boos. His draw decision was called fair and was popular with the crowd. The crowd was actually fair-sized, given the recent scandal, but still, half of the chairs were empty. It was thought that the Burns-O'Brien farce had hurt the gate.[490]

---

488 *Los Angeles Times*, May 12, 1907; *Los Angeles Express, Los Angeles Herald*, May 11, 1907.
489 *Los Angeles Times*, May 10, 1907.
490 *Los Angeles Express, Los Angeles Times, Los Angeles Herald*, May 11, 1907. Sullivan had the best of the first 10 rounds, outboxing Kelly, but Hugo came back strong in the last half and evened matters. Kelly dropped Sullivan in the 14th round with a left hook to the jaw, but Sullivan stalled and smothered and got out of trouble.

Jack (Twin) Sullivan.   Hugo Kelly.

Burns said that his and McCarey's "intentions were meant for the best, but I can see now where the whole affair was a bad break from beginning to end." The *Herald* said, "One thing is certain: A deep disgust has settled over patrons of the ring and future affairs will be attended with no small spirit of mistrust."[491]

Another story came out saying that O'Brien had once before been offered $42,000 to lay down to Joe Gans in Nevada. "O'Brien did not accept, but it is said that the reason he did not was because he did not want to stand the jibes of the world by losing in any way to a 'nigger,' according to his own alleged words." This also explains why so many fighters drew the color line. If they lost, they would be subjected to taunts and ridicule.[492]

John L. Sullivan said O'Brien was "far from being a first-rate fighter." His marvelous shiftiness was the only thing that saved him and kept him out of trouble in the ring, and enabled him to win fights. He said Corbett was the first of the big exponents of the shifty game, using quickness and agility to defeat stronger opponents.

Sullivan said Jeffries was the best heavyweight champion ever, because he was big and strong but also knew how to use the modern style of shiftiness. John L. said,

> Jeffries, being probably the quickest big man that ever lived – although when you saw him fight, he was so immense in bulk that his movements never seemed to be anything like as quick as they actually were – Jeffries, with his quickness and his impenetrable crouch, and

491 *Los Angeles Herald*, May 12, 1907.
492 *Los Angeles Times*, May 12, 1907.

his immense power of endurance, and his vast hitting power, and with all of the foot-shiftiness of the new style – there can't be any doubt that, had it been possible for Jeff and I to meet when we were both at our best, he would have sent it over on me. More than that, I never saw the man that I thought could stand a chance to lick Jeffries. If he's wise he'll not fight anymore. He's too big to get down to trim, and he's had a fine day of it, anyhow, and there has been a lot of effective new stuff introduced into the game even during the few years since he has been out of the ring.[493]

PHEW!!

As of mid-May 1907, Eastern sporting writers were practically unanimous in saying that Jack O'Brien should no longer be tolerated in the American ring, for he was a faker, pure and simple. McCarey's common sense in risking the possibility of what occurred was sadly commented upon. "Tommy Burns is criticized for having had anything to do with such a proposition, but escapes far better than the others." It would be seven months before Jack O'Brien again entered the ring, which was quite a long time for a fighter who had been as active as he was.[494]

493 *Los Angeles Times*, May 12, 1907.
494 *Los Angeles Herald*, May 17, 1907.

264

CHAPTER 10

The Australian Champion

In mid-1907, Tommy Burns began a championship phase where he took on the top fighters from different countries, and also began fighting in various places around the world. He wanted to establish the fact that he was the true world champion and not just the American champion.

A match with Australian heavyweight champion Bill Squires had been in the works even before the Burns-O'Brien rematch. There had been earlier attempts to get Jeffries to come out of retirement to fight Squires, but Jeffries insisted on receiving $25,000 of a $30,000 purse, and would not accept a 60%/40% split. Burns stepped up to the plate to face Squires for $8,000.[495]

According to secondary sources, since 1902, the hard-punching Bill Squires had racked up a string of at least 19 victories in Australia. His notable bouts included: 1902 WDQ4 Ed "Starlight" Rollins; 1904 WDQ4 Starlight, WDQ11 Peter Felix, LDQ8 Arthur Cripps (Squires' only loss), and KO1 Peter Felix; 1905 KO8 Bill Smith and KO7 Felix; 1906 KO3 Tim Murphy (Australian title), KO1 Peter Kling, KO1 Bill Smith and KO1 Mike Williams; and 1907 ND4 and ND6 Arthur Cripps.[496]

Bill Squires

---

495 *Philadelphia Inquirer*, January 4, 1907.
496 Boxrec.com.

Primary source accounts said Squires was undefeated in 24 battles. Two of the fights were fought with bareknuckle London prize ring rules. One bout was a draw, two were decisions, and the other 21 were won by knockout. He certainly had knockout punching power.[497]

James J. Jeffries would be paid $1,000 to referee the Burns-Squires championship bout. One question that comes to mind is if Burns was so upset over Jeffries' decision in his first championship match with O'Brien; why then allow him to be the arbiter of another fight? Perhaps he agreed to Jeffries because Jeff would attract fans to the fight, and also because the fight films might generate more income with Jeffries involved.

C.E. Van Loan wondered how much the "nauseous fight scandal" of the recent Burns-O'Brien bout would affect the game in the north, in the San Francisco area, where the fight would be held. Sports tended to have poor memories, and San Francisco, having been out of the championship boxing game for over a year owing to the earthquakes and fires, was hungry for a big fight. Some thought Squires had a chance to win, which helped garner interest. Bill's manager Barney Reynolds predicted that Squires would whip Burns easily.

Those who were eager to see Jeffries in the ring again were hoping that Squires would defeat Burns, for Jeff had promised to come out of retirement to fight Squires if he won, in order to bring the title back to the Americas. However, Jeffries "is not particularly anxious to fight again. Jim is a man who hates the grind of training – possibly because he trained harder than any fighter that ever conditioned himself." Jeff said it would take seven to nine months to get back into fighting trim. Van Loan opined, "Jim Jeffries was the greatest heavyweight fighter this country ever saw. He was probably the greatest fighter of modern times. At the time of his retirement he was at the top of his physical perfection."[498]

On May 30, 1907 in Tonapah, Nevada, Mike Schreck defeated Marvin Hart in the 21st round of their bout when Hart's corner threw in the towel. Hart had suffered a broken right wrist in the 6th round. Thereafter, Schreck took over the bout and administered punishment, despite Hart's fierce aggressiveness. They slugged like demons throughout, but Hart was not able to fight as effectively as a result of his best weapon being crippled. Still, Hart almost had Schreck out in the 18th round. However, Schreck recovered, and in the 20th round, only the gong saved Hart from Schreck's onslaught. In the middle of the 21st round, the towel was thrown in. Hart's pluck was admired, given that he had fought hard with an injury.[499]

For the Squires fight, Tommy Burns trained at Harbin Springs, north of San Francisco. For the most part, Squires trained in secret in San Francisco.

497 *San Francisco Examiner*, July 4, 1907.
498 *Los Angeles Examiner*, May 12, 1907.
499 *Los Angeles Herald*, May 31, June 5, 1907.

Initially, in Los Angeles it was said that Burns would be the favorite, for Squires was not able to hit hard without squarely setting himself first, so Burns would be able to avoid him easily.[500]

Because Squires kept his training camp dark, many thought he was another Jack Palmer and had been overrated. However, as his training progressed, and some saw him work, an increasing number of reports were favorable towards Squires. Interest in the fight gradually built.

The local San Francisco press began hyping the fight. The Los Angeles press said the bay area was head over heels in love with the coming bout, for the dailies were boosting the fight. Many great fighters had emerged from Australia, such as Bob Fitzsimmons, Peter Jackson, and Young Griffo. Squires was supposed to be the next big talent. Still, Burns was the early 10 to 7 favorite. In Los Angeles, reports were more mixed. One man told the *Los Angeles Herald* that Squires was a big dub, while another said that he was a real fighter.[501]

The Burns-Squires bout was scheduled for 2 p.m. on July 4, 1907, to be held in an open air arena capable of seating 10,000 people. Special trains would take fans to the arena.[502]

500 *Los Angeles Herald*, June 12, 1907.
501 *Los Angeles Herald*, June 20, 1907.
502 *Los Angeles Herald*, June 23, 1907.

On June 24, a crowd of spectators at Shannon's gymnasium watched Squires train. Joe Thomas sparred 3 rounds with the Australian. Observers liked what they saw. "Squires gave the impression of a man who can take a vast amount of punishment without being affected. ... There can be no question of his condition when he steps into the ring." However, "the question as to his ability must remain unsettled until he has exchanged punches with the Canadian." Squires had been in hard training in the U.S. for nearly four weeks.

The respected Parson Davies, who had seen Squires train, said, "Never in my life have I seen so great a piece of fighting machinery concentrated in 180 pounds of human being. ... [E]very ounce of flesh on the Australian is there for a purpose. ... A more cleanly built big athlete couldn't be found in any man's country." The fight was anticipated to be one of the biggest betting events in the history of the fight game on the Coast.[503]

Women were amongst the spectators who watched Squires train, and they would also see the fight. This was shocking to Squires, who said,

> I for one strenuously object to women attending prize fights. If I thought it would do any good, I'd request the management to bar them. Think of a fellow dancing about a ring with only a pair of tights on with a lot of ladies looking at him. They'd think the girls were pretty bold back home if they tried to do a thing like that.[504]

Training at San Rafael, Squires had no superfluous flesh, and was weighing about 185 pounds, looking quite strong. One source said Burns expected to weigh about 179 pounds on fight day. Another reported 175 pounds.

As the fight approached, as a result of many wagers being placed on Squires, the betting odds rapidly grew tighter, moving to even money, or with Burns as a slight 10 to 9 favorite. Apparently the bettors thought Bill had a good chance to win. Although this was probably a bit of hyperbole, it was said that the fight had more interest than any other for the past four years.

Squires could not understand why Burns was not a top-heavy betting favorite. "It's a mystery to me why Burns is not a strong public choice in the betting. He's the champion of the country and has fought his best fights in this vicinity." Bill was upset because he wanted to wager on himself, but would not win as much with the odds being so tight.[505]

On the evening of June 27 and the morning of June 28, an avalanche of money came in on Squires, causing the betting odds to shift completely and make him the favorite and Burns the 10 to 9 underdog. "This is a most unexpected state of affairs which can scarcely be accounted for when one

---

503 *San Francisco Chronicle*, June 25, 1907; *San Francisco Bulletin*, June 24, 25, 1907
504 *San Francisco Bulletin*, June 24, 1907.
505 *San Francisco Bulletin*, June 25, 1907; *Los Angeles Herald*, June 27, 1907.

takes into consideration the fact that Squires is practically an unknown pugilistic quantity." However, he was the Australian champion. Australia was known for producing some fantastic fighters. Also, Squires had an impressive record of knockouts, and had looked good in training. Still,

> Burns is the American champion. He has fought his way to the top of the fistic heap through the best of the present crop of heavyweights, and why patriotism has not asserted itself and influenced the betting in favor of the American (as it usually does in the case of an international battle), is indeed hard to understand.[506]

Upon completion of the construction of the outdoor fight arena, it was said to be the best open-air structure ever. Those who would pay $2 for a bleacher seat would be just as satisfied as those who paid $30 for a box seat. The seats opened for sale at Willis Cigar Store, 1515 Ellis Street, and almost immediately, $7,000 in tickets were paid for or held in reserve. "Uptown everything is forgotten but the Burns-Squires fight." Given the amount of local interest, it was anticipated that Coffroth likely would have a record-breaking house.

On June 28, Burns shifted his training camp from Harbin Springs to Oakland's Reliance Club, which charged 50 cents to those who wanted to see him train. He did his morning road work, jumped rope, punched the bag, shadow boxed, and sparred 6 rounds with his sparring partner, George Brown. Although Tommy looked small in street clothes, "he strips big, and produced a very favorable impression on the fans." He exhibited plenty of speed. "Burns has improved wonderfully as a boxer since he was last in San Francisco, and, pitted against Brown, who is a taller man, he made a good showing."

---

506 *San Francisco Bulletin*, June 28, 1907.

Afterwards, Burns said that just before he left Harbin Springs, he weighed 169 ½ pounds. "I probably weigh a little more than that now, and I think I will go into the ring weighing from 172 to 175 pounds. I can say honestly that I never felt better in my life."

When told about the current odds, Burns replied, "Squires is favorite? Oh, well, wait until the boys from Los Angeles arrive. You can bet that the odds will shift a point of two when they start sending it in." Burns and trainer Lewis were quartered at the Athens.[507]

Those who were visiting Squires' training camp said that he was not being overrated.[508]

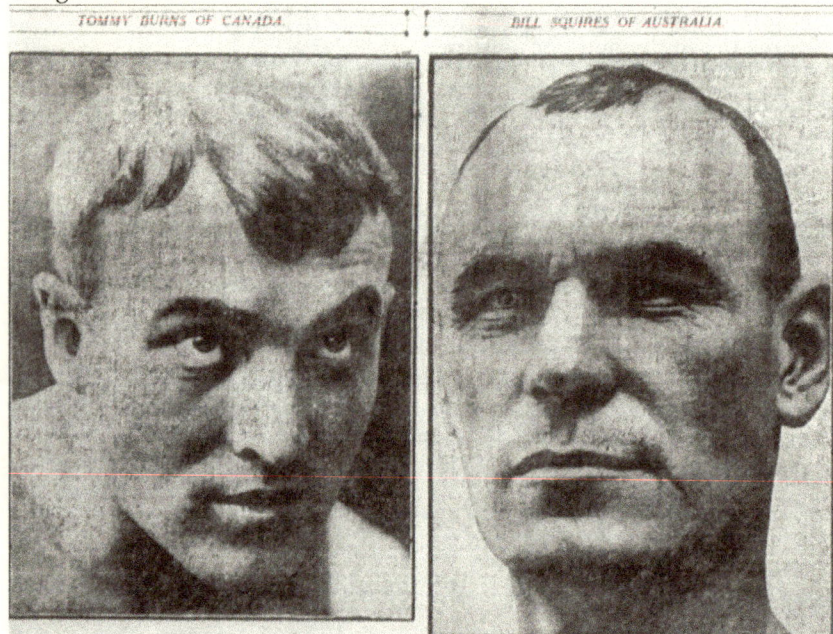

TOMMY BURNS OF CANADA.   BILL SQUIRES OF AUSTRALIA.

When assessing the bout, one writer said it would be a mistake to assume that Burns is not a clever man. Some believed he was a rough and ready smasher, owing to the fact that he attacked Jack O'Brien with little regard for what Jack might do. However, Tommy's earlier fights had shown him to be a boxer. He could stand up and slug, but he could also make it a runaway fight for several rounds. On the other hand, Squires fought in just one way – on the attack. His sole goal was to hit his opponent with a crushing blow.[509]

The week of the fight, interest in the contest fully awakened and the betting was brisk. The *Los Angeles Herald* said, "Whether this is due to Jimmy Coffroth's clever boosting and press work, or is accounted for by genuine interest cannot be determined." Much of the San Francisco press

507 *San Francisco Chronicle, Los Angeles Herald,* June 29, 1907; *San Francisco Bulletin,* June 28, 1907.
508 *Los Angeles Herald,* June 28, 29, 1907.
509 *San Francisco Chronicle,* June 30, 1907.

was into the fight. Still, most Los Angeles fans thought Tommy would defeat the unknown Squires in short order.

James Jeffries, who would referee the bout, confirmed that if Squires won, he would re-enter the ring in order to regain the laurels for America. Although Burns was a Canadian, he was from the American continent.[510]

Burns anticipated that he would defeat Squires within 15 rounds. The confident Squires said he would win within 10 rounds.

On June 30 at the Reliance Club gymnasium, nearly 600 fight fans paid 50 cents each to watch Burns box 3 rounds with George Brown, punch the bag, and go through his usual training routine. Burns anticipated that he would enter the ring at about 176 pounds, four pounds below his regular fighting notch. However, Tommy felt much faster on his feet at the lower weight.

At that point, Squires was the 8 to 10 betting favorite. Coffroth said the advance ticket sales had already exceeded the $11,000 mark. Clearly, fight fans were interested in the contest.[511]

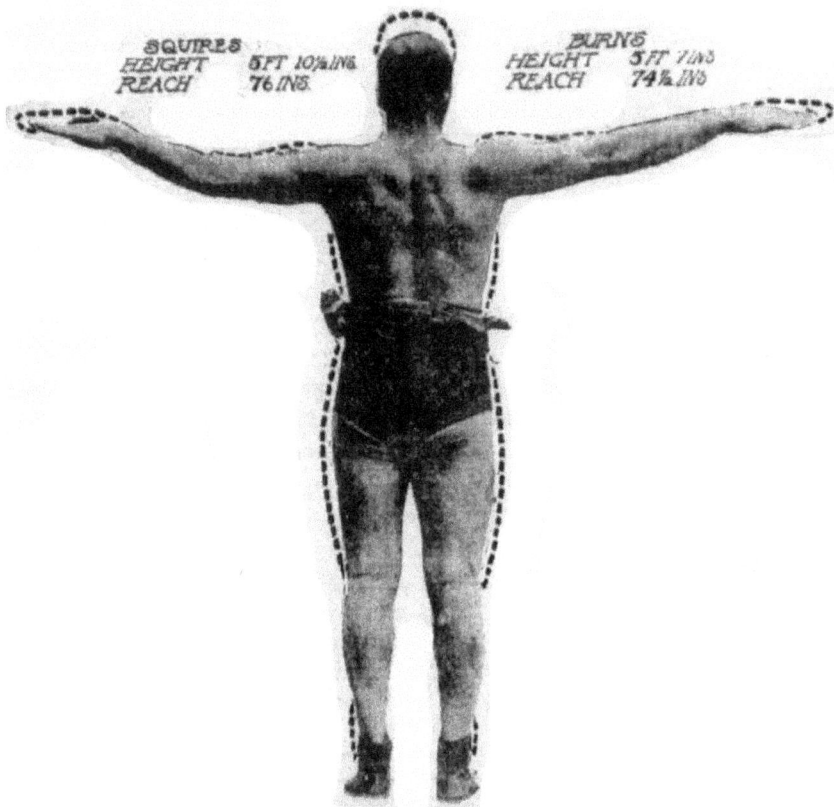

SQUIRES
HEIGHT 5FT 10½INS
REACH 76 INS.

BURNS
HEIGHT 5FT 7INS
REACH 74½ INS

---

510 *Los Angeles Herald*, June 30, 1907.
511 *San Francisco Bulletin*, July 1, 1907.

All those who had seen Squires in training just before the fight said he looked well, and had good speed and power. However, because he was an unknown in America, and local fans had never seen him in actual combat, they were not sure what to expect. All of that said, oddly enough, the Australian remained the betting favorite.

Jeffries said Burns was looking very quick and strong, and had improved as a fighter; his recent string of successes having increased his confidence. He said if Squires was the mixer that he was said to be; the fight should end in a knockout.[512]

The *San Francisco Evening Post* said the sports were loud in their praises of both men. Professor Lewis said Burns was in excellent shape. "From the way the brawny Australian appears he certainly should be a good one and Burns should have his hands full. ... The local colony of Australians is coming to the front and placing bankrolls on the man from the antipodes." Perhaps this explains why the odds shifted to make Squires the betting favorite. Australians who had seen Squires in action were fully confident in his prowess.[513]

The *San Francisco Bulletin* said that although it was the Australian's American debut, his Australian record entitled him to recognition. Many competent local critics who had seen him at work had come away favorably impressed with his style and hitting powers, sufficient enough to bet their money on him and make Squires the favorite.

> He is not a showy or flashy boxer, but is a sturdily built, aggressive chap, with tremendous driving force. While his muscles stand out like whipcords all over his body, he does not show any semblance of being muscle-bound. He has a free-and-easy method of moving around. ... [H]e has the necessary wallop to bring home the coin. ... Of course, the class of fighters he has been pitted against do not stand out in the limelight as champions, but he has done all that was asked of him in clean-cut fashion, having polished off twenty-four men inside of seventy-eight rounds, an average of three and a quarter rounds per fight. But two contests went over ten rounds. Jerry O'Toole lasted 15 rounds in 1906, while Peter Felix stuck for eleven rounds in 1904. As he cleaned up Felix in a single round in 1905, it shows that he is of the improving sort.

> Just how he will loom up against a speedy man like Tommy Burns is another question. The latter is much faster on his feet than the ordinary heavyweight and may keep the Antipodean on a steady run until he sizes up his style. It is utterly impossible to figure out the probable winner on past performances, as they have not met the same men, and sizing up a fighter on his gymnasium work is like

512 *Los Angeles Herald*, July 1, 1907.
513 *San Francisco Evening Post*, July 1, 1907.

trying to get a correct line on a ball player by his work in practice. ... Squires may be able to dispose of the Canadian in jig-time, or it may be a long-drawn-out bruising battle, and in the latter event the chances of Burns winning are more than bright. That latter has shown that he is capable of going at a fast clip for twenty rounds, and with his cleverness he may be able to systematically slash his adversary into ribbons and eventually put on the finishing touches with a decisive punch.[514]

At the conclusion of their training work on July 1, Squires weighed 180 ½ pounds, while Burns weighed 176 ½ pounds.[515]

Jim Jeffries at Squires' Training Quarters Examining the Australian's Powerful Forearm and Fist.

---

514 *San Francisco Bulletin*, July 1, 1907.
515 *San Francisco Evening Post*, July 2, 1907.

When Jeffries met with Bill to discuss the rules, Squires objected to Burns' wearing a rubber pneumatic girdle, which he felt blocked body shots. Jeff said he would inspect it and use his judgment as to whether it lessened the effect of body punishment, and if so, he would ask Tommy not to wear it.[516]

Burns said the rubber device was designed to protect him from low blows, not body shots. It did not cover the legal scoring area. Apparently, it was invented by Twin Sullivan and worn by him in his fights. Tommy agreed not to wear it if Jeffries told him not to do so.

Jeffries said that when he ordered the men to break, it meant that the boxer who was holding had to let go and step back, but that he still had to protect himself at all times, including on the break. Squires agreed and said he had fought that way his entire career.

Jeffries called Squires a tough, powerful, and likely looking fellow. Of course, he had never seen him in an actual fight, but only in training. "I have seen many a gymnasium champion who left his fight there and didn't amount to anything in the ring, and again I have seen many a sloppy gymnasium worker fight like a demon when he got into the ring."

Despite a large amount of local betting on him and talk that Squires would win, one writer felt there might have been false impressions as to his ability. This writer observed that Squires "seems to have little or no footwork and handles himself somewhat after the style of Jack Palmer, the Englishman who met defeat at the hands of Twin Sullivan."

Yet, as of July 2, two days before the fight, Squires was still the 10 to 8 and even 10 to 7 betting favorite over Burns. Very confident Englishmen were "backing him to a man" and offering to wager large sums of money on Squires. For whatever reason, Burns could not seem to shake the image of being a "mediocre" champion, as one writer had called him. Still, those who came from Squires' training camp had widely divergent views. Some were not impressed; though most appreciated Bill's obvious punching power.[517]

Squires had a lot of backing from his fellow Australians, as well as many of those who had seen him in training. The Australians thought their champion was unbeatable. They believed he would not only defeat Burns, but would also defeat Jeffries. "Able critics and competent judges of fighters have pronounced him to be a marvelous fighting machine."

It was said that four out of five fans fancied Squires in the fight. "They seem to think that a big surprise is on tap and that the Australian will prove to be another of those wonderful heavyweights whom the Antipodes keep shooting over here from time to time." "Boshter" Bill's modesty boosted

---

516 More referees today should do the same, given how many fighters in cowardly fashion wear overly large foul protectors whose main purpose seems to be to block legal body shots as much as they are to block low blows. They might as well wear headgear too. If a fighter cannot block or take a body shot, then he or she should not be in the game. Yet, many so-called champions are unwilling to use properly placed groin protectors.

517 *San Francisco Examiner, San Francisco Call,* July 2, 1907.

his stock. "Modesty and real fighting ability go hand in hand." Truly great fighters "were modest and not noisy, bombastic blow-hards."

Little was known about the caliber of Squires' opponents. "But we know he beat them all and in jig time, too." Seven of his knockouts were in the 1st round, six were in the 2nd round, and only three fights went over 4 rounds. Of the others, two went 4 rounds and six were finished in the 3rd round. "That is some hitting. … The public likes a fighter who keeps after his man and is willing to take a chance." However, it remained to be seen whether Squires was a false alarm or would turn out to be another Fitzsimmons.

The *Bulletin* opined that the fight's length would depend upon whether Burns would exchange punches or use his superior footwork and attempt to outgeneral Squires. The consensus of opinion was that if Burns mixed it up that Squires would win, but if he played a waiting game and darted in and out that he would eventually wear down the Australian. "Burns will undoubtedly pursue the latter course, but Squires may prove to be a shrewder man than he is given credit for being." The present indications were that Squires would enter the ring as the heavy betting favorite, though this was due to the entire lack of Burns money.

Fight experts' opinions were quite mixed:
Eddie Graney: "I think it will be a great fight and I think it will be an even battle."
Billy Roche: "Squires will surely win."
Sam Berger: "From what I hear of Squires I think it will be an even fight."
Billy Jordan: "I have not seen Squires work, but I like his looks."
Spider Kelly: "I think it will be a great battle. Too hard to pick a winner."
Eddie Hanlon: "Squires will win sure. He is the best man from his country in a long time."
Tom Corbett: "Burns is the best short end I ever saw."

Tim McGrath: "I look for Squires to win in ten rounds, sure."

Jack O'Brien: "Squires will win in short order."

Alex Greggains: "I like Burns. He is the goods."

Jimmy Britt: "Squires will knock Burns out inside of seven rounds."

Billy Gallagher: "Squires is a cinch."

Billy Nolan: "I think Burns will win, as he has the class."

Battling Nelson: "It is too hard to pick the winner."

Tiv Kreling: "I hope Squires wins inside of fifteen rounds, as I intend to tour Australia with the pictures and will make a world of money." A contract had been signed with the Miles Brothers to film the fight.

Harry Pollock: "My pal, Jack Johnson, tells me that Burns will win."[518]

On July 2, Burns worked his abdominal muscles, skipped rope, punched the bag, and worked with dumbbells for 20 minutes.

THE BULLETIN'S PHOTOGRAPHER CAUGHT JEFFRIES DISCUSSING THE RULES WITH TOMMY BURNS WHILE AN INTERESTED CROWD OF ASSISTANTS GATHERED AROUND.

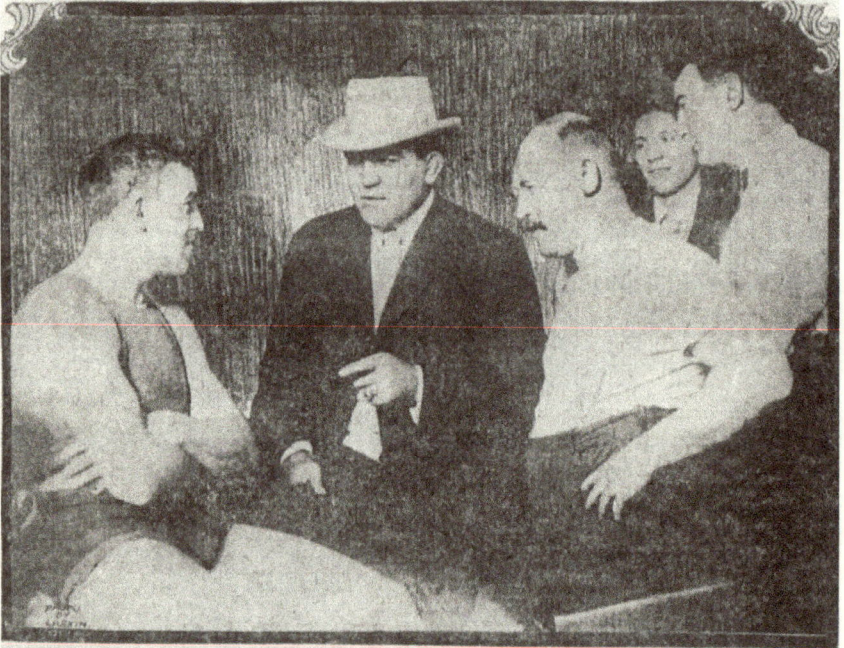

Reading from left to right—Tommy Burns, Jim Jeffries, who will referee; Trainer Lewis, Frankie Edwards, who beats Johnny Murphy in the preliminary, and George Brown, sparring partner of Burns.

When Jeffries met with Burns, he asked him not to use the pneumatic armor. Tommy replied, "That's all right. I'll leave it off in this fight." Jeff informed both fighters that straight Queensberry rules would govern.

Regarding the two combatants, Jeff said,

> I want to say that a pair of better trained heavies I never laid eyes on. Burns looks well, and knowing him as I do I expect to see him put up a desperate fight. Squires looks the part, and of course that's all I can

518 *San Francisco Bulletin*, July 3, 1907.

say about him from personal experience. If he lives up to his looks it will be a corking battle. … I couldn't help noticing the extreme confidence that exists on both sides. There will surely be keen disappointment for somebody when it's all over.[519]

One writer said Burns looked to be several pounds lighter than in the past, but was much faster, particularly with his footwork. He was much faster of foot than when he met O'Brien in the "lap race." "Burns is a better man than he was when he fought Barry. He has the 'winning courage' which comes with a few important victories." Burns was called a combination of boxer and slugger, while Squires was a pure slugger.

Professor Lewis, Tommy's trainer, said, "I have worked with Burns before several of his fights and each time he was in great condition. I want to go on record as saying that he is better and faster than ever before."

The champion said he used to overwork when trying to make the middleweight limit. He was much happier and more effective at a higher weight. Tommy planned to fight Squires from the start, but was not going to allow Squires to hit him with the right.

519 *San Francisco Examiner*, July 3, 1907.

I have never been stuck on this thing of working myself to death before any fight. I used to do enough of that when I was making the middleweight limit and I figure that it hurt me. Now I do just enough work to keep me feeling right all the time and I find that I can increase my daily stunts without tiring. ...

I intend to fight him from the opening bell. By this I do not mean that I am going to be sucker enough to stand up and let him wallop me with that big right hand of his. A knockout punch is all right provided you land on the other fellow. Marvin Hart had a fairly good right swing, but I never let him hit me with it once during the fight, and after the fifteenth round I was out slugging him at his own game.

Responding to those who said Squires would quickly knock him out, Burns said, "Nobody ever did that to me yet; no man ever dazed me with a punch to the jaw, and I'm not going to worry about it until after it happens."[520]

The *San Francisco Call* had a unique perspective regarding why Squires was the betting favorite. It speculated that the reason practically no one was betting on Burns was because the fix was in for Burns to lose in order to set up a Jeffries-Squires match. Folks smelled a rat when Coffroth hinted at matching Jeff and Squires should Bill win, feeling that the Burns-Squires match was just a set-up forerunner to the really big payday - Jeffries-Squires. Therefore, gamblers "do not see how Squires can possibly lose under the circumstances that exist at present." All of the wise ones were betting on the Australian, who was a 10 to 7 favorite owing to the fact that so much money was being bet on him and so little on Burns, even though Tommy was the champion and no one in the U.S. had seen Bill box in an actual bout.

The *Call* said Burns was a confessed crooked fighter, and in addition to the O'Brien bout, had other shady transactions. It printed a letter written by Burns to Billy Gee, a well-known eastern sporting man. It interpreted the letter to mean that Burns would not take a chance with any tough fighter, including O'Brien, unless the bout was fixed for him to win. Tommy felt that he had worked hard enough and was entitled to easy money at that stage of his career.

The letter, if authentic, was written on March 25, 1906, before Burns fought two men on one night in San Diego, and well before Burns fought O'Brien in their first championship bout. In it, Burns allegedly said:

Well, Bill, I am in San Diego. I box two fellows here Wednesday night, each ten rounds. Have it fixed, so ain't taking chances. I got two telegrams from Los Angeles wanting me to meet Root. Hart beat

520 *San Francisco Examiner*, July 3, 1907.

him in twelve rounds and O'Brien beat Kaufman, and you know Root isn't very game. ...

I want some one I can trust to make the match with O'Brien and get all the coin we can. ... Now, Bill, if you like, go ahead and match me with O'Brien and Ruhlin. Be careful with anyone else; as I am champion, I don't want to take any chances of getting beaten.

Get all the coin you can, either a purse or percentage, and fix it with O'Brien as I know he is O.K. now to get the coin. Also try to get me on in London, England. I can beat all those fellows over there. I got a letter from John Willie. He wants to box me. He wants some money. If he agrees to lay down I'll give him a match, but make him put up a guarantee. Take no chances at all. As I fought my way to the top, Bill, let's get some money now. ... I am in business in Long Beach, Cal. It's a few miles from the city. I have a Japanese art store. My intended wife is taking care of it for me while I am down here. She's as good as they make, and when you meet her you will agree with me.

I have met the whole family and stopped at their home in Portland for a month. They are very swell people. But they don't want me to fight. I told them just one more year and I would cut it out.

When you write send it to 231 Pine avenue, Los Angeles. That is where my store is. ... P.S. – Arrange O'Brien's go at once, and fix it.[521]

Naturally, this letter and article casts doubt on the integrity not only of both O'Brien bouts, but on the Burns doubleheader that took place on March 28, 1906. It made gamblers feel that Burns might very well have agreed with Coffroth to throw the Squires fight. At least, that was how they were betting their money, without many other reasons to do so, given Squires' relative local obscurity.

The day of the fight, the *Call* said rumors were swirling about. Many fight fans thought Burns would double cross Squires the way he did with O'Brien and fight to win. "The general opinion, however, prevails that Squires will be the victor at any cost." With Squires victorious, more money would be in sight when Bill fought Jeffries. "Everybody is on to Burns, and this is one of the principal reasons why he never could be seen in the same ring with the great undefeated champion." Fear about the fight's integrity was causing fewer folks to wager on its result.

Burns was still struggling to find any respect. The *Call* did not even grant that he was the world heavyweight champion. "Burns has not a clear title to the American championship, but with Jeffries out of the running he stands out as the most likely candidate for the honor."

---

521 *San Francisco Call,* July 3, 1907.

Squires, on the other hand, had the backing of well-respected folks like Larry Foley, the famous Australian trainer, who said that Bill was one of the best men who ever came from that country.

Still, it was conceded that in training, Squires did not show the footwork that Burns had. Tommy was a "marvel on his feet." It was admitted that Squires was strong and a hard puncher, but some questioned his ability as a boxer. Burns supporters opined that Tom was too clever to allow Squires to hit him. They also said that Burns was a hard hitter who knew how to land his blows. It was noted that Squires had defeated Peter Felix in 1 round, but so too had Jack Johnson. However, Mike Williams had defeated Jack Palmer in 9 rounds, while Squires had defeated Williams in 35 seconds.

Even Jeffries did not understand why Squires was so much of a favorite, given that he was an unknown quantity. "Burns is a good man. He is a better man than the Pacific coast fight fans think. … If Squires wins, if the public demands it and if there is enough money in sight, I'll fight him."

The confident Burns said that if he did not win, he would never again put on a glove. The versatile champion could box and move or he could stand inside and mix and rough it. He would measure his opponent and then select his fighting method. "I never felt more sure of winning in my life."[522] He also said,

> If Squires beats me I'll never fight again…. [I]f I don't win this fight I'll quit the game…. Last night I saw the motion pictures of Squires going through his training stunts, and if he isn't any better than they show I will have an easy time. He seems very slow. There is no possible way for him to beat me…. I think this fellow is overrated.[523]

On the day of the fight, Burns remained the 10 to 7 underdog. Some were even taking wagers at 10 to 6 odds. Late money on Tommy made him only a 10 to 8 underdog, though some were still taking 10 to 7. "The general public could not understand why Squires had become such an overwhelming favorite and were getting a trifle skeptical as to the exact nature of the encounter."

The championship fight was held on July 4, 1907 in Colma, California, in the San Francisco Bay area. The day of the fight, Squires was said to weigh 182 pounds, while Burns was weighing 179 pounds. Squires was said to stand 5'10 ½" and to have a reach advantage. Tommy was 25 years old to Bill's 28. It was Squires' first bout outside of Australia. The fight was scheduled to start at about 2 p.m. under the sun.[524]

The morning of the fight, Burns said,

> I feel fine and am confident that I will win. I think the fight will be short. My style of fighting will be governed entirely by the pace that

---

522 *San Francisco Call,* July 4, 1907.
523 *San Francisco Examiner,* July 4, 1907.
524 *San Francisco Bulletin, Los Angeles Express, Los Angeles Times,* July 4, 1907.

Squires sets. ... If he should succeed in landing one of his Australian punches on me and put me out it will be my last ring battle. I think I shall win in about fifteen rounds.

Squires said,

> I expect the fight to be over in short order, and that I will win in decisive fashion. I have instructed Referee Jeffries not to pay any attention to my seconds in case they should throw up the sponge. If Burns should get me in distress at any stage of the battle I don't want my seconds to get rattled and toss up the towel. I want to fight to the last ditch. ... My condition is perfect and I will put up a hard fight.[525]

Reports varied as to the attendance, some listing the venue as containing a crowd between 5,000 and 6,000 people, while others said there were 7,000, 8,000, and even up to 9,000 persons present. It was one of the biggest crowds ever seen in California. Not more than ten women were in attendance. The few women in the crowd were of the kind that one might expect to meet in the fashionable shops and at the better theaters, well gowned. The day was hot, so the crowd perspired, but there was a cool, brisk breeze which provided some mercy.

Entering the ring at 2 p.m., Squires wore green trunks, a faded dirty brown-gray sweater, and a shabby soft gray slouch hat. He had his wrists and hands bound with tape. Tim McGrath accompanied him, carrying Irish and Australian flags. Bill moved about the ring to test it, smiling at the crowd. One paper said Squires was advertised as being age 28 but looked at least 10 years older. His seconds were McGrath, Eddie Hanlon, Bill Russell, Judge Denton of Australia, and Martin Murphy.

Shortly thereafter, to the cheers of the crowd, Burns entered the ring with the American flag waving behind him. He was wearing a dingy bath robe. Underneath, he wore green and red tights with an American flag as a belt. With Burns were Professor Frank Lewis, George Brown, Earl Keating, and Mark Shaughnessy. Tom went to his corner, and then went over to Squires to shake hands.

Former world lightweight champions Battling Nelson and Jimmy Britt were in attendance and introduced. They shook hands. Also introduced were Al Kaufman and Jimmy Burns. They all bowed to the crowd. Al Kaufman challenged the winner.

Billy Jordan announced, "The rough diamond of Australia – Bill Squires." After the applause, he said, "The heavyweight champion of America – Tommy Burns." An American flag was waved over his head and the crowd applauded again.

Jeffries entered the ring to referee. Jordan introduced Referee Jeffries, "The great and only undefeated champion of the world." Jeff received an ovation.

Burns won the coin flip to choose corners. He took the corner that would place his back to the sun.

Squires wore bandages, but Burns wore light kid walking gloves under his boxing gloves. The two were photographed.

While they were squaring off, Tommy said, "How are you, Bill? I am going to make you travel some this time." Another quoted Tommy as saying, "I'm glad you're feeling good. I'm going to give you an awful run." Jeffries momentarily conferred with them.

When he stood erect, Squires loomed above Burns. Some actually felt sorry for the champion, feeling that there was a huge size mismatch. "It's a shame to put him up against a little fellow like Burns." Another observer said if Tommy was killed, that he brought it upon himself.

Once again, Burns was fighting for respect. At ringside just before the fight, Tommy was a 10 to 9 underdog, and it was even money that the American champion would not last 10 rounds.

Billy Jordan announced that it was a 45-round contest with straight Marquis of Queensberry rules to govern, the men to protect themselves at all times and to break upon the referee's order.

Announcer Jordan made his familiar cry of "Let her go" to start the bell and the fight. Squires rushed after Burns from the start as though he expected to sweep him off his feet. Tommy danced around the ring and kept away. Burns was "as nimble as a sparrow," backing around the ring as Squires followed. Bill focused on the body.

After a clinch, Tommy moved about, and then suddenly set himself and met the oncoming Squires with a perfectly timed right cross "which sounded like the crack of a whiplash," dropping Squires heavily to the floor, "making a positive thump as he struck the mat." "It was one of the cleanest knockdowns ever seen in a championship contest and there was an ugly red lump below Squires' left temple as he scrambled to his feet." He quickly rose at the count of two, failing to take the benefit of as much of the count as possible, showing that he was not ring-wise.

With his arms hanging loosely at his sides, Squires rushed at Tommy without attempting to guard himself or use any defense. Burns moved and watched him eagerly, looking for an opening. Squires rushed in and both men hit the body. Burns blocked several hard swings and returned with some clean blows. The Australian made no attempt to block, relying entirely on a chance to shoot in a haymaker. They clinched several times. Squires was rough in the clinches and landed some stinging blows to the "alleged champion of America."

Squires again lunged but fell short with a left hook. Burns stepped back and set himself and sent Squires to the mat with a hard right and left to the jaw.

Squires again rose in a couple seconds. "Burns was the coolest man in the arena at this time. There was a smile on his face as he stepped in close to his victim." Squires waded in, but Burns hit his "ungainly antagonist" with a right above the eye. Tommy landed some more ugly smashes.

Burns measured his man with his left and then another flush crushing right to the jaw caused Bill's hands to fall to his sides and he collapsed onto the brown canvas for the third time, like a deer that had been shot, limp and lifeless. He was counted out. Squires' poor defense had cost him. The local sources agreed that the fight had lasted 2 minutes and 8 seconds.

When the fight was over, an Australian who had just sat down into a $15 seat said, "I soy, o' chap, when's the fight going to begin, you know?" The man sitting next to him said, "G'wan. It's jolly well over."

The Miles Brothers filmed the fight, and the footage still exists. The film reveals that Burns began the fight cautiously, lightly bouncing and moving back from the attacking Squires, but keeping his balance well. Burns had a good sense of range, stopping momentarily to feint, continuing to move back, and then unleashing a right just as Squires moved into his range. The two clinched, and Burns attempted hooks to the body and head on the inside.

Burns continued to backpedal, but launched and landed a right on the advancing Squires, who was in the process of firing a hook. They went into a clinch. Because Tommy had landed, he sensed something, so he spun

Squires away to obtain some punching room, looked alertly at Bill, moved back slightly as Squires threw a right that fell short, and then countered with a pulverizing straight counter right that dropped Squires. Bill rose and continued coming forward.

Burns had a little forward-and-back bounce to his footwork, giving some room, flicking light jabs and using stiff arms, attempting to set up Bill for another right, which he launched and landed as Squires flurried. Bill went down, but rose yet again.

Burns advanced and, using a measuring left to set up the blow, snapped Bill's head with a right. He then followed with two more rights that were set up and landed in the same fashion, off the measuring left. Squires continued to flounder forward, and Tommy gracefully and fluidly moved backward to maintain his range, then grabbed the canvas with his feet, stepped forward and landed his fourth perfectly timed right in a row, dropping Squires for the third time.

Squires was counted out with Burns standing over him, his hands on his waist. He had impressively defended the title with a 1st round knockout. He had demonstrated keen boxing skill to set up the knockout. His balance, smooth movement, sense of distance and timing were expert.

The *San Francisco Examiner* said Squires "fought like another Palmer minus the latter's ability to take the gaff." Burns was "complimented on all sides on his clever fighting and it was generally admitted that he is well entitled to sign himself the champion of the world."

The *San Francisco Call* said Burns had scored a decisive victory over a man who had come to the country with a record of more than two-score clean-cut victories to his credit. "Squires showed glaring lack of judgment and of knowledge of up to date ring tactics."

The *San Francisco Chronicle* called Burns a shifty fighter with a punch. He had proven that he was a man to be reckoned with. "Tommy danced in and out, avoided the wild and therefore harmless rushes of his opponent, and was quick to take advantage of the opportunities as they came to him." Burns was a clever boxer who knew how to protect himself and at the same time deliver a hard punch.

The *San Francisco Bulletin* called Squires a novice and a "lemon" who was willing, but had no defense at all, and had an "egg shell jaw." He had power, but could not hit Burns. The gullible public had been fooled. The fight proved once again that a man may be a "crackajack in practice, but a veritable dub in actual combat."

The *San Francisco Evening Post* said, "Squires came here with a reputation as a possible second Bob Fitzsimmons, and so the public took the bait."

It was estimated that $72,000 in gambling wagers had changed hands. The 10 to 8 odds favoring Squires "were so palpably false that many people became suspicious and intimated that it was fixed for Squires to win." However, the fight was on the level.

Former lightweight champion Jimmy Britt gave his impressions. He said Burns' easy victory proved that American fighters were in a class by themselves. Jimmy knew all along that Burns would win (although the *Bulletin* had previously quoted him as picking Squires to win). Britt had sparred with Squires at Shannon's gym, and from those sparring bouts he had found that Bill was a good hitter and willing to mix it, but was sadly deficient in blocking and feinting. Burns far outclassed him, but it had to be said that at least Squires showed a willingness to fight (which was more than O'Brien had shown). The very large crowd proved what a wonderful hold the fight game had on the public.

Britt said Burns was as cool as a cucumber. He feinted and moved and landed his rights squarely on the chin as Squires came in.

> Burns, in the short spasm of fighting he indulged in, impressed me as being a cool, heady fighter with a terrific punch. He is as shifty on his feet as a lightweight and is quick with both hands. The best thing I noticed about him is his ability to hold himself in check and hit accurately when he has his man on queer street.

The *San Francisco Call* was much harsher in its assessment of the bout. It called the fight "the worst apology for a national boxing event" since Jeffries-Munroe in August 1904, and it noted that promoter Jim Coffroth was the perpetrator of both "expensive bits of humor."

It claimed that the *Call*'s previous expose on the fight forced a change to the program, and therefore instead of throwing the fight, the shackles were taken off Tommy's wrists and he fought on the level. The odds had been 10 to 7, with Squires the favorite, but then suddenly there was no Squires money, when only the night before there had been plenty of folks willing to bet big money on Bill. It felt this was evidence of the fact that word got out that "Faker Burns" would fight on the level, and therefore no one wanted to bet on "Unknown Squires" anymore. It took an additional dig at the champion. "Tommy Burns – he of the long record of fakes and proposed fakes – is a long way from being of the stuff of which topnotchers are made."

The *Call* claimed to be the only newspaper that stood up for the public and not the promoters. It had claimed that the fight would hurt the game, and its prediction came true. It was exposing the bald manner in which the public was swindled out of its money. All of the other San Francisco newspapers had boosted the fight for Jim Coffroth to swell the receipts and increase interest in the fight, but this was done with total disregard for the public, "even though the rotten character of the match was well known. Burns' foul-smelling record as a faker was glossed over or not mentioned, the fact that Squires never has whipped any one as good as a third-rater was excused, while Coffroth's enterprise was lauded to the skies." Ouch. It said the public was entitled to know from the expert sporting writers whether a match was a good one or not, as well as the character of the principals involved.[526]

---

526 *San Francisco Call, San Francisco Examiner, San Francisco Chronicle, San Francisco Evening Post, San Francisco Bulletin,* July 5, 1907.

According to the *Examiner*, Referee James J. Jeffries gave Tommy Burns full credit for his performance. Also, Jeff was not as harsh on Squires as many were. He said,

> The outcome of the fight certainly surprised me. I expected to see a longer battle, and hardly expected to see the go end in the first round. I must say that Burns is a much better fighter than he gets credit for being. He has done all that has been asked of him so far and is a greatly improved boxer.... It doesn't follow that Squires is not a good man because Burns beat him. There are lots of men who would be easy for Squires, but against a man who has studied the game as thoroughly as Tommy has in the last two years the Australian showed up very poorly.[527]

According to the *Call*, Jeffries said,

> Squires showed a lack of ring generalship by wading in without attempting to guard himself. He did not have a chance to get warmed up before he was on the mat for the count. The victory was not a lucky one, for Burns was waiting to put the haymaker over, and when he saw his chance he took advantage of it. Burns is a wise boxer and never overlooks an opportunity. He should be given all credit for winning. At that, Squires is not a stiff, like many now believe. As for me, I am still the retired champion. I will not meet Burns. So long as the belt remains in America I am satisfied. Had Squires won I would certainly have re-entered the ring just once more to defend my title.[528]

The *Bulletin* quoted Jeffries as saying that Burns proved that he had been greatly underrated.[529]

The *Chronicle* confirmed that Jeffries' retirement was qualified. Jeff said,

> If Squires had been the victor, it would have meant $100,000 to me. I would have gone into the ring and would have defended the title. As long as I am able to fight it will be kept in this country. Burns can have the title, unless he should be defeated by some foreigner. That's the only chance to get me back in the ring.[530]

Burns was a Canadian, but he was residing and fighting in the U.S., and was an American.

It was said that Squires' defeat meant that Jeffries would never again enter the ring. "Burns will be able to defend the title for some years and by that time Jeffries will have passed his athletic prime."

Squires' overconfident manager, trainer, and backer, Barney Reynolds, had bet and lost heavily on the fight, starting with a $5,000 side bet with

527 *San Francisco Examiner*, July 5, 1907.
528 *San Francisco Call*, July 5, 1907.
529 *San Francisco Bulletin*, July 5, 1907.
530 *San Francisco Chronicle*, July 5, 1907.

Burns. The press and even Tommy's opposition had continually underrated, and to some degree, denigrated the champion's fighting ability, but Tommy Burns was laughing all the way to the bank.

The receipts totaled $25,251.50, showing that boxing was still thriving in San Francisco. Burns received an $8,000 guarantee, in addition to the $5,000 side bet. He contributed $250 to the payment of the $1,000 that went to Jeffries for merely refereeing the bout. Squires earned $6,060.36 (40% of 60% of the receipts).

Trainer Reynolds blamed Squires for being obstinate in accepting advice. He pleaded with Squires to keep away from Burns for the first couple of minutes just to size him up. Although Squires initially promised to do so, "when I saw him look over Burns with a look of contempt plainly written on his face," Reynolds knew that he did not respect or fear Burns. "I am sure he was surprised that Burns was such a small man and also at his boyish roly poly appearance. I confess that I also thought he would not make a mouthful for Squires, but he did." Yet another example of folks underestimating Burns, this time much to their detriment.

Reynolds said Squires had been told that Burns could not hit hard, so he went at Tommy in an open manner, willing to allow Burns to hit him just so he could find an opportunity to land a bomb. Squires had once done the same thing in a fight in Australia and had won.

> Just to show his contempt he walked up to his opponent with his hands at his side. The fight lasted just 15 seconds, and there were three blows struck. This man landed a right and a left, blacking both of Squires' eyes. Squires then swung on him and the man went down. Squires never looked back at him, but as soon as he struck the blow he turned on his heels and started pulling off his gloves as he walked toward his corner. It was just this same spirit which seemed to possess him when he met Burns, as he certainly has more of a defense than he showed on Thursday, when he put up practically none at all.[531]

---

531 *San Francisco Call*, July 6, 1907.

When asked to make a statement, Squires said, "I'v 'ad a bloody good lickin' an' I'm goin' 'ome." Bill was greatly surprised, but had done his best. He had been treated fairly and squarely. Another paper quoted Squires as saying,

> The better man won, and I came a long way to get a good beating. I have no excuses to offer. ... I underestimated my opponent somewhat in believing that he did not possess a knockout blow, which he showed plainly he had. I went after him from the sound of the gong and figured on landing a punch that I have beaten so many others with. I made a mistake in not taking a rest of eight seconds when I went to the mat the first time. ... I could not regain my senses in time to put up a proper defense. ... I knew that I was being counted out. My brain was working, but my muscles failed to respond at the critical moment.[532]

Tommy Burns told the *Bulletin,*

> Immediately after the fight had started I realized that Squires was a poor ring general and decided to whip him as speedily as possible. I didn't want to take any chance of running into one of his punches, not caring to test his brand of knock-out jolts. ... I knew that he had no defense and, feinting him out with my left, whipped in three sharp right-hand jolts that met him squarely on the chin. As to my future plans, I have several theatrical offers and will go on the road for a while, but am ready and willing to box any man in the world, barring Jeffries. He is entirely too big for me.[533]

Burns had used motion pictures to prepare. "I saw the moving pictures of Squires in training which were placed on exhibition." Fight films made it possible for him to scout Squires without having seen him in action in person. Tommy told the *Call,*

> I felt confident all along that I could beat Squires. ... He never laid a glove on me... I did not take any chances of allowing him to score a decisive blow, which I knew he possessed. When I sent him to the floor for the first time with a right cross I knew that the victory was within my grasp. I saw the pictures of Squires in training the other night and I said, 'If I cannot beat this fellow I will never fight again.' ... Squires is a big, strong fellow, but I outgeneraled him. The decisive punch was what I might term a double blow. I started a hard left to the stomach, which reached its mark; then I finished him with a hard right to the temple.[534]

---

532 *San Francisco Call,* July 5, 1907.
533 *San Francisco Bulletin,* July 5, 1907.
534 *San Francisco Call,* July 5, 1907.

For the *San Francisco Chronicle*, Burns wrote his own article about the fight and his plans:

> I told them that if I didn't put him away in ten rounds that I would never put on the gloves again…. I didn't think it was all over when I gave him that first right-hand punch. After I gave him that one, I said to him, 'Remember, Bill, you are not in Australia now. This is no wrestling match.'… He doesn't know anything about boxing and had no guard…. Do you know the funny thing about it all? If this man had licked me, they would have all said he was another great, and only and now that I have handed him a sleep powder, they will say I have licked a dub…. I was prepared to go forty-five rounds if necessary…. I am a different fighter today than the time I fought Dave Barry. I was sick then and not able to do my best and I think that I have improved in the last few months…. I practiced a left today which I caught from Gans. I have been studying Gans' method of fighting, as I admire his style and think he is a good one to follow….. I think I will spend ten or fifteen weeks in theatrical engagements. But I am willing and ready to fight anybody and anywhere – if I can get the money. That's my business. Jeffries? No, nothing doing. You hear those other guys talking about fighting Jeffries, but not for me. I've got some sense. I wouldn't think of it.[535]

Burns told the *Examiner* that he had landed his right quite easily, but it was set up by his left. "I have seen Joe Gans fight a number of times and have spent considerable time learning a trick of his which I used today. Gans keeps his left hand out in front and keeps it busy, and waits for a chance to let go his right." Tom had drawn Bill's attention to his left, and "every time I sent in the right he was not expecting it and he got the full force of the punch."

Tom said the only punch that Squires had landed was a right to the ribs, which grazed his elbow as it landed and lost its force. "It didn't bother me at all." He also said,

> I will fight anyone if there is any money in it. When I say anyone I want to exclude Jeffries. Jim is too big for me, and I don't see where I would have a chance of beating him. I have several offers to go on the road with a theatrical show and I will probably spend the next fifteen weeks on the stage. After that I will take on any fighter who is anxious to box me, provided a suitable purse is offered by a responsible club.[536]

When Squires met up with Burns, Bill said, "Well, Tommy, old boy, you swung one on me and I got it. I got a good fair licking. You're the best man

535 *San Francisco Chronicle*, July 5, 1907.
536 *San Francisco Examiner*, July 5, 1907.

and you won. I feel all right and I am quite satisfied." Burns replied, "You'll get somebody else, Squires, as I got you and you can start again, but not with me." Bill said, "No, I am satisfied, and I'll go home now."

The Los Angeles papers declared that the fight was a fiasco and the public was sold again. Fight fans were disappointed because they had paid from $5 up to $20 for tickets, in addition to railroad fares to see the fight. Squires was overrated and his performance pitiable. "That the defensive skill of the Australian was exceedingly poor was speedily attested." Squires insisted that he had been led to believe that Burns was not a knockout puncher, so he was careless.

One L.A. paper blamed the *San Francisco Examiner* for providing fake boosting of Squires. "Squires is the protégé and proud discovery of W.W. Naughton, the well-known boxing 'expert' on the Hearst papers.... Misled by the Examiner's rotten fakes about Squires, thousands of dollars were lost on him."[537]

Some asked whether prizefighters earned too much money, more than they ought to. The analysis offered by the *Bulletin* is applicable to questions about athlete's salaries even today.

> The winner, according to sapient amateurs of pugilism, is not really a first-class fighter, and the loser is so inexpert that he has no class at all.
>
> Today a large number of persons who are not 'sports' are murmuring at the injustice of paying ignorant bruisers a fairly large fortune for a few minutes' work, while men of brains and education, who do work calling for a far higher grade of intellect than pugilism requires, earn only a pittance, at which a man like Tommy Burns would turn up his nose.
>
> These complainants are the same persons, or persons of the same sort, who declare on occasions no mechanic is worth $6 a day and no servant girl is worth more than $25 a month. They have a false notion of the basis of wages. They discuss wages as if there were some immutable standard not depending on times and circumstances. They have curious prepossessions about what wages for various classes of service 'ought' to be; as if wages were fixed by moral and not by economic laws.
>
> The amount of compensation to be paid for service is determined by supply and demand. As a rule, intellectual labor commands higher pay than manual labor, but not because it is intellectual labor, but only because, as a rule, the supply of intellectual labor is less in proportion to the demand than the supply of manual labor. ...
>
> Good prize-fighters are few and people are willing to pay large prices to see them fight. Consequently they earn very large sums. ... Obscure pugilists today are very poorly paid. But when a man mounts to the top, or nearly to the top, in his trade, whether the trade be law, or medicine, or acting...or prize-fighting...he gets his own price for his services and is entitled to all he gets.[538]

537 *Los Angeles Express*, July 5, 1907; *Los Angeles Times*, July 5, 1907.
538 *San Francisco Bulletin*, July 5, 1907.

Regardless of his impressive victory, Tommy Burns still struggled to obtain respect as a fighter and recognition as champion. The tough *Call* said,

> The status of Tommy Burns as the successor to Jim Jeffries has not been firmly fixed by his victory yesterday. It is conceded that no foreign boxer has a chance with him, but Jack Johnson is to be reckoned with in this country. Burns undoubtedly has been underestimated by many and the full measure of his ability is still a mystery, as it was not brought out by his fight yesterday. One thing was settled beyond doubt, and that was his ability to deliver a hard blow.

Another former lightweight champion, Battling Nelson, said that foreign boxers would thereafter be looked upon with suspicion. Like many others, he too was begrudging in giving Burns credit as champion. Although Burns was claiming the championship of the world, Nelson felt that he needed to meet other men, like Hugo Kelly and Mike Schreck, to clinch the title claim.

> If successful in defeating these two men he should take on the only real legitimate candidate for the championship honors, Jack Johnson. If Burns can defeat Johnson, the colored heavyweight champion, he will be proclaimed the undisputed heavyweight champion of the world beyond the question of a doubt, now that the only real heavyweight champion, James J. Jeffries, has retired.[539]

Potential next opponents mentioned for Burns also included Sam Berger and Al Kaufman. Everyone wanted to get a payday and a chance at the title.

Jack Johnson, who was training for a fight with Bob Fitzsimmons, also wanted to fight Burns, as did fellow black fighter Joe Jeanette. Johnson said,

> Didn't I tell you Squires was the biggest sucker that they ever sent over? Why, Jack Palmer could lick him. He never did anything, never had anything and never will amount to anything. ... I will fight Burns any way he wants – clean break, straight rules, cut the purse or winner take all. He is not a champion until he beats me, and I am recognized as the best big man in America today.[540]

When the question was raised to Tommy about fighting Johnson, he said that he was not sure whether he would be able to do so. He was perfectly willing to fight him to show the world that he was the "dusky" fellow's master, but his wife and family had something to say about it. They did not want him to engage in a mixed race title fight.[541]

---

539 *San Francisco Call*, July 5, 1907.
540 *San Francisco Call*, July 8, 1907.
541 *San Francisco Evening Post*, July 9, 1907.

293

Jack Johnson had scored an early March 1907 KO9 over Bill Lang. A couple weeks after Burns fought Squires, on July 17, 1907 in Philadelphia, the 29-year-old Johnson would knock out a 44-year-old Bob Fitzsimmons in the 2nd round.

The *Call* said that hereafter; in order to assure the public that it will receive its money's worth, every foreign fighter should be tested locally before being placed in a big match. It felt that the public had rewarded boxers well, but fighters had seldom shown their appreciation for the public's generosity, because they usually tried to pick easy opponents and found many reasons for dodging the tough ones.[542]

In the days subsequent to the championship bout, James Jeffries said that although Bill Squires could never beat Burns, he felt that Bill was better than many were saying. "Squires wanted to reach the top too soon and should have fought some of the second raters until he got accustomed to the fighting game in this country."[543] Jeff also said that just because Burns beat him quickly did not mean that Squires could not fight. In fact, Jeff said that many were underrating Tommy. Jeffries said,

> Burns can have the title of champion if he wants it and I think he will take care of it in a satisfactory manner. It will take a good man to whip him. He has unlimited confidence since he has whipped O'Brien and Squires and confidence counts more than many pounds of weight. Burns has ability to back his confidence. He can take a punch and can deliver a punch such as will win fights. Besides, he is clever and fast. He'll stay on top for a long time, barring accidents.[544]

Burns said he would be willing to fight Squires in a return match in Australia if he was offered a $10,000 guarantee. Reynolds felt that Australians would want to see the man who could defeat their idol so quickly. "The prestige he gained by his sensational victory would make him a big drawing card." Reynolds felt that the folks out there, upon seeing Burns, would be shocked that he was the man who had defeated their respected champion. They would say, "That's the man who beat Squires! What! That little fellow?"

Tommy was preparing to gather some easy money on the vaudeville stage to increase the size of his rapidly fattening bank roll. He was also considering a match with England's champion Gunner Moir.

Some called Burns the "one and only real active heavyweight champion," while others called him the "near champion."[545]

---

542 *San Francisco Call*, July 7, 1907.
543 *San Francisco Evening Post*, July 9, 1907.
544 *San Francisco Call*, July 9, 1907.
545 *Los Angeles Herald*, July 21, 1907.

CHAPTER 11

British and World Champion

After defeating Bill Squires on the 4th of July 1907, Tommy Burns traveled to Ontario, Canada to visit his relatives. He was given a parade in his hometown of Preston.

In early 1907, Marvin Hart had scored 2nd round knockouts over Harry Rogers and Peter Maher, but in late May, Mike Schreck stopped Hart in the 21st round. Schreck had earlier scored a KO19 John Willie and KO13 Tony Ross. Many wanted to see Schreck in a fight with Burns if Jack Johnson was not granted the opportunity. However, just when Schreck was hot, in late August 1907 in San Francisco, Al Kaufman knocked out Mike Schreck in the 7th round.

Despite the meaningful victory over Mike Schreck, Al Kaufman's stock only rose incrementally. The *San Francisco Call* said neither fighter showed any class whatsoever. It said the fight was a question of which one was the poorer fighter. Kaufman was big and strong, with wonderful hitting power, but he hit a man with limited defense. It said Al had much to learn in the art of boxing.[546]

In late September 1907, Tommy Burns returned to Los Angeles to exhibit the Squires fight films. He would make money with that venture, carrying the films around to various theaters and exhibiting them as part of a show in which he was the attraction. Burns was "attaining something akin to popularity and is gaining a large following."

On September 27, 1907 at the Naud Junction Pavilion in Los Angeles, in a world lightweight championship fight, Tommy Burns worked the corner of George Memsic (a.k.a. "cousin" Jimmy Burns) in his 20-round decision loss to Joe Gans. James J. Jeffries refereed and rendered the decision.

When both Burns and Jeffries attended the theatrical show "The Man of the Hour" on the same night, one newspaper commented, "so however you look at it, the heavyweight champion was in the house."[547]

There was some evidence that Burns might be willing to cross the color line if he was offered a sufficiently large financial inducement to do so. Tommy was trying to convince promoter Jim Coffroth to offer him $25,000 to fight Jack Johnson. Although this was quite a large amount of money, "under present conditions they would undoubtedly draw a big house and at

---

top prices, too." However, at that point, no promoter was willing to put up that much money for the fight.[548]

Following his victory over Mike Schreck, Al Kaufman went on to score an October KO3 over Dave Barry in Philadelphia. The power-punching Kaufman was a strong emerging contender at that point, although he had been knocked out by Jack O'Brien, so there wasn't a huge amount of pressure brought upon Burns to fight him, or a large public demand for the fight. Also, Kaufman's manager, Bill Delaney, was not yet pressing for a championship fight for Kaufman.

At that point, Tommy Burns did not take on top American contenders, white or black. Rather, Burns decided to take the show on the road to foreign countries. Some might say that he was meeting champions from those countries in order to establish himself as a true world champion, a policy which he had started with the Squires bout. After all, some believed that the way to gain full acceptance as *the* world champion was by defeating the champions of America, Australia, and Great Britain. Burns had won the American championship (if not the world championship) by defeating Hart and then O'Brien, and the Australian championship by defeating Squires. He could further solidify his world championship claim with a victory over the English champion, Gunner Moir, as well as the other British Isles champions.

Others might say that Burns was looking for what he thought would be easy paydays. Still others might say that all of the bad publicity surrounding Tommy's integrity and the recent Squires mismatch/blowout forced him to leave America and seek foreign fights in order to make the big purses.

Another perspective is that negotiations for foreign matches had been ongoing since earlier in the year, and would have taken place regardless. In mid-1907, it was said that boxing had found a revival in England. The money there had drawn an influx of American fighters, including black boxers like Sam McVey, welterweight Bob Scanlon, and Sam Langford.[549]

---

548 *Los Angeles Herald*, October 2, 6, 1907.
549 *Los Angeles Herald*, June 17, 1907.

Tommy Burns wanted in on the biggest paydays available, regardless of where they were. He was willing to fight the best fighters that the British Isles could produce, and on their home turf.

As of October 1907, Burns was scheduled to fight British champion James "Gunner" Moir at London, England's National Sporting Club. Moir was very well thought of in England, so there was money to be made in a championship fight held in England against the English champion.

Moir had been discussed as a possible Jack O'Brien opponent in late 1906, when O'Brien was looking to dodge a rematch with Burns.[550] The Brits had been negotiating with Burns since early 1907. A match between the two had been finalized.

On October 19, 1907, Tommy Burns was on an eastbound passenger train that derailed and wrecked at 5 a.m. at Earl, Colorado, just north of Trinidad. There were two deaths and several injuries. Burns' hip was sprained. His manager, Billy Neil, suffered an ankle sprain.[551]

Tommy stopped off in Kansas City to have his injuries examined. He intended to leave for England soon after arriving in New York.

Just five days after the train crash, on October 24, 1907, Burns set sail for England. The Moir fight was scheduled for December 2. Before he left New York, Tommy told the local press that he expected to clear about $9,000 on the fight, after purses and wagers were paid. When a reporter responded that he would only win that amount *if* he won, Tommy replied, "No if about it. I'll whip Moir sure."

Burns also said that he intended to fight Jack Johnson when he returned to the U.S.

> I haven't much regard for him. He is big, but he isn't as big as he looks. ... His body isn't strong, and I'm satisfied that he has a yellow streak. ... I'll give Johnson a fight, but I'll make terms. Gans demanded and got 80 per cent with Memsic, win, lose, or draw. I won't be that hard on Johnson, but I'll get mine.[552]

Some said Moir might prove troublesome for Burns. The Gunner was a rough and ready fighter with a bull neck, broad shoulders, deep chest, and muscular arms. However, he would not have any reach advantage, despite the fact that he was 5'10" and would have a three-inch height advantage over Burns. Tommy had long arms.[553]

Despite some hype surrounding Gunner Moir, the *Los Angeles Herald* said it was highly probable that Burns would knock him out inside of 10 rounds. His record failed to show anything that would indicate that he

---

550 *Police Gazette*, December 22, 1906.
551 *Los Angeles Herald*, October 19, 1907.
552 *New York Evening Word*, October 24, 1907.
553 *Los Angeles Herald*, October 26, 27, 1907.

could defeat Burns, despite the fact that London reports said Moir would outweigh Tommy by 30-35 pounds.[554]

In 1907, former Burns title challenger Jim Flynn had won a 20-round decision over Jack Sullivan and he had also fought him to a 20-round draw. That same year, Flynn scored a KO18 George Gardner, KO7 Dave Barry, and WDQ13 Tony Ross.

However, on November 2, 1907 in San Francisco, Jack Johnson knocked out Jim Flynn in the 11th round. Flynn's recent success after his loss to Burns made Johnson's victory over him all the more significant. Like Peter Jackson before him, Jack Johnson had distinguished himself so clearly that he was obviously deserving of a shot at the crown. Johnson said he was ready to fight Burns at any time. However, he would have to wait.

The champion might have been getting away from the West Coast fight scene at just the right time. It was said that the Los Angeles City Council had all but killed big fights in that city when it passed legislation limiting bouts to 10 rounds with no decision, and requiring the fighters to wear 6-ounce gloves. That, combined with the dissatisfaction from the O'Brien and Squires fights, meant that the foreign trip was well-timed.[555]

From England, Burns wrote that he had met James Moir, and the Gunner looked to be about 200 pounds. "He is very conceited. I hope to be able to take some of that out of him. I saw the moving pictures of how he knocked out Tiger Smith in one round. He ain't much of a boxer, but rushes all the time, and that's what I like, as there will be a collision before many rounds and the climax will be reached." Burns was a great analyst of fighters. He had watched footage of Squires sparring with Jimmy Britt before their bout as well, and had studied Bill's movements until he knew him like a book.

Tommy said that if he was successful against Moir, he had a match scheduled with Irish champion Jem Roche. Roche held a 1907 8-round decision over Charlie Wilson, and Wilson held a 1903 KO2 over Moir, four years ago.[556]

Burns was willing to bet $5,000 on himself against Moir. There would be plenty of folks willing to take the bet; owing to the fact that the British felt strongly that Moir would defeat him in their scheduled 20-round bout. Tom said, "I think I will stop Moir in about ten rounds."[557]

Burns wrote that there was a $5,500 purse and a $2,500 side bet. He was not at all concerned by the fact that Moir was a much bigger and taller man. Despite the fact that Burns was only 5'7", his arm span/reach was 7.5 inches longer than his height.[558]

---

554 *Los Angeles Herald*, November 4, 1907.
555 *Los Angeles Herald*, November 12, 1907.
556 *New York Evening Word*, November 14, 1907.
557 *Los Angeles Herald*, November 14, 1907.
558 *New York Evening Word*, November 19, 1907.

Former title contender Charlie Mitchell said that while he considered Moir to be a top-notcher, he felt that Burns would win.[559]

The Burns-Moir bout had some real significance. It would be the first heavyweight championship fight of the gloved era to be fought in England. The remarkably well-built Moir was the pride of England, and was said to be the best fighter there since the days of Jem Mace. The *New York World* wrote, "Burns, as champion of America and Australia, will have a clear right to the world's title if he beats Moir." Hence, the fight was a big deal.[560]

The *Los Angeles Herald* echoed the *World*'s sentiments. It said if Burns beat Moir, an American would again be the world champion. Burns had already won the American championship with his victories over Hart and O'Brien, and the Australian championship with his defeat of Squires. By adding the British championship; he would establish himself as the true world champion. Hence, the fight was more than just a payday, but a way for Burns to establish himself as the legitimate world champion.

It was noted that starting with Marvin Hart; heavyweight opponents had underestimated Burns, thinking that he was too small in stature to be a threat. Time and again he had proven them wrong. He was built along the lines of a "giant killer," like Sharkey and Walcott.[561]

While in England, Burns and the National Club had a dispute regarding who would referee the championship bout. Tom knew that Moir was the club's man, so he wanted to be absolutely certain that he would receive fair play. Tom insisted that he would not fight if a club member refereed the bout. However, the club always used its own referee. The tough negotiator Burns was obstinate. The club finally gave in, and Eugene Corri Holborn, a noted sportsman, was agreed upon.[562]

Back in the U.S., on November 28 in Colma, California, hot contender Al Kaufman won a 25-round decision over Jack "Twin" Sullivan, whom Al had defeated previously via KO1. Prior to Kaufman's victory over Sullivan, in late September, Sullivan had won a KO19 over Bill Squires in Bill's first fight since losing to Burns in July. The fact that Squires went 19 rounds with Sullivan showed that he was not so bad after all, and gave Burns' quick victory over him more credence.

Regardless, many said that Kaufman's decision victory over Sullivan was less than impressive. "The fight did not appeal to the spectators, who expected more action, and they took their revenge out on Referee Roche by jeering and booing him to their heart's content for his decision." They thought Sullivan had at least earned a draw. The *Call* agreed that Kaufman won on points by a small margin, but most were disappointed by his

559 *New York Evening Word*, November 23, 1907.
560 *New York Evening Word*, November 12, 1907.
561 *Los Angeles Herald*, November 25, 1907. "Burns was born in Canada, and therefore is an American."
562 *New York Evening Word*, November 27, 1907.

showing, given that he had nearly a 40-pound weight advantage. They did not consider Kaufman to be of "championship timber."[563]

In London, the Moir fight was attracting a great deal of interest. Seats were being offered for very high prices. High class ticket prices in America typically went from $5 up to $35. However, the London tickets were going for $15.75 up to $52.50. The majority of the spectators would be National Athletic Club members, limiting the number of seats available to the general public. Fortunately though, the fight would be filmed.

Owing to the confidence the Brits had in Moir, Burns was only a slight 5 to 4 betting favorite.[564]

GUNNER JAS. MOIR,

Since 1903, James "Gunner" Moir had won at least eleven fights in a row, if not more. His important victories included: 1904 W10 Big Ben Taylor and KO6 Bill Smith; 1905 KO2 Peter Felix; 1906 KO8 Jim Casey and WDQ9 Jack Palmer (British heavyweight title); and 1907 KO1 James "Tiger" Smith. Footage of the Tiger Smith bout shows that Moir was big, strong, and muscular, and very aggressive and active with combinations to the body and head, knocking down the much smaller-looking southpaw Smith multiple times en route to the 1st round knockout. Moir had a particularly powerful right. The British referee, dressed in formal dinner attire, did not enter the ring, but stood up on the ring apron outside the ring.

In May 1905, Moir was called a "big, husky fellow, with broad shoulders and a long reach. He has a stiff punch and can hit without getting set." Moir had knocked out in 2 rounds "Peter Felix, the negro, who is a giant in stature, and who has been the champion of Australia for a number of years."[565] The July 1905 *Police Gazette*

---

563 *San Francisco Call*, November 29, 1907. Regardless of the criticism, Al Kaufman was on an impressive win streak since the late 1905 LKOby17 loss to O'Brien, including 1906 KO15 Dave Barry, KO1 Jack "Twin" Sullivan, KO10 Sam Berger, and KO14 George Gardner; and 1907 KO7 Mike Schreck, KO3 Barry, and W25 Sullivan. Of course, Burns claimed to have dominated Kaufman in sparring, and Al had not been overly interested in meeting Burns back when Tommy had attempted to make the match.
564 *Los Angeles Herald, New York Evening World*, November 30, 1907.
565 *Police Gazette*, May 6, 1905.

said Moir was a member of the British Navy, who had made a great showing against the Australian champions.[566]

The day before the championship bout, in America it was said that Burns was the better boxer, but Moir was the larger man and a hard puncher. At that point, in England, the betting was at even money. Hence, the Brits thought highly enough of Moir that they were betting their hard-earned coin on their champion. This was no mismatch. In addition to the excitement over their champion, because it was the first world heavyweight championship there since the bareknuckle era, and because seating was limited, the high demand for attendance caused some seats to be sold for $100.[567]

James "Gunner" Moir

On December 2, 1907, at London, England's National Sporting Club, Covent-garden, Tommy Burns took on British champion Gunner Moir.

The rivals had been in training during the past month. Moir's headquarters were at Shepherd's Bush, while Burns trained at Wembley. Each day, Moir had walked 10 miles or run 5 miles. He would spar with three or four expert boxers, skip rope, work the punching ball, and climb rope, all of this taking about an hour and a half.

566 *Police Gazette*, July 2, 1905.
567 *San Francisco Examiner*, December 1, 1907.

The day of the fight, the *London Daily Telegraph* listed Moir as standing 5'9 ½" and planning to enter the ring at 13 stone, or 182 pounds. Some later reports said he was actually 193 pounds or more. Moir was a "splendidly-developed fellow, and is in perfect condition." He said, "I do not know whether I shall win, for I am not sufficiently acquainted with Burns or his methods. All I can say is that I am dead keen on upholding England's honour, and if I fail it will not be for the want of trying."

Although lighter than Moir, Burns was as "hard as nails" and a very fast boxer, "remarkably so for a heavy-weight." Therefore, he would no doubt "offer a very stubborn resistance, even if he does not win."[568]

The *London Daily Express* said,

> I know of no better representative of modern fighting than Moir. … His recent victories over Palmer and 'Tiger' Smith demonstrated that he has a terrible punch. … I think tonight he will surprise even some of his friends, as he is far quicker than most people think, and, so far as punishment goes, he will take as much as any man living. He is the old type of British 'bulldog,' game to death.

However, the *Daily Express* also recognized Burns as a good one too.

> Burns is a plucky man and a hurricane fighter. … It will be a great thing to win the world's heavyweight championship at about a stone over middleweight, and I see Burns states that if he does win he will fight Jem Roche, of Ireland, which is not very interesting news. No, Mr. Burns, if you do walk off with our championship, go back to your own country and add to your laurels by beating Sam Langford. … We shall have given you our best, and it will not add greatly to your reputation if you beat Roche as well. The colour line is overdone in America. … Although I would prefer to see white men win, let us be fair and say lots of men have saved themselves trouble by drawing the line at coloured men.[569]

The odds were 5 to 4, with Moir the slight underdog. The closeness of the odds demonstrates that the gamblers did not think Tommy Burns was taking on a soft touch, but rather a worthy fighter and the best man in the British Isles. Still, Burns predicted that Moir would not be able to stay against him for much longer than 6 or 7 rounds.

In America, it was said, "Both men are known as rushing fighters, with plenty of gameness and stamina. Moir has been in the ring several years and has won all of his fights with comparative ease." The prize money was $5,000 or $5,500, depending on the source. The loser would receive $1,000 of that amount.[570]

---

568 *London Daily Telegraph*, December 2, 1907.
569 *London Daily Express*, December 2, 1907.
570 *San Francisco Examiner, San Francisco Chronicle, New York World*, December 2, 1907.

One London source said they were fighting for an alleged substantial purse of 2,300 pounds. Another broke it down by saying the National had put up a 1,300-pound purse, but they were fighting for an additional stake of 500 pounds a side.

The London papers said, "An extraordinary amount of interest is being taken in the event." The *London Daily Telegraph* said there never had been such a high demand for seats, not even for the famous 1892 Peter Jackson-Frank Slavin fight. The *London Daily Express* agreed that not since that fight had there been anything like the excitement.

The afternoon of the fight, Burns sent a message to New York. "Am feeling fine. Hope to win. Will wear the American flag. Doing my best to defend it."

The Americans were backing Burns to win. They declared that English fighters, compared to Americans, were slow and cumbersome, and lacking in ring strategy. They felt that Burns would win because he was a great ring-master, very shifty, and resourceful in his tactics. The night of the fight, the odds were 6 to 5, with Burns the favorite.

The handsome theatre was packed to its utmost capacity. There were many men of high social standing in the audience, including noblemen. One report said 600 Englishman in evening dress filled the National Sporting Club auditorium.

The fighters entered the ring at 10:15 p.m. Moir was seconded by Harry Williams, Arthur Gutteridge, and Sid Grumley. Moir wore a heavy woolen dressing gown, which they removed. *The Telegraph* said, "Moir's record certainly justified his appearance last night for the heavyweight championship of the world." It said he had only suffered one prior defeat, to Charlie Wilson.

Burns wore a long loose overcoat. He had a stars and stripes flag around his waist. Tom was attended by Ben Jordan, Jim Styles, and Jim Lowes.

The fighters looked ghastly in the blue of the electric light. The ring was 18-square-feet, and surrounded by large arc lamps to enable the cinematograph recording of the bout.

Eugene Corri would referee and judge the contest.

After entering the ring, Burns immediately demanded that he be shown the purse money and stakes and insisted that they be deposited with the referee. He refused to commence the bout until this was done. This act was met with disfavor, and many hooted the American.

Burns later explained that he had heard about a British law called the Gaming Act, whereby a man did not have to pay on a bet if he did not want to do so. Burns had his own money at stake, and naturally did not want to risk it for nothing. Some of the National Sporting Club's officials suggested to him that if both of the side-bets were deposited with Mr. Blacklock and handed by him to the referee before the fight, to be given to the winner at the conclusion, there could be no possibility of trouble. Burns was quite keen about looking after his interests.[571]

Mr. Bettinson, the club's secretary, introduced the combatants.

At age 29, Moir was older than the 26-year-old Burns and stood 5'9 ½" to Burns' 5'7". The local sources said Moir scaled 13 stone (182 pounds) to the 12 stone 3 pounds of Burns (171 pounds). However, the Americans said Moir was actually closer to 200 pounds. Burns was probably larger as well. 6-ounce gloves were used. The bout was scheduled for 20 rounds for the world heavyweight championship.

The bout exists on film, so it can be compared with what the British and American press said about the fight. One caveat about film is that what exists today is not necessarily entirely complete or what was shown at the time, and you can never be sure about what editing has taken place over the years, or whether the film is being shown at the proper projection speed.

1 – The local *London Daily Telegraph* and *London Daily Express* reports said they started by sparring lightly. Burns worked around his man. He hit the Gunner fairly easily when he wished, but no damage was done. Three times the referee cautioned Moir for holding with his left hand, and was nearly disqualified. At the end of the round, Moir landed two nasty jabs and a swinging right.

In the U.S., it was said that Burns crouched low against the fairly erect Moir, who extended his arms widely, somewhat like a wrestler. Burns was able to land at will and cleverly avoid Moir's rushes. Two heavy blows to the neck and ear sent Moir staggering to the ropes. Moir held and hit in the clinches several times, causing the referee to warn him for hitting after a clinch had been declared. Overall, it was a tame round, but Burns was the better boxer, feeling his man out.

The film of the fight shows that the bout began with no referee in the ring. Referees were allowed to preside from outside the ring unless necessary. Overall, the larger Moir was cautious, moving away from the smaller but powerful Burns. With his legs bent, Tommy advanced with small but quick steps, with a springy quality to his footwork, bouncing forward and back as he continued to advance, incessantly feinting with his hands and entire body, always on the alert. Neither threw many punches, as it was a feel-out round.

Both men knew how to raise their guards to block or clinch to avoid blows. When close, the Gunner was more interested in holding and hitting, grabbing the neck with his left and throwing some rights. The tuxedoed Referee Corri stood up from outside the ring to warn Moir against this tactic.

Burns stalked Moir, looking to set up his sharp, snappy right. He quickly stepped in with a fast combination – jab to the head, right to the body, jab

---

571 Burns, *Scientific Boxing and Self Defence* at 171-172.

to the head, then right to the head, followed by another right to the head. Moir stepped back and Burns fired two quick jabs and followed with his right to the head. Moir grew more cautious and more inclined to hold and hit. Tommy returned to his corner with a smile on his face. Between rounds, his cornermen waved fans at him, while Moir's seconds waved towels.

2 – The English reported that there was more holding than fighting in this round. Burns scored, except when Moir held him. The American papers said the pace increased and they fought at close quarters, where Burns was superior and hit the body. He did receive a nasty uppercut though. Moir frequently clinched, and the referee, who sat outside the ring, warned the Gunner that he risked disqualification for hitting in the clinches and on the break. Little damage was done, but Burns had the better of matters.

The film shows that Burns started the round as the aggressor, but soon became the counter puncher, moving away on the alert. Tommy kept his arms or feet almost continually slightly moving in a semi-feinting action. The versatile champion could slide or lightly bounce around in a circle, or he could move forward on the attack, varying his tactics. Whenever Moir moved forward, Burns would move back or to the side, or he could clinch. He maintained his balance very well, regardless of what direction he was moving, and was always ready to stop and punch at any moment. He had a nifty side-step to the right, which he used on occasion throughout the bout, never allowing Moir to get a read on his position.

Moir's punches looked stronger and more vicious than they did in the 1st round, but Burns had the better punch form. They both often clinched in close, but Moir began holding behind Tommy's head with his left and punching with his right, sometimes behind the head. This caused the referee to stand up from his seat and caution him. Moir did not listen, for he continued his holding and hitting tactics. Burns put his head down just a bit on the inside, making it easier for Moir to hold his head and hit.

At one point, after Burns was hit during a flurry of Moir blows, he lost his balance momentarily and very briefly touched the canvas with his right glove. However, at that point the referee had stepped onto the ring apron and was admonishing Moir regarding his incessant flagrant holding and hitting tactics that he had used just prior to the flurry, so there was no count. Moir quickly turned and looked at the referee for the moment, and then approached him by the ropes.

Resuming action, Burns went back on the attack again with some jabs and rights. Moir held with his left and fired some right uppercuts and overhand rights. These tactics continued, while the referee stood up and hollered at him.

3 – At first, there was some hot infighting, and Moir scored good shots to the ribs. It then became a "patting match." Burns was too clever at long range. Moir threw a storm of blows, but they did not hurt or bother

Tommy. Near the end of the round, Burns suddenly sprang in with a hard jab and right that knocked the Gunner down. Tommy looked happy, as if he hardly had been touched at all. The champion's tactics suggested either that he had been holding back all along, feeling his man out, or allowing Moir to tire himself. The bell saved Moir.

The film shows that Burns was light on his feet, moving forward and back and choosing when to step in and fire or when to step away or off to the side. Each took turns being aggressive or moving away. When they clinched, while holding Tommy's head, Moir landed several rights, but the champion took them well. Both fired some shots on the inside, but Moir especially liked working in the clinches. Moir landed some good rights and right uppercuts and even a nice flurry, which kept Burns on the defensive more, looking to duck or clinch. The Gunner kept working at a good pace, throwing and landing several rights.

Eventually, Burns woke up, bounced forward and back in lively fashion, and then moved in, blasting away with a series of four sharp rights off lead left stiff arms that sent Moir to the canvas. Moir quickly rose and the bell rang before any more blows could be thrown.

4 – The English said Burns led with some hot ones, and Moir held again. The referee cautioned Burns for using his head. Moir did not hold with his left quite as much, but instead punched. Both landed some damaging blows. They seemed a bit tired. Moir had thrown many blows. Burns laid on him a lot.

In the U.S., it was said that Moir rushed like a bull with powerful blows, particularly his right, while Burns gave ground. Moir improved and landed his best blow of the fight, a right jolt to the chin. Burns took a break, which allowed the Gunner to have slightly the better of the round.

On the film, Burns began on the attack, bouncing forward and back as he moved in. He especially worked his right. Moir was still frisky, moving away and clinching, but also firing some very hard rights. Burns began walking in on Moir, allowing the Gunner to fire his right. Moir boxed and hit him from the outside, being more effective than Burns. However, Tom ducked down a bit and seemed unfazed by the blows.

The champion would continually alternate his style, sometimes sliding or walking in, and at other times bouncing and dancing around on the outside as Moir attacked. When Burns came forward, Moir landed some good rights and was fairly active, but Burns was not bothered, calmly moving in at will. Tom eluded some blows by moving around on the outside, or by clinching and smothering on the inside, combined with his ducking. Burns was not as active with his offense as was Moir.

5 – The London papers said Burns' lowered head made it difficult for Moir to hit him. The Englishman showed some fatigue, and Burns hit him hard in the face. Not much serious damage was done, though. Overall, Burns seemed content to punish Moir with his taps, taking the points lead.

The Americans reported that Moir drew first blood with a right to the nose. However, Burns came back hard and began forcing matters, and by the end of the round, Moir was in bad shape. A right on the jaw and a long left swing over the eye cut Moir. It was Burns' round.

From the film, it can be seen that Burns continued alternating between applying pressure by moving forward on the attack, or bouncing, sliding, and dancing around on the outside to make the Gunner's blows fall short. His footwork was very smooth. He was poised and seemed in command, carefully selecting his sharper punches from both the outside and inside. However, overall, it was more of a Moir round in terms of numbers of blows thrown and landed than the newspapers indicated. Moir demonstrated the more consistent offensive output, but the champion remained so calm and fluid that he appeared to be in control of matters. Toward the end of the round, Burns caught Moir with a very nice combination jab-right-jab-right that momentarily stunned the Gunner, who fought back and continued holding the neck and hitting.

6 – Burns led and hit Moir four times flush in the face, including a vicious left hook. The Gunner was not able to do much good, for Tommy avoided all of the punishment that Moir attempted to give him. Although Moir landed one very hard body blow on Burns, Tommy again replied flush on the mouth. Weak half-arm blows concluded the round.

The U.S. reports said Tommy's footwork baffled the Gunner, who became wild. Moir clinched to rest, and Burns allowed him to do so. Tommy had the advantage in the sparring. It was an even round, with neither doing much effective work.

The film shows that Burns glided in and out, circling and moving left and right, sticking several jabs on the taller fighter's damaged left eye. Even with old black and white film, it is obvious that Moir's left eye was cut and bleeding down his face. Tommy used forward-and-back baiting footwork and primarily remained on the outside, boxing away, picking apart Moir, who was slowing down. Burns could fire jabs even on the move, dancing or stepping to the left as he pumped his jab. Occasionally he fired off one of his famous hard rights. For the most part, Burns was able to pick off Moir's blows by raising his gloves or outstretching his arms, or he would clinch, or duck. Tom took a few rights, but did not seem to be bothered too much.

7 – Burns took it to him. This roused Moir, but the American led with his left and landed easily whenever he wished, although too lightly for any big effect. Moir was clearly out-generaled, and Burns' tactic of leaning his head forward appeared to bother Moir.

The Americans said Burns cut a gash in Moir's cheek. Moir started rushing, but towards the end, Burns set the pace and had Moir breaking ground. The British champion looked pained and tired, like a beaten man. The Gunner clinched often.

The film shows that Burns kept up his light bouncing footwork, keeping his hands in constant motion, remaining relaxed and ready. Burns stepped in more in this round and fired off a crisp shot on the way in, but did so by setting up his moment to attack with circling footwork. He primarily launched rights to the body and short lead left hooks to the head, along with his usual jabs. They continued their usual clinching, though Moir was not doing as much inside work as he had done earlier in the bout. Moir clearly could not get a read on Tommy's in-and-out work.

8 – The Brits said Burns was all over him. Moir was bleeding freely from the repeated blows to his face. Eugene Corri, a member of the London Stock Exchange, finally entered the ring to separate them when they hung together. Corri was active in getting them to break away. Burns hit Moir very hard several times, but the Gunner took the punishment well.

In the U.S., it was said that Moir came back gamely, but was badly punished. Burns changed tactics and met Moir's rushes with punches, splitting his lip. Tommy also drew blood from his nose. Burns landed many jabs and had the Gunner dazed. Several times a succession of blows had Moir on his way out. Moir reeled as he went to his corner and was a beaten man.

The film confirms that this is the round when the tuxedoed Referee Corri entered the ring. When Corri would break them, he would walk between them and continue to the other side and then turn around to face them again, rather than the usual break and step back that we see today.

It was obvious at this point that Burns was quite confident, choosing when to step in or when to bounce around on the outside. Tommy danced about as quickly and as lively as a cricket. He was pecking away. The referee would break them as soon as Moir held behind the head. Burns alternated between lying in on the inside and dancing around at a distance. He was landing relatively easily and boxing beautifully. Both of Moir's eyes were bloody. Burns landed a few solid rights, but Moir showed that he still had some fire left, fighting back hard and attacking, primarily working his right and right uppercut to the body and head.

9 – The English version said there was more clinching. Corri took off his coat and again entered the ring. Burns looked fresh. Moir's punches at close quarters seemed to have no sting. The referee had to break them repeatedly. Burns landed the best hits, and Moir remained puzzled by his tactics. He was the more fatigued of the two. Burns wound up with three savage jabs which sent Moir to his corner in a very groggy state.

The U.S. version said Burns continued meeting Moir with cutting, stabbing punches. Burns had him bleeding from the nose, mouth, and eyes. Moir backed and clinched and was groggy. Burns attacked unmercifully, setting a good pace, firing many blows, punishing the retreating Moir, who was saved by the bell and all but out.

On the film, the referee removed his tuxedo jacket to begin the round. Burns boxed similarly to the way he had in the previous round, choosing his moments to fire or move away, to fight on the inside or outside. He set up rights with jabs or measuring stiff arms, and threw some good right uppercuts on the inside. Whenever Moir would advance, Tommy was good at moving away, exhibiting his smooth gliding and quick bouncing footwork. It was more of a calm, gradual picking apart than what the print press indicated. Burns did not throw all that often, but when he did, he mostly landed, being very efficient. Moir kept trying to hold and hit on the inside. The Gunner's attacks from the outside were ineffectual owing to Tommy's ability to move or clinch.

10 – The Brits said Burns was all over him. He hit the Gunner with right and left whenever he liked. Twice Moir went down from heavy blows, and twice he tottered up again. Then came the finish, and Moir was counted out. The U.S. reports had several versions which were not entirely accurate.

The film shows that Burns continued boxing calmly and cautiously, taking his time and using jabs to set up rights, and sneaking in short shots on the inside. Burns' gliding and side-stepping footwork still seemed fresh.

There were three knockdowns. First, Burns dropped the fatigued Moir with a series of three rights; each off measuring jabs, over the top of Moir's outstretched arms. He threw a jab and right, double jab and right, then jab and right to deck him. After Moir slowly rose, Burns advanced as the Gunner survived for a while by moving about and trying to fight back. Burns eventually hit him with another right to the chin off a jab. At first, Moir seemed fine, continuing to move laterally for just a moment, but then in a delayed reaction, as if something suddenly triggered in his brain, he waived his right hand out as if to shoo Tommy away and simultaneously crumpled onto the canvas on his side. Moir rose again on shaky and unstable legs. Burns attacked ferociously, leading with his left and hitting him with a right to the body and following up with a couple rights to the head that sent Moir back. Tom then set him up, using a measuring jab to the chest and immediately following with a big right to the chin that literally spun Moir around, who then fell forward into the ropes and down to the canvas for the final time. The corner stepped in to stop it. Moir did not appear to be given a count, and possibly rose before ten seconds, but it did not matter. He clearly had enough and went to his corner.

As a result of his victory, all of the newsmen agreed that Tommy Burns had to be given recognition as the world heavyweight champion.[572]

The *London Daily Telegraph* said it was a poor contest for a heavyweight championship and not to be compared with the Jackson-Slavin fight.

---

572 *London Daily Telegraph, London Daily Express, Los Angeles Times, San Francisco Examiner*, and Associated Press reports, December 3, 1907.

The American was too clever in his defence especially; too tricky and too fast for the Britisher. He always looked a winner after the third round. He played the fox, letting Moir do most of the leading, his one idea being to land a knock-out punch. He was quick on his feet, and in the matter of ringcraft and generalship far in advance of Moir. The latter was splendidly game, resolute, and dogged, but his punch did not possess its old power, and he had but little speed. The American had an ugly habit of using his head...More than once [Moir's] seconds complained of their man being butted.[573]

The *London Daily Express* said Moir's friends were bewildered by his lack of punishing power. For several rounds he was a chopping-block for his shorter foe. "He preferred to spar, not to fight, and was beaten all the way because of his error in tactics." It felt that the fight might have been different had Moir fought from the start instead of sparring and boxing with his clever foe. Burns exhibited the greater cleverness throughout the contest. He was much quicker on his feet. He drew first blood, and eluded the Gunner's blows.

The crowd noise was so loud that the referee's voice was hard to hear. He struggled to get them to break. He had to warn Moir for holding with his left, and had to admonish Burns for using his head.[574]

According to the Associated Press reports reproduced on both coasts in the U.S., Burns had disposed of Moir in 10 rounds with relative ease. His victory was virtually assured early in the bout, and it was just a matter of time. Moir was cut up, while Burns left the ring with few marks. Burns was superior in science, generalship, endurance, agility, and punching power.

In New York, it was said that the result was a confirmation of the predictions. "Popular as the victory is, it would have been still more popular if Burns was not Canadian born and bred. His success is hailed, however, as another vindication of American methods of training, American strategy, and American tactics in the ring."

The *San Francisco Examiner* summarized that Tommy sized up Moir over the first 3 rounds, and then landed stingers that knocked him about. Moir's alleged wicked infighting consisted of nothing but clinching and trying to hit on the break, which drew cautions from the referee. "The fight proved what every American had known for years, that England has not even a second class heavyweight." It said the winner received $4,500 and the loser $1,000.

Jim Jeffries, who some still called "the real champion of the world," said Moir was a dub. Jeff was tending to his saloon business and would not consider a match with Burns. When told that the public would insist on his fighting, that it would be a big purse, and that some would accuse him of

---

573 *London Daily Telegraph*, December 3, 1907.
574 *London Daily Express*, December 3, 1907.

being afraid, Jeffries said, "I'm through with the game and they can all go to hell."[575]

In 1915, Referee Eugene Corri offered his thoughts on Tommy Burns. "Burns was every inch a man. Modesty was not his strong point. I doubt if there was an ounce of that quality in his composition, and I am sure he would not have regretted the omission had his attention been called to it." Tommy's self-esteem was "abnormally developed." "He got on my own nerves a bit, until I came to understand him and to discover that at heart he was all right." Tommy was not rude or unmannerly, but assertive, self-assured, and of a pronounced individuality. This came out especially when it came to choosing the referee and when he insisted before the fight that the money be given to the referee to hold. Tommy was a well-dressed man who "could not easily be turned from his purpose."

When Corri told Burns that he resembled Napoleon Bonaparte, Tommy smiled and said, "I have been told this on the other side. But I don't think he would have had a dog's chance with me in the ring. He might be very clever at getting other men to fight for him, but I like to do all my own fighting myself. That is where Napoleon and I differ."

Corri said Tommy's original name of Brusso was pronounced "Broozo, not unlike 'bruiser', and when all is said, Burns could 'bruise' with the best."

The night of the fight, Burns entered the ring with his dressing gown and cap on instead of being stripped and ready for the fight, as was customary in England. He kept Moir waiting for a while, dallying, tying his shoelaces, etc. Corri urged him to hurry up. Tom then demanded that the money be handed to Corri. When told that it was not the custom for the referee to hold the money, Burns replied, "That cuts no ice with me. I want the referee to hold the money." Mr. Bettinson then handed Corri the money, and he put it in his dinner jacket.

As for the fight, "Burns immediately proved himself to be the better boxer, while Moir took his punishment heroically." Burns was clever and had enough skill to avoid Gunner's terrific lunges. Tommy was in and out all the time, and his science made him look like a sure winner throughout. Although Corri had heard that Burns was in the habit of taunting his opponents, the referee did not recall hearing him do so with Moir. The Gunner landed one very hard right in the 2nd round, and also landed several others, but he never landed in quite the right place. "Moir was game to the last – and, although beaten, was far from being disgraced."

Afterwards, Burns told Corri, "By George, that fellow can take some punishment! And though he never hurt me very much, I believe he could have hurt me if I had let him." Tommy said to Moir, "Don't take it so badly

575 *San Francisco Chronicle, New York Daily Tribune, Los Angeles Times, San Francisco Examiner*, all December 3, 1907;

to heart, Moir; we've all got to be beaten some day. My turn will come next."[576]

After Burns defeated Moir, talk of a Burns-Jack Johnson bout continued, and the champion was not ruling out the possibility of such a match. Tommy said, "I hope now to arrange a match with Jack Johnson upon my return to America…. I am also willing to box Roache [sic], the Irish champion, if there is money enough in it…. What I want just now is to take a vacation trip through France, Germany and Italy with my friends."[577]

Burns had defended the title three times in 1907, against O'Brien, Squires, and Moir.

> Burns is under promise to come back to the United States and give battle to the negro heavyweight. Johnson, who doesn't bank altogether on what Tommy has said in the connection, says he will be waiting at the dock. … [T]he Johnson-Burns match now seems inevitable.[578]

Tommy Ryan said, "Tommy Burns, a good fighter, is a joke for a champion. Really I must consider this fellow Johnson as a sure enough black peril. I doubt if there is a heavy today that can stand him off. He is getting better all the time, too."[579]

In February 1908, Burns offered to fight Jack Johnson, but insisted on receiving 75% of the proceeds, win or lose. Johnson's manager, Sam Fitzpatrick, turned down that offer. Johnson had already made an offer to stop Burns within 20 rounds or forfeit his share of the proceeds if he failed to do so. However, Burns was well aware of the fact that he had all of the negotiating power. Clearly though, Burns was willing to fight Johnson for a very big payday, of which Johnson wanted his fair share.[580]

The Burns-Moir fight films were exhibited in the United States. A February 8, 1908 advertisement said the fight pictures would be shown in San Francisco for a week. Adult admission was 10 cents, while child admission was 5 cents.[581]

During 1908, Tommy Burns remained on his lucrative foreign tour. The English liked what they had seen of him, and wanted Burns to fight there again. Another title fight was scheduled to be held in London again, in February, against another British fighter named Jack Palmer. The purse was $7,500, with 75% going to the winner and 25% to the loser, with a side bet of $2,500.

Although the bout was scheduled for 20 rounds, Burns predicted that he would stop Palmer within 6 rounds. Very little money was wagered on

576 Corri, Eugene, *Thirty Years A Boxing Referee*, Edward Arnold (London, 1915), 130-139.
577 *San Francisco Examiner*, December 4, 1907.
578 *San Francisco Examiner*, December 3, 1907.
579 *Los Angeles Herald*, December 8, 1907.
580 *San Francisco Examiner*, February 10, 1908.
581 *San Francisco Examiner*, February 8, 1908.

Palmer. "After Burns gets through with Palmer he will give a number of public exhibitions and then prepare for his fight with Jem Roche, the Irish champion. The American has just received an offer of $10,000 to go to Paris and meet a French boxer during April."

Burns was a 6 to 4 betting favorite in clubs, and was even a 2 to 1 favorite to stop Palmer within 6 rounds. Tommy said that he intended to stop him quickly, for he had a number of exhibitions scheduled the following week. He was also set for a March 17 match in Dublin, Ireland with Irish champion Jem Roche.

The *New York Herald* wrote, "Palmer is considered a somewhat better fighter than 'Gunner' Moir…but has a reputation for hitting low, it being on an alleged foul blow that Moir was given the decision over him when they last met."[582]

The 27-year-old Palmer had been fighting since he was 17 years old. He had won the British middleweight title in 1902. He won the British heavyweight title in 1903 with a KO12 over Ben Taylor. He fought Jack "Twin" Sullivan in 1903 to a 15-round draw. That same year, he also had a WDQ2 Frank Craig. In 1904 against Mike Williams, Palmer was stopped in 8 rounds, but then won via 7th round disqualification in the rematch to win the South African Heavyweight Championship. In 1905, he KO'd Geoff Thorne in 5 rounds.

By 1905, Palmer was being called "the best big boxer in England."[583] In early 1905, there had been some talk of Jack O'Brien fighting him. At that point, Palmer was the champion of England. It was said that he was a harder hitter than O'Brien and had just returned from a trip to South Africa, where he had defeated a number of fighters.[584]

Palmer lost the British heavyweight crown with a 1906 LDQby9 to Moir. On March 26, 1907 in a rematch of their 15-round draw, Jack "Twin"

Jack Palmer

582 *New York Herald*, February 10, 1908.
583 *Police Gazette*, July 2, 1905.
584 *San Francisco Bulletin*, February 13, 1906; *Police Gazette*, March 31, 1906.

Sullivan stopped Palmer in the 9th round. At that time, Palmer was credited with heart and being able to take punishment, but not much more. Burns witnessed that fight. Palmer had not fought since then.[585]

On February 10, 1908 at Wonderland, a big music hall on the east side of London, Tommy Burns fought Newcastle's Jack Palmer. Burns entered the ring with a smile and looked confident. Palmer seemed very fit, and was also brimful of confidence. Still, even in England, at that point Burns was a 3 to 1 favorite, although some said the odds were 6 to 4 in Tommy's favor. 2,000 people witnessed the bout, which began at 10:30 p.m.

According to the *London Daily Express*, in the 1st round, Burns completely outgeneraled and outpaced Palmer. Tommy was constantly on the attack, and did as he pleased.

In the U.S., it was said that Palmer was outclassed from the start. "Burns shot in the blows so fast it was impossible to keep count of them. At the end of one minute Palmer was on his knees taking the count." Palmer demonstrated gameness though and lasted for a while. A minute later, he was down again from a hard right to the heart. He covered and backed away and lasted the round. He was bleeding from the nose, his eyes were puffed, and his lips were swollen.

Another report said Palmer crossed his arms over his face and doubled up his body so that the smiling Burns could not land often, but each time that he did, the contest almost ended. A punch to the ribs and left uppercut combination dropped Palmer twice in the 1st round.

Still a third report said Palmer was initially dropped by a right hook to the jaw. He rose and was put down again. Twenty seconds later, a left dropped him.

The next 3 rounds were a repetition of the 1st round. Palmer was unable to land a blow or to defend himself. He was dropped two or three times in each round.

According to the *London Daily Express*, in the 2nd round, the quick-footed champion again dominated. So heavy was the punishment and bewildering his skill that Palmer once fell to his knees.

A U.S. report said Palmer went down from a left over the heart, but managed to run around and survive. Another said Burns landed jabs from a crouch, and then dropped Palmer with a right.

The London report said in the 3rd round, it was obvious that Palmer recognized that he had met his master, and it was only by dropping to the floor on several occasions that he lasted out the round.

The American report said Palmer tried to hit Tommy, but received a smash to the jaw that decked him for a nine-count. A left to the heart dropped Palmer again and the gong sounded.

---

585 Boxrec.com; *Los Angeles Herald*, March 27, 1907.

The *Daily Express* said that when the 4th round began, it was obvious that Burns had made up his mind to finish him quickly. He forced the exchanges at a rapid pace. Palmer clinched, which drew a caution from the referee. The onlookers called upon Palmer to make a fight of it, but he was often on his knees, and eventually fell at length and was counted out.

The U.S. report said Palmer was dropped several times. A right to the body set up a left hook to the head that knocked him out for the count.

Another report said Burns decked him three times in the 4th round, once with a heart punch, the second time with a left hook to the jaw, and the third time with a swinging right. Palmer was hissed off the stage.

The *London Daily Express* said that by quickly and easily defeating Palmer, Tommy Burns was fighting his way into the good opinion of English boxing circles. Still, the bout was pitiful. Palmer would neither box nor fight. During the 4 rounds, Jack continually dropped to the floor, while Tommy laughed aloud. There was not the slightest doubt as to the difference in class between the two men, and Burns won like a champion from the start. Although the result did not cause much surprise, the locals were keenly disappointed in Palmer's performance.[586]

The *London Daily Mail* said the fight was so farcical that it was accompanied by loud hooting. It was scheduled for 20 rounds, but nowhere near that many were necessary. For most of the bout,

> Palmer, with his back curved like a railway arch, held his gloves tightly pressed to his cheeks, while Burns endeavoured to find an unprotected piece of face to hit at. Under a storm of vituperation Palmer occasionally dodged out of distance; once or twice he took the liberty of flapping a tentative glove in the American's face, after each of which "incursions" he hugged Burns like a long-lost brother and permitted himself to fall in a mass at his opponent's feet.

Burns was "good-humouredly complaisant" and "seemed to be rehearsing his accompaniment to the cinematograph." Humanely, instead of punching Palmer on the unprotected body, he pushed his man around the ring and occasionally threw and landed a blow. He did not administer much punishment at all. However, he did not have to do so. Tom occasionally landed on the back of the head or neck, or landed with moderate strength to the chest. Palmer went down again and again.

In the 4th round, Palmer went to the floor for the sixth time and failed to rise before the ten seconds were counted. He only started to rise after the count was concluded. The referee handed Burns a check and Tom smiled. Palmer sat in his chair, talking to his seconds. He showed no symptoms of

---

586 *London Daily Express*, February 11, 1908.

the punishment. "Burns won easily. Palmer lost more easily. It was the poorest fight ever witnessed."[587]

London's *Lloyd's Weekly News* called the fight a farcical fiasco, one of the most one-sided matches ever seen. It took place at Wonderland, East London, on Monday night, to the jeers of the crowded audience. From the start, Jack Palmer of Newcastle commenced strange tactics. He covered up as much of his face as possible with his hands and arms. Burns would move around looking for an opening, and coolly landed to his selected spot. Palmer went down several times and took 8-counts, with his eyes bright and watchful for the signal from his seconds to rise. He never seemed able to avoid the merest fraction of the force of the blows. He took all that was sent his way, and received many vicious digs on the back. It wasn't a fight at all, being totally one-sided. Palmer seemed too afraid to fight back.[588]

Jem Roche, Burns' next scheduled opponent, was at ringside, and said, "Palmer fought like an old woman. Burns is a master of the art of pugilism and in addition to this, was in splendid physical condition."

Burns has to be credited for his quick and dominant 4-round knockout performance against a man who had lasted 15 and 9 rounds against the highly respected Jack "Twin" Sullivan (who could give even large heavyweights like Al Kaufman some trouble).

An English report said the winner took 75% of the purse, which was 80% of the gross gate receipts, with the loser taking the 25% remaining balance. They also had a side bet of 500 pounds a side. The U.S. papers said Burns and Palmer fought for $2,500 a side and 75% of the gate receipts.

W.W. Naughton wrote, "The American public will forgive Tommy for taking on these easy marks if he will keep his promise and come home within a reasonable time to fight Jack Johnson."

A Burns acquaintance said Tommy wanted to meet several men of different nationalities so that there was no doubt as to his right to call himself world champion when he finally met and defeated Johnson.

Joe Gans said Johnson would easily defeat Burns, and was willing to bet $5,000.[589]

One month after the Palmer fight, on St. Patrick's Day, March 17, 1908 in Dublin, Ireland, Tommy Burns defended his heavyweight championship crown against Irish champion Jem Roche. The *Irish Times* said the Wexford blacksmith Roche had a 16-3-1 record, which included: 1900 KO4 Jack Fitzpatrick; 1905 L20 and KO18 Young John Sullivan; 1906 W20 Young John Sullivan; and 1907 KO8 Charlie Wilson (who held a knockout victory over Moir). Roche was well thought of in Ireland, and was "strongly fancied by his compatriots."

---

587 *London Daily Mail*, February 11, 1908.
588 *Lloyd's Weekly News*, February 16, 1908.
589 *San Francisco Examiner, San Francisco Chronicle, New York Herald, New York Times, New York Daily Tribune, Los Angeles Times, Los Angeles Herald,* all February 11, 1908.

The fight was held at the Theatre Royal on a Tuesday night. Roche arrived in Dublin from Wexford, and was in excellent fettle. Burns reached the city from London, and also looked very fit.[590]

The day before the fight, at Dublin's Dolphin Hotel, Burns told a reporter that his right eye was still inflamed from a recent accident. Still, he was very confident. He bet 900 pounds on himself in order to win 300 pounds. He ran 7 miles.

The day of the fight, the *London Daily Express* said Roche was 30 years old, stood 5'7 ½" and weighed 12 stone, 9 pounds, or 177 pounds. In photos, Roche looks much heavier than that, and is obviously far heavier than Burns. Burns was listed at 12 stone, or 168 pounds, although he too likely weighed more than his listed weight.

In England, Tommy was a 3 to 1 betting favorite. However, in the opinion of the local Irishmen, "Roche cannot lose. He was never better in his life, and has gone through his training in a thorough business-like manner." Once again, the locals thought highly of their champion, and were backing him to win. The confident Irish champion Roche said, "The odds laid on the American are absurd, and I wish I could afford to take the money to thousands." Roche appeared to be of hard muscle. He was fit and in good spirits.[591]

The *Irish Times* said, "Never has a boxing match excited such interest in this country." The Irish felt that their champion was good enough to win the heavyweight title. Roche was fitter and stronger than ever before. He had trained hard and conscientiously for eight weeks. He was burly and had great power and stamina.

However, Burns' abilities were respected. "Burns has a great record, and, the easy manner in which he disposed of the English champion, Moir, gives proof of his ability." It said Burns had laid 500 pounds on himself to win 200. They were fighting for an alleged 2,500 pounds.[592]

According to the local *Irish Times*, the attendance at the Theatre Royal was magnificent, and included many notables from the world of sport. "The receipts probably constituted a record for the United Kingdom." The match had been ratified as far back as January 6, for a purse of 1,500 sovereigns, of which 80 percent was to go to the winner, and 20 percent to the loser, with a side bet of 500 sovereigns. The fight was scheduled for 20 rounds.

Prior to the bout, the Master of Ceremonies, Mr. King-Morgan, introduced Bill Squires to the audience, and Bill announced that he wanted to fight the winner.

Roche came on first, with the orchestra playing the "Boys of Wexford." Burns came out to the tune of "Yankee Doodle." They both met with a great reception. Burns had as his seconds Pat O'Keefe, Ben Jordan, Billy

---

590 *Irish Times*, March 16, 1908; *London Daily Express*, February 11, 1908.
591 *London Daily Express*, March 17, 1908.
592 *Irish Times*, March 17, 1908.

Neil, and H. May. At 10:15 p.m., the referee, Mr. R.P. Watson, ordered the seconds out of the ring, and the men faced each other. The excitement was intense.

Jem Roche and Tommy Burns

They sparred cautiously to start. Burns kept on the move for a while. Roche kept his left arm well extended and the right guarding his chin. The American landed lightly with jabs to the face and forehead, and Roche twice led for the body in attempting to return, but was short. More cautious sparring followed. Burns moved all the time. Roche landed a tap to the body, but Burns then dashed in and following a left to the wind he brought across his right half-arm jolt to the point of the jaw and down went the Irishman. He was counted out. Roche was on his feet again a couple of seconds after the ten-count had concluded.

The bout had ended with such startling suddenness that the audience was in shock that the fight was over. "The hope of Ireland had gone down before the superior prowess of the invincible visitor from the States." The fight had lasted just 1 minute and 28 seconds, or 88 seconds.

The *Irish Times* said Burns was very fast and very clever, with plenty of dash and resource, "and beyond all doubt he is a worthy holder of the Championship." He had arrived in England the past October, and had been victorious in three contests inside of four months, defeating Moir in December, Palmer in February, and Roche in March, all by knockout.[593]

In the U.S., it was said that despite the big local build-up, it was not much of a fight, for it only required about half a round and one punch for Burns to knock him out. Roche was sluggish. They sparred for a while in the 18-foot ring, with Roche on the defensive and Burns trying to find an opening by using feints and light jabs. Tommy was trying to draw his opponent out. Roche landed two blows to the ribs. Tommy maneuvered cleverly, feinted with his left and landed a short, sharp right to the jaw that dropped Roche like a log. He was unable to beat the count. After he had been counted out, Roche offered to renew the fight, and Burns agreed, but was overruled. The official time was 1 minute and 28 seconds.

Burns said it was the easiest fight he ever had. "I gave Roche the same blow on the jaw that knocked out Squires. It was the first and only punch I landed. I fitted about a bit and jabbed him lightly with the left and sent a right to the jaw and Roche was out."

The surprised crowd hissed Roche. Some cried "Fake." Naturally, they were upset by the rapidity of the ending, having paid good money to witness the bout. The crowd had paid admission prices ranging from $4 up to $100. Roche later said, "He did it too quick, that's all."

---

593 *Irish Times*, March 18, 1908.

One source said about 3,000 people witnessed the fight, while another said every seat of the 4,000-seat theater was taken. Yet another report said 5,000 folks saw the bout.

The U.S. reports said the fight was for a purse of $7,500 (of which the winner took 80%) and a side bet of $2,500. Burns also bet $7,000 on himself at 1 to 3 odds. The ringside betting was 2 to 7 on Burns. Tommy said he had too much money riding on the outcome to take any chances, so he went in to make the fight as short as possible. "I will fight any one if there is enough money in sight."[594]

The *London Daily Express* said the theatre was packed with folks from all over the United Kingdom. Burns' confidence was backed by his willingness to bet almost any amount of money on himself at any reasonable odds. He did not find it difficult to locate folks willing to accept his wagers, because the Irishmen were not to be denied in their high opinion of their own champion, and so money came from all quarters. However, it was not a fight at all.

Burns was scheduled to be in Paris on Saturday to officiate a boxing match between Walter Stanton and Jack Costello.[595]

The wealthy Tommy Burns in dapper poses.

594 *New York Times, New York Herald, New York Daily Tribune, Los Angeles Times, San Francisco Examiner, San Francisco Chronicle*, all March 18, 1908.
595 *London Daily Express*, March 18, 1908.

CHAPTER 12

Earning the French Franc

In early April 1908, Tommy Burns' manager, Billy Neil, said Burns would remain in Europe for several more months, for the money there was too good to turn down. He claimed that Tommy had already made $53,125.

> I don't think even Jim Jeffries made money as fast as Burns is making it now. You have no idea what a lot of money there is in the fighting game in England and France this year. They are all worked up over the game. Tommy has set a minimum of 300 pounds a week for his theatrical engagements. That's about $1,500, and he can get all he wants of it.[596]

Neil was also trying to arrange a match with Jack Johnson. Burns wanted the fight, and was willing to allow his $2,500 deposit money to remain in the stakeholders' hands from nine to twelve months in order to give promoters an opportunity to arrange the contest. Burns demanded $30,000 as his share of the prize money regardless of the result, and was willing to box Johnson before any club that would pay him that amount. He preferred a fight to the finish or one of 45 rounds. Burns was out for easy money, and if he was going to take a risky fight, he wanted to make a bundle.[597]

Initially, Johnson's manager Sam Fitzpatrick had resisted accepting terms so strongly in Burns' favor, feeling that Johnson was entitled to a greater share of the proceeds, but Johnson insisted on the match, realizing the future value of winning the title.[598]

Just before Burns' next bout, in mid-April it was reported that articles for a fight between Burns and Johnson were to be signed. The agreement was for Burns to receive $30,000, win or lose, and for Johnson to be guaranteed at least $5,000. The only challenge was to find a promoter willing to pay that amount.[599]

Some criticized Burns' large monetary demand as a way of pricing himself out of the market so as to avoid the fight, but Burns believed the fight was worth that amount, as other very big fights had been, and that some promoter would eventually put up the money. Before the end of the year, he would be proven correct.

596 *New York Evening World*, April 11, 1908.
597 *Los Angeles Herald*, April 11, 1908.
598 *San Francisco Examiner*, December 24, 1908.
599 *San Francisco Chronicle*, April 14, 1908, April 15, 1908.

About that time, via a London publisher, Burns wrote and published *Scientific Boxing and Self-Defence.* In it, he discussed his thoughts on boxing tactics, training, and technique, as well as his career. He noted that he only had three losses in his career, all of which were via the decision route as a middleweight. No one had ever put him down for the count. His losses to Schreck and O'Brien were essentially avenged, and he explained away his loss to Sullivan as the result of being weight drained, something which he proved in his very next bout by going up in weight and clearly defeating champion Marvin Hart.

Burns felt that he had established his firm right to the world championship by defeating the Australian and English champions, "as well as those of my own country (for, although born a Canadian, I am an American citizen, and have never sought to disguise the fact)." Tommy also responded to the criticism that his championship career had received.

> I have been styled a third-rate champion, and may, possibly, be such; but, if that be a fact, then all the other boxers knocking about just now must be only fourth-raters, and I wouldn't like to class them as such, despite all that the critics have to say. It's curious, but the *de-*merits of my rivals are only discovered after I have done with them.

Burns complimented his hosts. "You Britishers are men, white men, and as good sportsmen as there are in the world. All I hope is that you will allow that I, too, have tried throughout to be as white as you are."[600]

The *New York World* quoted Burns from his book as saying,

> I am not twenty-seven years old, yet I have fought over fifty battles since the year 1900. ...

> Get rid of the idea that boxing is brutal. It isn't. It's a business in which brains count more than anything else.

> The first essential of a scientific boxer must be quick and clever footwork. I have always considered my success to be primarily due to the fact that lacrosse and hockey taught me to be spry and smart on my feet before I ever thought of donning a pair of boxing gloves. ...

> My road work rarely exceeds five miles and consists of a brisk mile walk as fast as I can go, then sprint for 100 yards or so at racing speed, then a fast walk again, and so on.

> A lot of boxers who are matched to fight at catch weights, and even other boxers, who have no difficulty in getting down to scale, devote far too much attention, in my opinion, to getting off what they imagine to be superfluous flesh. This, I feel sure, is a mistake, for if a

---

600 Burns, Tommy, *Scientific Boxing and Self-Defence*, Health & Strength (London, 1908), 166-172.

man trains himself down too fine he is bound to feel tired and get slow. If you feel tired knock off for a day. …

Why is it that so many promising boxing careers are cut short? … Boxers are more prone, perhaps, than other people to the disease known as 'swelled head.'[601]

The *London Daily Express* described the good-looking Burns as a clever fighter, a fairly clever writer, a great advertiser, and an astute financier. "Burns never runs down his opponents, knowing well the difference of a good and bad gate." Bill Squires was again on his track. Trying to build up interest in a return match, Tommy was telling folks that Bill nearly had him out at one point during their one-round bout.

This paper said that fights with black fighters Jack Johnson, Sam Langford, or Sam McVey would be of far more interest than a rematch with Bill Squires. "Surely there is nothing unsportsmanlike in saying, 'You've beaten our best. You are too good for us. Don't stop and fight inferior men, but take on men more worthy of your powers." Although Tommy had a very good record, the *Express* opined that his opponents had not been in the same class as the giants of old. However, the clever Burns knew that he was a drawing card in Europe, and was making easy money without having to extend himself.

Still, the *Express* also opined that it could not be said that Burns was a coward. He was willing to fight the best men if good money was offered. He was even willing to fight Jim Jeffries. A 7,000-pound offer had failed to draw Jeffries out. Jack Johnson was spoken of as a dangerous opponent, so Burns wanted sufficient financial remuneration to fight him. "One cannot question Burns' pluck or common sense. As a fighter he is well worth seeing, and as a writer his book is worth reading."[602]

Burns had made a great deal of money in Great Britain, and wanted to earn the big money that was being offered in France as well.

One month after the Roche bout, on April 18, 1908 at the Neuilly Bowling Palace in Paris, France, Tommy Burns boxed another British/English/South African boxer (sources vary) named Jewey Smith, in a scheduled 10-round fight. A big crowd paid high prices for seats. Fully one-third of the spectators were women. Hundreds of women came with escorts, and many came alone. The women took it for granted that they would be given admittance, which was not usually the case in the U.S. The fight was for 60,000 francs and the world championship.

According to American dispatches, Burns was the well-trained and clever pugilist, while the red-headed giant Smith depended entirely upon his brute strength. In the 1st round, Burns felt him out for a while and made an exhibition of him. Smith had minimal science and was puzzled by Burns'

601 *New York Evening World*, April 19, 1908.
602 *London Daily Express*, April 15, 1908.

tactics. When Tommy twice floored Smith with straight punches to the jaw, the crowd loudly cheered, especially the women.

Jewey Smith

Smith proved to be rugged and game, and remained aggressive in the 2nd round. Tommy mixed it up and landed at will. Jewey's guard was of no use in stopping the quick jabs and myriad of punches.

Although Smith landed several heavy body shots in the first two rounds, he was a beaten man from the start, for Burns showed much more skill. Tommy toyed with and outclassed Smith, as a general rule hitting him lightly for the first couple rounds.

In the 3rd round, Smith attempted to use his great strength and mix it. This forced Tommy to discard his exhibition tactics and get down to real fighting. Smith became winded. He clinched to avoid punishment, but Burns threw him to one side and then dropped him with a right to the jaw, although another source said it was a left.

While the referee was counting, a flashlight for the moving picture machine set fire to the paper flowers girding the balcony of the crowded Neuilly Bowling Palace. Another source said that at the end of the round, a photographic apparatus exploded, setting fire to the flags and decorations. A cry of "Fire!" was raised. A panicked stampede of spectators rushed for the doors, and some were knocked down in the flight. The fans were encouraged to remain in their places, which most did, and the fire was quickly extinguished.

While all this was taking place, Referee Luis Phelan calmly continued his count over Smith, who rose at eight. He was showing the effects of the punishment. The spectators who had run away quickly rushed back into the building. Some American women shouted, "Don't spare him, Tommy!" Some French women cried, "No mercy! Knock him out!" They were into it, although the English women sympathized with Smith. Despite the calls for a finish, the gong saved Smith.

In the 4th round, Burns again toyed with Smith, hitting him when and where he pleased. Tommy was smiling. The referee asked, "Why don't you finish him?" One source said Burns shook his head and refused to send in the knockout blow. However, another source said Burns dropped Smith twice and administered severe punishment. Smith was tough, and took it.

In the 5th round, despite having absorbed a great deal of punishment, Smith rallied gamely. However, he could not succeed in reaching the agile Burns, who finally ended the fight with a terrific right to the jaw that put Jewey down and out for the count. Tommy was awarded the bout amongst the cheers of the crowd.[603]

Burns agreed to meet black boxer Sam McVey, who was then living in Paris, if the money was right. The Parisians liked McVey, and wanted to see him fight Burns.[604]

Fighter Willie Lewis offered his thoughts on Burns, Johnson, and McVey, as well as the Jewey Smith fight.

> I went to see Tommy Burns fight Jewey Smith the other night. I was in Burns's corner, seconding him. Smith was a big fellow (over 200), and he looked tough. Before the fight started Burns said to me, 'If this fellow is a stiff I'll knock him out in a round, but if he is a game chap and can fight at all I'll let him go a while and give the crowd a run for their money.' And that's what he did. He played with Smith and he would occasionally drop over a left hook or a right cross, and down would go 200 pounds of English beef. Believe me, Burns is a terrific puncher. He dropped this fellow Smith with little hooks that didn't travel six inches. He's a corking good puncher, and the fastest big man I ever looked on. If you want my opinion, he'll whip Johnson to death certainly. Anyone who picks Burns for a sucker is a sucker himself for doing it.

> Burns came here a few days before the fight and we worked together – I for my fight with Harry Collins on Friday and he for Smith on Saturday. This gave me a chance to get a line on him, and, believe me, he was a big surprise. He is a large edition of Terry McGovern when Terry was 'Terrible Terry.' He carries a sleep pill in either mitt, and fights with a crouch that makes it hard for an opponent to get to his jaw.

> He is very short and put together compactly, but he's got an awful reach. That's the secret of his fighting. His reach is 74 ½ inches, about the same as Bob Fitzsimmons. He is a fast puncher, quick to

603 *New York American, New York Herald, New York Daily Tribune, San Francisco Chronicle, San Francisco Call*, all April 19, 1908.
604 *New York Herald, New York Daily Tribune, San Francisco Chronicle*, all April 19, 1908.

take advantage of an opening, and he is the jollying kid in the ring, for while fighting Smith he kept encouraging the latter to fight by saying, 'That's right, Jewey, keep coming,' and 'Oh, you forgot to block that one,' and 'That's right, put more steam in it.' This got Smith's goat, and he had barrels of confidence when he entered the ring.

You may be surprised to know that Sam McVey, the big Los Angeles negro, is the Parisians' fighting idol, and as soon as Burns got to Paris he was pestered to death with challenges from McVey and his followers. They offered a purse of $20,000 for the match, and Burns said to me:

'I had made up my mind that I would fight only one negro – that's Johnson – but I hate like the deuce to let this money get away from me.' At the fight Saturday McVey and his backers again challenged Burns, and Tommy replied:

'Give me a purse of $25,000, split $20,000 to the winner and $5,000 to the loser, and a side bet of $5,000, and I'll fight McVey here.' If they fight the scrap will draw an awful mob. Everybody in this town is crazy over McVey. They never saw anything else as big and ugly. ... You ought to see that coon. He's got clothes that would make a Sixth avenue darkey dude look like a rag picker. Last time I saw him he wore a cream-colored suit that looked like silk – sort of a pajama rig. He goes to fights in a carriage with a dress suit on and a bouquet in his hand, and they say society has taken him up, and he is taken around to dinners in the swell houses, and let sit at the table without putting a muzzle or a chain on him.

The frogs will go crazy when Johnson comes home. And they will think we're a dingy nation for fair when those two big smokes go down the boulevard at the same time.[605]

In late April, Jack Johnson arrived in England along with manager Sam Fitzpatrick, hoping to arrange a meeting with Burns.[606]

In early May, it was said that Burns was hoping to meet McVey for $25,000 and a side bet. However, the McVey bout never took place, for negotiations fell through. Burns was not going to take the fight for less than what he demanded. On May 23 in France, McVey scored a KO3 over Jewey Smith.

Also in late May, from London, Burns sent a cablegram to Jack Curley accepting an offer to fight Jack Johnson on Labor Day in Nevada for a guarantee of $30,000, win or lose.[607]

The *Los Angeles Herald* wrote,

605 *Los Angeles Herald*, May 6, 1908.
606 *Los Angeles Herald*, April 28, 1908.
607 *Los Angeles Herald*, May 20, 1908.

Tommy Burns may be stalling in his long drawn out negotiations with Jack Johnson, and again he may be in earnest. Far be it from the humble layman to decide the matter at this distance from the present scene of action. One thing is sure, however, and that is that the rotund Thomas is as clever as they go in the fight game. Probably no other fighter at present in the ring would be tolerated if he procrastinated about the match as has Burns. He is the legitimate champion, however, and he is making good use of his title to bring in the shekels.[608]

When for four days there was no reply to his cablegram accepting the Johnson fight, Burns told the press that in view of Curley's silence, he decided to accept an offer out of Australia to fight Bill Lang in Sydney during the visit of the American fleet. He said that he would earn $20,000 in Australia, regardless of result.[609]

The Australian syndicate deposited $10,000 to bind the match between Burns and Lang. The syndicate also had the option of arranging two additional fights at $7,500 each. It was too much money to resist.[610]

Most knowledgeable sportsmen wanted to see Burns versus Johnson. The *Los Angeles Herald* wrote, "Tommy Burns, of course, stands out as the leading light in the heavyweight class, though the dark cloud created by the appearance on his trail of Jack Johnson has somewhat dimmed his star. The title seems to lie between these two, however, and should be so confined for some time."[611]

World lightweight champion Joe Gans said Burns was harming the boxing game by holding out for $30,000, win, lose, or draw for the Johnson fight. He said,

> There never before was a champion fighter…that insisted on such impossible terms as this man Burns. … Mind you, I am not criticizing Burns because Johnson is a man of my own color. That makes no difference to my way of thinking, as I firmly believe and always have that Burns will give Johnson the fight of his life and probably beat him. I am figuring that Burns' stand is hurting the boxing game just at a time when it needs the most friends.[612]

Of course, Burns' defenders might call Gans a hypocrite, given that he had demanded 80% regardless of outcome against George Memsic, and Gans had been implicated in fixed fights. Furthermore, Gans had previously gone on record as opining that Johnson would defeat Burns. Certainly

608 *Los Angeles Herald*, May 23, 1908.
609 *Los Angeles Herald*, May 24, 1908.
610 *Los Angeles Herald*, May 29, 1908.
611 *Los Angeles Herald*, June 7, 1908.
612 *New York American*, June 14, 1908.

though, Burns had both his supporters and his detractors regarding his insistence on such financial terms for a Johnson bout.

TOMMY BURNS FEELS SAFE IN HIS NEW CYCLONE CELLAR

In the meantime, in his second fight in Paris, back again at the Neuilly Bowling Palace, just under a month after the Jewey Smith bout, on June 13, 1908, Tommy Burns took on Bill Squires in a rematch. Since being stopped by Burns in the 1st round in 1907, Squires had later that year been stopped in the 19th round by Jack "Twin" Sullivan, and was also knocked out in the 6th round by former Burns title challenger "Fireman" Jim Flynn. In late April 1908 in Dublin, Ireland, Squires knocked out Jem Roche in the 4th round. Roche had already suffered the LKOby1 to Burns.

Obviously, Squires had not really earned a title shot. One report even said, "The fight was alleged to be for the heavyweight championship." However, given the high frequency of his defenses, much superior to most of his predecessors, Burns deserved some leeway. To his way of thinking, he was still earning very good money, without a huge risk of losing the title.

Jack Johnson was present at ringside. Before the fight, he challenged the winner.

This time, Squires did much better and lasted much longer. Some said the first 4 rounds were relatively tame, for Burns did not extend himself at all. Another report said Squires easily won the first 3 rounds, landing left jabs almost at will. Tommy was not concerned with the jab, but was watching out for Bill's famous right, which the champion made sure did not land. Bill's aggressive tactics kept the pace fast and won him points, though such a pace eventually caused him to tire.

Most of the 4th round was very tame. Both men took matters easy. However, the slower pace might have lulled Burns into a false sense of security. Near the end of the round, Squires hooked in a terrific right to the jaw that sent Burns reeling across the ring, all but out. Another source said Squires scored a flash knockdown with a hard jolt to the nose. Before he could land another blow, the gong rang and saved Burns.

When the 5th round started, Burns bounded out of his corner with a leap and jabbed Squires three times, perhaps to show Bill that he was all right. However, thereafter, Burns was content to let Squires do most of the work throughout the round. It was another Squires round. It appeared that Burns was not concerned with points, but was fighting to let Bill tire himself out from his own exertions. Burns continued fighting cautiously and defensively.

In the 6th round, Squires began showing some signs of fatigue. Conversely, it soon became evident that the champion was as sound as ever. Overall, the pace had slowed, but Burns had awakened and put forth more steam into his blows. He also began increasing the rapidity and frequency of his attacks. Still, Squires held his own, hitting hard and fast, constantly landing his jab, which deterred Tommy's attack.

In the 7th round, perhaps realizing that Burns was in better shape, Squires tried to end the fight with a single hard wallop. He swung his right for the head several times, but each time Burns would either duck, sidestep, or block the blow. Squires forgot all about his left, which he had worked with such good effect during the early rounds. The only time Bill was able to touch Tommy at all was in the clinches.

The round was all Tommy's, for he did most of the punishing. He started rushing Squires all over the ring. Just at the gong, Burns whipped in a terrific right to the body, and Bill appeared very weak as he wobbled to his corner.

The 8th round did not last very long. Burns jumped out of his corner, feinted a left, and then shot a tremendous short right to the ribs or solar plexus which dropped Squires to the mat for the ten-count. It was fully five minutes before he recovered. Many smartly dressed women were amongst the first to shake Burns' hand and congratulate him.[613]

---

613 *New York American, San Francisco Chronicle*, June 15, 1908; *Washington Herald, New York Sun*, June 14, 1908. Most American newspapers reported very few details regarding the bout. Not too many in America cared.

Within days of their rematch, it was announced that an Australian sporting syndicate had arranged for a third bout between Burns and Squires for a very large $15,000 purse.[614]

After returning to London, Burns said he planned to leave no later than July 1 for a tour of France and Italy, and would sail from Naples for Australia on or about July 7.

Stories circulated to the effect that some believed Burns had carried Squires in their recent match, allowing him last 8 rounds and look good in order to satisfy the Parisians, and also in order to justify a large purse for yet another fight with Squires in Australia. Some thought that Burns' quick recovery from the 4th round knockdown was odd. The thinking was that Burns intentionally allowed Squires to deck him so that Bill could brag to his hometown fans in Australia about how he had almost knocked out the champion, which would increase the demand for a third bout there. The *Los Angeles Herald* said,

> Simultaneously comes stories from Americans in Paris to the effect that Burns permitted Squires to stick eight rounds and make a good showing merely to influence the Paris representatives of the Australian fight club to accede to his demands for a $15,000 purse for the fight with Squires at Sydney. In justification of these rumors is the story that Burns recovered so speedily from the effect of the knockdown in the fourth round that it looked 'fishy' to ringside spectators who had seen real fights in America. It is argued that Squires can return home and proudly boast of almost knocking out Burns and thereby boost the box office receipts amazingly.[615]

It is possible that Burns carried Squires. After all, the fans and press enjoyed a competitive and entertaining fight. Tommy had been given little credit for blowing through Squires the first time, and maybe he did want to justify a third lucrative bout in Australia.

However, it is also certainly possible that Squires was better than was originally thought, that he had benefitted from his first experience with Burns, and had shown his true form this time. He had lasted 19 rounds with Jack "Twin" Sullivan. Squires likely adjusted his tactics and was more respectful of Tommy's power and paid more attention to defense. Also, Squires did have a legitimately hard punch. Most of his victories were via knockout, so it is certainly possible that the puncher simply caught Burns, and that Tommy wanted to fight cautiously.

The *Herald* also said,

> Burns is the most pronounced globe-trotting champion the world ever knew. No other champion undertook the worldwide tour that

---

614 *Los Angeles Herald*, June 16, 1908.
615 *Los Angeles Herald*, June 22, 1908.

the Los Angeles fighter has undertaken, and the great success he is experiencing in mopping up with all the ambitious heavyweights in Europe, after cleaning out the American stable of would-be champs, justifies him in his hunt for easy game, big money and a glorious good time. Reports from all his fights indicate that the stocky chap never has been extended in any of his European engagements and as the Antipodes hardly can offer fighters any better than Bill Squires in the heavyweight division Tommy should continue shaking the golden tree indefinitely.

When he returns to America next fall he undoubtedly will be ready to take on Jack Johnson and all other fighters who want his game. Never lacking in cool courage, he is not afraid of any of them, and his good judgment in passing up the hard game for the soft money engagements should not be construed as cowardice on his part. It merely is an exhibition of good sense in taking easy money where no chance is involved, in preference to taking the same money where a materially greater chance of losing exists.[616]

Furthermore, despite some of the press urging Burns to fight Johnson, it cannot be underestimated how much the color line was a part of American life. The entire society was segregated. Most every sport other than boxing was totally segregated, and even boxing only had its rare exceptions in non-title heavyweight fights and in just a few lower weight class championship fights.

The *Los Angeles Herald* noted in a headline that the Negro fighter was passing away, and had been eliminated from championships, which were now held by all white fighters. George Dixon, Joe Gans, and Joe Walcott had all been defeated and lost their world titles, having fought once too often. "The negro of today in the ring occupies a decidedly less conspicuous position and will find it remarkably difficult to get engagements. Jack Johnson alone stands in a position to command the admiration of the fight world for his prowess, real or imaginary, as it may be." Hence, despite the push by some for a Burns-Johnson fight, there were just as many or more of others in the population who did not care to see such a fight and would be perfectly happy never to have such a bout take place. There were even some who would be angry if such a fight was allowed. No American promoter would put up the money necessary to make the Johnson match, although they probably could have done so.[617]

What Tommy Burns made clear at that point in his career was the fact that he was willing to break the color line if enough money was involved. He was in the game to make as much money as possible, and if he was making good money taking on softer challenges, he was going to do it. If he

---

616 *Los Angeles Herald*, June 22, 1908.
617 *Los Angeles Herald*, July 6, 1908.

was offered very big money for a very tough fight, sufficient enough to risk losing the title, he would take that fight as well. Clearly though, regardless of what some said about his opponents, most of Burns' European bouts had garnered a fair amount of pre-fight interest, and the local champions and opponents were sufficiently well thought of such that promoters and fans had wholeheartedly backed the fights. Tommy Burns was making good money with his foreign tour.

CHAPTER 13

Australian Admiration

After Tommy Burns defeated Bill Squires in their June 1908 rematch, Burns and Squires were engaged to meet again in Squires' home country of Australia, where a third bout between them would garner the most money, owing to Bill's local popularity.[618]

Apparently, an Australian syndicate put up $25,000 for two matches there; one between Burns and Squires, and another between Burns and current Australian heavyweight champion Bill Lang. For Squires, Burns was to be paid $10,000, win or lose, and $2,500 for expenses. Squires would receive $4,250. Burns would then earn an additional $5,000 for the Lang fight, win or lose.[619]

Burns was scheduled to arrive in Australia in early August 1908, to "scrape another financial platter clean." Before he left Rome, Italy, Tom sent a letter assuring his Los Angeles friends that he was too careful to be caught out of condition and would train aboard the ship.

> I'll bring back a few more medals and have a few more dimes for my bank account when I return, as well as having cinched my claims upon the title. Give my regards to Spring street and tell the doubting ones to cage Johnson and hold him until I get back. I don't want this mess of gravy spilled before I return.[620]

Burns arrived in Sydney, New South Wales, Australia on August 11, 1908, thirteen days before his scheduled title bout. Wanting to see and welcome Burns, at Bateman's Hotel, a large crowd extending to the other side of the street blocked traffic for an hour. One man gave a speech about boxing. The crowd applauded each of his statements and replied, "Hear, hear." He said that boxing was a manly sport, a great and national pastime. Some called it bad and brutal, but they did not know anything about it. It made a man full of vim, as he should be. He would much rather see a man defend himself with his fists than take a knife, dagger, or revolver.

Mr. Hugh D. McIntosh said he was proud to be associated with the enterprise that had brought Burns out. Tommy was prepared to fight any white man living, and so far as the syndicate was concerned, if the fights they had arranged were financially successful, they were prepared to make him a match with Jack Johnson. "Of course he demanded a large sum, but

---

618 *New York Evening World*, June 15, 1908.
619 *San Francisco Chronicle*, August 24, 1908; *New York Times*, August 24, 1908.
620 *Los Angeles Herald*, August 5, 1908.

after he had fought all the best whites offering he believed Burns was prepared to meet Johnson for the largest sum obtainable." Burns had signed an agreement binding himself to meet Johnson under certain conditions.

Bill Squires added a word of welcome and assured Tommy that he would have a good time and receive fair treatment. Bill hoped that on the 24th the best man might win.

Burns thanked them for their reception and echoed Bill's sentiments. "I also wish to say that Squires is a good, game boy, and a dangerous boy for anybody to crack."[621]

A special stadium at Rushcutters Bay was erected especially for the bout.[622]

While preparing for Squires, Burns told the Australian press that it was well within probability that he and his colored challenger, Jack Johnson, might decide their differences in Australia.

It was also said that Burns might meet Stanley Ketchel, who was on a meteoric rise. The 22-year-old world middleweight champion Ketchel had recently scored a May 1908 KO20 Jack "Twin" Sullivan, June W10 Billy Papke, and late July KO3 Hugo Kelly.[623]

The *Sydney Bulletin* noted that both Squires and Burns were extremely polite, respectful, and gentlemanly when referring to one another. Squires was training at Lake Toronto, and said to be in excellent fettle.[624]

Just three days before the championship, on Friday August 21, 1908, for the first fight held in the stadium erected at Rushcutters Bay, Tommy Burns refereed a 20-round boxing match between Sid Russell and Peter Felix. At the bout's conclusion, Burns awarded the decision to Russell.[625]

On Monday August 24, 1908 at Rushcutters Bay in Sydney, Australia, Tommy Burns fought Bill Squires for the third time. The fight was scheduled to start at about 3:30 p.m. There had been a tremendous rush for tickets.[626]

According to the *Sydney Morning Herald*, over 15,000 spectators were present inside the arena and over 24,000 outside the enclosure. The *Sydney Daily Telegraph* said the stadium was filled with a huge crowd which paid admission from 10 shillings up to 5 pounds. It estimated that by the time they entered the ring, at least 16,000, and up to 18,000, were seated within the roofless enclosure. The *Referee* said 17,000 people were on hand to watch the battle. The *Sydney Bulletin* estimated 16,000 - 17,000. Dozens of American naval officers were present, hundreds of American sailors from the battleships in the harbor, as well as many leading citizens of Sydney and other Australian cities.

621 *Sydney Daily Telegraph*, August 12, 1908.
622 *Sydney Morning Herald*, August 19, 1908.
623 *Sydney Daily Telegraph*, August 19, 1908.
624 *Sydney Bulletin*, August 20, 1908.
625 *Sydney Morning Herald*, August 22, 1908.
626 *Sydney Morning Herald*, August 24, 1908.

The fight had been in the making for several months. Hugh McIntosh wanted to induce Burns to come to Australia to fight the best they had, and had deposited 2,000 pounds with the *Referee*, to be given to Burns, win or lose. They fought for a purse of 3,000 pounds, of which 2,000 went to Burns win or lose, and 1,000 pounds to Squires. Many anticipated that such a large purse would lead to a financial loss, but the huge crowd made the venture a big success.

Several bookmakers offered tempting odds of 5 to 1 against the underdog Squires.

The principals appeared at 3:45 p.m. Squires entered the ring first, heralded by a tremendous outburst of applause which terminated in three ringing cheers. He was clad in a bath wrapper and attended by his trainer Jimmy Russell, sparring assistant Arthur Cripps, ex-Australian heavyweight champion Billy McCall, and Charlie Frost.

Burns followed a little later with trainer Pat O'Keefe, Manager J.J. Kelly, Jack McDonald, M. Burke, and Arthur Scott. He was also accorded sufficient applause and a flattering reception.

When Burns stripped, he did not look well. He was pale, and the statement that he had been under medical attention, suffering from a cold, was easily realized. It was said that Tom had hurt his arm in sparring, and then a couple days later, caught a cold when he refereed the Felix-Russell bout. He spent the next day in bed, with Dr. Maitland, as well as Mrs. Burns, attending to him. Tom was in the ring for the championship fight a mere two days later.

Squires and Burns shook hands and the crowd cheered. Bill was in splendid condition and never looked better. Tommy's round form made him appear a bit fat, but he was fit. Burns wore maroon trunks and the American flag for a sash. Squires wore blue trunks, while the colors of his waist-sash were red, white and blue.

The champion won the toss for selection of corners, which was of considerable importance, considering the bright sun. Burns chose the corner where the sun would be behind him, while it glared into Squires' eyes.

L. Harry Nathan, a very experienced official and former amateur boxer, refereed the bout. The timekeeper was W. T. Kerr. Strict Marquis of Queensberry rules would govern, so each man could hit at any time he had his hands free.

The locals did not give out the weights, likely owing to the fact that weigh-ins were not required for heavyweight fights.

The round-by-round account is from the local *Sydney Morning Herald*, *Sydney Daily Telegraph*, and the *Referee*, which was also based in Sydney.

1 - At first, they moved warily and made some half-hearted leads. Burns showed much tricky footwork and was continually dancing on springs, looking cool and confident. Squires looked nervous and anxious. They eventually got going and there were some exchanges and a good deal of clinching. Referee Nathan had to interfere to part them. Burns was plainly sparring for opportunities, while Squires was endeavoring to make them. The aggressive Squires landed several rights and an effective blow to the solar plexus. However, overall, it was three minutes of fast work with no harm done. Neither man had an advantage.

2 – This was an exciting round, as the boxers quickly got going and became rough. Squires was the most eager. Several of his punches made impact, but they had no effect. Some said Squires no longer had the punch that he once did. However, it would be more accurate to say that his punches were powerful, but that Burns shifted and moved away from them nicely with skillful footwork and therefore deprived the thumps of much of their sting.

Burns acted as if he was on springs, and kept dancing in and out and shifting about in a manner that might bewilder the oldest ring general.

Squires looked determined to land a good hard punch. Bill kept throwing lefts, and now and again landed heavily, though he missed several uppercuts. Squires was piling up points with right and left, fighting the battle of his life. He forced the pace and was always going at Burns.

However, Burns looked as if he could do more if he so chose, and appeared cool. Tommy cleverly blocked many blows, and landed some good ones at close quarters, as did Squires, though not to the same extent. Burns landed his hard right to the ribs, which had a palpable effect. Still, Squires showed improved cleverness, eluding several blows.

Once, when Squires ducked, his head struck Burns' left eye hard. Burns was momentarily dazed and a mouse and bump appeared on his face. One source said Squires even brought blood from Tom's nose.

The pace was quick, and the crowd cheered the willing and determined fellows. It was a very fast and interesting contest already, marred only by the frequent clinching and inclination to remain there until the referee broke them.

3 – Squires fought with more confidence and used his left freely, landing some blows, but missing most as a result of Burns' superior skill. Tommy's shiftiness proved a revelation. Squires kept him on the move all the time. Bill's friends were applauding excitedly on a frequent basis. He was determined, only allowing himself to be set back momentarily when Tom threw something hard his way.

They did a good deal of work in close, locked together in frequent clinches, something which occurred quite often in every round. Referee Nathan's shirt was smudged with the blood that was coming from Tommy's nose. He struggled to part them, for they enjoyed close-up punching. Both did good work in close, though Squires did not land anywhere near as often as the bulk of the spectators imagined, for Tom had a good defense. In a clinch, Burns landed short blows to the jaw and some rights to the body that were solid thumps.

Squires kept coming in with the love of war, firing his left and then following to the body. Tommy shifted away from the blows so as not to feel their full impact. Bill was determined to land. Tom used finesse and waited, engaging his footwork and blocking skills. He also ducked some blows and side-stepped. Squires was doing better than Burns as far as points went, but Tom was poised and calm. He took his opponent's blows without being troubled or shaken.

Squires was an improved fighter. His footwork was better, as well as his guarding and timing. It was a good, clean, entertaining fight, despite the excessive clinching and occasional holding and hitting.

4 - As a result of his success to that point, Squires looked very confident. He still forced matters and was more active than Burns with his punches, showing to great advantage. "Squires had landed often enough to flatten out most ordinary boxers, but Burns was still going strong, and smiling here and

there, though by no means in a flash way." Burns feinted and backed away a good deal, looking confident, though patient. They ducked each other's swings. They came together and punched until the referee broke them.

Referee Nathan was busy separating them from clinches. They clinched and hit heavily. The pace was terrific. Burns brightened up considerably and put more vigor into his fight. He brought blood from Squires' mouth. One source said a right to the jaw momentarily dropped Squires, but the other two did not mention this. The effect of Tommy's handiwork was already evident on Bill's puffed face, though the challenger continued his aggressiveness.

Squires hit Burns with a right uppercut. Bill did considerable damage with punishing rights to the ribs, one or two of which made Tom squirm. After a hot rally, a solar plexus blow shook up Burns. However, Tom showed his marvelous recuperative powers, which were manifest throughout the fight. He clinched to save himself, but after breaking away he still danced around in the same lively fashion, looking cool and sure, despite the fact that Bill was dangerous all the time.

The fans were pleased by the good pace and the always present possibility of something decisive occurring at any moment. Nothing more exciting had been seen for many a day, especially given the skill level. Squires saw to it that every round featured lively, hard fighting.

5 – For the first minute, they fought in the clinches. Squires was eager as always. They engaged in some fast exchanges of heavy blows. Squires continued swinging hard lefts and rights, and even some uppercuts, connecting sometimes, though failing to land on other occasions due to Burns' good defensive measures. In fact, both exhibited skillful evasive tactics.

Squires prevailed in the out-fighting, landing a succession of hard punches, but Burns got in several effective hits at close quarters. It was an exciting contest, and the thousands applauded continually as the men scuffled. Burns worked the ribs and body well, particularly with his left. Bill hit the stomach and jaw, though Tom just smiled. Burns landed a fine hook to the body, which caused Squires to clinch so hard that Referee Nathan found it quite difficult to separate them.

One opined that on the whole, the round was even. Another believed the round ended with the points being a good deal in favor of Squires.

6 - This round was similar to what had preceded it. Both were busy again. Burns' lefts to the body in the clinches made a palpable impression, which helped Tommy to do better, but Squires kept going strong and never lost heart. Clinching was still a feature of each round. Squires landed a right cross which made Burns fall forward onto Bill's shoulder and clinch to save himself. Squires was doing very well, but the smile remained on Tommy's lips. Whenever he was hit hard, Burns just smiled and wore his same cool expression.

The *Referee* opined that the bout's nonstop action would bring heaps of coin to Geach and MacMahon, who had purchased the moving picture rights for 1,000 pounds.

7 - Squires started operations as usual by sending in his left to the neck and driving his right to the ribs. Bill landed heavy blows with both hands to Tommy's jaw. The spectators imagined that Burns was about to collapse, and they went wild, rising and cheering with excitement. Squires followed Burns again, punching him with right and left. However, Tom danced about as lively as ever. Burns then took a turn at fighting like a tiger, driving some shots between Bill's punches, rattling him. Blood from Tom's nose and Bill's chin spread over the referee's shirt. Both men seemed a bit fatigued at the call of time. They were about equal for most of the round, but the Squires section was jubilant.

8 - Squires continued leading and scoring in a sustained fashion. He landed repeated blows to the jaw. Their effect, however, was only momentary, for the sound of the blow had scarcely died away before Burns looked as well as ever. Some saw the champion's downfall, but Burns husbanded his resources and absorbed the blows. Halfway through the round, the referee cautioned Squires for holding and hitting. Bill rushed with vigor, and did some good work before Burns landed a telling left to the ear and twice sent his right to the stomach.

9 - They were both busy. Squires was still battling desperately and carrying the war to Burns. More than once, Bill appeared to be on the verge of getting Tom into trouble, but Burns was always cool and on the alert. The champion got the better of some hot exchanges, landing some effective body blows which caused Squires to clinch. Squires turned the tables with a right uppercut to the chin that drove Burns back for a moment, though it affected him but little. Tom fought hard with both hands. His left hook to the ribs and right to the face rattled Bill, whose badly puffed face gave him a sick and sore appearance. They continued exchanging hard blows. Tom's nose bled freely again.

10 - Despite the fact that he continued landing several blows to the head, Squires was weakening more perceptibly than at any other time, for his punches had lost their steam. Tom treated Bill's blows with contempt, taking them without wincing. As the challenger's vigor fell away, the champion appeared stronger.

However, Squires rallied gamely, and the thousands urged him on. The fighters banged away, toe to toe, and the crowd cheered uproariously. Squires focused on the body, while Burns hit the head. Tom landed some uppercuts, but Bill did not budge.

Burns' desire to conserve his power and energy was noticeable, fighting hard here and there. Waiting for his moment, Burns landed a nasty blow to the body. Squires held him, but Tommy worked himself free and followed up with several heavy punches. A wicked right just brushed Bill's jaw. Squires weakened a bit, while Burns looked as strong as ever. However, overall, Squires was the more consistent with his offense, while Burns only fought in spurts.

A blow to the temple appeared to temporarily daze the American, who stood with his arms hanging to his sides to receive three or four punches about the face without making an effort to stop them. However, just before the gong, a left to the solar-plexus hurt Squires.

11 - Squires missed more than he scored, but he landed often enough that the spectators were worked to a high pitch. Whenever he landed a solid blow, the crowd cheered him on. Burns continued working on him, trying to wear Bill down. They were both fighting at a furious clip at the bell. The crowd tumult and intense excitement over the fierce rally was so great that neither fighter heard the gong.

Another source opined that at this stage of the fight, Squires was tiring, and his face was badly puffed. The end was near, yet still he followed and fought, and tried hard to give as well as he received. However, Burns knew too much to run into harm's way.

12 - Squires opened up by rushing, apparently fully recovered. Burns warily skipped around and watched for an opening as Bill eagerly attacked. They exchanged blows, and were a bit wild. Squires landed a left to the jaw and stomach and they clinched again. He continued landing, but without sufficient power to do any damage. Still, the challenger's earnestness and the manner in which he scored evoked rounds of frequent applause.

Burns skipped in and out and shifted about. At last Burns saw his chance and shot out his solid left, and though Squires countered well, the champion had all the better of the scuffle that followed at close quarters. Tom did his most telling work in the clinches, always placing his punches to vital spots. The referee stepped in momentarily to adjust the champion's sash, which had become loose.

Squires landed, but he did no harm. Burns hooked his left to the throat, which more than made up for the several blows that he had received. Squires was waging a desperate battle, but his power was ebbing fast, while Burns seemed just as strong as when the struggle had commenced. "All the force had pretty well left Bill now; he had drawn too heavily on his resources by making the fighting and endeavoring to keep going with a man who is an artist on his feet."

13 - Bill was dog tired through his own exertions, and it seemed as if Tommy knew it, for Burns lost no time in getting down to business. He landed repeatedly on the body in holds, and led when they broke away. Squires was manifestly weak in the knees and groggy. However, after some exchanges and clinches, they were again pegging away at close quarters with both hands, and the excitement was high.

Suddenly, while Bill's head was almost against Tom's breast, Burns landed a short jolting right uppercut to the chin that caused Squires to go down to a sitting posture. As he leaned over in a dazed state, blood trickled from his mouth.

Squires rose at the count of eight and tried to mix it. The crowd cheered. Burns landed long punishing hits on his unsteady foe. Another forceful right uppercut and left hook dropped Squires to one knee. He rose at eight, but was rocky, tottering, and swaying about.

Tom came right after him. Squires ducked an imaginary blow. Burns then crashed his right on the back of his neck and Squires fell flat on his stomach and was counted out. However, another local source said it was a hook to the jaw that finished him.

Great excitement prevailed. The crowd had enjoyed the immensely exciting fight, and cheered them in appreciation. A squad of American seamen stood up and cheered. Squires had given a gallant effort, and so the universal applause was as much for the vanquished as the victor.

Neither man was much the worse for wear, though Squires had a very puffed face. Another source said Squires showed distinct signs of wear and tear. Both eyes were very much discolored and he was cut beneath one of them, and another cut was on his chin. Still, Bill treated the damage as trifling, and said he felt well otherwise, all things considered. Burns had a discolored eye as a result of the bump that he sustained in the 2nd round.

The *Sydney Morning Herald* said Squires had put up a splendid struggle, while the champion's methods were a revelation. "The fight was one of the most exciting that Australia has seen for many years." It was full of movement and action from start to finish, and both pugilists secured the crowd's admiration. "The fortunes veered to and fro, and though Squires prevailed during the first ten rounds – at times almost overwhelmingly – Burns showed such marvelous recuperative powers that at no time did the contest appear one-sided." Still,

> The issue leaves no doubt as to the respective merits of the two men. Barring accidents, Squires would be beaten by Burns every day in the week, and that in spite of the fact that the Australian prevailed during nearly the whole of yesterday's fight, and at every stage was the undoubted winner on points. The difference between the two men is that Squires is a pugilist – a pugilist who has developed his powers to a high degree, but still only a pugilist. Burns is a scientist, who has applied his brain to solving the problem of the knock-out. ... Added to his scientific precision of boxing is a capacity for taking punishment which is almost superhuman. It may be possible to hurt Burns with a battle-axe, but most of those who witnessed his performance of yesterday would be inclined to doubt it. Squires rained upon the apparently soft, boyish face of the champion

sufficient blows to satisfy any three followers of the game whom Australia can remember. But they did not trouble Burns.

Essentially, Burns could knock out Squires, but Squires could not knock out Burns.

The fight was compared to a contest between a bull and a matador, with Squires the bull and Burns the matador. However, unlike the matador, Burns did not simply elude, but was also willing to tire out the bull by allowing him to pound on him. "When he stepped in to deliver the final stroke Squires was already a beaten man – beaten by the awful exertion of banging his fists against the basalt countenance of Mr. Noah Brusso." Burns had allowed Squires to throw his showy artillery of straight lefts and swinging uppercuts, but Tommy was always confident in his resistant powers, and was content to pound away with his infantry of half-arm shots until it was time to bring up the cavalry.

One thing this paper noted about the American method and interpretation of the rules was that hitting in holds was not only permissible, but to a degree astonishing to Australian followers of the game. Throughout the bout, in the clinches, the men hit one another wherever there was an opening, and, even when the referee dragged them apart (for the men were reluctant to separate), they continued swinging at one another. Mr. Nathan had several narrow escapes from their blows when he broke them.

Up until the 10th round, the Australian crowd was happy. The fight had been well contested, but it looked as if Squires would avenge his previous two losses to Burns. However, "Then Burns – the Burns who had been battered unmercifully for half an hour – seemed to mysteriously develop a faculty for hitting Squires." Up to that point, Tommy had scarcely delivered any long range punches, and most of his short inside blows had passed unseen. On the other hand, Squires, who had spent a glorious half-hour inflicting the blows, suddenly and mysteriously grew weak. His own hard work had apparently exhausted the Australian.

When the 12th round opened, Squires appeared like the runner who had just broken the tape after a ten-mile race, whereas Burns seemed like the fresh boxer straight from the training room. He was like a new man. Burns not only accepted with a smile the few blows that Squires still inflicted, and continued his own short-arm inside blows in the clinches, but Tom also demonstrated a new faculty of being able to stand off his opponent and send in long, well-aimed hits which went straight to their marks like the thrusts of a lance.

When the 13th round began, almost everyone knew that Squires was about to lose. They exchanged and clinched, and on the inside Tommy landed some heavy blows. They scuffled, and Squires made a final desperate attempt at a knockout. They clinched again, and from sheer exhaustion as much as the blows, the Australian sank to the floor. He rose at nine to cheers, but Burns, with cool confidence, struck him three times, and he fell again. He rose at eight. The final blow was scarcely a second later. Burns sent in a left hook and Squires crumpled up and fell face down. His seconds threw in the towel, but it was not until long after the expiration of the ten seconds limit that Squires was able to stand again.

The *Morning Herald* concluded that the fight was Burns' from start to finish, despite the fact that Squires was all over him. It had little doubt that had Burns seen the necessity, he could have applied aggressive tactics at any point. His method was plainly to let Squires tire himself out before making his own effort. "As for Squires, his boxing was never seen in Australia to better advantage. He has developed tremendously since leaving Australia." The press and the crowd had enjoyed and appreciated the fight.

The management had a telephone at ringside, and all through the fight, Mr. McIntosh had communicated the varying phases of the battle to Mrs. Burns. After the fight, the receiver was handed to Tommy, who said, "Is that you, Jewel? This is Tahmy. It's all right."[627]

One writer in the opinion section of the *Sydney Bulletin* wrote,

> Brutality is what people want when they attend a fight to a finish. They are not happy until they get it, or seem to get it. Let them once be persuaded that they don't get it, and there'll be an end to the enormous fees that prize-fighters receive for practicing the noble art of false pretence.[628]

The fans had paid good money and had enjoyed the Burns-Squires fight because it had been brutal.

Speaking of the fight, the *Bulletin* said,

> Squires was the better boxer, Burns was the superior fighter. He never wasted a blow, and his two targets were the heart and the chin. Occasionally he smote over the kidneys, but he never tried for that target. On points Squires won easily, but he hadn't the stamina to last 20 rounds, and the long succession of chips on the point of the chin hastened his collapse. But there was no knockout blow. Burns won simply because Squires led for 12 rounds and, piling up points galore, exhausted himself in doing it. Burns is not so much a fighter as an anatomist. He destroys his opponent's blows either by dancing away as they come or by coming in closer and tapping the arm or shoulder that is delivering the blow, thus destroying the aim. It was a case of brains and immense lung power against brute force, great skill and marvelous quickness. Brains and lung power triumphed.

> Burns recovered more rapidly and did not tire nearly as quickly as did Squires. Burns did not hit as hard, but, "When a man uses a cold chisel on a piece of iron, one sees very little impression after each

---

627 *Sydney Morning Herald*, August 25, 1908.
628 *Sydney Bulletin*, August 27, 1908.

blow, but in time the iron is severed." So Burns wore him down, combined with the exhaustion that resulted from Squires' own efforts.

The man who beats Burns will be either too quick or too scientific for him. He will either get his blows in so quickly that Burns cannot dance away from them or destroy the aim by tapping the biceps or shoulder, or he will have such marvelous dexterity that he will be able to feint a blow, draw Burns' defence, and then, while Burns is tapping the firing arm, cross suddenly with the other and land on the jaw. And that man doesn't seem to be on deck just now.[629]

The *Bulletin* also said that despite being listed at 5'7", Tommy looked even smaller. He was plump, round, and cherubic, with a waist. Squires was big and muscular and looked as strong as a horse. But Tommy was not soft on the inside. He was terrific at infighting. Squires led, but his leads mostly landed against the leather walls of the gloves and arms, while Tom's jolts at close quarters did their deadly work on the body. "This power Burns has of dealing terrific hits with either hand at a distance of about a foot, combined with his amazing footwork, make him the wonder he is."

Still, Squires had landed some vicious shots. Burns endured smashing blows that would have settled 99 out of every 100 pugilists. The fact that Squires did not rattle him was attributable as much as anything to the fact that Burns had a wooden head which could not be injured. Some of the blows that Squires landed on him "were enough to slay an adult gorilla in robust health." But Burns took it all. "Notable points about Burns were his condition (he never once lost the spring in his step) and his stolid calm. He knew the precise moment he had his man beaten better than anyone in the audience."

Squires had shown a heap more fistic science than when Australians had last seen him, up to 40% more. "And on Monday afternoon, for all his misfortunes, he did his country proud." Squires was in the fight until the middle of the 10th round, when the hurricane of stomach blows told, even on his iron frame.[630]

In a post-fight interview, Burns said,

I had one of the hardest fights of my life. I was not well; the climate has affected me, and I have been suffering from a heavy cold. ... I have not been myself at all, and have felt slow and tired. My right arm is not too good, as I wrenched it while sparring, and could not use it as I would like to. You can take it from me, Bill is one of the gamest and strongest fighters I have ever met. He is certainly no 'false alarm,'

---

629 *Sydney Bulletin*, August 27, 1908.
630 *Sydney Bulletin*, August 27, 1908.

as the American press called him, and he could beat most of the heavy-weights in the world.[631]

Another paper quoted Burns as saying,

> Things hadn't been going well with me in my training. There was that jarred arm and the cold on my chest early last week, as well as the chill suffered in the ring on Friday, and I kinder thought it would be best to save myself as much as possible, as I knew Squires to be dangerous, but he set me a livelier go than I expected, and had me on the move always. It was to my mind, better to let him rush and tire than to stand up and mix the work, as he possibly might last longer than I, and there were visions of that close call in Paris before me all the time. Bill is a brave fellow, as I told you Sydney people before, and he put up a great fight, but I had the punch when the opportunity came.

Tommy also thanked Hugh McIntosh for the magnificent organization of the event, and thanked the Australian audience for its fairness.

Squires said,

> On my previous battles with Tommy Burns and what I consequently knew of his fighting, I rated my chance this time particularly good, and after we had been at it a few rounds my confidence was greater. He gave me some hard knocks in those clinches and about the ribs, but I knew at least a few of mine told. Burns is a good hard fighter, and one who will take a whole heap of beating, no matter who he faces. I may not be able to hit with the force that I used to, but I fancy many of those punches which landed on Tommy Burns would have a much more severe effect upon other men. ... Burns is a man in thousands. He is very quick on his feet, a hard puncher, a shrewd fighter, and has a frame of iron.[632]

Squires said to Burns, "By Jove, Tommy, you gave me a very heavy punch on the throat in the twelfth round." Tom replied with a laugh, "Sorry for that, but a man had to do something to stop you, you know." Good-natured Bill laughed too.[633]

Current Australian heavyweight champion Bill Lang, who had witnessed the fight, said, "Yes, I've watched Burns closely, and I'm convinced that there'll be a new champion on September 2." September 2? That was in only nine days. Actually, they wound up fighting on September 3. Yes, Tommy Burns was actually going to defend the title yet again only ten days after going 13 grueling rounds. Amazing! How many fighters today would or could fight 13 pro rounds and then fight another scheduled 20-round

631 *Sydney Morning Herald*, August 25, 1908.
632 *Referee*, August 26, 1908.
633 *Referee*, August 26, 1908.

bout a mere ten days later? Furthermore, Lang would have the advantage of having seen Burns in action, whereas Burns had never seen Lang box.[634]

The biograph machine had successfully filmed the fight. It was taken from the shaking of the hands to the finishing knockout blow. The management intended to show the complete bout at the stadium a mere two days after the fight. It was also arranged that the moving pictures would be shown in Melbourne and Brisbane.[635]

AMUSEMENTS.

PALACE   THEATRE.

SPECIAL AFTERNOON PERFORMANCE,
SPECIAL AFTERNOON PERFORMANCE.
TO-DAY, AT 2.30.
TO-DAY, AT 2.30.
and
DAILY AT 2.30.   DAILY 2.30,   DAILY 2.30,
DAILY AT 2.30.   DAILY 2.30,   DAILY 2.30.

THE BURNS-SQUIRES BIOGRAPH BOOM.
THE BURNS-SQUIRES BIOGRAPH BOOM.

                LADIES' MATINEE,
TO-DAY.   LADIES' MATINEE.   TO-DAY.
                LADIES' MATINEE,
which Gentlemen will be permitted to attend.

PALACE.

THE BURNS-SQUIRES BOOM.

THE MANAGEMENT Regret the limited
capacity of the Palace Theatre, and begs
to state that
ALL LAST NIGHT'S OVERFLOW TICKETS
ALL LAST NIGHT'S OVERFLOW TICKETS
Will be Available any Night till Friday.

PALACE   THEATRE.

SOLE LESSEE ..... EDWIN GEACH.
(There is absolutely no free list.)

SENSATIONAL SUCCESS SCORED NIGHTLY.
SENSATIONAL SUCCESS SCORED NIGHTLY.
SENSATIONAL SUCCESS SCORED NIGHTLY.

Many Many
HUNDREDS REFUSED ADMISSION LAST NIGHT,
HUNDREDS REFUSED ADMISSION LAST NIGHT.
HUNDREDS REFUSED ADMISSION LAST NIGHT.

MACMAHON AND CARROLL'S SENSATION,

THE BURNS-SQUIRES STRUGGLE.
THE BURNS-SQUIRES STRUGGLE.
THE BURNS-SQUIRES STRUGGLE.

Remember,
THE LAST DAY BUT TWO.
THE LAST DAY BUT TWO.
THE LAST DAY BUT TWO.

3/. 2/. and 1/.
EARLY DOORS until 7.30 to Back Stalls and Gallery,
6d extra.
Secure your Seats—The Best is Good Enough—at
Nicholson's.
Doors open at 7. Performance at 8. Curtain 10.

---

634 *Sydney Morning Herald*, August 25, 1908.
635 *Sydney Daily Telegraph*, August 25, 1908.

The day after the fight, both Burns and Squires were given a private viewing of the biograph pictures of the training and the fight. The camera had been contained within a 4' x 4' enclosure. Three men were in that tight spot for over an hour. The length of film taken was about half a mile.[636]

After a showing of the fight in Melbourne at the King's Theatre, one reporter described the motion pictures.

> The film is certainly a realistic one, and every point in the great encounter is brought out in a manner that takes the spectator right to the ringside. What a splendid battle Bill Squires put up is plainly manifested in the moving picture. Up to the tenth round at least the Australian seems to be well ahead, and scoring points in every round. That his blows lacked their old true force there can be no doubt, for the picture shows Squires landing on Burns's face and head scores of blows, any one of which, with the old steam behind them, would have summarily ended any fight. In the seventh and ninth rounds in particular Squires is shown taking most astounding liberties with his opponent's head with both hands but quite ineffectively; but from that time onwards Burns did all the hustling. According to the film Squires had the points, and Burns had the punch, and if the apparatus can't lie, the blow that finally put the Australian out of commission was a prod behind the ear, nearly on the back of the neck, struck downwards as Squires was ducking down for a clinch.[637]

Speaking of the reasons why Burns had not yet fought Jack Johnson, one writer opined, "Racial pride counts for something in pugilism, and one great reason why Burns would not give Johnson a chance to wrest the championship of the world from him was a ferocious hatred of the idea of the negro being the bruising monarch of the earth."[638]

However, putting racial prejudices aside, given that Burns had drawn very well for the Squires fight, and that Australians had seen Johnson defeat Peter Felix and Bill Lang the previous year and were well aware of his prowess, it was within the realm of possibility that Hugh McIntosh might be able to meet Burns' financial demands for a Burns-Johnson title fight.

The Burns-Lang championship bout was scheduled to take place in Melbourne. Win or lose, Lang stood to earn 600 pounds, while Burns would earn 1,000 pounds.

Since his March 1907 KOby8 loss to Jack Johnson in Melbourne, Bill Lang had been on an impressive thirteen-fight win streak, which included KO9 Peter Kling, KO1 Mike Williams, KO12 Peter Felix (vacant Australian heavyweight title), KO8 Arthur Cripps, KO7 Peter Felix, KO1 Bill Smith, and July 1908 KO5 Jim Griffen. Some had recently criticized him for

636 *Referee*, August 26, 1908.
637 *Melbourne Age*, September 1, 1908.
638 *Sydney Bulletin*, August 27, 1908.

requiring 5 rounds to stop Griffen, whom the 190-pound Lang had outweighed by two stone, or 28 pounds. However, Bill was not in good health that night nor well trained, and yet he defeated a good man relatively quickly.

BILL LANG,
CHAMPION OF AUSTRALIA.

The *Sydney Bulletin* said of Lang, "The man is Mighty, and, like the truth, he should prevail. Truth doesn't always prevail, but it is worth backing in a fight to a finish." Australians thought very highly of Lang.

Lang's original name was Swiss – Lanfranchi. His mother was Irish. He had formed his muscles working as a blacksmith, and had an athletic build. He stood 6 feet tall and weighed 13.5 stone, or 189 pounds. He was 26 years old.

Lang had vastly improved since his loss to Jack Johnson. "He was quite a novice, as he says, when he stood up against Johnson, the tall nigger whom Burns, thus far, has avoided." Bill had only 2 years of experience when he met the colored champion. Johnson's manager had bet that Jack would knock out the relative novice within 3 rounds, but Lang had lasted 8 rounds before his second threw up the sponge. At present, Bill was nearly a stone heavier than when he fought Johnson, and much more knowledgeable of the science of the game.

It was said that Lang had never taken the count. Over a year ago, Lang had often sparred Bill Squires, but Squires' vaunted punch never put him out.

Lang had not lost for nearly two years. He reckoned that he was improving every week. Having seen the champion in action against Squires, he was confident that he would defeat Burns. Bill remarked, "Wait and see!"[639]

---

639 *Sydney Bulletin*, August 20, 1908.

Many Australians agreed that Lang had a better chance to defeat Burns than did Squires. "There are more than a few followers of the game who feel confident Lang will test Burns' powers much more severely than did Squires." Hence, given how good the Squires bout had been, the Australians were just as excited or even more so to see the Lang fight.[640]

Six days after the Squires fight, on August 30, Burns left Sydney for Melbourne. Tom said that although he had not quite shunted his cold, he felt much better than he did when he had faced Squires. After fighting Lang, if a match with Johnson could not be arranged, the champion intended to return to America to fight Stanley Ketchel.[641]

Burns said he had bet 1,300 pounds on himself before the Roche fight in Ireland, and had won $13,000 on the second Squires fight. He was paid 2,000 pounds for the most recent Squires fight. Squires was paid 850 pounds. Tommy was making good money on the road.[642]

Increasingly, the American press was warming up to Burns. Some took Tommy's side against fighters who were challenging him, particularly Jack Johnson, who had fought only once in 1908, in England against the local Big Ben Taylor, who had lost more fights than he had won, including losses to George Chrisp, Jack Scales, Jack Palmer, Gunner Moir, and Sam McVey. Sam Langford, who had racked up many impressive victories in the two and a half years since his April 1906 decision loss to Johnson, was also seeking matches with either Burns or current middleweight champion Stanley Ketchel.

THE WORLD'S CHAMPIONSHIP
Will be Contested
THURSDAY,
10 o'Clock a.m.,
At the STADIUM,
CITY ROAD,
SOUTH MELBOURNE.
WET OR FINE.

Take South Melbourne Tram or Train to Montague.

TOMMY BURNS,
Undisputed Champion of the world,
Who has never refused to meet any man, and has beaten every man he ever met, meets

BILL LANG,
Undisputed Heavy Weight Champion of
Australia,
In an Encounter of
10 ROUNDS,
ONE TO WIN.

Jack Johnson is making a big noise about claiming the heavyweight championship from Tommy Burns, because Tommy deemed it his duty to keep his contracts with the Antipodean promoters to go to Australia and whip all the heavy crop in that neighborhood. These big blacks consider themselves of extreme and exclusive importance any time they desire to talk and evidently believe that because they are black they should have first call on any of the champions they desire

640 *Sydney Daily Telegraph*, August 27, 1908.
641 *Sydney Daily Telegraph*, August 30, 1908.
642 *Referee*, September 2, 1908.

to fight. If they are as anxious to fight as they proclaim themselves to be, why in the world do they not arrange a match between themselves? Both Langford and Johnson are hotfooting it after Burns…. It is a cinch that Burns and Ketchel will mop up with the fighters who are in line for their titles, as neither is afraid of any fighter in his class, black or white. In the meantime, it would be an excellent idea for Langford and Johnson to prove themselves in the heavyweight division by an elimination contest…. Johnson never has whipped a real classy fighter when that fighter was in his prime, unless his decision over Langford can be so termed. Langford has whipped a few classy men. If Langford is the demon he claims to be, he should trim the big black noise without trouble. … Black fighters have the same fault they charge to the white fighters. They draw the color line. … [N]obody ever has heard of Langford chasing Johnson all over the country with defis, although both Langford and Johnson are hurling challenges every hour at Burns and Ketchel. If either is sincere in his desire to fight for championships, it will be no great trouble to arrange a Johnson-Langford match, and this fight would draw almost as well as a Langford-Ketchel fight. And if Langford ever gets the big saffron in the ring, the fight world will have heard the last yawp from this noisy individual whose mail is addressed to Jack Johnson. …

Those who are criticizing Burns for going to Australia to pick the lemon crop in that country are making an error that they readily will admit any time they think it over without prejudice. Burns has had a hard climb to the top rung. Easy money is the rule now, instead of small purses and hard fights, as he experienced in his climb up the ladder. Having attained that prominence that is the goal of all fighters …he has the right to accept all the emoluments of his office, and a few easy scraps and big money are among them. Nobody ever has accused Tommy of being a coward, as he has accepted fights with bigger and heavier men and whipped them, and has done all that has been asked of him since he claimed the championship. He has begun a fighting tour of the world, in order that he may become a legitimate world champion, and has whipped everything in sight of any consequence. … He will return to America in November or December, and after he gets home there will be considerably less talk by fighters who now are seeking matches (in their minds) with him.[643]

During his short time to prepare for Lang, Burns, who was recovering from his cold, told one newspaper, "I can say I am better today a good bit than when I fought Squires. Lang will have to be moving round some to

---

643 *Los Angeles Herald*, September 1, 1908.

win, but he is a big fellow, and big fellows are always dangerous, especially when they have the punch which I hear Lang has." Although Tom's right arm was still a bit sore, it had recovered wonderfully through massaging.

Burns also said he hoped that he and Jack Johnson would be brought together, and that if they did, win or lose, he would retire. He had made ample money, enough to live very comfortably.

Bill Lang was very confident. He said that he was weighing 13 stone, 7 pounds (189 pounds), at least over half a stone heavier than Burns. He was five or six inches taller than Burns, just as long in the reach, about the same age, and just as strong.

> Why shouldn't I have a good chance? I know they are laying 5 and 6 to 1 on Burns, but that won't win the contest, and I tell you I have been improving fast lately. Jim Griffin wouldn't have lasted half the time he did had I not been ill during the afternoon of the match, and also followed the advice of my seconds to stand off.
>
> I only weighed 12 stone 6 pounds and was a comparative mug when I fought Johnson. No matter what anyone tells you about him letting me stay nine rounds, they bet a lot of money he would knock me out inside four rounds. I am a great deal better man now. I saw Tommy Burns fight Bill Squires, and if I don't win or surprise a lot of people by my showing I will be very much disappointed.[644]

Dan Creedon said Lang had developed a very dangerous body jolt which, when landed fair, would put out any man.

Two days before the fight, on Tuesday September 1, a crowd of half men and half women got a chance to watch Burns train at his training quarters at the Hotel Victoria, Beaconsfield-parade, Albert Park, South Melbourne. Even a dozen clergymen were amongst the crowd which delighted in the clever exhibition of physical training.

Burns was both graceful and "one of the most compact men alive. ... His frame is just a store house of strength and energy, and his endurance is remarkable." Clothed from neck to feet, Tom wore maroon woolen tights and an American flag around his waist. He punched the ball for five minutes, gradually increasing his pace and varying his strokes. He also skipped rope a couple thousand revolutions, demonstrating all sorts of tricky footwork, and then he shadow-boxed. Ground exercises followed, and then more punching ball. He apologized for not doing any sparring.

Unlike American boxers who liked to open their training quarters to the public; Lang was training privately at Carlton.[645]

The day before the fight, on the 2nd, Burns treated an audience, which again included clergymen, to a splendid exhibition of ball punching, rope

644 *Referee*, September 2, 1908.
645 *Melbourne Age*, September 2, 1908.

skipping, shadow sparring, and other physical exercises for nearly an hour. He was "warmly applauded on his remarkable cleverness and activity."

Burns said, "I have come thousands of miles to this country to win, and I am going to win, and when I do win Australia may still keep the championship, for I like your country so well that I am ready to become an Australian." Tommy wanted to remain in Australia.

Regarding a potential fight with Jack Johnson, Burns said,

> All that is needed to fix that battle is Johnson's signature, and that has yet to be obtained. My terms have been stated, and they go. I shall not alter them. ... This I now wish the world to know – my fight with Jack Johnson will be the last fight of my life. ... I want to meet Johnson, and have done with it; but I don't want to have done with it till I meet Johnson, or till he says he will not meet me.

From his training quarters, Bill Lang said,

> It is usual for a boxer before a big mill to say he never felt better in his life, but honestly I never did. I am hitting harder, and seem to be more alert and springy than I ever did. ... I can say with sincerity that if I don't win I will lose absolutely on my merits, but I am very hopeful, and after having witnessed the Sydney encounter I know that my chance of success is an exceedingly good one.

WORLD'S BOXING
CHAMPIONSHIP,
THIS MORNING,
10 o'Clock,
At
THE STADIUM,
CITY-ROAD,
SOUTH MELBOURNE.

TOMMY BURNS
(Champion of the World)
Against
BILL LANG
(Champion of Australia).
20 POUNDS. ONE TO WIN.

PRELIMINARY.
CRIPPS VERSUS NELSON.
Prices, £3, £2, £1, 10/; and a limited number of seats at 5/, to be had at the Stadium.
Doors open at 8 a.m. Seat-holders are requested to take their places early.

HUGH D. M'INTOSH,
Governing Director,
The Scientific Boxing and Self Defence Co. Ltd.

The day of the fight, the local *Melbourne Age* said Burns would strip at his usual weight of about 12 stone 6 pounds (174 pounds), while Lang would scale 13 stone 4 pounds (186 pounds).[646]

Hugh McIntosh's octagonal-shaped stadium was specially built on the City-road in South Melbourne. The stadium was even bigger than the one at Rushcutters Bay, with huge circular stacks of benches which were spread over a wider area than Rushcutters, though they did not rise quite as high. The seating could

---

646 *Melbourne Age*, September 3, 1908.

accommodate 16,000, and had room enough for 3,000 more to stand.[647]

The Burns-Lang championship fight took place on Thursday morning, September 3, 1908 in South Melbourne, Australia; ten days after the Burns-Squires bout.

A couple sources said 7,000 or 8,000 were seated in the stadium, which began to fill before 8 a.m. Another said 10,000 spectators were in attendance. Present were hundreds of men who had never even seen a fight before. Once again, a Burns title fight in Australia would be a financial success.

When Burns arrived, he realized that he had forgotten his arm band – the elastic support for his jarred right forearm, so it had to be sent for via motor car. This caused a delay in the start of the main event.

Meanwhile, after the preliminary bout concluded, rain fell from the clouds, and topcoats were donned and umbrellas spread out. In a short while, the rain ceased. The announcer informed the crowd the reason for the delay, which wound up being about 20 minutes.

At 11:50 a.m. the audience loudly cheered the 6-foot-tall Lang as he appeared in the ring with his trainer, Joe Stokesbury, and his seconds, Loy Lacey, Andy Dowling, and Alf Boyd. He looked nervous and anxious. Lang waited quite a while in the ring for the motor car to return with the bandage for Tom's right arm.

Finally, seven minutes later, at 11:57 a.m., a burst of applause preceded the advent of the champion, whose seconds were trainer Pat O'Keefe and several bottle and towel men that included Pat Burke, Harry Claydon, and the jockey Geoff Ross. His entry was like the arrival of a potentate. Burns did not look like a fighter, wearing a motor cap, sweater, trousers, patent leather shoes, and a coat to keep warm. "He looks more like a barrister or a surgeon than a prize-fighter. That is when he is not fighting."

Bill Squires entered the ring, challenged the winner, and was cheered, even though he then claimed that he did not have sufficient time to prepare for his last battle with Burns. His claim was a reach, given that he was 0-3 against the champion.

The boxers shook hands and disrobed. Lang did not wear colors or trunks, but just a stomach supporting band. Tom wore maroon trunks and his adopted country's colors.

Joe Stokesbury objected to Tom's elastic arm bandage on his elbow, but the referee, Mr. L. Harry Nathan, said that since Burns was not going to hit with his elbow that he would allow the bandage. Stokesbury also protested the glove's laces being tied on the front part of Tom's forearm. He was again overruled. The referee announced that strict Marquis of Queensberry rules would govern.

Inspector Biggs examined the gloves and was satisfied.

---

647 *Referee*, September 2, 1908.

The announced weights were 13 st. 4 lb. Lang and 12 st. 6 lb. Burns, or 186 pounds Lang to Burns' 174 pounds. However, two days prior to the bout, Lang had told the *Referee* that he was weighing 13.7 stone, or 189. As usual, no one knew for sure because they did not step on a scale.

The round-by-round account is an amalgamation of the *Sydney Morning Herald*, *Sydney Daily Telegraph*, *Weekly Times*, *Melbourne Argus*, *Melbourne Age*, and the *Referee*.[648]

1 - When the gong sounded, Lang immediately commenced to dance away from Burns. He was big and not as graceful as the champion. Lang backed away with his left shoulder covering his chin. Burns moved to his opponent with the glide and poise of a panther ready to spring. He followed, wary and watchful, trying to provoke a lead. "There was something grim and terrifying in the slow, cool, determined way in which Burns followed him round, for all the world like some fierce animal stalking its prey."

Burns eventually cornered Lang, who clinched. In a rough rally and scramble, Lang tripped and fell with Burns toppling over him. After resuming, Tom missed a left uppercut and they clinched again.

Burns forced the infighting and Lang learned about his inside abilities. Tommy worked the ribs and stomach in a cool and deliberate fashion. Lang seemed tense. After a rally, while Lang was holding, Burns landed a couple left uppercuts to the chin. Burns jolted in body blows and followed with a right uppercut to the chin. Tom continually hit him with uppercuts. The American's hands worked like flashes of light, up, down, and across, all the time. Whenever there was an opening, Burns found it. Lang fought back gamely, but his height was a disadvantage at the inside game. Bill rested his full weight on the champion, hanging on.

Lang tried jabs from the outside, but Tommy would get inside and work. The champ drove a right to the body and quick as a flash threw the same punch to the head. Bill rocked a bit but fought back. Tom feinted and landed a heavy right to the ribs or stomach which shook Bill badly. Lang held and they wrestled roughly.

Hundreds stood and applauded the round. Bill had faced him in plucky fashion, but the opening round was pretty well all the champion's. One opined that the round ended "with the Australian beaten pointless." Another said,

> Burns stood out above his opponent by sheer force of energy, and this force seemed almost superhuman. In clinches he simply ripped his arms free, and tried to tear away through Lang's guard in on to his body and face. Again and again he succeeded, though Lang managed by skillful stopping to rob the blows of most of their power. Still,

---

648 *Sydney Morning Herald*, *Sydney Daily Telegraph*, *Melbourne Argus*, *Melbourne Age*, September 4, 1908; *Referee*, September 9, 1908; *Weekly Times*, September 12, 1908.

Lang was being made to work hard. Burns undoubtedly counts on his own wonderful stamina to last him through.

Lang tried his best to keep away, but Burns was always watchful for an opening.

2 - Overconfident, as Burns came charging in with contempt and led with his left, he carelessly kept his right hand low. Lang landed a splendid well-timed snappy left hook under the side of the chin and Burns went down with a heavy thud onto his back. It was a big surprise. Thousands stood up and screeched. The crowd was beside itself with joy, shouting themselves hoarse. Tom quickly sat up with an expression of surprised amusement and undisguised admiration. He smiled. Sources varied as to how long he was down, some saying six seconds, while others said eight or nine seconds.

After Burns rose, Lang rushed at him with confidence and scored on the jaw. Burns was as alert as ever, although inclined to keep away a bit until he fully recovered. Lang landed a left uppercut to the chin and hard right to the body. Burns showed more caution and worked around him. Tom landed a jab that rocked Bill's head back. Going in close, Tom landed a right uppercut to the chin.

Having quickly recovered, Burns began forcing the fighting again and was willing to mix it up. Tommy had learned his lesson though, forcing matters with more caution. He blocked blows and worked on the inside. Burns clearly preferred the inside game. They exchanged hard blows. A clinch and sharp rally ensued in favor of Burns, though he was hitting rather wildly when they broke. More clinching followed, and then Tom chased Lang around the ring.

Lang blocked or eluded most of Burns' blows and retreated rapidly before the attack. Tom was vainly endeavoring to get to close quarters. Finally, he stood still in the middle of the ring with his hands down, trying to draw Lang in, but Bill would not take the bait. When they finally clinched and Lang was holding on, Burns dealt out short-arm body punishment until Bill was beaten out of the clinch.

3 – Emboldened, Lang gamely came at Burns. The round opened with a sharp rally. Bill landed some hard body shots. Burns retreated, drawing Lang after him. However, suddenly Burns bore in with both hands and drove Lang about the ring, giving him no rest. The champion scored repeatedly on Lang's face. Lang had a wonderful capacity for absorbing punishment. Burns was as active and eager as ever. He continued rushing Lang around the ring. Tommy finally cornered him and worked his short-arm pounding to the body, every now and then whipping one over to the head. A left brought blood from Bill's wounded nose. Lang simply held on the inside and made ineffectual attempts to stop Tom's blows.

The referee annoyed Burns by stepping between them when they clinched. Tom wanted to work on the inside, and snapped, "Don't come between us like that."

Lang struck back, but could not get the steam into the short-range blows that Burns could. There was some hot infighting, with Burns doing all the effective work. Close in, he hit the ribs with uppercuts. The heavy body assault shook up Lang. A left on the jaw jolted Lang very badly, and his counter was weak.

Lang broke away and Burns followed him all over the ring. Bill seemed to be weakening, and just before the gong, a heavy right to the side of the face or temple badly staggered Lang. Some skin had gone from Bill's nose. Another account said the right swing to the temple dropped Lang for eight seconds. Lang weathered the rest of the round.

Between rounds, Lang's corner poured advice into his ears, while Burns' corner was practically silent.

4 - Lang appeared somewhat weak and nervous, anxious to keep away from Burns. Tom's blocking, dodging and persistent following provoked Bill into attacking. Tom kept coming, no matter what hit him, even though Lang landed some good rights. In remarkable fashion, Burns smothered a shower of hits. When Tom cornered him, Lang rallied and landed to the body. However, Burns fired long straight hits that distorted Lang's face, one of which cut open Bill's eyebrow, half blinding him.

Finally, Burns decked Lang. The *Melbourne Age*'s version said a Burns right cut Lang's left eyebrow and then almost immediately another right-clip on the chin dropped Lang for eight seconds. The *Melbourne Argus'* version said a powerful swing to the ear brought Lang to the boards looking limp for eight seconds. According to the *Morning Herald*, the champ feinted and swung his left heavily to the jaw, knocking him down. According to another version, Tom threw a left which missed, but then followed with a right to the ear with such force that Lang went down for three seconds.

When he rose, Lang swung hard blows which Burns ducked. Tommy smiled and then swung his right and left to the face. A punch to the stomach caused Lang to bend over. As Lang clinched, Tom landed a strong uppercut that rattled Bill, but he fought back gamely. Lang's trainer shouted, "Get away! Keep away! Run away!" Bill seemed too weak and dazed to obey the instruction. He took a lot of body punishment. His left eye just over the brow was looking bad. On occasion, Tom verbally objected to the referee's being too eager to go between them and break them, when there was no need to interfere. Tom liked to work on the inside.

Lang ducked to avoid some blows, but Burns landed a left and powerful long-range right to the jaw that sent Lang down to the boards for the second time in the round. He was down for eight or nine seconds before rising.

Lang landed a right, but was showing signs of the punishment. Tom landed a left and right hook which drew blood from Lang's left eye. Burns looked confident. Bill missed an uppercut and landed a right to the ribs, but Burns countered with the left uppercut and also sent a straight left to the forehead.

One source claimed that in his anxiety to finish, Tom left himself open, and being slightly off balance, was sent down by a straight left to the neck. He rose at once, clinched, and cut loose. However, other sources strongly disagreed, saying that Burns went down from the force of his own blow, and was not knocked down.

Bill was still blocking and returning the blows, but one writer felt that he was plainly demoralized, and only the gong saved him. Another writer claimed that Burns hit Lang on the side of the face and knocked him down as the gong sounded.

5 - There was a great deal of ginger in this round, although the contest had already been fast up to this point. Lang kept away. Tom followed him. There was no escape. Lang was not confident, but still he showed pluck.

Burns maneuvered Lang into a corner and then rained a terrible series of blows upon him. A right to the jaw made Lang shiver and shake. Tom's right to the ribs sent Bill to the ropes. Burns continued hitting him, and Lang was practically helpless. In succession, Burns swung two rights to the jaw and Lang went down. One source said it was an uppercut that dropped him. At eight, Bill rose.

Lang was at Burns' mercy. The champion fought at high speed and landed his right to the stomach. His masterful right uppercut to the chin (one said chest) dropped Bill again for an eight count. Lang gamely rose and waded in. Tom took a few feeble blows but landed a severe left to the body. Burns had discarded defensive tactics at this point, increasing the vigor of his attack.

Burns missed a powerful right which Lang ducked and therefore Tommy fell to the floor from the impetus of his own blow. Some incorrectly said he was sent down by a blow to the neck. "The imaginations of some scribes are fertile indeed." This writer said that occasionally in the fight, Burns went down from missing a swing, but was only dropped once in the contest, in the 2nd round.

Down for no more than a second, Burns rose instantly and pounced upon Lang like a tiger. He planted right and left to the face, and again the Australian champion went down, but he was saved by the gong at the count of four.

6 - Burns was fresher than ever, determined to finish the fight. His feet and hands worked like lightning, and he dodged about Lang in a disconcerting way. He badly rattled Bill with a heavy left to the ear. Lang was kept on the move, but he fought back hard. Burns showed some clever tricks with his head in evading blows. Tommy did not appear much hurt by what he received.

Burns twice landed his left to the chin, and left and right to the head and left to the chin again and Lang was forced into a corner. Tom struck hard and often. Every blow told, and Bill could not escape. He fought back in exciting fashion, but was ineffective. Lang got back to long-range again, but was shaky and demoralized. Tom landed some hot lefts and rights.

Lang seemed weak. He retreated, but a right cross to the side of the face dropped him for eight or nine seconds. When he rose, Tom rushed him, and a heavy left to the body sent him down again by the ropes. He rose in a couple seconds and went to work.

Burns forced Lang to rally. Lang landed a hard left to the ribs, and Burns feigned being badly rattled. The crowd cheered as the champ's hands dropped and he swayed weakly in front of Lang, who hit him on both sides of the face. "You've got him, Bill – he's done," yelled the crowd, and, "Burns is done, finish him, Bill." To everyone's astonishment, Burns allowed Lang to smash at his head with both hands, with no reply. Tom took a dozen blows in succession. However, Burns began smiling and the cheering suddenly stopped. His broad grin caused Lang to sense danger and he backed off. Burns was alternating between a fierce attack and "contemptuous fooling." It was like a cat playing with a mouse.

Burns followed Lang with surprising springiness and speed. "Never at any time of the fight had he appeared stronger and fresher. More quickly than it can be told Lang was penned in a corner of the ring and a smashing right swing on the jaw sent him down and out." Another version said Burns feinted at the body, which caused Bill to drop his arm, and then Tom followed with a right to the jaw and Lang dropped like an ox. While he lay there being counted out, Joe Stokesbury also threw in the towel. Two minutes and fifty seconds of the round had elapsed. Lang was assisted to his corner, while Burns danced to his.

Burns received 1,000 pounds and Lang 600 pounds. Promoter Hugh McIntosh noted that Lang was the first man in all of Burns' championship bouts to drop him. However, this was not true, if reports are to be believed about Squires decking Burns in their second bout.

Bill Squires said that from the start, Lang never had a chance. His best opportunity was when he downed Burns with a lucky blow, but he wasn't swift enough to take advantage of the occasion.

The *Sydney Morning Herald* said Burns completely outclassed Lang, administered severe punishment for several rounds, and won a decisive victory via 6th round knockout. Strict Queensberry rules helped Burns, for he was a superior infighter.

The *Daily Telegraph* said Lang had made a courageous effort, but was overwhelmed. Burns did not have a scratch on him.

The *Melbourne Age* was very impressed with Burns. "There is probably no boxer alive who has been more perfectly equipped by nature for the game he follows than Tommy Burns. He is a big man packed into the smallest possible space, and overflowing with strength and endurance." He was able to smother Lang's punches, close right in and smash away at short range. Burns "sought Lang's embraces, so that he might cuddle right in and use the full freedom of his own two hands in hammering away like a contract carpenter. It was the force, the speed and the roughness of these close range attacks that wore Lang down." It recognized that Burns was a "ring general and a brainy fighter." He studied his man, found the one area where he was nervous, and then brought forth all of his craft to work to heighten the effect.

Although beaten, Lang had made a "mighty and courageous effort. ... Lang has earned every right to be considered a champion. He is a clever, cool game fellow, with a great big, generous punch." However, Burns was just too much.

The *Referee* said Burns did not bounce around as he did with Squires, but circled like a panther watching for an opportunity to spring. Tom slowly but surely crept after the ever-retreating Lang. Burns obviously wanted to fight. "I have seen all the best men Australia has known during the past quarter of a century, but I can't recall one who had the combative instinct so strongly prominent. Burns would beat a cleverer man."

The champion was described as having "headiness," a "sustained tenacity of purpose which enabled him to keep at his man all the time," and as being "strongly constructed everywhere." He was the aggressor, intently watching his opponent's every move in order to find a weakness and quickly pounce, generally scoring when he did. Tom sometimes gave his head to several hard punches, and the crowd watched and marveled, sometimes thinking that Bill had him, but soon realizing that it was Lang who was about to be gotten. Tom usually treated Bill's punches as mere nothings and tossed them aside with ease or ignored them.

The Burns inside work was a revelation, for Lang could not overcome it; hence his desire to try to fight at long range. Up close, the blows came from everywhere. "Australian boxing has forgotten all about in-fighting, the most exciting and attractive (to onlookers) part of the business – mainly through the ignorance of most referees." Such a statement is equally applicable to modern boxing and refereeing, much to the detriment of the sport. More referees should be slower to break fighters. The *Melbourne Age* agreed that Australian boxers had too long been used to referees pulling them out of trouble with monotonous calls of "Break," when the rules allowed for the men to work on the inside. Hence, the Australians had failed to properly learn this aspect of the craft.

Afterwards, Burns said, "Gentlemen, I've travelled the world, and must say you're the finest sports I have ever met." Considerable cheering followed.

Burns said his strategy was to have Lang fight himself out. He felt confident throughout, even when decked. "I could have got up easily in two or three seconds, but I thought I'd take the full time."

Burns thought Lang had dropped him with a right, but others had him questioning himself. Tom said the pain was on his left cheek, but someone said that the shock from the left hook landing on the right side was felt on the left. "Today was the first time I have been knocked down since I have been champion of the world."

Tom did not want to shake hands afterwards because his right wrist was slightly damaged. He put ice on it. He intended to rest for a couple of months.

Burns said Lang could punch and was tough. "There's material for a good fighter in Lang. He's a great game fellow, and clever in his way, but he must learn how to infight to be successful. Of course, I hustled him a lot, and he contributed considerably towards his own undoing." Tommy tried to get Lang to be more aggressive, to fight himself out, and to leave more openings, but usually Lang tried to keep at long range. Burns claimed that when he allowed Lang to hit him in the last round, it was an intentional trick. "You've got to use your head as well as your hands in this game." Tom also said,

> No, I didn't take him cheap a bit. He's a good game fighter who only needs experience to do a lot better. That knockdown punch was the biggest surprise of my career. ... Yes, Squires and Lang will put up a great fight if they meet, and I couldn't tip the winner with any confidence.

Someone made an adverse comment about Lang's courage due to his moving away as much as he did. Tom said that such a comment was wrong, that if Lang wasn't a thoroughly plucky fellow he would not have stood half of the punishment that he gave him. He said Lang moved around as a result of the fact that he realized that he knew less about infighting than Tommy did. "He did exactly what I would have done had I been similarly placed." The chivalrous retort was heartily applauded.

In the afternoon, after he had been out in the gardens with his wife admiring the flowers, Burns said,

> I am just as fresh as when I entered the ring this morning. To be successful in this infighting a man must be trained for that particular kind of work, and Lang has not trained that way. He is a grand, game, clever fighter, but wants the proper kind of experience. … He will be a much better man after this.

The Australian press liked Burns. It was said that Tom and his wife had a happy marriage and were very attached to one another. Mrs. Burns was a charming hostess, putting folks at ease. Tommy was a very genial and good fellow, and as candid and straight as a schoolboy.

Lang was very sore about the ribs, and a doctor said his tenth rib was fractured. Bill said it happened in the 1st round, when Tom hit him with a right to the ribs. "I got the punch which damaged my ribs while breaking from a hold. There was a whole heap of devil in it, and I always felt weak and sore afterwards." He also said that he jarred his left elbow. Bill had marks on his ribs, nose, and eyebrow.

Lang further said, "I did my best, but found him too good; he knows more than we do about infighting and is an unusually strong bustling fellow going all the time. I thought I had a chance when I knocked him down, and once or twice afterwards." Another paper quoted Lang as saying, "I thought I had him in that second round. It was a great punch; but Burns is a solid fellow. Still, I never gave up hope, and more than once afterwards, it seemed to me as if I might finish up Champion of the World." Bill wanted a rematch, but also said he was satisfied that he was beaten by a great fighter, and that was all there was to it.

Burns' manager J.J. Kelly said he was concerned when Tom was dropped, but knew he was all right when he rose and shook his head. "I was scared a bit, too, while Squires had the upper hand at Paris a few months ago, but the Rushcutters' Bay battle never caused me the suggestion of a pang."

Trainer Pat O'Keefe said Burns had a great chin, and would never be beaten until someone knocked him limp. "I don't think the man lives who has the necessary weight in his punch."

The next day, Burns said he was not going at top speed at any time in the fight. "I had a lot of energy in reserve all the time, but I dare say I'll put it all into the Johnson encounter whether it is needed or not – that is, of course, if I have the good luck to meet him, and I hope to meet him here."[649]

In the following days, the *Sydney Bulletin* said the reports about Burns before he came to Australia were misrepresentations. He had been pictured as a small-sized champion dancing around his adversaries like a cat on hot bricks. His strength was less noticeable than his agility and ring-craft. This paper felt that in fact, Burns was a big, very strong, aggressive fighter, willing to mix it up on the inside. He had a bull neck, heavy shoulders, and thick waist. "To be clinched by Burns was to be punched in the region of the heart, kidney, liver, lights or spleen." He was stronger than the larger Lang, who could not save himself other than by using his height and reach and offensive tactics. "Tommy is a 'born fighter,' to be sure, and God gave him a stocky figure and a quick eye and more brains than most men in the stoushing business." The fact was that Tommy Burns could be a bull-like attacker or a fancy dancing boxer.[650]

Bill Lang would go on to score a 1909 KO17 and KO20 Bill Squires and KO12 Bob Fitzsimmons (in the films Lang looked strong, though 46-year-old Fitz looked shot), and 1910 KO7 Squires, but would lose a 20-round decision in a rematch with Burns that same year.

As of early September 1908, Tommy Burns wanted and needed a rest. 1908 had been a very busy year for him, for he had successfully defended the title six times in that year alone.

> No more work for me for two months, anyhow. I've been working now for nine months on end, fighting and giving theatrical displays, and to finish up with I have fought two world's championship battles in ten days. I think I've earned a spell, and I will leave Melbourne on Monday to take a rest in the mountains.[651]

---

649 *Melbourne Age*, September 5, 1908.
650 *Sydney Bulletin*, September 10, 1908.
651 *Melbourne Argus*, September 4, 1908.

CHAPTER 14

The Payday and Functional End

Following his victory over Bill Lang, Tommy Burns said he wanted his next and final fight to be against Jack Johnson.

> I particularly want to meet Johnson and get out of the boxing game for ever. I want to meet Johnson, firstly, to make it plain that I draw no color-line, nor bar any man in the world; and secondly, to establish my own opinion, that I am Johnson's superior; and thirdly, to quit the game as champion of the world.[652]

To that point, since winning the title in early 1906 from Marvin Hart, Tommy Burns had made 13 successful title defenses, 11 by knockout, over the two and a half plus years that he had been champion. He should be applauded for being a very active fighting champion who defended the crown frequently. He solidified his claim to the championship with his victory over Jack O'Brien, who was then considered to be the only other claimant to the title. In his world tour, Burns had established himself as a true world champion.

However, although most of the men whom Burns fought were the champions of their respective countries, many had been bested by other contenders, and were not better than the best American contenders of the day. Still, Burns was often the underdog in those bouts or only a slight favorite, so the fights were perceived as competitive in their inception. Also, he was quite an active fighter, so one has to credit him for that.

Burns can be mildly criticized for failing to defend against some top contenders, such as Mike Schreck. Schreck had a 1903 10-round decision win over Burns, but a 1904 D6 in which Burns was considered superior. Schreck knocked out George Gardner in the 20th round in 1905, and in 1907 stopped former champion Marvin Hart in the 21st round. However, Schreck had in 1904 lost a 15-round decision to Jack O'Brien, whom Burns had bested as champion. Also, Schreck was stopped by Al Kaufman in 1907, and lost a decision to Tony Ross in 1908. Ross had a loss to Flynn, whom Burns had defeated. Furthermore, Burns had agreed to meet Schreck, but the promoter withdrew the offer.

Burns also didn't fight Al Kaufman, who had knocked out Jack "Twin" Sullivan in 1 round. In Burns' defense though, Kaufman had lost to O'Brien via KOby17 in 1905, and Burns had defeated O'Brien. Yet, Al had some

---

652 *Referee*, September 9, 1908.

very good subsequent wins: 1906 KO14 George Gardner, 1907 KO7 Mike Schreck and W25 Jack Sullivan, and 1908 KO9 Jim Flynn. Flynn was coming off a 1907 KO6 Squires and 1908 W10 Sullivan. Certainly, Kaufman was as good as or better than many against whom Burns defended the title. Still, Kaufman had his chance to fight Burns early in Tom's championship career, and declined the opportunity. No one disputed that Burns had gotten the better of Kaufman in their sparring. Kaufman's manager never pushed for a Burns-Kaufman match, nor did the press.

Burns had defeated Hart and O'Brien, as well as the international best, successfully defending quite often, more often than anyone before him other than John L. Sullivan (who mostly only fought 4-round bouts), and more times and more frequently than most who have reigned after him, so his championship career has to be considered worthy of praise.

Tommy Burns was interested in making money. Perhaps American sports had become a bit soured towards him after the second O'Brien match and the Squires bout. Performing too well against Squires had actually hurt him, because instead of applauding Burns' performance, the press denigrated Squires and the fight. It made sense at that point to take the show on the road for a while. Burns found that he could earn as much or more money in other countries, against easier opponents, and with much greater appreciation.

Tommy Burns always stood ready to take a tough title defense against the era's best contenders, and even to break the color line to do so against Jack Johnson, Sam McVey, or Sam Langford, as long as there was a sufficient financial reward. The promoters had to be willing to put up big purses, but apparently the demand was not great enough, and in the case of Johnson and other black fighters, racial/socio-political considerations factored into the lack of offers as well. Foreign countries paid Burns well to fight their champions. Furthermore, in other countries, Burns did not have to live in the shadow of James Jeffries.

Jack Johnson had been eager to fight Burns for the past two years. However, Burns had easily defeated Marvin Hart, the man who had defeated Johnson, albeit controversially. Since losing to Hart in 1905, Johnson had won 15-round decisions over fellow blacks Joe Jeanette and Sam Langford in 1906, and in 1907, knocked out Bill Lang in the 9th round, former champion Bob Fitzsimmons in the 2nd round, and Jim Flynn in the 11th round (after Burns defeated him). Johnson also held victories over Sam McVey. He was clearly the top contender for the crown, race excepted. Yet, no American promoter was willing to financially back a Johnson-Burns fight with the type of money that was required to make such a fight, likely in part because of the color line.

However, Australian promoter Hugh McIntosh came up with the money to support the articles of agreement that Jack Johnson and Tommy Burns had signed back in April 1908. He was going to pay Burns a minimum of

$30,000, win or lose, to fight Johnson. That was all that Tommy needed. Johnson was guaranteed a minimum of $5,000, which was sufficient to induce him to fight as well.

The Australians appreciated and admired both fighters, so there was a sufficient demand for the fight, and they did not have the same issues with the color line as did the Americans, at least not when it came to heavyweight championship boxing. Since Burns had been a big gate draw in his two prior Australian fights, McIntosh believed the fight would be financially successful.

Tommy Burns had been true to his word, and at last had been proven correct in his contention that the Johnson fight was worth that much. The shrewd businessman had held out for $30,000, and he got it. As one paper wrote, "Burns is not afraid of Johnson, but he realizes that a match with the saffron streak would be worth more to him financially than any half a dozen fights in which he could engage, and he means to make the club that stages it stand a tap. And he is right as a fox, too." Ultimately, Burns was willing to fight and did fight the top contender to the crown.[653]

The long-awaited mega-fight with Jack Johnson took place on December 26, 1908 at Rushcutters Bay in Sydney, Australia. It would be the last time that Burns entered the ring as champion, for in the 14th round of their bout; the police entered the ring and stopped the fight. Despite wanting to continue, Tommy Burns was not allowed to go out on his shield. Referee Hugh McIntosh awarded the bout to Johnson, who clearly had been in control of the fight up to that point. Johnson was too fast, big, tall, long, strong, and defensively skilled for Burns.

To his sporting credit, Tommy Burns had taken on Jack Johnson for his final 1908 defense, doing something no heavyweight champion of the gloved era had done in an official title fight – break the color line. Burns has to be commended for being willing to fight the era's best contender, when no other champion before him had defended his title against a black man. That decision gained Burns a great deal of money, but it also separated him from his title.

Burns' loss to Johnson and decision to fight a black man in a championship fight also cost Burns heaps in terms of his legacy, particularly by those who regretted or were even angry that Burns had broken the color line. Violation of the social taboo would cost him in prestige. Furthermore, those who for various reasons did not want to acknowledge Johnson as a great fighter had to denigrate Burns. The backlash, particularly by the American press, was quite harsh. No white heavyweight champion would defend against a black fighter again until 1937.

The fact is, though, that Tommy Burns was a very good boxer and an underrated fighter, who could both stick and move on the outside and

653 *Los Angeles Herald*, September 3, 1908; *San Francisco Chronicle*, December 6, 1908.

attack and fight on the inside. He was quick, strong, durable, and well-conditioned. He had knockout power in both hands, a very good chin, fast feet, and was quite skilled. He was a versatile ring general who could do it all, and deserves more respect than that which history has afforded him. Those who underestimated him based on his height and weight usually came to regret it.

Burns essentially retired after the Johnson fight. He had plenty of money, and no longer needed to fight. He had planned to retire after that big payday, win or lose. His heart was no longer in it, or at least not to the extent that it had been. However, like many retired fighters, he couldn't remain away from the game forever. After over a year of inactivity, in April 1910, Burns fought Bill Lang in Australia again, and this time he won a 20-round decision, much different than the previous KO6 victory when he was at his best and was active and sharp.

Following the Lang rematch, Burns did not fight again for over two years, when he scored a 1912 KO6 Bill Rickard in Canada. Ironically, it was his first boxing bout in his native country. He occasionally came back to fight again after lengthy periods of inactivity, but he was never the same again, given that the once extremely active fighter was only fighting about once per year, if that. In 1913, again in Canada, he fought a ND6 against Arthur Pelkey.

Perhaps telling regarding the ill-will towards Burns for having fought and lost to Johnson, his late January 1914 KO4 Battling Brant in the remote town of Taft, California, an insignificant bout, was Burns' first fight in the U.S. since his July 1907 KO1 Bill Squires, six and a half years earlier. He did not fight in the U.S. again.

After only three fights in three years (or four in six years), Burns did not fight again for nearly five years (in part owing to World War I) until a late 1918 KO4 Bob "Tex" Bracken in Canada. His final fight was almost two years after that, in 1920 in London, England, a LKOby7 to Joe Beckett, when Burns was 39 years old. Essentially, his boxing career had functionally ended with the Johnson fight.

Appendix:
Tommy Burns' Record
(a.k.a. Noah Brusso)

BORN: June 17, 1881; Hanover, Ontario, Canada.
DIED: May 10, 1955, Vancouver, British Columbia, Canada, at age 73, one month shy of his 74th birthday.

1900?

Burns claimed a KO5 Fred Thornton, but this is unconfirmed.

1901?

Burns claimed knockout victories over Billy Walsh, Archie Steele, Ed Sholtreau, and Walsh again. These bouts have not been confirmed.

1902

Jan 16	Fred Thornton	Delray, MI	KO 5
Feb 5	Billy Walsh	Detroit, MI	KO 5
Mar 3	Harry Peppers	Detroit, MI	KO 2
Mar 5	Archie Steele	Detroit, MI	WDQ 2
Apr 4	Billy Walsh	Delray, MI	W 6

This was possibly a knockout.

Apr 18	Ed Sholtrau	Detroit, MI	KO 1

Newspapers used various spellings, including Sholtrau, Sheltrau, and Sholtreau.

May 16	Ed Sholtrau	Detroit, MI	W 10
Jun 27	Dick Smith	Mt. Clemens, MI	KO 2
Jul 9	Dick Smith	Mt. Clemens, MI	W 10
Sep 19	Jack O'Donnell	Butler, IN	KO 11
Oct 24	Earl Thompson	Detroit, MI	EX 5
Oct 24	Billy Moore	Detroit, MI	EX 5

Brusso's main sparring partner at that time was Jimmy Duggan.

Nov 6	Reddy Phillips	Lansing, MI	KO 9

Phillips retired after the 9th round.

Dec 9	James J. Corbett	Detroit, MI	EX

Corbett sparred with Brusso during that week.

Dec 26	Tom McCune	Detroit, MI	KO 7

1903

Jan 16	Mike Schreck	Detroit, MI	L 10
Feb 13	Jim O'Brien	Delray, MI	W 10
Mar 25	Dick Smith	Delray, MI	KO 3
Mar 25	Reddy Phillips	Delray, MI	WDQ 2
Apr 18	Horace Thompson	Detroit, MI	EX

There are unconfirmed claims that Brusso scored a KO3 Earl Thompson on this date.

Sep 25	Jimmy Duggan	Houghton, MI	KO 9
Oct 12	Jack Hammond	Sault Sainte Marie, MI	KO 3
Oct 24	Billy Moore	Houghton, MI	D 10
Nov 8?	Jack Butler?	Sault Sainte Marie, MI?	KO 2?

This bout has not been confirmed by a primary source. The local newspapers did not mention the bout, although subsequent semi-primary sources list the victory on Brusso's record.

Nov 25?	Jack O'Donnell?	Evanston, IL?	KO 11?

This bout has not been confirmed with a primary source.

Dec 31	Tom McCune	Detroit, MI	W 10

1904

Jan 28	Ben O'Grady	Detroit, MI	KO 3

Subsequent to the O'Grady bout, Brusso changed his name to Tommy Burns.

Feb 26	George Shrosbree	Chicago, IL	KO 5
Feb 27	Mike Schreck	Milwaukee, WI	D 6
Mar 18	Tony Caponi/Camponi	Chicago, IL	D 6
Apr 9	Tony Caponi/Camponi	Chicago, IL	W 6
Apr 26	Joe Schildt	Tacoma, WA	EX 4
Apr 26	Bobby Johnson	Tacoma, WA	EX 4

Back in Chicago, Burns began sparring with Otto Sieloff.

On May 17, Burns and Sieloff arrived in Utah, and sparred and trained in Ogden for one week.

May/Jun In the last week of May (after May 24) and throughout June, Burns gave exhibitions with Jerry McCarthy in Salt Lake and Ogden, Utah.

Jul?	Joe Wardinski	Salt Lake City, UT?	KO 1?

This bout has not been confirmed by a primary source, though semi-primary sources list it.

Jul 8	Hans Erickson	Kemmerer, WY	KO 3

Jul 18 Burns took up a position as a sparring partner for Cyclone Kelly.

Jul 20	Willard Bean	Salt Lake City, UT	EX 2

Aug In Seattle and Tacoma, Washington, Burns trained and sparred with Jean Wilson and Tommy Kane on a daily basis in preparation for the Cyclone Kelly bout.

Aug 19	Cyclone Kelly	Tacoma, WA	KO 4

Burns sparred with Louie Long and Warren Zubrick (a.k.a. Zurbrick) in preparation for the Woods bout.

Sep 16	Billy Woods	Seattle, WA	D 15

Burns continued sparring with Warren Zubrick.

Oct 6 Burns sparred with John Willie in Milwaukee.

Oct 7	Jack O'Brien	Milwaukee, WI	L 6

1905

Jan 31	Joe Schildt	Ballard, WA	KO 6

Burns boxed with Larry McKenna in preparation for the Sullivan match.

Mar 7	Jack Sullivan	Tacoma, WA	D 20
May 2	Dave Barry	Tacoma, WA	W 20
Jun 7	Hugo Kelly	Detroit, MI	D 10

Burns sparred with Warren Zubrick in preparation for the Kelly rematch.

Jul 28   Hugo Kelly   Los Angeles, CA   D 20

Everyone agreed that Burns had the best of the bout, including the referee, but the fighters had made a pre-fight agreement to call it a draw if there was no knockout.
Bout advertised as being for the World Middleweight Championship.

Burns continued sparring with Zubrick in preparation for the Barry rematch.

Aug 31   Dave Barry   San Francisco, CA   KO 20

Burns sparred with Zubrick for the Sullivan rematch.

Oct 17   Jack Sullivan   Los Angeles, CA   L 20

1906

In January, Burns sparred with Al Kaufman.

In February, Burns sparred with Jack Sullivan, who trained him for the Hart fight.

Feb 23   Marvin Hart   Los Angeles, CA   W 20

World Heavyweight Championship. Burns age 24, Hart age 29. Reported weights: 175 Burns, 195 Hart.

Mar 28   Jim O'Brien   San Diego, CA   KO 1
Mar 28   James Walker   San Diego, CA   KO 1
Burns was attempting to stop both within 20 total rounds.

Burns engaged in vaudeville to make money.

Apr 24   George Blake   Los Angeles, CA   EX 4

Burns tried to make matches with Jack O'Brien, Bob Fitzsimmons, Mike Schreck, Gus Ruhlin, Hugo Kelly, Al Kaufman, and Sam Berger, but they all fell through for various reasons.

Aug 22   Abdul Malgan   Arcadia, CA   EX 3

Burns was sparring and exhibiting with Malgan on a daily basis.

Sep   Burns sparred with Billy Woods and George Memsic (a.k.a. Jimmy Burns) in preparation for the Flynn bout.

Oct 2   Jim Flynn   Los Angeles, CA   KO 15

Oct 26   Dan Long   Los Angeles, CA   EX 3

Oct 27   Dan Long   Los Angeles, CA   EX 3
Burns and Long gave both matinee and evening exhibitions.

Nov 4   Billy Woods   Long Beach, CA   EX
Nov 4   George Memsic   Long Beach, CA   EX

Burns regularly sparred Memsic and likely Woods in preparation for the O'Brien bout. He also did some work with Abe Attell and Arthur Collins.

Nov 8   Abdul Malgan   Long Beach, CA   EX

Nov 28   Jack O'Brien   Los Angeles, CA   D 20

1907

Jan 10   Joe Grim   Philadelphia, PA   EX 3
One-minute rounds were used.

Burns was traveling with a theatrical company. He also visited his family in Canada.

Apr   Burns trained for the O'Brien rematch with Frank Lewis, Billy Woods, and George Memsic.

Apr 25   Billy Woods   Long Beach, CA   EX 3

Apr 30   George Memsic   Long Beach, CA   EX 4
Apr 30   Billy Woods   Long Beach, CA   EX 4

May 2   George Memsic   Long Beach, CA   EX 3

May 2	Billy Woods	Long Beach, CA	EX 3
May 5	George Memsic	Long Beach, CA	EX 3
May 5	Billy Woods	Long Beach, CA	EX 3
May 6	George Memsic	Los Angeles, CA	EX 2
May 6	Billy Woods	Los Angeles, CA	EX 3
May 8	Jack O'Brien	Los Angeles, CA	W 20

In preparation for Squires, Burns sparred George Brown.

Jun 28	George Brown	Oakland, CA	EX 6
Jun 30	George Brown	Oakland, CA	EX 3
Jul 4	Bill Squires	Colma, CA	KO 1

Burns visited family in Canada.

Oct 24	Burns set sail for England.		
Dec 2	James Moir	London, ENG	KO 10

1908

Feb 10	Jack Palmer	London, ENG	KO 4
Mar 17	Jem Roche	Dublin, IRE	KO 1
Apr 18	Jewey Smith	Paris, FR	KO 5
Jun 13	Bill Squires	Paris, FR	KO 8
Aug 24	Bill Squires	Sydney, NSW, AUS	KO 13
Sep 3	Bill Lang	Melbourne, Victoria, AUS	KO 6
Dec 26	Jack Johnson	Sydney, NSW, AUS	LTKO by 14

1909 Inactive

1910

Apr 7	Bill Lang	Sydney, NSW, AUS	W 20

1911 Inactive

1912

Aug 8	Bill Rickard	Saskatoon, Saskatchewan, CAN	KO 6

1913

Apr 2	Arthur Pelkey	Calgary, Alberta, CAN	ND 6

1914

Jan 26	Battling Brant	Taft, CA	KO 4

1915 Inactive

1916 Inactive

1917 Inactive

1918

Sep 19	Bob Bracken	Prince Rupert, B.C., CAN	KO 4

1919 Inactive

1920

Jul 16	Joe Beckett	London, ENG	LKO by 7

Acknowledgments

I want to thank all those who helped in some way with the research, photographs, editing, promotion, or general support of my endeavors:

Randy Essing

Sergei Yurchenko

Tracy Callis

Stephen Gordon

Clay Moyle

Steve Compton

Tom Seemuth

Cheryl Huyck

Katy Klinefelter

Zachary Daniels

Ron Marshall

Margaret Leask

Cyberboxingzone.com

Boxrec.com

Pugilibri

Eastsideboxing.com

University of Iowa Interlibrary Loan Services

Library of Congress, Prints and Photographs Division

INDEX

McDonald, Frank, 98, 198, 206

McGovern, Terry, 20, 21, 325

McGrath, Tim, 276, 281

McIntosh, Hugh, 333, 336, 343, 345, 347, 352, 359, 364, 365

McKenna, Larry, 43, 71, 82, 368

McVey, Sam, 296, 323, 325, 326, 349, 364

Memsic, George (see also Burns, Jimmy), 44, 174, 193, 198, 206, 242, 295, 297, 327, 369, 370

Miles Brothers, 193, 200, 276, 283

Miller, William, 231

Mitchell, Charley, 299

Moir, James "Gunner", 201, 231, 240, 294, 296-313, 316, 317, 319, 349, 370

Moore, Billy, 17, 18, 26, 29, 367, 368

Munroe, Jack, 51, 70, 93, 286

Nathan, L. Harry, 336-339, 342, 353

Naud Junction, 97, 119, 129, 135, 143, 166, 168, 170, 179, 191, 193, 206, 225, 229, 230, 232, 233, 241, 242, 245, 262, 295

Naughton, W.W., 78, 92, 151, 152, 153, 202-204, 209, 210, 212-215, 221, 245, 252, 253, 262, 292, 316

Neary, Charlie, 55, 57, 193

Neil, Billy, 51, 65, 168, 297, 317-318, 321

Nelson, Battling, 276, 281, 293

Nolan, Billy, 240, 245, 259-261, 276

O'Brien, Dick, 23, 70

O'Brien, Jim, 23, 162-164, 367, 369

O'Brien, "Philadelphia" Jack, 19, 23, 30, 38, 39, 41, 42, 47, 53, 60, 61, 64, 70, 72, 80, 86, 87, 92, 93, 108, 113, 116, 118, 128-132, 134, 138, 152, 154-158, 160, 162, 165-168, 170-172, 175, 179, 185, 188-191, 194, 196, 197, 202, 204, 205, 218, 221, 231-233, 240, 253, 254, 261, 264, 270, 276, 296, 297, 313, 363, 368-370

O'Connor, C.A., 198, 231

O'Donnell, Jack, 16, 31, 367, 368

O'Donnell, Steve, 70

O'Keefe, Pat, 317, 336, 353, 361

Olympic Athletic Club, 128

Pacific Athletic Club, 95, 97, 106, 116, 117, 119, 126, 131, 135, 143, 162, 168, 170, 179, 190, 206, 229, 245

Palmer, Jack, 70, 231, 233, 267, 274, 280, 284, 293, 300, 302, 312-316, 319, 349, 370

Peppers, Harry, 11-13, 15, 20, 21, 169, 367

Peppers, Irene, 15

Phillips, Reddy, 16-18, 23, 27, 367

Plumb, Dido, 65

R.C. Smith, 31

Reilly, Tommy, 44-46

Reliance Athletic Club, 269, 271

Reno, Charley, 52, 56, 57, 60, 62, 63

Other Books By Adam J. Pollack

John L. Sullivan: The Career of the First Gloved Heavyweight Champion

See mcfarlandpub.com or amazon.com

In the Ring With James J. Corbett

See lulu.com

In the Ring With Bob Fitzsimmons

See winbykopublications.com or amazon.com

In the Ring With James J. Jeffries

See winbykopublications.com or amazon.com

In the Ring With Marvin Hart

See winbykopublications.com or amazon.com

Adam J. Pollack is a staff writer for Cyberboxingzone.com, a member of the Boxing Writers Association of America, and an attorney practicing law in Iowa City, Iowa.

www.ingramcontent.com/pod-product-compliance
Lightning Source LLC
Chambersburg PA
CBHW020406100426
42812CB00001B/221